Try the Damascus Road

For Judy

William W. McDermet III

William W. McDermet III

Eagles Publishing
Jamestown, NY

To secure copies of this book
e-mail to: samnox@madbbs.com
or
write to: 504 Panama Bear Lake Road, Panama NY 14767

Introduction

If there is a theme to Try the Damascus Road it could be captured in the words: journey, pilgrimage, trip, path, adventure or way. Each person will have many religious experiences along their journey. How we do, and do not, react to them, along with our ongoing relationships to God, and others, will result in a meaningful or meaningless pilgrimage. Experiencing one's personal pilgrimage is a spiritual journey.

The vast majority of this collection of articles, meditations, prayers and poems has been selected from those published in magazines and newspapers. An editor deemed them worthy of inclusion in their journal. The publication where each piece appeared, is given at the end of each writing. Some items have been in more than one publication. A list of these publications is at the back.

As I put these items together, and re-read *what* I have written over the past 40 years, I find much of my thinking and understanding concerning biblical and theological perspectives has changed. My, *how* they have changed! I considered "going-back" and changing some concepts. Then, I thought, "No, what I wrote *then,* is what I thought *then.*" Thank God, we can all grow in our understanding.

William Wallace McDermet III is a native of Nebraska, growing-up in Lincoln. He is a graduate of Nebraska Wesleyan University, BA; Brite Divinity School, the graduate seminary of Texas Christian University, BD (now MDiv); and Christian Theological Seminary, DMin. While at CTS he was selected to Theta Phi, scholastic honor society in religion, as a degree student.

From 1960 to 1989 he served five congregations: United Christian & Baptist of Kalona, Iowa; Blue Ridge Boulevard Christian of Independence, Missouri; First Christian of McPherson, Kansas; Downey Avenue Christian of Indianapolis; and Prairie Avenue Christian of Decatur, Illinois. One of the enriching experiences of his life was the opportunity to serve as senior pastor at Downey Avenue for 14 years. At that time most of the national staff of the Christian Church (Disciples of Christ) worked out of Missions Building located one block from Downey Avenue; and 71 ordained clergy were members. This made life far from dull. From 1989 to 2000 he served as interim pastor to congregations in southeast Iowa and west central Illinois. He and his wife, Sheral, make their home in Chautauqua County, New York.

Traveling the Road

Advent Adventures

Meditations for the Trip

Prayers Along the Journey

Maps for Traveling

The Newspaper Route

Traveling the Road

Messenger

the christian MINISTRY

THE CHRISTIAN

Christian Theological Seminary

Vanguard

Catalyst

PREACHING

World Call

DisciplesWorld

The Des Moines Register

Try the Damascus Road

Acts 9:1-9

Have you had a religious experience lately? Have you ever had one? Jameson and Westfall, in their "irreverent guide to churchology" called Bull at a New Gate, note:

> There was this Jew named Saul, and what a corker he was! . . . He was on the road to Damascus one day to get some more Christians to persecute, and all of a sudden, bang, he was struck down blind like he was hit with an atomic bomb or something.
>
> And when he came to, he asked what had happened. And a voice answered, and there was a change in Saul like you never saw before . . .
>
> Moral: Most people nowadays avoid the road to Damascus.

When one speaks about a religious experience, what does that mean?

You may think only of wild, way-out, almost supernatural happenings. Is it someone espousing weird sounds that cannot be understood? Maybe it was the time evangelist Aimee Semple McPherson rode a motorcycle onto her California Angelus Temple stage. She was dressed in a police uniform, blew a whistle, and shouted, "Stop, you're speeding to hell." Then she preached on the subject, "The Green Light Is On."

Or maybe a religious experience is when you touch the television at the request of Oral Roberts to make your "point of contact" and are healed. Hmm.

Consider all the religious experiences recorded in the Bible. It's almost overwhelming. In the Exodus event we find water looking like blood, water separating. Hebrew children remaining healthy while Egyptian children die, and many other unique experiences.

In the New Testament we see Jesus healing the blind man, Jesus causing wholeness – instead of a legion of evil spirits – to dwell within the "mad man" among the tombs; a transformed Peter preaching boldly at Pentecost.

Can religious experiences be a part of contemporary happenings? While walking one dark evening, Peter Marshall "accidentally" tripped over a fallen tree, but the short fall kept him from plummeting over a steep cliff. He interpreted the experience as an opportunity to reexamine the priorities in his life.

Can an authentic religious experience happen in the 1980s while you simply attend a presentation of a wonderful choral presentation and you are transformed by the power and majesty of the words and music to begin to experience the depth of the very meaning of life? Yes.

I want to challenge three common conceptions about religious experiences.

(a) Religious experiences happened only in Bible times.
(b) Religious experiences are always ultra-dynamic.
(c) Religious experiences happen only to other persons.

Wrong, wrong, and very wrong.

Let us take a look at Paul's experience. He started on his journey as Saul, breathing threats and murder against the disciples of Christ. He is no 40-hour-a-week worker. He enjoys his persecuting work. Never mind the double-time pay; let's get on with it. But on that trip he had an encounter with Jesus. And because of his past lifestyle, of course others found it difficult believing he (of all people) could have a religious experience.

En route to Damascus this young Pharisee came to a crossroads and to a personal crisis. Accumulated influences caught and crushed him until he was emotionally unhinged, spiritually bleeding, and physically blinded. It was at that moment, when he could go no further within himself, that he found help beyond himself. He found God. From that experience he arose, still blinded, to follow the living Lord of his vision. The details are not important. What is important is that he was transformed by that experience and became a new being.

The God that was present with Paul is present with us. Biblical personalities do not have a strangle-hold on religious experiences. Our God is a God of creation and re-creation. We can be guided by the same Spirit that guided Paul. Jesus' spirit was alive then and is alive now.

Religious experiences can happen in the here-and-now, and they can happen to us. We need to be prepared to receive them. We need to cultivate a receptive attitude and be aware of God's continuing activity.

I'll use myself as an example of one who has experienced happenings that I would now, after reflection, claim and call religious.

The year is 1957. I have just eaten a great meal and I have walked out to the front yard of the Theta Chi fraternity house. It is a beautiful May evening, and everything seems to be a lush green. I am surrounded by friends. In a few days I will graduate from college. In three months I will be married. Standing in that front yard I am immersed in a powerful affirming feeling that includes good food, an exciting world, education, friendship and love. (All gifts from God.) Twenty five years later I still recall that exhilarating moment.

The year is 1959. My wife, Sheral, and I are in the worship service of a small black church in Waxahachie, Texas, a first for both of us. The choir performs with a soloist singing to "Dear Jesus" who seems to be about 10 feet above her. I am captured by the moment. I am asked to preach. What can I, a young seminary student, say? Yet I "have at it," and I receive a number of "Amen's." Talk about support from those in the pews! It is a taste of God's Kingdom.

A religious experience has its beginning in amazement and willingness to experience God's continuing activity. The religious person wonders at the phenomenon and lives within that wonder. No other knowledge or information or interpretation can change the amazement of God's involvement.

The year is 1964. I am in a training session for directors of summer youth conferences. At our closing worship experience we participate in a service where we "pass the peace" (of Christ). I am standing next to Don Manworren who turns to me, holds my hands, looks at me, and says, "Bill, may the peace of Christ be with you, and with your spirit." It is so genuine that I am almost unhinged by his sincerity and warmth, and I am almost unable to pass the peace to the next person.

Religious experiences are simply what happen – in so far as they come to persons who are capable of receiving them, or prepared to receive them, as religious experiences.

The year is 1980. I am to have eye surgery. I have known this for a number of months and I am worried. This type of surgery is done on one's eye under local anesthetic. "My God, they are going to cut into my eye and I'll still be awake." However I am also aware that a number of persons within the congregation have said to me, "I'll be praying for you when you have your surgery." And I know by their look, and tone of voice, and touch, and past history, that they are not making flippant comments. They mean what they say.

On my surgery day I am still filled with dread. I am wheeled into the operating room and the ophthalmologist shoots anesthetic in three places around my eye. Somehow I fall asleep and do not awaken until I am back in my hospital room. Hmm, another religious experience.

Now sisters and brothers, what about you? Can you tell of similar experiences? Indeed can any birthday or reconciliation or even funeral service be a religious experience? Yes! And, of all places, the church ought to be the place where you share your religious experiences.

Paul provided us with excellent guidance. "When you come together, each one has a hymn, a lesson, a revelation, a tongue, or an interpretation" (I Corinthians 14:26). He says, "Therefore, if any one is in Christ, he (she) is a new creation; the old has passed away, behold, the new has come" (II Corinthians 5:17). Yes, we are always passing through the experience of becoming.

Maybe you have already had religious experiences. You simply don't couch them in "religious" terminology. Thank God once again for them. Be ready to participate in more of them – both as giver and receiver. Touching, holding, speaking in hope, a family reunion; all can be religious experiences. That Easter worship when you were captured by the thrill of the day as you sang the hymn "The Strife is O'er, the Battle Done" and realized some moisture was on your hymnbook – it came from your eyes. You had a religious experience.

Open yourself and allow the experiences to happen. If necessary, shift gears. Get yourself out of neutral or reverse, into the position where religious experiences can happen.

Paul's testimony was that on a dusty Damascus road, in a moment of truth, he found God. Jameson and Westfall facetiously and sadly note: "Most people nowadays avoid the road to Damascus."

Let's prove them wrong. Amen.

(Messenger, July 1982)

Understanding My Own Miracle!

Can you be thankful for something that happened years ago, and is only recently fully understood and appreciated? Yes and Amen!

Recently I completed class work on a second seminary degree. One of my papers centered on the Old Testament topic – "God and the Natural World, the Problem of Miracles." The Exodus "Red Sea" Crossing received special emphasis. Thus, my guided study and research gave vivid theological insight and meaning to a personal experience that happened 22 years ago.

The Exodus event is *the* event in the Old Testament. When the writers of ancient Israel used the word "Miracle" they were not thinking of acts that went against nature. They referred to acts that aroused a sense of wonder in the eyes of the beholder. The only miracle was God, who was an ever present and wonderful God, whose works inspired gratitude and joy. And because there is no limit to God's power, everything was miraculous!

For the Old Testament writer the essential part of a miracle does not lie in its "miraculous" character, but in the power of revelation that the event contains. The Exodus is the central example of the way in which the Old Testament accounts for the relationship between God and persons. The near-tragedy of the Crossing became a remarkable triumph, and it remains for Israel today the classic example of God's love for God's people.

The Exodus Crossing became a miracle only by a combination of circumstances. First, by the presence of the Israelites at that particular moment, and then by Moses, who gives to these circumstances a religious interpretation. It was thus understood as an act of God. What about my own experiences? What do they say to me?

It is the summer of 1959. I am student pastor of the Christian Church at Ringgold, Texas. One Sunday afternoon that August, my wife, Sheral, and I are returning to Fort Worth. We are in our 1949 Chevrolet, traveling south on US 81. I am driving between 60 and 70 miles per hour. (Then, within the speed limit.)

We are almost at the top of a hill when suddenly two cars appear side-by-side, coming toward us. The passing car will not be able to get around the other car without hitting us! In a split second I get the car off the road onto the right-hand shoulder. I'm not sure how I did it. We just sit there for a few minutes and are thankful that no accident occurred. It seemed to be a miraculous escape.

That event happened in a few seconds on a north Texas highway more than 22 years ago. Reflecting on that event, I can gain some insight into the problem of miracles – or at least to some understanding of the difficulty that arises in recording them, analyzing them and speaking of them.

I come from a long and deep religious background. I've been immersed in the life and work of the church since I was in junior high. I'm a believer. (Whatever that may mean.) I must be both honest and thankful about the Ringgold event. Was the other car really *that* close? Sheral says: "Yes!" Does that event grow larger through the years? I had to look up some of the details. Did it really happen as I tell it? Did I see and feel God in that happening? As I find purpose and meaning in life, I look back on the Ringgold event and find deep meaning in it. I've alive. I tell the story.

The idea of miracle from the historical point of view has its beginning in amazement. The religious person wonders at the overpowering phenomenon and lives with that wonder. No other knowledge or information or interpretation can change that amazement! Great turning points in religious history are based on a natural phenomenon or an historical event, or both. Reflecting on that happening the believers experience wonder and a miracle.

Miracle is that which happens – in so far as it comes to persons who are capable of receiving it, or prepared to receive it – as miracle. One cannot take out of the Exodus experience the intense belief that God is accompanying, preceding, and guiding Israel out of Egypt. And, one cannot take out of my Ringgold experience the belief that God was also present. My study of the Bible coupled with my readings and understanding, provides insight to what once happened in my own life.

A response to such events is a renewed dedication to God. I say in both faith and works: "Thank You, and Amen!"

(The Disciple, October 4, 1981)

The Woolly-Worm Parade

I missed one, at lest I
think I did.
Some of them were going right
to left, but not all.
Why do they cross the
highway anyway?
Is it worth the possible cost
to get to the other side?
There were so many one autumn
cars slid off the road.
If they stay on one side they
are safe, and will become
beautiful moths.
Why adventure, there are
eighteen-wheelers out there!

Are we like woolly-worms?
Should we play-it-safe, or
journey into the unknown?
Is God with us – here, there,
everywhere?

A Grave Affair

The year was 1959, and I was in my third year at Brite Divinity School, the seminary of TCU. I was also the student pastor of the Christian Church at Ringgold, Texas.

I received a phone call from a woman living at Wichita Falls. Her mother, a member of the Ringgold congregation, had died. In detail she shared what was to happen. The service would be at the Ringgold Church. Her United Methodist pastor from Wichita Falls would bring the "message." Her mother had lived across the road from a retired Baptist preacher, and he would read scripture. As the student pastor, would I come and give a prayer? I responded I would be glad to share in the service. I had never "had a funeral" so I felt this would be an excellent way to break-in.

While driving to Ringgold, I rehearsed my prayer a number of times. Once there, I played the role of custodian, and arranged the chairs for the funeral. Then I stood on the front steps, waiting for the procession from Bowie. The small church was beginning to fill. Finally the procession came over dusty north Texas roads.

As the family moved into the church I introduced myself, welcomed them, and asked "who is the United Methodist pastor?" "Oh," replied the daughter, "didn't someone phone you, he can't come." I then stammered, "the Baptist preacher?" She said, "He's sick, didn't anyone talk with you, you're to do the service."

It was decision time. I could get into my 1949 Chevy (details remain vivid) and go back to Fort Worth; or try to stumble through the service.

Somewhat pale, I decided to give-it-a-go, and I took my place behind the pulpit. A few months before, Russell Bythewood, pastor of Tabernacle Christian when I made my profession of Faith in 1949, at Lincoln, Nebraska, had given me A Service Manuel, a how-to small black book put out by funeral directors. It held a potpourri of funeral service goodies. During the piano prelude I flipped through the Manuel and located some scripture passages.

A local tradition was that a community choir rendered funeral "specials." This group was ready in the choir loft, and they started the event with "Beyond the Sunset."

Then it was my turn. I shared with the congregation that there had been a mix-up and I was not informed, nor prepared for the service; but I would do my best. My honesty proved to be most helpful, for friends and family viewed me with understanding. I read some scripture; I read one of the Manual's poems, probably "Crossing the Bar."

It was choir time again, and they groaned through "In The Garden." Then I gave *my* prayer – the one part I had perfected. I had visited the deceased, and thus was able to make some personal reflections; and we had shared communion together. The choir gave their rendition of "Peace Perfect Peace" and I gave a Manuel benediction.

Not knowing what my role was, I allowed the funeral director to station me beside the open casket. I obediently stood there while the people filed-by. One distraction was a very determined fly – determined to make its home on the nose of the deceased. Each mourner would discreetly shoo the fly off its perch, only to have it return for the next person to perform the act.

As I took my seat in the funeral coach, I fumbled through the Manuel looking for suitable cemetery remarks. I recall asking the director what I should do when there, and I believe he replied: "Oh just read a little Bible and have a benediction." At the back of the Manuel I found material under "Committals" and used one as the final part of "my" service.

I was finished but the gravediggers were just beginning. Two men started filling in the grave while the family were but a few feet away. The dirt landed with a resounding "thud!"

Finally the whole event was laid to rest, and I headed home trying to appreciate that my on-the-job-training was an opportunity to believe: experience-brings-wisdom and even grave events can be met with humorous humility.

For the Birds

Doves always appear
  at new beginnings
  carrying olive branches
  and attending baptisms.

Maybe God is a bird-watcher
  calling to me
  in my spiritual pilgrimage,
  "Hey, you turkey, fly!"

(alive now! – July/August, 1982)

Use More Four-Letter Words

We were in need of a speaker for our church business meeting. I suggested a friend from a neighboring community. He would be all right, just so his talk wasn't too long. In securing my friend to speak, I instructed him to, "Just say a few words, keep it short!"

At that meeting my friend, George Good, stood before us and said, "I've been told to watch my words, and keep this brief." He then said, "I love you," and built a thought-provoking ten-minute talk around those three words.

Some four-letter words just add to the noise pollution. What about your language? At the end of a day, if you were to write down the words you most frequently used, what would they be? Would an analysis of your conversation show an emphasis on the weather, or yourself, or talk about others? Could you possibly be boring to others?

Rudolf Flesch, author of The Art of Plain Talk, encourages us to use simple language and to put a premium on short words and sentences.

Consider some short action words. "Help." It is not a sign of weakness to say, "I need help." People basically want to be helpful, but they have to know of a need. "I'll help you," are significant words to the one speaking and to the one hearing. The psalmist said, "Our help comes from God who made heaven and earth." "Care." "I care what happens" (to you.). "Bear." "Bear one another's burdens," a theme from Paul.

Note the use of four-letter action words in hymns we sing: "*Give* of *Your Best* to the Master." "*Lift High* the Cross of Christ." "*Rise* Up, O Men of God." "*Take Time* to be Holy." "*More Love* to Thee, O Christ."

The word *love* is used over eight hundred times in the scriptures. Jameson and Westfall in their book, Bull at a New Gate (Fortress Press, © 1965), say:

> *Love is the biggest word in the Bible, and I don't care how many words are longer, there is no other word as big. Love is more things than your words or mine or anybody else's can describe. Love is what it took for creation . Love is what was involved in the creation of mankind. Love is what Jesus Christ . . . is. . . . Love is . . . the Holy Spirit. . . . Love is God.*

Hope. The football coach says he has hope that this year the team will win. Hope needs to be there especially if in this case that team lost all its games last season, and the upcoming schedule is more difficult. On a deeper level, contemporary Christians are talking about a theology of hope – a forward-looking and forward-moving kind of faith, seeing the future as dynamic and open. The full reality of God is yet to appear. Hope is what breaks down barriers, walls and borders.

How often each day does your vocabulary include the words: life, dear, gift, kind, or Lord? Do you use sentences such as, "You are dear to me." "All life is a gift from God." "I should be kind and good because Jesus Christ is Lord."

Some persons are afraid to speak kind words. If so, they do not adhere to Paul's challenge in *Acts*. He says, "Do not be afraid, but speak." Paul's rule of thumb was that *we* speak, not to please man, but to please God.

How do you use words? Consider the use of the word "save." In these two examples the person reveals their philosophy of life. First person, "If I get more money, I can save more for myself." Second person, "If I get more money, I will give it to save lives."

When should you speak? Speak a supporting word at the time of death, or marriage, or when success or failure has come to a friend or neighbor. Include four-letter words in your everyday conversation. Make a list at the end of the day; what words did you use?

Watch your language, use more four-letter words, words such as: help, love, life, kind, amen, need, care, give, live, Lord, able, feel, bear, hope, dear, nice, soul, save, lift, dare, more, sing, pray. Who knows, maybe others around you will pick up the habit and use them: family, children, neighbors, relatives, friends. Maybe someone will even write them on walls where others may see them.

(Catalyst, November, 1973, also World Call, February, 1973 and Messenger, November, 1991)

Table manners

A loaf on the table
is only some wheat,
but shaped with those hands that care.
So we take it and eat
a symbol so sweet,
that God's loving son would share.

But if we should gorge
while others have none,
and see nothing but juice in the cup.
We still missed it all
down to the last crumb,
and the meal is not holy we sup.

(The Mennonite, February 2, 1982)

Jesus: Superstar or Gentle and Sweet

(Editorial note: This sermon was prepared especially for graduating high school seniors at the First Christian Church, McPherson, Kansas.)

Some years ago I was on the program for the ordination service of a friend. The minister giving the sermon said he would say some things to the candidate, and the rest could listen. This is what I am going to do this morning: talk to you who are wearing red gowns, and the others may listen.

This past year the rage has been over the rock opera *Jesus Christ Superstar.* As it is with many issues, people divide into two camps. You are either for or against "it." At a recent Ministerial Alliance meeting one man noted with much displeasure that *Superstar* had been played at our junior and senior high schools. Those clergy split into two camps. One group said the opera was unfaithful to the New Testament, and they could no longer fellowship with other clergy who disagreed with them. The rest felt that *Superstar* was not the whole Gospel story but did render a service as it communicated the person of Jesus vividly, and by being contemporary, provided a helpful service.

A close look at the New Testament reveals that many different terms were given to Jesus: Messiah, Son of God, Son of Man, Prophet from Galilee, Man from Nazareth, Carpenter from Nazareth, The Christ. History also records him as a troublemaker, revolutionary, and friend of sinners.

Is the Man of Nazareth a superstar? The definitions found in the dictionary are helpful: Super – "of superior quality, extremely fine, great, stately, majestic, grand, admirable fine, or excellent;" star – "rare, influencing mankind and events, one who plays the leading role in a performance." These definitions do not seem to discredit the Gospel narrative of Jesus. Assuredly, he had *the* leading role in the performance – mankinds. To call him superstar does not discredit; it may clarify for you the role of God's Son.

We all have an image of Jesus. It is unfortunate that the church may have fostered an image unfaithful to the gospel. Too many see Jesus as a meek, milk-toast do-gooder. The Gospel does not record this. We see Jesus praying in anguish, weeping, irritated, disappointed but with compassion for all. A look at the Gospel according to Luke reveals Jesus as an inquisitive youth, preaching the good news, living a disciplined life, healing, eating with sinners, forgiving, and overcoming death. Therefore, he is able to be called superstar. He plays the leading role in a performance; he influences mankind and events.

Can Jesus be a superstar to you and also serve as inspiration to individuals of your grandparent's vintage? I believe so. I use the example of myself and my grandfather. Recently, I attended a meeting at the Christian Church state office in Topeka. I had never been there. As I walked into the building, I saw pictures of former state ministers in the foyer. The middle picture was my grandfather; it made a deep impression on me. After that experience, I returned home and looked at an old, worn file an aunt had given me last Thanksgiving. It contained material that W. S. Lowe, my grandfather, had used in his ministry.

What did we have in common outside of our vocation? The material in that file was for the most part the type that I would not use. His sermons were always classic: introduction, three points, and a conclusion. I generally do not use such a form. His illustrations and themes were not those I would select. He might mention Theodore Roosevelt, Jane Addams, and the then President of the

YMCA. I would use Martin Luther King Jr., Malcolm Boyd, Harvey Cox, and Robert McAfee Brown. The music selected by my grandfather is not what I would choose today. (At family gatherings we might get around a piano and sing, in fun, music from my grandfather's era.) There is a great deal of difference between my grandfather and me. Or is there? One of the poems from his file is titled, "Love Your Neighbor as Yourself."

To love your neighbor as yourself
Has such an easy sound
But it is not so easy,
As most of us have found

We can excuse our own mistakes
Find reasons for them all,
But it is very difficult
If someone else should fall.

We think he could have stronger been;
And fled temptation's lure,
We would have done so in his place,
Of that we are quite sure.

And, so to our dismay we find
It harder than we thought;
To ever keep fresh in our minds
The lesson we've been taught.

Each day we must resolve to try
More earnestly to show
The charity to everyone
That we ourselves would know.

That poem will probably not win any prize. However, a special note following the poem says, "Written by an invalid for over twelve years in a hospital in Omaha. Written lying in bed." Today, someone in a hospital for a week complains, and he or she thinks it is forever. Yet this poet's attitude is charitable. That poem had meaning for my grandfather, and it has some meaning for me.

Now I would select different material. An example would be the poem: "Love Enough to Last the Winter." It was published in the May 1971 Catalyst. It speaks of love between two persons lasting through rain, tears, hellos, and goodbyes. It was written by Judy Hanna, who two years ago, sat where you sit today. It has meaning for me. It might have meaning for my grandfather. Our lives are the same as we serve the same Jesus.

Can Jesus have a deep relationship with everyone? Jesus, superstar, can be something to you and something to grandfather, or grandma.

Grandma needs to be treated gentle and sweet. She has lived most of her life; perhaps her husband is dead. Her eyesight is failing; her friends are gone; those pains are too frequent; the doctor won't allow her to eat the foods she wants. She needs someone sweet and gentle, and that someone is Jesus.

Yet you might need a superstar, and he is that. Develop a strong relationship to him on your journey through life. You might say, "Well, I don't think so. What I see in those who call themselves Christians paints a discrediting picture." You are correct, so what. What if the Church, the Jesus people, are sinners and bums: we all are.

In developing a good relationship, I encourage you to be normal and natural. Our Silent Meditation that appeared on the worship bulletin on Palm Sunday said, "Christ, you know I love you, did you see I waved? I believe in you and God, so tell me that I'm saved. Jesus, I am with you, touch me, touch me, Jesus. Jesus I am on your side, kiss me, kiss me, Jesus." — *The Crowd on Palm Sunday* by Webber and Rice. If the identification had read "from *Jesus Christ*

Superstar," which it was, someone might have said, "Oh my, that shouldn't be on the worship bulletin." Don't let that type of comment stop your growing relationship to Superstar.

Be normal and natural in your relationship to Jesus. If you choose the traditional style in prayer, you might simply repeat the 23rd Psalm, you cannot beat it. That's fine, nobody can argue with that. Grandma might use it often. However you may select to converse with God in another way. An example would be: "Here I am, God. It's been a tough week. I've gotten angry at persons. I've done a few things that I know were wrong. Yet I'm here. I guess I'd like to have a spiritual shot-in-the-arm. I'm ready. Sock it to me, maybe in a scripture, a hymn, a poem, a prayer, even in a sermon."

Jesus Superstar is real. Develop a real relationship with him. You know the classic quote from the coach who is giving a pep-talk to his players. "They (the other team) put their pants on like we do one leg at a time." Jesus didn't wear pants as we know them; but he was (and is) just as real as you. He had (and has) the same hopes, desires, and dreams that you do. Jesus Superstar is always present.

A number of words describe Superstar's life and work, such as: understanding, acceptance, forgiveness, compassion, inner strength, obedience to God. I hope these words will become an active part of your vocabulary.

A Christian Church pastor, A. W. Fortune, whose ministry was during the last century; said, "Our fathers served their time, and we must serve ours." My grandfather served his generation; I'm serving mine; and you will serve yours – hopefully all of us with a good relationship to Jesus. He loves your grandma and he loves you.

In our recent worship-through-the-arts month, one of the creative entries in the arts and crafts division was a banner by a woman from St. Louis. It depicted the song "Bridge Over Troubled Waters." The woman constructed a bridge formed by three crosses. The words on the banner were: "Go, ye, Bridge the Troubled Waters." That commission comes from Jesus Christ, Superstar, to you. "Go, ye, bridge the troubled waters." Amen.

(Catalyst, June 1973)

Can Anything Good Come from McPherson?

(Editorial note: The author is the pastor of the First Christian Church, at McPherson, Kansas. This article is adapted from a sermon he gave at a joint worship service of his church and the McPherson Church of the Brethren. The Scripture reference was John 1:43-46.)

Outside our immediate area, few persons have heard of McPherson, Kansas (it often comes out "McFearsome"!). It's a small community, like Norfolk, Nebraska, Mt. Pleasant, Iowa, Paris, Texas, Chillicothe, Missouri and Durant, Oklahoma. On a visit to Pittsburgh, Pennsylvania, we found that friends there had heard of Kansas City and Wichita, but McPherson doesn't mean much to Pittsburghers. Some asked, "Isn't that out close to Dodge City, where Matt Dillon is?"

A recent magazine article about decorating small homes and apartments says, basically: "Think big in small places." And, more and more, each one of us needs to expand their horizons to include the ideas and needs of our world.

If ever a person needed to expand his living space, it was Jesus of Nazareth! He was born in an obscure suburb of Jerusalem. He grew to maturity in an unimportant village called Nazareth, a place so insignificant and unpretentious that Nathanael doubtfully questioned, "Can anything good come out of Nazareth?"

For many people, Nazareth today is Podunk. For me, it was Unidilla, a town of about 200, southeast of my home town. In high school, if you did something stupid, someone would be sure to say, "Go back to Unidilla!"

Regardless of size, some of the world's most significant thinking was done in the town of Nazareth, and from it came one who is known as Lord and King and Master. What mattered most was not the size of the town, not the quality of schools, not the nature of the community or the strength of the synagogue, but rather the Person who found in the town, the school, the community and the synagogue something more vital than anyone else found. Jesus captured from his own small environment all the values it offered and then enriched it with his own insight and depth.

Historians would have been amused if told that a baby born in Bethlehem and reared in Nazareth would play a greater part in history than a Caesar. Indeed, the historians of the day were unaware of the importance of the wandering preacher and teacher of Nazareth. So, when they wrote of the period, most of them failed to mention Jesus at all. They were victims of the fact that there are so many who make loud noises that the humble great are quietly ignored.

True today! If we are asked to name a dozen sports figures or a dozen movie stars, most of us could. But what about the great teachers, scientists, lawyers, clergy, social workers, writers; how many can we list?

It was a small band of followers in New Testament times that became close to Jesus. Philip brought Nathanael, his friend, to Jesus. Good news was scarce then, and surely good news is scarce now. I have read about a painting in which a man is walking through a vast landscape of fog, and the picture speaks of the vague and ill-defined world. But the most important part of that picture is not a world that has lost its shape and meaning, but rather, that the artist left the man with nothing but a blur for a face. Are there persons living today in McPherson, Kansas, like that faceless figure?

Can anything good come from McPherson? Who asks this question? God? Other persons? Do we ask it ourselves?

Just what is McPherson noted for? Minneapolis, Kansas, capitalizing on prehistoric rocks nearby, calls itself the Rock City. Dushler, Nebraska, is known as the Broom City. Wichita, which used to be known as the Air Capital, now calls itself the Fresh Air Capital! Salina is the "City on the Move." (I'm not sure just where it is going?) Well, what about McPherson? We are the "Light Capital!" We have a nice park, a nice high school building, McPherson College and Central College. Is that about it? What about spiritual light? Are we known for that?

I have a habit of stopping to see if I can help stranded motorists on our highways. My friends say it is a bad habit, and that some day I'm going to get clobbered. Anyway, recently I stopped to help a man stalled on the Kansas turnpike. He doesn't know me. He doesn't know my vocation. All that man knows is that I live in McPherson and I stopped to help him; after he had been there for some time and nobody had offered any assistance. What do you think his feeling will be toward us McPhersonites, the next time he goes through the "Light Capital?"

Honors have come to three college youth from our Christian Church. Carol Zimbelman was elected Representative Phillipian by her fellow students. Her election "to the most prestigious position a student can hold" was announced at the annual Awards Assembly. She is also listed in Who's Who in American Colleges, is president of the Comet Social Club and is a recipient of the Oreon E. Scott Memorial Award made to students in The Graduate Seminary of Phillips University. Donna Nickel received the Gertrude Major Award as the outstanding student in education at Phillips. Julie Chinberg recently earned the highest grade on a nursing exam received in the past ten years at Texas Christian University!

Here are three individuals in three important fields: social work, education and nursing. They came from McPherson. They show promise of being vital in their fields. Maybe you know them; maybe you helped shape their lives. Maybe they will be part of the answer to the question, "Can anything good come from McPherson?" You Brethren friends can give like examples. Didn't you help in shaping those lives?

Small Christian groups, "small" only in that their numbers are not large, are noteworthy. Unitarians are in the forefront of social work. Quakers make an impact on the religious front far above their numerical strength. The same may be said for the Brethren, with your emphasis on the simple, meaningful religious life and the dedication to reconciliation which is one of your greatest strengths. A small group, the Nazarenes, leads American denominations in per capita giving to church work, with $213 a year. We Disciples have been noted for giving leadership to the ecumenical movement. Often a local or state Council of Churches executive will be of Disciples background.

It seems incredible now that a handful of men and women who had been touched by Jesus carried their faith and their hope around the world. They did it in a very undramatic way. "Philip found Nathanael." Nathanael found someone else, and that someone else found a friend. Their mission was to share the hope they had found from the Man of Nazareth. That is our mission, also. So, if you have found faith and hope in a faceless, fogbound world, share what you have found!

Kitty Hawk, North Carolina, was unheard of before the Wright brothers made it famous. A small cabin in Kentucky is meaningless until you think of Abraham Lincoln. *What really matters is not where a person came from, but what that person is doing, and where that person is going in life!*

Essentially, it is a relationship to Jesus, the Nazarene, which makes good individuals, whether they come from Little River or London, Chicago or Unidilla, Kansas City or Hope, McPherson or Nazareth. When individuals begin to "think big" with Christ, wherever they live, the place where they are is transformed by the power of the Spirit of God, and small places become as large as the Kingdom of God. Amen.

(The Christian, December 19, 1971)

from Prelude to Postlude

They sat in the pew
ahead of us.
She with snow-white hair,
he with little.

My wife noticed first.
They gently held hands
through the entire service.
How many years had they
    sung hymns
    uttered prayers
    given offerings
    drunk cups
    heard sermons
    enjoyed anthems
    greeted friends
    cherished scripture
    and held hands?

I do not recall anything
special from that Sunday.
Except their touch.
Tender, silent love.

(The Secret Place, Summer 1999)

So You Have Called James Christian

(The author, pastor of the Downey Avenue Christian Church in Indianapolis, Indiana, gave the sermon from which this article is adapted in the final weeks of a pastorate at First Christian Church in McPherson, Kansas.)

The word is out that James Christian is to be your new pastor. The first item of business is to give the Pulpit Committee a word of appreciation for the past nine months of hard work. They spent many hours in talking, thinking, considering the mission and purpose of the church, praying, visiting and traveling, and we are grateful. They worked in the proper manner with Ron Reed, our Regional Minister.

When they visited James Christian, they were open, honest and sensible as they pointed out the strong and weak points of the congregation and its desire for a team ministry. They did not go out and get the cheapest person they could! So, hats off to them for a strong piece or work!

Now for some suggestions, as you contemplate that new ministry. Remember, that indeed, it must be a team effort. I mention the success of Bob Devaney and the Nebraska football team. Bob Devaney does not suit up and score points. And the members of the Cornhuskers team do not coach from the sidelines. However, they both have the same goals in mind, and both contribute to achieving those goals.

I never fail to be amazed at how many church members think the pastor of a church has one goal and takes one direction; while members wander off toward different goals. Friends, it is a team effort! Great things can be accomplished if pastor and people see themselves on the same team, working and loving together as they move toward the high calling of Christian discipleship!

Some church members call a pastor and then do absolutely nothing to help the pastor improve the church. They just sit back and see if the new pastor can do anything.

A good healthy attitude toward James Christian (and pastors in general) is needed. Showing one attitude toward pastors was a notice originating in Great Britain in 1939, as the nation prepared for war, reading: "All persons in the above age group are required to register for national service except lunatics, the blind, and ministers of religion." The vocation of the ministry will never be much with attitudes such as that!

Another example comes from Rollin Fairbanks in *Pastoral Care.* While he was serving his first pastorate in a small town, he entered a shop. The owner, a friendly young man, recognized him as the new preacher. After the usual questions as to how he liked the town, he asked, "What musical instruments do you play?" When told that the new preacher did not play an instrument, he said proudly, and with some pity: "My brother is a preacher, and he can play the guitar and the mouth organ at the same time!" James Christian is a pastor, not a circus entertainer!

As you come to know your new pastor, be aware of some "givens" A "given" is when you go to summer camp and the director says that lunch is at 12:00. If you come at 11:30, you'll have to wait. If you come at 12:30; sorry, there's no more food. That's a given; it's something understood in advance.

Let's illustrate: If you are the general manager of a professional basketball team, and Wilt Chamberlain has just been hired, you do not sit Wilt down in your office and ask, "Have you played any defense in basketball?" He has! Or, if you are the director of a TV program, and Julie Andrews has just been hired, you do not ask Julie, "Have you ever done any singing?" She has, and she does it very well.

Now, when James Christian comes, please do not ask him: "Are you a Christian?" "Have you ever conducted a funeral?" "Is the Bible important?" "Do you love God?" These are givens. And, the sooner you see, in your own eyes, that James Christian is a Christian, and loves God, the better for all of you.

Allow me to give you some guidance in supporting the new pastor. There will be times when you do not feel you can agree with his interpretation, his stand, or his way of presenting the faith. Enter into dialogue with him about any concerns. And when you do agree, tell him and support him. By seeking out places of agreement, you can be supportive and still remain honest to your own convictions.

Some years ago a staff person from our Disciples Pension Fund wrote an article on our subject. I've revised his suggestions to apply to your anticipated team ministry.

1. Treat the pastor as an important person who is engaged in the most urgent, important work in the world.

2. Support the pastor's leadership and direction of the mission and purpose of the church.

3. Encourage the pastor for standing for high Christian ideals, even to the point of loving enemies; even when he substitutes "The Gospel: Love It and Live It" for "America: Love It or Leave It."

4. Earn a share of the joys and satisfactions that come from Christian service.

5. Listen to the pastor. He might even get over some of his *crazy* ideas if he could share them with a real good listener – or they might turn out to be not so crazy, after all!

6. Make an effort to be as understanding of the pastor as you desperately want someone to be of you.

All this will result in such a harmonious relationship that, in four or five years, there will be no small group saying, "It's time to send James Christian down the road."

May I encourage you to distinguish sharply between minors and majors in the ministry. The minors are James Christian's own thing, and none of your business. I list a few.

He drives a red sports car; he votes for the Vegetarian Party; he wears bow ties; he hasn't bought anything from your store in six months; he has a good-looking wife; he likes mustard on his fried-egg sandwiches. These are minors. Say nothing about them!

Now, here are some majors, and if he should stub his toe on one, he might be in need of some well-planned suggestions.

He feels that blacks are inferior; all Roman Catholics are bad news; God is worshiped only at daybreak; women elders are out; your next child will be a girl, if you pray hard enough. If such major statements as these come out, action needs to be taken. If he says all those in the church down the street are going straight to hell, that's major, and a "No-no." But if he likes to eat rhubarb pie and pizza at eleven at night and can still be alert for a ten-o'clock funeral service the next morning, that's a minor.

When James C. acts and speaks out like a Christian – support him! Some years ago, a fellow pastor supported open housing in his community. That church held a nine o'clock and an eleven o'clock service. At nine, he preached that all are brothers and sisters in Christ, supported this with scripture, and said anyone should be able to live wherever they desired if they could afford it. After the early service, the church leaders held a meeting with him and said that if he preached that sermon at eleven, he was out. He preached the same sermon, and he was out! God help us! But thank God for that pastor! The Christian faith is stronger because of him!

In November, 1965, an editorial from *Missions,* the American Baptist publication, listed some ways to "kill your pastor." I've selected two to mention for your meditation: ignore him, or love him to death. To illustrate the latter, more positive point, the story is told that a "famous" church known for great pulpit men was open. The congregation called a young man, and, after a year, a group met with him and diplomatically indicated that he was not living up to their past strong reputation. The new pastor said, "I'm sorry; I'll resign." To that statement he was told, "Oh no; it's our job to make you a great preacher and pastor!"

Let me be even more personal and pointed. Eleven years ago, when I was the pastor of a small church, death came by way of suicide to a young man who was a member. The memory is still clear of sharing that experience with the bereaved mother. For the funeral service that small church was packed with friends, fellow students, and the curious. Afterward, the comment was overheard, "I wonder who they brought in to do the service." They brought in no one! A young pastor, two years out of seminary, did it, and afterward the mother complimented me on the "good job." She was mistaken. A "good job" had been done because she had had confidence that I could bring hope into a very difficult situation.

If great pastors are made, they are made by church members who have given them the proper care and love.

Many of you looked puzzled when I announced that James Christian was to be your new pastor. Please do not call your Presbyterian friends and say so. "James Christian" is fictitious; but, hopefully, these comments are not. "*Ponder anew what the Almighty can do,*" in a team ministry, with your cooperative attitude and active support; complemented by the grace and love of God. Amen.

(<u>The Christian</u>, September 23, 1973)

Those Tabernacle Teams

Church league basketball usually brings a yawn from most people. Yet I found the mid-1950's to be exciting as a player, coach and hustler for Tabernacle Christian Church in Lincoln, Nebraska. The Lincoln Church Leagues were divided by ages into Classes A, B, C, D. The public school did not allow games between junior highs, so boys played for Class C church teams. The high school coaches would drop by to see key players of this "farm-system."

My own fame ran toward coach and hustler. Not content with church league games, we scheduled high school teams from small southeast Nebraska towns. In 1952, Unidilla High School played us. At 6'3" I was somewhat of a giant in small towns, but twice I let a bounce pass go right through my legs, and the crowd laughed. Brad Warner got burned on a heating stove close to one of the baskets when he went in for a shot. The game was on my birthday and later at the dinner for the teams in the Unidilla Christian Church they sang "Happy Birthday" to the clumsy ox. We lost 27-29.

In 1954 we scheduled a game with Hallam High School, playing on their tile floor. We dressed above the floor on a balcony. One team member decided to see what was on the other side of a temporary door. It fell, exposing our team, but gratefully not the players as we were almost dressed. We won 57-49 in a polio benefit game.

Our 1955 B team beat Greenwood High 72-55 and Douglas High 70-64. Douglas was ranked in the top ten of their Class. I recall the Douglas cheerleaders cart-wheeling around the gym yelling "sink-'er Bobby, sink-'er." Bobby didn't sink enough shots because we outscored them in the last quarter 24-12. Jerry Amen (a wonderful name for a church team member) arranged a date with a cheerleader. I'm sure his baby-blue 1949 Pontiac convertible scored more points than his floor play. Later our Class C team would play, but lose to Otoe High.

Yet the church league was our real meat. We were a church with a gym which really helped. And how I would hustle and recruit. All very proper and ethical. The league requirements were that a player must attend worship services twice a month, and our players did.

Our B team won the city championship in 1953, 1954 and 1955. Our A team won every year from 1955 to 1958. Our C team won in 1956. That team played "one of the games we're glad we didn't see" listed that March in the Lincoln Journal. We beat St Matthew's Episcopal 76-5 with the game being stopped after the third quarter. The quarters were seven minutes with a running clock. Being more greedy than benevolent, I was irritated that the referee had stopped the game. I wanted to get 100 points. But he was a Pennsylvania-steel-bred-Nebraska-football-end, so I said, "Sure, you're right, it should be stopped."

Church leagues are not run like the NBA. In 1956 the referees did not show for a game. Trying to reschedule the game would be difficult, so I volunteered to ref. The other coach agreed, and while the game was on I blew the whistle; during time outs and at the half, I was the coach. My own team questioned my calls more than the opposition. We won the game by 9 points. The other coach congratulated me on calling a fair game. I did not submit a fee to the league office.

Teams were pointing for us. Against our 1956 A team First Presbyterian used Stan Matzke, a former three-year letterman from the University of Nebraska, along with Ted Conner, an all-stater from Hastings. Yet we prevailed

36-34. That same team played Nebraska Wesleyan's Freshman team winning 59-54; and the Wesleyan Reserve team, losing the first time 45-51, winning the return game 51-49.

Between 1951 and 1957 we won 86% of our games, mostly against churches with memberships up to five times our size. At the end of each city tournament, All-Tournament teams were named and listed in the Sunday Journal-Star. In 1955, 1956 and 1957 we placed 19 out of a possible 45. Our 1958 A team played in the national YMCA tourney at Salina, Kansas.

Having been successful in basketball we thought we would try softball. I coached the 1955 Girls team, with the help of Brad Warner, we won the city. Our 1956 Midget team, also a city champion, was built around our pitcher, Roger Campbell who had a 9-1 season and batted .667. Our catcher was Brian Thoms, a left-handed throwing Catholic. I hadn't hustled him. He lived in the immediate neighborhood and wanted to play. "Yes, it's okay" said his parents, and "he'll come to your worship." Talk about ecumenical fellowship! Brian got Roger a lot of strike-outs. As soon as the ball left Roger's hand Brian would yell "SWING!" and most batters did just that.

Yet the team I will always remember was the 1956 C basketball team. We won our three tournament games 63-35, 59-26 and 69-38,

Four of that team made the all-tournament team and were just starting their sports careers. Doug Osterholm would star for Lincoln High in basketball. Dick McCoy would be a varsity standout in gymnastics. Dick Harr made the Southeast High basketball varsity as a sophomore. He would later be All-City in football, twice city player of the week and win letters in football, basketball, track and baseball. Dave Wohlfarth would become state tennis doubles champion for the state of Nebraska. Later he became sports editor for the Dayton Journal-Herald; and the Lincoln Journal-Star.

Then there was Don Burt. He would make the Lincoln High varsity basketball team as a sophomore. In 1958 and 1959 he would be selected All-City, All-State and All-Tournament as he led Lincoln High to consecutive state championships in Nebraska Class AA. As a senior he was selected winner of the Harry Sidney Dobbins Memorial Award, based on achievements in athletics and scholarship. In our final Class C game for Tabernacle he got 29 points.

In the fall of 1957 I moved to Texas Christian University and Brite Divinity Seminary. The 1962 C team would have a winning record, and the 1962 and 1964 A teams won city championships. But Tabernacle would never be the power they were in the mid-1950s. In the late 1960's they would change the church name to Southview and in the early 1970's they dismantled the third floor gym.

To what extent we exemplified Christianity in our sports program, one really can't adequately measure. I do know that our 1957 Athletic Committee report stated: "Through all our success we have tried to maintain a policy of 'what profit is there in winning, if youth do not learn to love God and their neighbor.'"

Even as church teams we never attempted to invoke God's blessing; or to encourage Divine intervention on the final score of the games. Learning that God has more important things to do than direct a ball into a basket is a positive learning experience. I believe in some individuals there was "spiritual success." At least there was growth in the human encounter.

A few years ago I was back in Lincoln, and I found and kept, a brick from the old gym. It reminds me of some church teams that were really very good.

(The Disciple, January 18, 1981)

Watching the old clock die

It came from the family farmhouse, and had
been refinished.
But you could tell it was old.
Then it made a strange sound, as if something
snapped.
The big, bruised pendulum kept moving, but
you could feel it was about to quit.
The spark from within went out, and so the arc
of life grew shorter and shorter.
You could detect movement for about ten more
minutes, then nothing.
Until loving hands started it again.

My friend is like that old clock.
The loving hands are God's.
And resurrection is the important word in
God's vocabulary.

(The Disciple, April 4, 1983)

The Schools

(Editorial note: Walter Knorr, a member of Downey Avenue Christian Church in Indianapolis, is one of seven members of his city's school board. An accountant, he has been a member of the congregation for thirteen years. His pastor, William W. McDermet III, interviews Mr. Knorr for The Disciple.)

McDermet: Walt, how did you become involved with the schools?

Knorr: In 1973, our oldest son was bused to an inner-city school. There were hard feelings in the community concerning schools. But we made up our minds very early that it was not our job to protest or march against the judge and the school board, but to work as hard as we could to make a success of the situation. We felt that our children's education was much more important than the school building or area to which they were sent. We became quite active in the new school. I was later elected president of the PTA.

McDermet: How did you get your name on the ballot?

Knorr: In a lighter moment, talking with another member of Downey about what was going wrong at the school, I said, "I guess the only way to get it straightened out is to run for the School Board." I did not know that my friend had met some people who were forming a group to slate people for the School Board. I was contacted by them to go through the slating process. Out of 54, I was selected as one of seven to run.

McDermet: All seven were elected!

Knorr: That's right. It was a real change for Indianapolis. For forty-some years the same group, really under the control of one man, selected candidates. They took control in 1930, following strong KKK influence. They were conservative, basically; it was quite an upset when we won.

McDermet: Financing came from where?

Knorr: We sold memberships for $10 for CHOICE (Citizens Helping our Indianapolis Children's Education). We contacted business people, we took donations from anybody – a grass roots type of thing. The laws make it very difficult for the average citizen of Indianapolis to run for School Board.

McDermet: What's the size of IPS?

Knorr: We have 75,000 students and 4,000 teachers in 103 elementary and junior high schools and ten high schools. There are an additional 4,000-5,000 support personnel. Our budget is $125 million.

McDermet: Racial balance in the public school system is a complex concern. How do you view this?

Knorr: We are not ordered to balance racially by a percentage. That bothers many people. I think the courts are trying to say that we do not want to be left with "black" or "white" schools. We still have eighteen schools defined as "black" – 95 to 100 percent black. We know we are going to have to eliminate that. We still don't know what the court will demand of us. The courts will probably give us some guidelines, saying, "You can have no less then ______ percent black or white children." *If* there is busing, it needs to be two-way busing.

McDermet: What comments do you have for the concerned church member who supports a good learning process in the schools?

Knorr: Anyone who wants to support a good learning process has to become involved. Parents and other taxpayers need to get into the schools, to see what's happening. And when they find things they don't think are right, they need to get all the facts and put pressure on those who are running the schools to get things changed. Involvement is critical. People need to find out how the school system is run.

It's unbelievable that many people don't know what the school board's job is. For example, when it snows, it is not the school board that decides if schools should be closed. Someone in an administrative position will make that decision, not the board.

McDermet: What is the school board's job?

Knorr: To set policy and evaluate the job being done by those carrying out the policy.

McDermet: What are your personal hopes as a board member?

Knorr: My hopes have changed after two and one-half years on the board. Originally I hoped that by the time I got off the board the desegregation case would be settled. In the election campaign I said I was not going to argue about the right or wrong of busing and the use of money to supply buses. But we have been found guilty and by law we have been ordered to correct that situation. We've been in court for more than ten years over the desegregation issue. It's taken time and money, and we have not done our job because of the uncertainty of the future. Long-range planning has all but ceased. I hope we can end this situation and get back to educating children.

I would like to see teachers, students and parents in Human Relations Workshops. I also wish each local school could share in school budget decisions.

Another hope is for strong parent involvement, which now is lacking. Another is the use of public school buildings by the public. Instead of opening at 8:00 and locking at 4:00, I would like the buildings to be used by the community. We now have pilot programs in five schools, where the community will decide how the building can be used.

McDermet: What are some of your biggest frustrations?

Knorr: No matter what your decision, some people will say you are wrong. I try to do my homework, but when it comes down to a vote, we're wrong in the eyes of some of the public. Another frustration is pressure groups. The group that sponsored us is putting on pressure in a certain direction. Teachers are organized and they put on a lot of pressure. Such groups mean well, but when I vote, I have to base my vote on what I feel is best for the *whole* school system, not for that one group. Negotiating with the teachers is frustrating. The state legislature determines what our resources are. This is public information, yet it takes six to eight months of negotiations to decide on teacher salaries, when we already know the limits.

McDermet: Can you list some satisfactions?

Knorr: Yes, there really are some. Our school system did not have an Affirmative Action program. We now have one. Affirmative Action programs offer employment to minorities, either race and/or sex. We give all an opportunity to compete for jobs. We also give minority persons already employed additional training. We require building contractors to have similar programs or we don't do business with them! We have adopted new testing programs to measure the growth of children, and we share these results with their parents.

McDermet: Does the church have a role in public education?

Knorr: Church members need to know what is happening in education so they can support when support is deserved and demand change where change is needed. School systems are dealing with the lives of a lot of people and church members need to be involved in that.

McDermet: Would you or the other six board members be interested in discussing issues with church members?

Knorr: I would, and I think many board members in any community would. I've never refused to talk with any group.

McDermet: We hear of school systems being restrictive in what textbooks are used. What happens here?

Knorr: The state approves a list of textbooks. We give those books to volunteer committees composed of administrators, teachers and parents. We use their recommendations in purchasing books. In forming any committee – since I've been on the board – we have teacher and parent representation. This was not done in previous years. I know of no books that have been banned.

McDermet: Have you felt support from members of your church?

Knorr: One of the most rewarding things has been the support I've had from the members of Downey. A number have come to me and offered their support. Others have written notes. Some may not have agreed with the stands I have taken, but they have offered their support.

(The Disciple, August 5, 1979. This article included two pictures: one of Walter Knorr and one with Walter and his wife, Sue, with their Sunday school class at Downey Avenue.)

Suffering and the Righteousness of God

I

> I am tired of living. Listen to how bitter I am. Why, God did you let me be born? I should have died before anyone saw me. To go from the womb straight to the grave would have been as good as never existing.
>
> Job, before his dialogue with God

In the early 1960's, I attended the wedding of Jerry and Karla. They made a lovely couple. Twelve years later Karla died. She died after suffering great physical pain for months and months. The suffering process of dying in her case lasted for about five years. For the last three months she let only Jerry and a sister-in-law be with her; she did not want to have others see her suffer. They suffered anyway. Why does a good God let it happen? How can God be close and yet do nothing?

It is characteristic of the Old Testament that its central problem was undeserved suffering. The Old Testament writers believed that everything centered in Yahweh. Thus every experience of suffering was believed to be the will of Yahweh. The very presence of suffering implies that somewhere there is a moral sin.

Sin in the Old Testament is seen as a rebellion against God and the moral law which God sets before man. To the Old Testament prophets, sin is disobedience to the moral requirements of God. Suffering is seen as the result of sin.

A main idea held for a long time within the Old Testament was the belief that if there was evil within the Israel nation there would be suffering. One could always find some evil, usually without looking too far. And the prophets could point to the sin as the cause of suffering. Yet with the growing rise of individualism, this corporate explanation of suffering left much to be desired.

Jeremiah states in 12:1, "Why does the way of the wicked prosper?" He has no answer. Again in 15:18 Jeremiah says, "Why is my pain unceasing, my wound incurable, refusing to be healed?"

By far our greatest insight to suffering in the Old Testament is the book of Job. It is a masterpiece of a book, and it is the one which in every age is felt to be modern. Today the view is generally accepted that Job is the name of an ancient worthy, and that there was a historical person behind the book, but that the work as we have it is the artistic creation of the author, or authors, who simply used the figure of Job as the vehicle for his message.

II Some Insights into Suffering

The book of Job deals somewhat with suffering. The mystery of human pain is discussed. But this is not the purpose of the book. Job goes beyond the suffering problem to the larger concern of finding a way of consecrated living.

To assume that the aim of Job is to furnish some kind of philosophical answer to the problem of innocent suffering is to miss the writer's purpose. The Hebrew mind was not primarily a philosophical mind; primarily it was a religious mind. Even when it asked philosophical questions, it gave religious answers.

The idea that suffering ennobles is very easy for the one who does not suffer. It explains somebody else's problem! Much more than physical illness is seen in the person of Job. He becomes estranged from God and knows enough of God to evaluate his loss. Were Job to become an atheist his real problem would cease to exist. His physical problems with undeserved evil would stay, but any spiritual torture, which is the real issue, would end.

One insight that comes from Job's suffering is his ability to talk out his problems. He does not curse God. He does admit to a lack of understanding to all his sufferings. God allows the eternal-human dialogue. This is a far better approach than damning God, or sulking in silence. Frank argument is always better than brooding silence, for silence breaks the bond, while words heal the relationship. From Job we can learn that God invites man to be frank with Him. Silence implies that we recognize no one to whom we can go to for strength or insight.

God's words in Job, and God's words in much of the Old Testament, have a central theme that is expressed in the words, "the fear of the Lord is the beginning of all wisdom." Some would substitute the word "love" in place of fear. The theme is that man should be reverent and submissive to God. God has hidden glory and hidden majesty that passes all human understanding. These attributes can never really be understood fully by man. Job's friends had believed in a God who was easy to understand, a God who rewarded goodness and punished sin. But God to Job was One who causes the sun to shine on good and evil alike, who causes the rain to fall on the righteous and the wicked. It was this God who had humbled Job, and who taught him to keep faith even in adversity.

Unfortunately in the first part of the book Job believes not in God, but in his own self-made conception of God. Job wants to meet God, but on Job's terms. He tries to become God's equal.

Some writers have supposed that the purpose of the book was to solve the mystery of suffering. If this was indeed its purpose it must be pronounced a failure. The mystery of suffering is too great and too complex to be solved in so short a study, even if any writer thought he could solve it at all. The dialogue nowhere penetrates the true reason for Job's suffering, and if the purpose of the debate was to solve this problem, it nowhere comes within sight of the solution.

The Bible has no simple solution to the problem of suffering. There are some whose sufferings are self-entailed; but there are some whose sufferings are not. Jeremiah insisted that some suffering is not innocent; the book of Job insists that some is.

One purpose of the book of Job is certainly to protest against the idea that misfortune is the evidence of sin, and to affirm that there is a problem of innocent suffering. But this is not where the author's originality is to be found. In this he is but reaffirming what is to be found in the Law and the Prophets and the Psalms. The author of Job was concerned less with theology than with religion. So far as any theological or philosophical explanation of the mystery of suffering is concerned, he has none to offer. The reader is told the explanation in Job's case, but that was necessary in order to establish that Job was really an innocent sufferer. Neither Job nor his friends can deduce the reason, and when God speaks from the whirlwind to Job, He does not disclose.

That the book of Job can speak to modern man can be illustrated in the success of Archibald MacLeish's, *J. B.*, a modern day version of Job. Part of its success is because suffering is as much a part of our time as any time.

Suffering may lead to faith, or a deeper level of faith. The Old Testament writers may be attempting to note that indeed we trust God, but in the suffering God is trusting man to be faithful.

Suffering seems to have a place in God's plan for us. It has value, not only for the sufferer, but also for others. Through suffering, mankind is lifted from lower to higher levels of understanding. This is one of the explanations why the righteous suffer. It applies with equal truth to our suffering, and to God's. Those who suffer much, are too often obsessed with what they have undergone. The secret of deliverance from this painfully general preoccupation with our own misfortunes is the discovery that they can be a source of insight.

In the end Job's problem is left unsolved, except that in the infinite wisdom of God undeserved suffering must have an explanation beyond our comprehension. This is the simple idea of faith, which does not insist upon explaining everything, but trusts the fundamental love and care of God in both prosperity and adversity. Job's inward experience of God at last satisfies him that there is a deeper justice and a deeper meaning in life than we can sometimes see. God speaks to him and he is satisfied.

III *Chapter Four of Job*

Friendship is still one of the strongest forces in this world. In the fourth chapter friendship may not be seen as even part of the answer to suffering, but friendship is not rejected. Job's friends traveled many miles to comfort him. At first their silence is not due to rejection, but to respect and compassion. Friendship is a strong theme of the Hebrew wisdom literature. Eliphaz apologized for having remained silent for so long.

Eliphaz says to Job what most of us would say. He tries to get at the bottom of the matter. To put the issue in modern language his friend is saying: "Job, you are very, very guilty; you are a horrible, immoral person. Your friends have stood with you, but now we should not because you are a sinful person and God is therefore punishing you. The only thing for you to do now is to face up to your sin, and take God's punishment and die."

The element of faith becomes the major issue. The sixth verse says: "Is not your fear of God your confidence, and the integrity of your ways your hope?" One wonders if the word "faith" might here be substituted for the word "fear?"

The progression in this chapter is very smooth. At verse 12 Eliphaz speaks of a vision that had come to him which revealed the truth, that no one is so perfect that he does not sin and therefore there is no one who does not deserve some punishment.

The mystery of suffering is the theme from verse 12 to the end of the chapter. Eliphaz believes he knows why the righteous suffer. The impact comes to him by revelation. He falls into some type of deep trance and understanding it by much inner-searching. A Spirit-vision visits him. He thus believes that whatever happens to man, he deserves it. Men are not God. In Eliphaz we see a picture of God that is very orthodox. In Eliphaz we see God "right and proper." But Eliphaz's God is a God removed from the real situation. God is majestic and pure and shows mercy, but is distant and is not involved in His world. Job will have none of this type of explanation, and of course the reader is the better for it. Eliphaz's God is only Eliphaz's God; he cannot be Job's God!

IV *Chapter Forty-two of Job*

A key part of the book of Job is 42:1-6. Job does not have a meaningful experience with God until he gets himself out of the center of the drama.

Life for some is seen as a mystery, but not a dark one, but one of light. This is seen at its best in Job. After much debate with his friends, and with God, Job comes to understand that the ways of God are meant to be a mystery to humans, a mystery to which the proper attitude is to be trusting and humble before God. The author of Job has Job take this attitude in his final statements (42:1-6). When we take the book as a whole we are led to see this possible answer to suffering. At the end of the book Job's fortunes are restored because of faithfulness to the mystery of suffering. Job simply must endure the suffering. Nowhere in Job is there ever spelled out any answer to explain his suffering. The writer Job wants the reader to understand that suffering is a necessary condition which can bring about deep religious belief. This could not be comprehended by simply reading about the subject, it has to be experienced first hand.

Job was suffering to vindicate more than himself. He was vindicating God's trust in him. He was not so much abandoned by God as supremely honored by God. The author wishes to make it plain that the actual cause in any given case cannot be deduced by man. The cause or reason for the suffering is hidden in the heart of God. Job, by suffering, was serving God, and the reader can identify with this.

The author very boldly gives God human words, and thus makes Job aware of the reality of God. He also allows God to become a creator and ruler of the world that bends toward Job, thus granting Job a vision of God's ways. Then, in the presence of God all pain becomes bearable, for God's grace is sufficient. Job becomes aware of his sinfulness at the very instant of his reconciliation with God. He is saved at the moment of his surrender. Indeed, he receives all when he surrenders all. Probably *the* key verse of the total book is 42:5: "I had heard of thee by the hearing of the ear, but now my eye sees thee." This is the culmination of a deep religious experience.

By the time we are finished reading the final chapter we realize that there is no spelled-out answer to suffering. However when the reader has gone through this ordeal *with* Job, and experienced the total event, no statement may be necessary. By the time the total book is digested and experienced there has developed a deep sense of the nearness, beauty and strength of a God in whom faith is the answer. The answer is rooted in hope, a hope that sees God in any and all situations. The situations however do not control God.

Job's response to God's speech is in a mood of complete humility. When Job said "I heard of thee," or as Today's English Version puts it: "Then I know only what others had told me," he is saying that he understood only a religion based on past tradition. When he says, "but now I have seen you with my own eyes," he is referring to a direct communication with God.

Job gives the reader the feeling that all the (doubt, death, and destruction) was worth it. He finds meaning in life. He finds meaning in suffering. He finds meaning in God.

Coming to grips with Job, and the whole problem of suffering is not something to be done in an afternoon when one has nothing else to do. The issue may continue through one's lifetime. There are different levels of insights to Job. The most superficial level has to do with the suffering of the innocent.

Deeper insights reveal that there is for Job a place where the problem is not solved, but answers seem to be appearing. The question "why?" is ever present, but it is not overpowering. Job is coming to understand that faith is the final word.

Still the greatest insight appears when Job comes face to face with God. At this point, for the first time he rids himself of his own concerns. When Yahweh does come, Job's walls of self-centeredness disappear. His small little world of suffering crumbles. He stops focusing on himself, and he thinks about God. In the divine-human dialogue new life is born, even out of the suffering.

So the answer to suffering is no answer, but something more. As P. T. Forsyth said: "We do not see the answer; we trust the Answerer. We do not gain the victory; we are united with the Victor" (Wesley C. Baker, More Than a Man Can Take [Philadelphia: Westminster Press, 1966], p. 118).

The concluding happy epilogue seems to spoil the story for many. As we come to understand that more than one writer had a hand in the book of Job, a different person may have tacked-on the section of the final seven verses. Modern man must remember that it is Old Testament man, so how else was an author to show the final happy-ending of a faithful Job, but to restore his fortunes on this earth.

V *The Major Purpose of Job*

The book of Job does not set out to give, and does not give, a philosophical solution to the problem of suffering. Instead, it asks, "What will a truly religious man do with the fact of suffering?" and "How will his suffering affect his relation to his God?" (Dwight E. Stevenson, Preaching on the Books of the Old Testament [New York: Harper & Brothers, 1961], p. 93).

Under the strong pressure of suffering, man discovers his true relationship to God; and if he is mature he will move from a traditional, second hand faith, through pride and rebelling to a genuine depth relationship with God.

But what the book of Job says is that there is something more fundamental than the intellectual solution of life's mysteries. The author has a message for the spirit rather than for the intellect. When one is suffering it may be good to understand the cause; but it is better to be sustained than to endure.

That Job is able to accept a God whom he cannot understand undergirds the belief that he has experienced faith. Through the total event he has experienced a new concept of God. Job may not be able to understand God's purposes, but he comes to the place of accepting God's purposes. Job comes, through suffering to an understanding that he is related to something beyond himself. Since Job considers integrity of greater value than himself, it can overcome all selfish considerations.

In the form of the book of Job the author is conveying that human dialogue (Job and his friends) and monologue (Job talking with himself) must stop and the important factor is the eternal and human dialogue (Yahweh and Job). Job must have a religious experience with Yahweh himself. It is at that moment that he understands. He understands when he does not attempt to meet Yahweh as an equal. The author expresses the meaningful relationship between Yahweh and Job with the words, "I had heard of thee by the hearing of the ear, but now my eye sees thee."

Sin is separation from God. And in the case of suffering, the sufferer felt cut-off from God, or so Job thought. But the author is saying that in innocent suffering the sufferer must not feel deserted by God. That God has not deserted the sufferer is a truth of Job.

Job finds a new relationship with God, through suffering. Knowing that God is with him he rests in God even in his pain. This is not to explain the meaning of suffering. It is to declare to the reader that even such bitter agony as Job endured may be turned to spiritual profit if he finds God in it. The author gives the feeling that the suffering person is better off than the prosperous wicked – because he still has God.

H.H. Rowley feels there are no better insights in the New Testament to this problem than in the Old. Paul has a thorn in the flesh, but God says, "my grace is sufficient, for my power is made perfect in weakness." Paul finds enrichment in his suffering. Job has the same experience.

The main question is not suffering, rather, what is the meaning of faith? Job finally looked beyond the wisdom of men to find this answer, to the wisdom of God.

VI

There is no answer to the problem of suffering. The only possibility is to declare in faith that God may be known in suffering, for indeed God has been there all along.

The book of Job offers several suggestions in dealing with suffering, but there is no real conclusion. Suffering may be retribution, testing, discipline, or mainly inexplicable. What really matters is the strength of a person's relationship with God. The relationship must be strong through both times of success and failure. The book of Job insists that God is to be worshiped solely because God is God, and that faith comes only with his divine presence.

The whole issue is the concern of life on earth where both happiness and misfortune come to man; and that man simply cannot, nor need he continue to attempt to find out why. The religious man is made to suffer so as to strengthen his faith and to deepen his belief. Perhaps Job has been too smug in his righteousness and had to be humbled before he was repaid with interest for his sufferings. If the story is taken in this light then Satan is no longer the fallen angel who goads Yahweh into doing evil, but he becomes Yahweh's special instrument for strengthening man's religious growth. Here in the book of Job the worst punishment was not the underserved misfortune as the doubt that went with it. God had no doubt about the final outcome.

The greatest dramatic action in the book is within the mind of Job. There is the battle ground, and it is the same with modern man as it was with Old Testament man. From start to finish the point is not what man thinks of God; but what God things of man.

The problem of suffering seen in Job is never really solved. To understand the book of Job will not stop anguish and despair, but it may direct a person's experience of suffering toward a deep understanding of religious faith. Coming to grips with Job requires the reader to become a participant in the dialogue. God speaks to man when man is able to hear. Coming to grips with Job causes the reader to discover deep meanings in God.

With a keen sense of suspense and an insight to psychology, the writer withholds until the end of his work the secret of the total story of Job; which is to show the divinity of God, the humanity of man, and the special relationship between a God who is truly God and a man who is truly man. All of this is seen with faith.

In the final analysis, we can only believe that God is good and that some day God will make plain what we understand only now in faith.

(Encounter, Fall, 1979)

The "Old" Testament as Revelation for Contemporary People

I believe that God is constantly searching for human beings, endeavoring to get through to us God's own purpose and will. Revelation is defined as God's own self-disclosure of God's will and purpose. Revelation is the act of revealing or disclosing. To this end what is usually referred to as the "Old" Testament is the record of a group of people with whom God was particularly successful.

The Disciples of Christ, of which I am one, is a communion that has espoused such slogans as, "Where the Scriptures speak, we speak; where they are silent, we are silent." Also, "No creed but Christ, no book but the Bible, no name but the Divine." Please note that Bible and Scriptures are used here with no distinction between the two Testaments. I feel comfortable in understanding God's revelation in both Testaments, noting that I am Christian, and thus find a very special revelation in the person of Jesus of Nazareth.

However many contemporary people have a minimal regard for the stories and concepts expressed in the "Old" Testament, and most people find little if any revelation of God there. That is most unfortunate. One of the major problems that prevents us from taking the "Old" Testament seriously is the very label we have given it: "old." This long Christian tradition robs the Hebrew scriptures of any independent meaning and credibility, for most people insist on interpreting the "old" through the "new." Seen in this context the "old" is believed to be out-of-date, outmoded, passe or no longer necessary. Therefore in this article I will use the term "the Hebrew Bible" for the first thirty-nine books of the Bible.

Many Hebrew Bible questions and concerns are those of today, and the Hebrew Bible speaks to those ancient and contemporary concerns. The Hebrew Bible reflects prayer, fear, passion and pleasure. All scripture contains the record of revelation of divine will and purpose, without which life cannot be rightly lived on this earth, or peace, justice, and goodwill among all be attained. (1) People of the Hebrew Bible lived, loved, laughed and were as lethargic as people are today. The sayings and insights of Amos, Hosea, Isaiah, Jeremiah and Ezekiel were not only a revelation to people of the Hebrew Bible; they are a revelation to contemporary people.

The Hebrew Bible reveals that individuals will find their proper development only through wholehearted service to something greater than themselves, and to the Hebrew Bible writers, that "something" is God.

We see in the Hebrew Bible that when God calls people to be righteous it is because God is righteous. Or when God calls people to show a tender and gracious spirit toward the weak, it is because God shows that spirit in the Exodus event. In the Hebrew Bible we are reminded that God enters into experience with people, and teaches them about God, when they are sensitive to learn. Even "enemies" in the Hebrew Bible were within God's control.

People in the Hebrew Bible came to know God through living. Life for them was good. There is only one case of known suicide in the Hebrew Bible. The Hebrew Bible writers said in effect, "God knows me, and I know God in the experience of living."

In the Hebrew Bible I find a growing revelation of God. At times those within the story have a childish or immature insight of God, and at other times we see clearly an adult or mature nature of God. Yet the Hebrew Bible writers were probably correct in allowing the reader to see all levels of understanding, and the childish experiences are not withheld.

The great events in the Hebrew Bible (the covenants, the Exodus event, the gift of new land, the presence in the Exile) are all interpretations of historical memories and data which see God at work to save people. Our directing and saving God has created a people out of the lost, and thus has established deep relationships. In kindness God has given life and land, and the people thus have a relationship of gratitude.

II

One degree of the revelation of God recognized in the Hebrew Bible is seen keenly through the prophets. In every account of a Hebrew Bible prophet's call the initiative is with God. Amos says he was "taken away by God" and rejects any relationship with professionals. Yahweh requires Hosea to marry Gomer. Isaiah reports on his overwhelming vision of God. Jeremiah feels the hand of Yahweh on him as a youth.

The prophets saw themselves as God's spokesmen. They felt many revelations of God, which established a permanent relationship with God. The Hebrew Bible prophets also felt a real kinship between God and humans. Humans are presented in the Hebrew Bible as spiritual beings, akin to God who is Spirit.

The prophets give to God human attributes. They speak of God as sorrowing and rejoicing, loving and hating, pleased and angry, proposing and then modifying or changing God's purpose, for that is the way they conveyed their meaning. H. Wheeler Robinson says it is a travesty of that meaning to try to transform it into the Greek philosophic pattern, as Christian theology has often done. (2)

For the prophets, humans should judge their conduct by the goodness of God. Yahweh wants the best moral conduct from every individual. They made God's thoughts known to the highest earthly leaders at the risk of their own lives. In all their activity, the prophets remained hopeful. They believed that humans had the power to discern right from wrong; they believed there was one God for all peoples. All of this came from a faith in God intuitive, reasoned, tested, and applied. (3)

For us the word of the prophet becomes revelation only when it finds intelligent and obedient response in receptive persons – both then and now.

III

For myself, I comprehend God's revelation in the Hebrew Bible as I thoughtfully come to grips with specific events.

One such event is Moses' encounter with God at the point of the burning bush. God spoke to and through this shepherd. In some places in the Hebrew Bible God was a God of the mountains, or fire or stars. But here God is concerned about people, persons who are under oppression. The flame signifies the bodily manifestation of God's actual presence. Moses is visited by a living God. Later, Pharaoh saw only the rights of those who ruled over the slaves. Moses saw the right of his people to freedom and happiness. We thank God for such persons then and now. When we measure the words of a prophet we ask, "How does it square with God?" Out of the unusual form of the burning bush Moses found God's content. Most would assume that if they would have been there, they too, would have seen the burning bush. But this is not necessarily so. Moses was prepared to see. So too must contemporary people be ready to receive revelation from God.

Another revelation is the event of Noah, the flood, and the rainbow. It is generally recognized that this story is based upon the Babylonian story found in the Gilgamesh Epic, and similar flood stories are found in other cultures. Yet here we find a revelation of God. The writer is saying God's own creation is doing a pretty lousy job of living within God's creation. This story may be partly myth, yet it is also a parable of terrible reality. There comes a point, when evil and sin are so heavy that something has to break. When that time comes, the forces of decency left upon the earth are not strong enough to hold back the deluge.

For Noah it was 40 days. For contemporary people it might be the time it takes to fight a war. In our time the flood is not of water, but it is of blood and tears. Noah was faithful and built the Ark, even though he did not fully understand why. God spoke through the signs of the times to everyone, but Noah was the one who heard. Why, because as the Genesis writer says, "He was a just man and walked with God."

The revelation from this event is that we are not left alone to face the seemingly impossible conditions which God created. The writer said, "God remembered Noah." The long wait was worth it. When the Ark rested on land Noah's first act was an act of worship to God. Then it was that God made a covenant with Noah and his family. Today we are that family.

> I have set My bow in the clouds, and it shall serve as a sign of the covenant between Me and the earth. When the bow is in the clouds, I will see it and remember the everlasting covenant between God and all creatures. – Genesis 9:13-15

The rainbow given by God then is not an accident or a fleeting hope. It is a sign of the covenant made by God's eternal goodness that will not fail.

A growing insight is seen in the Hebrew Bible event of Abraham's attempted sacrifice of Isaac. As a 100 year old man he was given a son. But when Isaac was a young boy Abraham was given a test to sacrifice Isaac. One can imagine the anguish that confronted Abraham, yet he must be obedient to God, for in II Kings the King of Moab burned his son as a sacrifice for a winning battle. The followers of Yahweh could do no less.

Here was a great soul living in a crude age. The climax is not the attempted sacrifice of Isaac, but the word from God that Isaac should not be sacrificed. Abraham was not blessed for correctness in conception of God's will; he was blessed because when he *thought* he knew God's will he was willing to obey it to the limit. The primary intent of the story was to explain that human sacrifice has no place in the worship of God. Later in the Hebrew Bible Hosea states: "For I desired mercy, and not sacrifice; and the knowledge of God more than burnt offerings." A final Hebrew Bible example of revelation is the story of Jonah. The form literature into which this book fits most naturally is that of parable. It came at a time when Israel was bitter toward others and Nineveh was a specific illustration. Only three verses are about the whale, while 45 verses are about the mission of God's people. Here the role of the prophet is to seek the will of God. The revelation is that on the ship Jonah saw hated foreigners as persons, and was willing to be sacrificed for them. The point is that there are second opportunities. The emphasis is not on Nineveh or the whale, but on Jonah. The question to be considered both for people of the Hebrew Bible and for contemporary people is: "How many have bought a ticket to Tarshish when the call is to Nineveh?" "How many ignore God's calling?"

There is much in the Hebrew Bible which, taken by itself, would never be accepted as a revelation of God. But this does not mean that it can be detached from the historic record. "To select certain portions of the Old Testament as Revelation and to reject others is to make the anthologist the inspired voice of God." (4) I am not totally comfortable with this statement by Robinson. Still I would be careful in a pick-and-choose-cafeteria-style digestion of the Hebrew Bible. However I note that humans decided what would be Hebrew Bible canon.

In the fifth chapter of Judges we read, "Most blessed of women is Jael, the wife of Heber the Kenite, of tent dwelling women most blessed." Why should she be blessed? When a man came, fleeing for his life, she welcomed him, and then while he slept, she drove a tent peg through his head. Part of Psalm 137 is good, "By the waters of Babylon, there we sat down and wept, when we remembered Zion." But part is not so good, "Happy shall he be who takes your little ones and dashes them against the rock." Part of Psalm 139 is good, "O Lord thou hast searched me and known me. Thou knowest when I sit down and when I rise up. Whither shall I go from thy Spirit? When I awake, I am still with thee." But part of the same Psalm is not so good, "O that thou would slay the wicked, O God."

I am satisfied that when one eats fish you eat the meat, and put the bone aside. You do not need to eat the bone! Also, you do not throw the fish away simply because there are some bones. (Driving pegs into human heads; dashing little ones against rocks; slaying the wicked.) I believe in the Hebrew Bible there is a great deal of meat, and a few bones.

IV

I want to take note of the strong and meaningful relationship between the Hebrew Bible and the New Testament, both which show revelation. In early New Testament times the Church considered itself as an old established religion, thus their dependence on the Hebrew Bible. No where is the Hebrew Bible called Old Testament in the New Testament. In early New Testament times the Hebrew Bible was an asset with no doubting of it until the second century.

The Hebrew Bible is the background or foundation of the Christian religion. Jesus, and in general the New Testament writers, took for granted an understanding of the major Hebrew teachings. Hebrew Bible ideas, illustrations, and references permeate the New Testament. Some investigators profess to find more than a thousand references and illusions to the Hebrew Bible in the New Testament. (5)

Luther has rightly perceived that Jesus, in so far as he engaged in teaching, is not different from the Hebrew Bible prophets; like them, he proclaimed the Law.

In the fifth chapter of Matthew, Jesus states before a large crowd that he has, "Not come to abolish the law and the prophets; but to fulfill them." True, he gives new insights to the law; however they are not a rejection, but a positive expansion of it. Through the remaining part of the chapter he reaffirms the proper stance of a believer: do not commit adultery, do not participate in divorce, do not swear falsely, do not hate your enemy; he embraces all this, yet gives an expanded, broader insight to all these Hebrew Bible revelations.

If a person feels that historical reflection is necessary for gaining a clear view of one they can not simply embrace Christianity and discard the Hebrew Bible. We must hear the Hebrew Bible, dialogue with it, and see it as *our* history. The Hebrew Bible can be called prophecy, the New Testament fulfillment. Hebrews 10:16-17 is simply the inspiration of Jeremiah 31:31-34 when the writer says that, "Yahweh will be their God and they will be his people."

For the Christian, the whole history (Hebrew Bible and New Testament) in its variety and multifamily, comes to final fulfillment in The Christ Event. The essential relation of Christ to the Hebrew Bible is, for example, the explicit theme of Luke 1-2. In the coming of the Deliverer the promises of the covenants are fulfilled. In language quite akin to the Hebrew Bible here it is told how the waiting people of God of the old covenant (the poor, and the shepherds) find the promise of salvation. Here "promise" is understood in a manner which corresponds exactly to what we found to be the essential features of the basic forms of the salvation oracles in the Hebrew Bible. (6) The detailed accounting in the opening of Matthew is to show Christ's genealogy linked with the Hebrew Bible.

In the fourth chapter of Luke the writer says that Jesus returned with God's power to his home community and following the established custom, on the Sabbath he stood and read in the synagogue these words:

> The Spirit of the Lord is upon me, because he has anointed me to preach good news to the poor. He has sent me to proclaim release to the captives and recovering of sight to the blind, to set at liberty those who are oppressed, to proclaim the acceptable year of the Lord.

After reading this passage Jesus said to those at worship, "Today this scripture has been fulfilled in your hearing." Of note for our purpose is that what Jesus quoted and placed so much emphasis upon was not any new revelation, but the exact words recorded in Isaiah 61:1-2.

The Hebrew Bible is the beginning and background of the New Testament. There is one God, one message, one revelation, one Word, one covenant. The new covenant extends the old. The revelation of God is real and effective only in the totality of its occurrence. The understanding of the Hebrew Bible is the criterion and the basis for understanding in the New Testament.

The Hebrew Bible Passover is an event to remember the goodness of God in deliverance. The Lord's Supper is also a memorial feast. Jesus linked the Last Supper as a Covenant, with the thought of a completion of much found in the Hebrew Bible. (7)

V

Contemporary people suffer from thinking that anything that has meaning must be "new and modern." For indeed the Hebrew Bible is a revelation of a maturing, growing and understanding insight of God.

Yahweh is the central figure of the Hebrew Bible. The name Yahweh occurs 6,700 times. God is an ever active and ever present Spirit. In our own time we find Dr. Martin Luther King Jr., spokesman for an oppressed people, turning with a passion to the Hebrew Bible and challenging our nation with the words of Amos: "But let justice roll down like waters, and righteousness like an ever flowing stream."

God was revealed to those who were ready to receive that revelation. People have a place in interpreting revelation, but people remain people, they are not God. The Hebrew Bible writers report a deep fellowship with God. The Hebrew Bible is the mother of Christianity.

Because the Hebrew Bible confronts us as no other source can with the creative God who acts in history, it remains an authoritative work. The writing leads us into Christ, and yet does all this not by its own pretentious claims, but by setting forth God, who alone can be the ultimate authority for life.

Notes

1. W.F. Lofthouse, Record and Revelation, H. Wheeler Robinson (ed.) (Oxford: Clarendon Press, 1938), p. 460.

2. H. Wheeler Robinson, Inspiration and Revelation in the Old Testament (Oxford: Clarendon Press, 1946), p. 189.

3. W.A.L. Elmslie, Record and Revelation, p. 292.

4. Robinson, op. cit., p. 273.

5. W.W. Sloan, A Survey of the Old Testament (New York: Abingdon, 1957), p. 9.

6. Bernhard W. Anderson, The Old Testament and Christian Faith (New York: Harper & Row, 1963), p. 222.

7. H.H. Rowley, The Re-Discovery of the Old Testament (London: Clarke, 1945), p. 214.

(Encounter, Summer, 1983)

Welcome to the Christian Pilgrimage

(Editorial note: This statement is taken from a sermon preached on Palm Sunday, 1977 as junior high youth were received into membership at Downey Avenue Christian Church, Indianapolis, Indiana. Mr. McDermet is pastor of the congregation)

The word "pilgrimage" is defined as, "*a journey of great distance, to some sacred place, as an act of devotion.*" Let us consider our Christian pilgrimage, on a day when we recall the triumphal entry of our Lord into Jerusalem, a part of his earthly pilgrimage.

My thoughts are especially directed to those young persons who, for the past eight weeks, have been considering church membership. Today they begin their Christian pilgrimage with their confession of faith and the receiving of Christian baptism. You "old-timers" in the faith can listen in, and see where you might assist young Christians in their journey, and reflect on your own pilgrimage.

Will you receive baptism as a mere formal act, or as a meaningful experience? This act is witnessed in the presence of the *whole* church. Our Orthodox friends believe that when we worship, we are surrounded by all Christians of all times. You are not alone. Your fellow travelers are called *the faithful*, the people *of God*. You are a treasure in earthen vessels.

In your high school years some of you may lose interest in the church. What happens on Saturday night will be more important than what happens on Sunday morning. We of the church need to make Sundays, and all times, exciting so that Saturday nights and Sunday mornings will be important. Many of you will marry, and you will probably stand before a clergyperson (and God) and be told about love as expressed in the Bible. After that, the sad facts are that some of you may drift away from the church, and your Christian pilgrimage will be in a dormant state.

All of you will have problems and joys and concerns in your family or job. Maybe you will return to the church, or to the Bible or to Christian friends for support. We hope you will find insights about suffering and growth, forgiving, sharing and caring, going a second mile, and not throwing stones.

Death will come to relatives and friends. You will again enter a religious atmosphere and probably hear the words, "I am the resurrection and the life."

In the pilgrimage you will recognize denominational differences. This is Christianity at its worst. Too many have forgotten that the church was one before it was many. You may experience arguments, bitterness and fights within the church. What will be your response? Adding fuel to the fire? Washing your hands, Pilate-style and having none of it? Or working within, trying to bring harmony out of difficult situations?

I want to call you – and all others – to make the Christian pilgrimage at the deepest possible level. The trip can be exciting. Excitement was seen at Palm Sunday. There was an outpouring of joy. There is always a joy in dealing with persons at deep levels, in sharing experiences, in the knowledge of the power of God that even overcomes death.

Not everything will be ice cream and cake. The journey will see many ups and downs and numerous in-between times. You will see Jesus presented in new ways. In the early 1950's there came the Revised Standard Version of the Bible. We have seen and heard "*Jesus Christ Superstar*" and "*Godspell.*" We have experienced the TV special "*Jesus of Nazareth.*" Be glad for these, for they are contemporary expressions of Christian insight.

There are six good disciplines to practice on your pilgrimage.

Worship together as the people of God.
Read and study the Bible.
Pray and meditate about God and God's world.
Give of your money and time.
Serve the local and world wide church.
Witness, remembering that witness is sometimes what you say, often what you do, and always who you are.

Some day others of the Way will die and *you* will take over the leadership role in sharing the Christian faith. May you realize the awesome fact that the church is always one generation away from extinction!

In the difficult times of the pilgrimage recall the parable of the Prodigal Son. It is never too late to start over.

One never becomes too old to enjoy the trip. Recently I heard one of your fellow pilgrims, at age 74 say: "That's a new insight!" What will be the depth of your relationship with God as you make the Christian pilgrimage? Will it be shallow, a once-a-year relationship? Or will it be deep and lasting?

Two boys were ready to leave their home town and venture into the world. Before going they visited the old hermit at the edge of town for insight. They asked him, "What will the people be like out in the world?" The response was, "What are the people like in your town?" One boy answered, "They are self-centered, greedy and cynical." The hermit replied, "That's how the people will be out in the world." The second boy, replying to the hermits question said, "The people at home have been good, kind, sincere and full of love." The hermit responded to the second boy, "That's how the people will be out in the world." Each person is the key to how he or she will find other persons on the Christian pilgrimage.

When you end your pilgrimage, may these words be said, "Well done, good and faithful servant, . . . enter into the joy of your master." Amen.

(The Disciple, November 20, 1977)

Who Is Welcome At Our Table?

Your past Thanksgivings were no doubt very much like mine – everyone was welcome. I recall those of the 1940's and 1950's with great joy. Ina and Austin came from a few miles away, Villa came from Denver, Aunt Margaret and the four M's came from Chicago. Margaret told me that she sang the Doxology with tongue in cheek, as she believed more like a Unitarian. From Missouri came Uncle Bill and his family. As President of the United States Chamber of Commerce he always seemed to be at the other end of the religious and political spectrum than Margaret, and he was not shy in expressing his views.

Some of the adults at the table were single by choice; some were still "looking." One aunt enjoyed the friendship of other women, and there were some snide comments, yet she was included.

I look back on those Thanksgivings with thanksgiving and appreciation. One of the main ingredients was acceptance. There was a strong welcome for cousin Fred from Beaver Crossing, who always seemed odd; and acted-out that oddness at family gatherings. Yet if he had not been present he would have been greatly missed.

Prior to one Thanksgiving a cousin phoned me on World Communion Sunday afternoon. They had a Korean congregation using "their" building on Sunday afternoons; but as it was World Communion Sunday, both congregations worshiped together, and a Korean served as an Elder. I thought this was a splendid way to celebrate the day, however as the phone call continued I sensed my relative did not share my feelings. A few weeks later when we shared that Thanksgiving meal I felt our conversation was a bit strained; we simply had to work on our relationship.

To some extent my family Thanksgivings were a gathering of strange bedfellows. So it was at the first Thanksgiving. Pilgrims invited Native Americans to a pitch-in meal. Ninety natives came, and they brought most of the food! They ate together, participated in games, and enjoyed each other. The cause of that Thanksgiving celebration was the fact that good rations had increased from five kernels of corn a day; thanks to the agricultural insight of a Native American. It was a day of harmony.

The incidents of open table fellowship are endless. In the Hebrew Bible we find Moses at Midian where he performs a simple act of kindness. He is invited to eat bread with the family of Jethro: "Come over and eat at my place." In the New Testament we read that Jesus was constantly breaking bread with anyone and everyone. In one parable Jesus portrays the host as one who sends his servants out to invite the wretched and forgotten to a meal. He says the down and out will have the choice places at the banquet table. He experiences intimate table fellowship with Zacchaeus. No one is denied the cup and bread at the Last Supper. No one is excluded. No one.

However, excluding persons creeps into our life style and we may not even recognize that fact. A recent example was the statement by a community leader inviting residents to participate in a Thanksgiving event. He said, "All Catholics and Protestants were invited." Did he mean our Jewish friends were excluded? Probably not, but if I were Jewish or followed another faith tradition, I might not have felt welcome.

Luke states, "This fellow [Jesus] welcomes sinners and eats with them." That is an inclusive statement. If we profess to be followers of the man of

Nazareth, will we also follow his inclusive life style? Who do you welcome, or exclude, from your table, your home, your life?

Jesus was labeled by his detractors as "a glutton and a drunkard," and we can easily picture the joyful occasions that called forth that charge. Jesus had the audacity to suggest that the table-fellowship shared with disciples, tax-gatherers and sinners constituted an anticipation in the Kingdom of God. He proclaimed the presence of the Kingdom in the eating and drinking and talking and laughing of those occasions.

The Kingdom of God as a feast? The tax-gatherers and sinners and disciples of the world gathered around a common table, sharing bread and wine in joyousness, posing arguments and swapping stories, experiencing the release of freedom in realizing that they were forgiven, joining voices in praise? That's my kind of Kingdom. That's God's kind of Kingdom!

Can the open-table fellowship of Biblical time and Pilgrim time be experienced in our time? In the late 1970's and 1980's our family Thanksgiving meal was shared with 150 new friends at Our Lady of Lourdes parish hall in Indianapolis. Those good people from Lourdes knew there were many in the neighborhood who lived and ate alone. Some senior citizens found it difficult to prepare a full meal for Thanksgiving. Thus, Lourdes provided the place and the food at cost. Others of us helped with the details. Downey Avenue Christian was across the street and down the block, and we wanted to participate. Neighbor friends from other congregations shared in the event. We set up tables and set places. We carried meals to shut-ins. We sang songs, we prayed, we laughed. One Downey family provided a musical program. Favors were given to all. We had a great time, we loved being together, and we were God's people.

This was our new family. My mother was victim to a stroke, and could not travel. Uncle Bill found it difficult to leave his home. My relatives were scattered, and Aunt Margaret had gone to be with the Saints, full time. One year when our out of state family did come for Thanksgiving, we discussed if we should have our own meal, or go to Lourdes. We went to Lourdes, for our family circle had expanded. It was a grand time.

We who say we are the People of God, how might we expand the places at our tables? Who is – out there – who needs to be invited in – to our table? We *can* practice a belief that any community that is truly a community must be able to suffer fools gladly and even to embrace the heretics that threaten its tranquility. We need to constantly be about asking the question: "Who is welcome at our table?"

(The Christian Ministry, January-February, 1996)

Was She Foolish?

Mark 12:38-44

Jesus was very serious about a person's stewardship! He was concerned that individuals use their life and money wisely. Recall the many parables that deal directly with this subject.

Jesus was teaching: "Beware of the scribes." Jesus attacks the practice of religion of the scribes as hypocritical. They wore long robes; the clothing of the well-to-do. They used the best seats, while most stood in the synagogue. They held the places of honor which went to those "prominent" in the community.

However, Jesus sees it as a show – without meaning. The scribes' calling as interpreters of the law made their behavior even more reprehensible. The scribes were living examples of external signs of religion. Jesus was not interested in *outward appearances* but *inner character*.

Immediately following this observation on the scribes Mark (also Luke) records the stewardship of the widow.

Gifts for the temple were received in trumpet-like metal horns. They were voluntary offerings. Jesus is standing close, observing, when the two coins were given. How Jesus knew "she put in everything" is not known. In many places in Mark Jesus is painted as having supernatural insight.

The widow's gift moved Jesus. It was the real thing. And so he called his disciples together and shared it. It was her next meal. Jesus had heard the noise of many coins on the metal, but this was very special. The gift that counts is the gift that costs. It was one of the world's greatest financial transactions: two coins.

What Jesus was noting was that lives, not gifts, were being reflected. Some with money gave. That was fine, but it was out of their abundance or surplus. The poor widow's gift was special.

The word "poor" comes from a Greek word that suggests "one who has to labor hard for a living." Paul sheds some insight from his writing in II Corinthians: "We work with God, as poor, yet making many rich, as having nothing, yet possessing everything." Indeed, in Romans, Paul says, "God did not spare his own Son, but gave him up for us all."

*****

How do we identify with this event? Most of us are not really rich or poor. I grew up with a boy whose family was rich. There were maids and butlers and chauffeurs in his house, which was connected to a seven-car garage. The family name was on a downtown theatre and a seventeen-story office building. He was rich. But I was not poor. The only time I really missed a meal was when I was snowbound on a bus. Yet while we are not wealthy, we are not poor. If we want to see the poor, we can go across town and go "slumming." Still, what we may consider to be average for us, most of the people of the world cannot dream of having. However, rich or poor is not the point – *giving in a loving attitude is the point.*

You need not feel inferior in giving when you give of yourself, for this kind of giving is not dependent upon the size of a salary or bank account. A big heart is more important than a fat check book.

The offering of our gifts depends upon our lives for its value. The largest gift is profitless when it is not mixed with love by the one who gives it. The act of giving has worth for the giver if they delight in their gift.

Percentage is the important issue instead of amount in dollars and cents.

Jesus complimented the widow who gave out of her living and he censured others who gave out of their comfortable margins. The widow believed enough to give all; others did not. Her gift was an act of faith; theirs a gesture. Thus she felt that she had given; they felt nothing. Her act of faith made her gift a noble deed and left a shining example for all to follow.

*****

We know persons like this unnamed widow. Their attitude toward money is a living-out of this biblical event. For me it was a 92-year-old woman in central Kansas. I first met Peggy in the basement of the church. I was in the role of a prospective pastor; she as the oldest active member of the congregation. She wanted to look me over, and when we parted that evening she remarked: "I think you'll be all right as the pastor."

I moved into her town two months later and discovered that poor health forced her to make the hospital her home. Yet even there she made good use of her time. I found her with two pieces of reading material: a large print edition of The New York Times and a book on beginning Spanish. She did not know Spanish and felt it was time she started. Friends reported that she always made good use of her stewardship of time.

She had been a widow for many years, yet she was one of the major givers to the church. In fact, some years earlier – when the issue was raised if a new structure should be built – it was Peggy who made an impassioned speech at the special congregational meeting: "Let's get on with it. This old building has served us well, but its 100-plus years old. I'll give $1,000 now and more later."

But death waits for no person, even kind widows, and later that year she died. As I was preparing her service I found she left suggestions for the event. She selected hymns and scriptures and mentioned her love for her church, ending with "keeping this membership to the last."

A few weeks after her funeral her son informed me that the total amount of her estate (while not large) would go to the church. All her copper coins went to the church. "She put in everything."

*****

And what of Mark's widow. Was she foolish? Most would reflect that she was not practical. The dictionary says of the word foolish: "Without good sense or wisdom; silly, imprudent, unwise, ridiculous, and absurd." But toward the end of the definition Webster uses the word "humble." By *whose* standards was she foolish? Should we, can we, move toward her example? What does this recorded event mean to us? Contrast the widow with the rich young man also mentioned in Mark (10:17-22). Jesus said to him: "You lack one thing; go, sell what you have, and give to the poor, and you will have treasure in heaven; and come, follow me." Yet he went away sorrowful. Which one made the Who's Who In the Kingdom of God?

Some years ago there lived in a small English village a woman who always gave herself in helping others. On her tombstone in the village cemetery are the words: "She Has Done What She Couldn't."

Mark's widow had only two coins. She might have thought: "What difference can two coins make? They are so small, especially when measured by other gifts. Let those give who can afford it. I really don't have anything to spare. No one will ever notice if I drop in anything or not." If she had thought like that, she would have walked away with the two coins still in her hand.

No gift of love is too small to count, but no life can be excused from the duty of sharing. Nothing escapes the notice of God, from whom no secret is hid.

In the 1980s, as in New Testament times, it is impossible to slip into the offering receptacle a casual coin bearing no relation to our income or to the object for which it is given. Our giving becomes the expression of our attitude to the Christian philosophy of life. Giving, like living, is a matter of faith. It is not a matter of finances.

(Messenger, July, 1980)

On Being A Hostage

Psalm 137

Recall the agonizing time you spent waiting in a surgical waiting room. Would the physician bring bad, sad news; or good, joyful news? The waiting time was excruciating. We have been waiting for 444 days – and this week we received the happy, joyful news – the American hostages in Iran are coming home! Many searched for a way to celebrate. We paraded flags, and shouted slogans, and honked horns and tied yellow ribbons on anything and everything. Often we have to be disciplined to wait for peaceful solutions to difficult situations.

One component of living was intensified during these times – we felt a close relationship to those who suffered. We agonized for those separated. We united our attention, our effort, our focus on those involved. We offered our prayers. We shared empathy/feelings for those in need. We were keenly concerned over the treatment the hostages received. (However we ponder: when have prisoners *ever* been treated well – anytime, anyplace?) We thought of revenge. No, correct that, most of us *wanted* revenge. We saw car bumper slogans telling Iran where to go! In frustration we wanted to push them in that direction.

One thing we do know for sure, which hopefully will capture our future action: the end result was accomplished without violence!! Unfortunately the only forceful rescue attempt ended in the death of eight. The waiting did take 444 days, but freedom was accomplished. There was anxiety, there were hardships, and there may be possible psychological problems. But let it be shouted, that the end result was accomplished without violence!

Our situation is not new; one similar is recorded in the Hebrew Bible, in Psalm 137:1-6.

> By the waters of Babylon, there we sat down and wept, when we remembered Zion. On the willows there we hung up our lyres. For there our captors required of us songs, and our tormentors, mirth, saying, "Sing us one of the songs of Zion!" How shall we sing the Lord's song in a foreign land? If I forget you, O Jerusalem, let my right hand wither! Let my tongue cleave to the roof of my mouth, if I do not remember you, if I do not set Jerusalem above my highest joy!

However, this becomes a cursing psalm, one with emotional appeal, the only example of its kind. It is the experience of distress, persecution and bitterness that calls for revenge. In this Psalm we are made keenly aware of the mood of those in Exile who remained loyal to faith, tradition and country, resisting foreign pressures. The writer put into words the burning feelings that surged in their souls. "We sat down" – in the posture of mourners in the ancient East. "And wept" – for their condition, and longed for home. "We hung up our lyres" – there was no reason for joyful song. It was a heartless request of the captors asking for a song that would stir homesickness and then indignation.

But note the language in the final two verses of Psalm 137:

> Remember, O Lord, against the Edomites the day of Jerusalem, they said, "rase it, rase it! Down to its foundations!" O daughter of Babylon, you devastator! Happy shall he be who requites you with what you have done to us! Happy shall he

be who takes your little ones and dashes them against the rock! (7-8)

My God. What have we here; in the Bible? We find a curse that is uttered against the Edomites, who in 587 BC had rejoiced over the destruction of the temple and the city of Jerusalem. In Psalm 137 we find intense patriotism, some of it flamboyant and aggressive. It is one thing to decide to uproot and go to a foreign land, but another thing to be taken by force. This Psalm causes many to shudder. It begins so nobly and ends so brutally. We cannot defend it, that is impossible. It is so contrary to the life and teachings and example of the one we call Lord, Jesus Christ. So we try to understand its context. With God's help we come to know that few things are more necessary than freedom from the spirit of vindictiveness.

We have vengeful feelings in our land today. Those feelings do not lead to peace; they are not God's ways! There are strong signs of a resurgence of ethnocentrism – the feeling that one's group or country is better, stronger, and more right than others. That feeling comes in patriotic slogans and T-shirts against Iran. As we think about the last part of Psalm 137, we might think of a recent song by the Charlie Daniels Band titled "In America."

> Well, the eagle's been flyin' slow, and the flag's been flyin' low . . . This lady may have stumbled, but she ain't never fell, and if the Russians don't believe it; they can all go straight to hell.

Does that type of song say anything for peace? Is that what we Christians ought to be about? Is that in tune with the will of God? Is ethnocentrism what Jesus preached? Does God call for action that "dashes little ones against the rock?" Or should we journey in a different direction?

Listen to other words found in the Bible.

> Let every person be quick to hear, and slow to anger, for the anger of man does not work the righteousness of God. Therefore put away all wickedness and receive with meekness the implanted word, which is able to save your souls. – James 1:19-21

Those words are appropriate as we rejoice over the return of any hostages. Those New Testament words are for our guidance.

Still other questions beg an audience. Can we be that audience? Who are those yet held hostage, in this land and in other lands? Who are in exile today, weeping, and refusing to sing? How shall we treat them? There are today hostages in Africa, in Latin America, in Asia, in our own country – those who are poor, the homeless, the powerless, those in prison, those millions of adults who cannot read, those who are trapped in dead-end jobs. All these conditions may lead to violence, and beg peaceful solutions.

As we ponder the peaceful ending to a difficult situation we may realize our national policy was probably wrong in supporting an oppressive Shaw of Iran. Maybe we can learn from that. Maybe we can learn to follow what is best for our world, not just for our nation. We must always encourage our government to support those governments that protect human rights.

What about the hostages in our own prison system? (I am not saying that we should simply excuse those who commit crimes; some type of true rehabilitation and change in life-style is necessary.) Yet Jesus calls us to minister to those hostages in his name. The Indiana State Supreme Court Justice, this very week, called on the legislature to take measures to stop the cycle of prisoners. We must support that.

If we truly want peace in our world we can learn and apply insights from the Iran hostage experience. We need to understand the customs, needs and desires of those in other nations. We need to apply those words from the musical, "The King and I" where west met east:

> Getting to know you, getting to know all about you.
> Getting to like you, getting to know you like me.

When I think of that song I think of examples from my own life. I never knew a black person until high school when a young black, Corny White, and I played on the sophomore football team. I met my first Jew when Herb Friedman joined our Boy Scout Troop. The first Catholic I knew was Pat O'Gara, we were in the same home room. Guess what? They laughed and got mad, and enjoyed, and ate, and played, just like I did. When I got to know them I liked them. That "getting to know you" continues to this day. Recently a Missouri Synod Lutheran pastor came and fully participated in our local ministerial association. A Missouri Synod Lutheran? Yes, and he's a very nice guy. We need to keep at "getting to know you," both individually and nationally. It leads to good relationships and a peaceful world.

After the American hostages came home we heard much about revenge against Iran, just as that super-patriot in Psalm 137 called for little ones to be dashed against the rock. Yet we claim the name of Jesus, and Jesus calls for another attitude, one found in the first gospel.

> You have heard that it was said, 'You shall love your neighbor and hate your enemy.' But I say to you, love your enemies and pray for those who persecute you, so that you may be sons (and daughters) of your Father who is in heaven. Matthew 5:43-45a

Following the Iranian ordeal one of the keenest insights came from the *wife of a hostage.* She said, "Now is not the time to talk about revenge. Now is the time to participate in rejoicing. Now is the time to work to see that we create a world where this does not happen again." To which I say, "Amen."

(Messenger, August, 1981)

A Way Out of Hell

In one scene of the movie "Gandhi," a young Hindu from the slums confronts Gandhi. In vengeance for the death of his own son at Moslem hands, the Hindu has killed a Moslem boy, crushing the child's head against a wall. "I am going to hell," he says. His tormented face shows that he is already there.

Gandhi is lying on a cot near death from the fast he began to protest the Calcutta riots of 1947. Looking at the Hindu, he says, "I know a way out of hell. Find a child whose parents have been killed in the riots, adopt and love the child as your own. But let it be a *Moslem* orphan, and raise the child as a *Moslem.*" The haggard man kneels by the cot and rests his head in Gandhi's knees.

What is hell? Where is hell? The word is used often. People talk about a "hellish world" or a "hellish condition." What does the Bible say about hell? Can Jesus provide an insight?"

The Hebrew Bible offers no formal doctrine concerning the destination and fate of the dead. It talks about the abode of the dead being underground, a place where persons suffer constant thirst, and where it is always dark.

There are many parallels to this concept in other Near Eastern cultures. But nowhere in Hebrew Scriptures is the place of the dead a place of punishment or torment. The word "Sheol" is used 66 times in the Hebrew Scriptures, such as in Psalm 139: "If I make my bed in Sheol, thou art there!"

In the first century, some believed in a hell of fire as a place for sinners. The name "hell" is from Hinnom, a community southwest of Jerusalem where human sacrifices had been offered and today garbage is burned. At this location there was a potter's field, bought, says tradition for the burial of the poor with Judas' 30 pieces of silver.

Within the New Testament, we find the word "hell" used 13 times. Its use is vague; the word is usually used not as a place but in reference to broken relationships and separation. That may suggest the right direction to consider getting out of hell.

Surprisingly, we do not find much reference to hell in hymns. John Rippon does use the word in "How Firm a Foundation": "That soul, through all hell should endeavor to shake, I'll never, no never, no never forsake!" For Rippon, hell is a condition of one's spirit, but God will not forsake one even in a hellish state. Charles Wesley refers to hell in two Easter hymns. In a stanza not usually found in "Christ the Lord is Risen Today," he has penned, "Christ has burst the gates of hell, alleluia." In "Rejoice, the Lord is King" he says, "The keys of death and hell to Christ the Lord are given." Thus Wesley boldly states that Christ can unlock doors that hold a person in any prison-like hell.

In Sabine Baring-Gould's "Onward Christian Soldiers," Christ and the church are linked together. "Gates of hell can never 'gainst that Church prevail; We have Christ's own promise, and that cannot fail." (I shall leave it for another time to ask the question: "Is the image of a Christian soldier an oxymoron?")

So what is hell? Some people believe that hell is other people. A wise Disciples uncle-clergyman, Austin J. Hollingsworth, once remarked at a family-reunion in Lincoln, Nebraska: "Heaven and hell are here on earth, and I've experienced some of both!"

One thing is certain: we read about hell daily. Hell comes in the form of suffering, killing, conflict, hopelessness, meaninglessness, and brokenness. Hell seems to be a condition and an attitude.

Hell is made by humans. It is seen in suffering, class systems, racism, and the lack or loss of human rights. God did not make any of these conditions, and God did not create hell. Indeed, just what kind of a God do we worship? Why would God create hell - so that "bad" people would have a place to suffer after they die? Would that please a loving God? Who needs God to create hell? Humans seem to do an adequate job by themselves. Even if we did not create hellish conditions, do we do anything to help those who are in hell to get out?

Gandhi put it this way:

> I suggest that we are thieves in a way. If I take anything that I do not need for my own immediate use, and keep it, I thieve it from somebody else. In India we have millions of people having to be satisfied with one small meal a day. You and I have no right to anything that we have until these millions are better fed.

Consider the subtle little ways even the church promotes what may be hellish. On Mother's Day we often praise and glorify motherhood. Fine, but how do we do it? (A flower to the oldest mother present, the youngest, the one with the most children, etc.) However do we ever consider the conditions of all too many in the pews? How about those who did not have a good relationship with their mothers? How about those women who dreamed in their younger years of becoming mothers, but never did? Or women who tried everything to conceive, but some biological or psychological condition did not allow them to become mothers? Are we sensitive to them, or have we simply caused a hellish condition to hurt and fester?

Even in 2004 the Body of Christ may create a hell-like atmosphere for some children of God when congregations do not consider women, or gays and lesbians, or people of color, or left-handed persons as pastors; or withhold church membership to some who were "dry-cleaned" without an "adequate" amount of water in their baptismal experience.

So how does one get out of hell? If hell is a condition made by humans - frequently dealing with attitudes, conditions, and relationships - then Jesus provides an insight. In the fifth chapter of Matthew, he says that anger and broken relationships may cause a person to be in hell. "You shall not murder; . . . if you are angry with a brother or sister, if you insult a brother or sister, . . . if you say, 'You fool,' you will be liable to the hell of fire." (Matthew 5:21-22 NRSV) Murder and name-calling result from human anger, and Jesus would prevent crimes of violence by rooting out the elements in human character that allow us to kill.

Hear Gandhi again:

> In my humble opinion, non-cooperation with evil is as much a duty as is cooperation with good. But in the past, non-cooperation has been deliberately expressed in violence to the evil-doer. I am endeavoring to show to my countrymen that violent non-cooperation only multiplies evil, and as evil can only be sustained by violence, withdrawal of support of evil requires complete abstention from violence.

A way out of hell is abstention from violence. In fact, healing broken relationships takes precedence over religious gift-giving. "Leave your gift there in front of the altar, go at once and make peace." (Matthew 5:24). Making peace gives one no time to create hell. But do it soon, "while there is time." (5:25b)

For Matthew's Jesus, love was the key. Loving is the way one gets out and keeps out of hell. We often make our own hells, but with God's help and grace, we can get out. To mend a broken relationship is to get out. This applies not only to individuals, but to families, groups, and countries. We get out of hell by giving our attention, concern, and love to others.

Reuel Howe once was asked, "How can I find God?" He replied, "Go find someone to love and you will find God." We could add, "and a way out of hell."

(Messenger, August 1984)

Running Through the Pain

Hebrews 12:12-14

Jogging is in, but it can also be painful. A friend recently remarked that for years he had jogged daily without suffering any of the multitude of aches and pains that so often afflict the amateur athlete. In a burst of enthusiasm, he doubled his weekly mileage from 10 to 20. There was no problem doing 15; when he reached 20 miles a week it began – aches in his knees and thighs so painful that his running was done in agony.

My jogging friend was afraid he would have to stop altogether, but suddenly the pains disappeared. His running became smother and easier than ever. Elated, but puzzled, he told his story to an experienced runner.

"You ran through the pain," she said. "As you go from one level of fitness to another you often have 'growing pains.' It's as though your old body is fighting the higher standards of the new, healthier body. You just have to grit your teeth and run through the pain."

In the twelfth chapter of Hebrews, the wise writer is challenging us to live within a disciplined life. Then he says, "Therefore lift your drooping hands and strengthen your weak knees, and make straight paths for your feet." That admonition to run through our pain is not an isolated Bible statement. The Bible is full of examples of people who did overcome.

Zacchaeus' size was not his major problem. Zacchaeus constantly felt the pain of being alone and hated. Yet he climbed that tree, and his climb led to a direct spiritual encounter with Jesus. His story is the story of God's search for us. The powerful acceptance of Jesus was met by the painful honesty of Zacchaeus. We can identify with Zacchaeus and his pain – for this is our story, with God's grace as the ending.

Infamous debater Job finally realized that God may be known, and even understood, in suffering. Job dealt with the deep issue of the meaning of faith, and he finally believed that in pain one can strengthen faith and belief. Through suffering, Job found a new relationship with God. He rested in God even in his pain. This is not to explain the meaning of suffering. It is to declare to all that even such agony as Job endured may be turned to spiritual profit if God is found in it.

Mary Magdalene knew the pain of bereavement. Yet in grief she came with the spices for his body, and then encountered Jesus in a different form. Peter knew the pain of denial. But Jesus forgave him, allowing him to "feed my sheep." Paul knew physical pain. Three times Paul asked God to take that thorn from his side, only to be met by spiritual insight, "My grace is sufficient for you, for my power is made perfect in weakness."

These biblical characters – real people – are representative of countless persons who established relationships with God, and within those relationships they were able to run through their pain.

What about your pain? Is it always around, and are you always hurting? Did someone else get the job promotion? Does "what if" continue to consume your thoughts? Is there the gnawing pain of a broken relationship? Are you bereaved?

I once visited a couple who had been married for over 55 years. They showed me the room where their only son had died at age five from a health problem that is easily overcome today. The room was the same as the day he died, 47 years earlier. They had nurtured their pain for almost five decades; they could not run through it.

George Fredrick Handel had been a well-accepted organist in London; but then the public tired of his work. He was financially broke and partially paralyzed when a "second-rate" poet brought him words to what would become the "Messiah." Life had been painful, but he became enthused over the work, and in twenty-four days (and nights) he composed the music. It was presented in Dublin, and then in London from 1743 to 1750 but it was not well received. Those who did not like Handel had his posters announcing the presentations torn down. Finally the London public accepted it. He would take no money for performances simply remarking that "Messiah fostered the orphan, fed the hungry, clothed the naked, relieved suffering." He had worked-through his pain.

Helen Keller could work through the pain of being blind and deaf, to the place that she found joy in a handclasp. Her reflection was:

> The hands of those I meet are humbly eloquent to me. I have met people so empty of joy that when I clasped their frosty finger tips it seemed as if I were shaking hands with a northeast storm. Then there are hands that have sunshine in them; so that their grasp warms my heart. There is as much potential sunshine in it for me as there is in a loving glance.

The writer of Hebrews states that strength and courage come from God, a strength that provides both physical and spiritual healing. Hardship may be God's way of preparation for the long pull – both in this life, and the next. Insight and support that provide healing come from each of us within our Christian communities. The writer-coach pushes us to see that Jesus needs more than drooping hands and weak knees to help others.

And what is this running leading to? The Hebrews author states it clearly: "Strive for peace with all. . ." Strive even thought it may be a painful experience.

Last summer, our Presbyterian friends (United Presbyterians and the Presbyterian Church is the US) voted to end 121 years of separation. Noting that the two denominations have adopted a common commitment to the task of peacemaking, one of the co-chairpersons of the reunion committee suggested it was futile for Presbyterians to seek to convince governments and peoples of the world to make peace "until we are able to make peace in our Presbyterian family. It was a war that separated us. Perhaps it may be peace that brings us back together."

As we set our bodies, minds, and spirits to run through the pain, we might contemplate at least four training rules.

1. We have the splendid example of those from the scriptures who ran. Study and learn from them.

2. We are supported by those sisters and brothers running within our Christian communities.

3. We must consider the great resources that are within each one of us, yet to be tapped.

4. God is with us in our running. Let us run "so that what is lame may not be put out of joint but rather be healed" (Hebrews 12:13).

On your mark. Get set. Go!

(Messenger, June, 1983)

Where Are the Nine?

Luke 17:11-19

It was almost impossible to describe their condition. They had swelling and lumps over their bodies, and some parts lacked any feeling. Their skin was covered with ulcers. For some there was deterioration of the nose and throat, for others hands and feet were eaten away. Leprosy is a living hell.

Some medical experts believe emotional stress may cause leprosy, and surely those with the disease felt stress. Whenever another human being came their way, lepers were required to shout, "unclean, unclean." They were segregated from society, and ordered to dress distinctively. Within their hell they longed, hoped and prayed for readmission to society and remission of their dreaded condition.

Luke says that on that day when Jesus entered their village those ten lepers "stood at a distance." In reality it was a tremendous gulf, for leprosy was the AIDS of the biblical world.

Somehow they had enough energy and hope to cry out in unison, "Jesus, Master, have mercy on us." He did! They were cleansed. Yet, the amazing element in the story is not that the ten were healed and released from their horrible state; but that only one returned to the source of that healing, to give thanks. Jesus then asks his question which was never answered, "Where are the nine?"

I can answer that question.

The first leper had a flourishing family shipping business at Joppa. Two years ago he was banished as a leper-outcast, and his wife and son tried to keep the business going. His competition took advantage of his absence. So following his cleansing, he headed post-haste for Joppa, as fast as his renewed body would take him.

When the second leper was questioned as to why he did not return, he made this statement. "I didn't want to be healed, because I don't want to live. I find life too difficult. Life is just a rat-race, everyone trying to get their piece of manna. I don't want any responsibility. I'd rather die than have to face the difficulties of living. But now – thanks to Jesus – I am forced back onto the old treadmill. Now I've got to find a job, and keep it."

After his encounter with Jesus, the third leper started immediately for Legio, his home town. He knew his family and friends prayed daily for his cure, and he wanted to show them that prayers were answered.

The fourth and fifth lepers were close friends. Excitedly they left for Caesarea. After about one hour of travel they realized they had forgotten to thank Jesus. So they retraced their steps, but by the time they returned, Jesus was gone.

The sixth leper knew he was healed, but he didn't care how it happened. He felt he got lucky, and he just wanted to get out of that seemingly God-forsaken village, so he took his exit.

The seventh leper had three grandchildren whom he has never seen since his banishment from society four years before. Those years seemed like a lifetime. As soon as he felt the change in his body he headed for those grandchildren at Dotham.

The eighth leper felt the whole experience was probably just temporary – a momentary remission. How could any *one* person make a difference in human suffering anyway? Why thank anyone for getting involved. So, after going to the priests, he simply went to the next valley, feeling he would probably be forced to return to the leper village when the sores reappeared.

A burning love is the reason the ninth leper did not return. Two years, one month and 14 days earlier, on the last night of his freedom from the leper colony, he spent a moon-lit evening with a young woman in Jericho. Knowing his state, she yet had said, "I'll wait for you." Those words had kept him alive. Now he headed for Jericho, on the run. He went with both fear and hope; in fear that she might not be waiting, and in hope, that she was.

Why did those nine not return to the source of their healing? The answer is of course as old as Adam and Eve – because they were human. They thought first about their own condition, and then about their relationship with other humans, and maybe finally about the source of their renewed life.

What follows is the "rest of the story." Two years after the Jesus encounter, lepers four and five accidentally meet leper seven in Jerusalem. Overjoyed, they decided to plan an annual reunion-celebration-thanksgiving event at Jerusalem every year. They did, and over the years others who had been in their suffering/healed circle joined them with their families. Before, they were forced to be together; now, they chose to be together, in the breaking of bread and prayers.

So, what is your reflection? Is this explanation simply an outburst of my wild imagination? Maybe, maybe not. I cannot prove it, you cannot disprove it. Also there is the possibility that you have given your energy to identifying with the Samaritan who *did* return. Oh? Is your faith that strong? If so thank God for it.

A friend, Melissa, provides an insight. Melissa grew-up in a county seat town in east central Indiana. Following her college days, and her venture out-into-the-world, one weekend she returned to her home town and was shopping for her mother in a grocery story. By chance she met a former classmate, one whose name she was hard-pressed to remember. They exchanged greetings, and the usual where-are-you-now questions and answers, and then they parted.

Later that week Melissa received a letter from this woman that read: "When I bumped into you at the store this week I don't know why I didn't say something, but now I will. Do you remember that weekend when we were seniors and you invited me to attend your church youth retreat? That event changed my life, and I've never told you. During my senior year I was experiencing some deep family problems, and that retreat really saved my life. For some reason I've never thanked you, but now I am. Thank you Melissa for caring and asking me to participate."

Can we be thankful, and express that thanks, after the fact? Yes we can, and we should.

What were those healing experiences in your life that made life not only bearable, but enjoyable? Maybe you just failed to see the hand of God entering your life. Jesus says it this way, "Rise and go your way; your faith has made you well."

Only God knows how many times those nine told their story of healing in later years. Maybe what they did, and what we need to do, is carve out a tell-God-time: a time where we express to God our thanks for God's loving acceptance and strength; a time that results in a yet stronger faith and more loving service to others.

It is never too late for us to give thanks to the source of our healing and being. Amen. (Messenger, April, 1988 and Preaching, November/December, 1993)

Any Bite Left in the Bulldog?

(Annual Cotner College Dinner, Cotner Center – Lincoln, Nebraska
June 8, 1984.)

Thank you Carl for the introduction, but the "real" facts of my life are (1) while growing up in Lincoln I played in the same German Band with TV personality Dick Cavett, (2) our family lived next door to *Mrs* America, Romona Deitemeyer. (3) and I was the "sitter" for Gary Glassford, son of Nebraska's football coach Bill Glassford. Not to be out-done, my wife Sheral was the "sitter" for the present Governor of Nebraska, although she would like to forget the evening the very young governor kicked her.

I also need to clear-up one item of information as printed in the recent Cotner Newsletter. It noted that I attended undergraduate school from 1945 to 1957. Now some of my friends may think I'm a bit slow, but please, that's a typographical error and should read 1954.

I bring you greetings from Kenneth L. Potee, class of 1919. Ken came to Cotner in 1915 from Great Falls, Montana. Following graduation from Cotner, he and classmates Church Smiley and Ira Crewdson went to the College of Missions, located one block from Downey Avenue Christian Church. Except for his many years in India, Ken has been an active member of Downey Avenue.

Eighteen months ago Carl Burkhardt asked me to come and be with you. So I've had more than ample time to think about my relationship with Cotner, and what I want to say. If you look in the 1929 Bulldog, the college yearbook, on the same page you find my mother Grace Eleta Lowe, my father William W McDermet Sr. and my mother-in-law Lucille Linebaugh. Father-in-law Elmer Yates came to Cotner later. Pete Cope, longtime fieldman for Cotner, and his wife Hazel, were friends of Sheral's. Hilda Chowins, Cotner instructor in Piano, was my piano teacher. She was the organist/choir director for the old Tabernacle, now Southview, church when I joined the choir. During my college days I took four classes at Cotner School of Religion.

For many years this Cotner Bulldog pennant was in my parent's home; and when they recently moved to Foxwood Springs I asked if I could have it. Do you know the story of the preacher who preached too long? His wife said, "Next Sunday when I think it's time for you to stop I'll wave my hanky." During next Sunday's sermon the wife indeed did wave her hanky. Whereupon the preacher said, "Would you all please stand so I can dismiss my wife!" I'll give this Cotner pennant to Sheral and when she thinks it is time for me to stop, she can wave the pennant.

About six months ago I informed Carl that my title would be "Any Bite Left in the Bulldog?" Cotner College "died" in 1934. Is everything over? Is this a coast until we come to the "Last of the Bulldogs?" Is there no bite because of a style of living that "chews on life" with dentures? Can you/we do anything yet with our lives? One reason we are gathered is because of our love for community. What are the expressions of community today? Friends, it only takes one to bite, and maybe you are that one!

In the Dictionary I found next to the word *bulldog:*

> A short-haired, squared-jawed, heavily built dog That has great courage and a strong, stubborn grip. British usage – a university attendant employed to Enforce the rules of behavior

for students.

Maybe you can recall a university staff member who acted like a British bulldog.

I looked up *bite* in the Dictionary and found:

> To seize, grip, a tight hold to cut into – as, there's a bite to her words. Synonym – incisive – cutting into, sharp; keen; penetrating; piercing; acute; as, an incisive mind.
>
> Incisive – is applied to speech or writing that seems to penetrate directly to the heart of the matter, resulting in a clear and un-ambiguous statement.
>
> Biting – implies stinging quality that makes a deep impression on the mind.

What can you yet do with your bite?

Being old, yet having bite has been happening for centuries. After 110 years of living Joshua encouraged the people to respond to God, and they did with the words: "We will serve God." Abraham found Sarah when she was 65. They were married, and at age 90 Sarah gave birth to Isaac. Abraham died at age 175, as the writer of Genesis said, "full of years." Enoch lived 365 years; but while he lived he walked with and pleased God. The Lord blessed the latter days of Job more than his beginning – and those days numbered 140 years. I'm not here to debate the actual age of these Biblical personalities; I simply believe they were senior citizens in the Household of God.

At an older age, these persons had bite in their living.

Let's look at the three phases of the biting Bulldog.

(1) The first phase is Cotner as a liberal arts college from 1888 to 1934. What do you recall when you think of this phase? People. Classmates, professors, friendships, events dealing with people. It was a time for students to consider new concepts and ideas. My parents recall the day that Professor Charles Lockhart went to the blackboard and wrote – "Keep an open mind and a suspended judgment." That's timeless! Those words had meaning in the 1930's. They have meaning for our day. That statement will have meaning years from now.

(2) The second phase is the Cotner School of Religion from the late 1940's to the early 1970's. What do you recall when you think of this phase? People. I think of Bill Moore, now in Webster Groves, Missouri; Dick Duckworth in Enid, Oklahoma; Ron Irons in Tulsa; and Charles McKinsey, now in Des Moines. I know that Cotner had good instructors. A Rabbi taught Hebrew. A class I had in Christian Education was taught by the pastor of Second Baptist Church.

In 1955 I took a class in the Harmony of the Gospels taught by Raleigh Peterson. One person in that class was Raymond Alber who was pastor of the East Lincoln Church. Raymond once preached in my home congregation. I remember that he always preached in a bow tie and was quite aggressive in his preaching. He almost shouted: "When I'm dead and lying there in my casket and people are filing by and saying, 'O poor Raymond's dead,' I'm going to rise up and say 'no I'm not dead!'" You could have scraped me off the floor.

What's the point? It is that Raymond Alber and I probably viewed scripture in a different light; we had a different style in preaching, even dressing – but at Cotner we could come together and share and learn and grow. Cotner School of Religion was interested in their students.

In 1957 I was approached by Raleigh and asked if I would like to be considered for a Rockefeller Scholarship for those who might consider the ministry. I said I didn't think so, which was unfortunate for me; for eight months later I was in Brite Divinity School. Yet Cotner was concerned about students.

Is there any bite in Raleigh J. Peterson Jr? At the General Assembly of the Christian Church (Disciples of Christ) last August in San Antonio, the representatives were spiritedly discussing the issue of abortion. From the microphone at the back of the arena we heard: "Raleigh Peterson, Lincoln, Nebraska, Madam Moderator I note that all speakers addressing this subject are men. Would the Moderator please see that we have speeches from women." Raleigh J. Peterson Jr. is alive and biting. He did not retire from life. I thank God for him, a Christian who has continued to keep before us the issues of peace and human rights and love and compassion.

(3) The third phase of Cotner is the present Cotner College Commission on Continuing Education.

Please consider in your mind's eye a woman in a basement classroom in a church building in Humboldt, Nebraska. She is learning, growing and coming to the place where she feels better about herself, her family, her church and her place in life; all because of a four-week seminar sponsored by Cotner.

See the pastor in Scottsbluff, Nebraska who has a better grasp of what to do when all hell breaks loose in a church board meeting because of a workshop in human relations – a part of Cotner's Continuing Education.

These are ways to bite today. When I informed Carl Burkhardt of my title – "Any Bite Left in the Bulldog?" he wrote "We hope so." Yes, because there is. The bite comes with the same content, but in new forms. And, I'm happy to note it comes in connection with our United Church of Christ friends. When you think of this third phase of Cotner what do you note? People.

When we consider our place in both education and the Christian faith, we must not be afraid of change. People are always in the process of becoming. We can foster growth in our own lives and we can encourage it in others. When we realize this, we will appreciate the importance of our own development as children of God. When we understand that God's love and grace are active in our lives, we open the door to adventures.

The trip – our journey through life – may be as important as the ending. We need to be heading in the right direction ultimately, but we need also to remember that today we are in the process of becoming. Bulldogs with bite, need to look at life as an adventure – a gift from God.

A few years ago some of us in this room gathered for the memorial service of Marian Lowe, Bulldog, class of 1929. In that service, instead of giving a meditation, I had five persons simply share incidents from her life – some were given with laughter, some with tears. It was a good experience, with a different form.

Some of us may think there is no bite in the present Cotner program, because of a misconception of the style of learning. This is often like how one thinks about a church. If I were to ask you, "Where is your church" you might say, "My church is at 16th and "K" or 22nd and South; it has many bricks, some stained glass windows, a minister and a mortgage." That is the church building. But the church is people, often in many different places, living, loving, and helping.

Friends, you don't do any biting before birth nor after death. The most important part on one's tombstone is that dash between your date of birth, and your date of death. We had nothing to say about when we were born. We can say nothing after our death. *Our time* is that dash between – that is the time we can bite.

Bulldogs are not parochial in their world outlook. This is a letter to the editor from a high school paper, this spring

> To the editors:
>
> The "Letter to the Editor" which appeared in the Jan 20 issue of The Owl expressed a political-view so prejudiced and narrow-minded that it demands a rebuttal. The attitude of its authors is a dangerous one; not an uncommon one, but a very dangerous one. The letter states that wearing clothes bearing symbols representative of other countries was a disgrace to America. Now do the authors come to this conclusion? Why must being pro-American necessitate being anti-Japanese or anti-British? At the present time, the United States is maintaining peaceful relationships with both countries. How can America continue to maintain positive, constructive relations with the rest of the world if its citizens reject anything which is not entirely American?
>
> America's greatest trait is its diversity. How many Americans are of entirely American ancestry? Indeed, this is a nation of immigrants and refugees. The different influences which these people have provided are the factors that have made the United States the great nation it is. Let us support diversity in America by continuing to advocate a free exchange of ideals between this country and the rest of the world.
>
> — William W. McDermet IV

I read that letter, not simply because it was by our son, but it captures a world vision greatly needed in our day.

Being a biting Bulldog can happen: anytime, anyplace.

Walking down the hall in the hospital you notice a woman in a chair obviously unhappy. You simply say – "Can I help you?" Your simple act of concern is very supportive – in fact you have said to the person – I see you, I acknowledge you, I really want to help you if possible. (True, one runs the risk of sticking a nose in where not wanted.) Bulldogs care.

A woman in her seventies taught in the school for 49 years. After retirement she goes back to volunteer. She enjoys it. Another retired teacher-friend thinks she's nuts. Her friend would work, only if money was involved. Bulldogs volunteer.

I close (has Sheral waved the pennant?) with two items. The first is a paragraph found in the 1931 Bulldog.

— Dedication –

> To the Cotner College of the past, present and future for which men and women have striven and sacrificed unto their lives in furthering her sacred task of molding the lives of her young people into characters with unwavering Christian ideals, of sympathy and brotherhood with all mankind, of con-

secrated service and love of God, the Giver of all; for her task of instilling in the lives of all who come within her walls a sense of humbleness and adoration of all that is noble and ideal in life; to the Cotner College of tomorrow with her greater possibilities and achievements, her greater service and inspiration as a result of all endeavors, all prayers, and faith of the past, we share the joy of all true Cotnerites who have gone before us and dedicate The 1931 Bulldog.

Goodness, that was one sentence, but the words must be considered.

One year ago this evening, four of us in this room attended the graduation ceremonies for Carleton College at Northfield, Minnesota. After sitting for two and one-half hours, listening to speeches and watching 438 seniors receive diplomas, the college chaplain pronounced the benediction, using the words of Dag Hammerskjold. "God, for all that has been, thanks. For all that is yet to come, yes." Amen.

We Were Family to Brad Long*

In its lifetime, Downey Avenue Christian Church has helped resettle over 150 refugees. Recently we began looking at the economic situation of persons in our own city. "What about people who are poor, lonely, and unemployed right here?" Could we find and minister to a "domestic refugee" – some individual in our county?

Thus a committee met and talked and brainstormed, and contemplated: "How could we implement this ministry?" One member contacted social workers she knew in community agencies. After several weeks she received a call: "I think I have a person your church could sponsor." He was an individual who had just "blown up" in her office! He had constantly been seeking employment, but every time a potential employer saw his record – which noted a heart problem – they said, "No," because of physical disability.

The first contact with the congregation was when members visited Brad Long in Wishard Hospital – the heart problem had recurred. Here was an individual who considered himself a loser and a loner. Brad had physical problems; his wife died thirteen years ago; and he could not find employment since 1979, although he constantly sought it. After his hospital stay he moved to a new apartment with the help of church members. Other Downeyites helped: visiting, altering clothes, providing transportation.

Two members, Violet and JoAnn, had weekly contact with Brad and developed a support system. Brad began to attend worship. Although he had very little income he always put something in the offering. He was an inner city individual who was living on food stamps; a little from the township trustees; with the church paying $100 a month rent and providing him with some spending money.

After a number of months Brad approached me rather timidly and said, "I have something I want to share with the church." What he brought were four pictures taken in 1965 in Dodge City, Kansas. Evidently this represented a happy event from his past, and he wanted to share that part of his history. We put them on our bulletin board.

In February his life began to change. He received his first disability check from Social Security for $300. A banker helped him establish a checking account and Brad was proud of it. Then in April, because of the diligent work of people in the congregation and his social worker, he received a lump sum disability payment of $9,300.

Now our friend Brad Long could give instead of receive, and he wanted to buy a plaque and place on it names of the individuals who had helped him. Members kindly steered him away from that, and then he said, "I want to give a religious picture to the church."

Thus one Sunday morning Brad brought his religious picture and presented it, in my office. Now, one person's da Vinci is another persons K-Mart paint-by-number. I thought we were receiving some type of "Bleeding Heart Jesus" picture and I mused about where to put it, and how I could graciously display it. But, when it was unwrapped, I held a picture of "Jesus and the Two Disciples on the Road to Emmaus." Very nice! So much for my "worrying."

Then our friend Brad wanted to give money to members. He tried to give money to Violet and JoAnn and they said, "No, we represent the church. We do not need and cannot receive your money." He persisted, and went to his banker and said, "I want a cashier's check made out to myself and the minister." In April he presented a check for $1,000 to the church. What he said as he made his gift to me is important: "The church people didn't tell me what to do." Then he said, "The church never asked any questions, they just helped." He concluded, "Nobody else cared, but the church did." In fact, during this process one of the social workers said to our people, "For medical and social reasons he needs to stop smoking. You church people tell him you're not going to be his friend and you're not going to support him unless he stops smoking." Our people agreed it would be good if he stopped but we were not going to tell him he had to.

JoAnn and Violet started to note a complete change in the lifestyle of Brad. He began to take on a good image of himself. The center where he lived had monthly birthday parties, but he never went; now he did. He developed confidence; he made new friends. He and Violet and JoAnn went out to eat and he picked up the tab! As they drove back to his apartment he saw an older woman on the street. Brad said, "That's Rosie. When I was down and out Rosie gave me quarters. I've heard that Rosie is down and out and is looking for a place to live. Maybe I can help her."

On Friday, May 4, 1984, JoAnn phoned the church that Brad had died from a heart attack. The day before he died he phoned the church and told our secretary that he had a phone and wanted his friends at the church to know the number. The very day he died he had been to see the case worker to say he no longer needed food stamps. He was a person who evidenced honesty and was proud to be moving toward independency. After he died his friends were looking through his belongings and they came across his address book. Almost all the names in his book were the names of members of the congregation.

Yes, it's sad that he died just when he was starting to blossom as a person. Yet, as Violet said, he died on top – feeling a deep relationship to this congregation, who were his family.

One important question needs to be asked: "Who really benefited from this relationship, Brad Long, or we of the church, or did both of us grow together?" I think those words of Francis of Assisi are correct: "It is in giving that we receive." In this community ministry, we found a sense of purpose for our being, and a living-out of the gospel of Jesus Christ. That ministry is open to other congregations, if they choose to seek it.

*(Fictitious names are used in this article. Vanguard, J/A/S, 1985.)

My Aunt Margaret: A Silly Saint

Funerals can be fun? Funerals can be fun! At least we can share joy and thanksgiving as we recall the fun times we shared with those who loved us and whom we have loved.

Recently my wife and I drove to the windy city to share in "A Service of Thanksgiving" for the life of Margaret Lowe Metheny, my Aunt Margaret. We indeed can learn and grow from such events.

Margaret was my silly and full-of-life relative. In her case "Lowe" was a num de plume for "humor." She was a PK (preacher's kid). She and my mother grew up together, and they stayed very close all their years. Mother told about life in the church parsonage. The two young sisters frequently played "church," my mother at the piano, and Margaret was the preacher. They used salt and pepper shakers for communion. When their dad performed a wedding in the parsonage parlor, the two girls sold standing-room tickets to neighbor kids for one cent to watch the ceremony from outside the picture window on the porch.

When my family lived in Lincoln there was an annual Lowe family reunion, and we could hardly wait for Margaret's family to arrive, for then the fun really began. Five Lowe sisters gathered in the kitchen and laughed and reminisced with funny stories until I thought they would fall down from laughter. I always stationed myself in or close to the kitchen.

Death comes to all of us, and there we were in University Christian Church (DOC/UCC), in Chicago, remembering Margaret. She died a month earlier, and per her request her body was given to science. Later her body was cremated, with her ashes placed in a lovely church garden next to Disciples Divinity House, and there a rose bush will be planted. (Probably with some thorns?).

Prior to the service, Marilyn and Marcia, her two daughters had requested the service be enriched with humor, which was Margaret's trademark. The service began with majestic organ music by Buxtehude and Bach. Following the pastors' Call to Celebration, we sang "Dear Mother/Father of Us All." One of her daughters put together "Highlights" of their mothers' life, read by the pastor. Per Margaret's request we read in unison a special version of the Ten Commandments. One of the Ten was: "Thou shalt not take problems to bed with you for they make very poor bedfellows." Another: "Thou shalt be a good listener, for only when you listen do you hear ideas different from you own. It's very hard to learn something new when you're talking."

We enjoyed readings from Psalm 100, Ulysses S. Grant and Ralph Waldo Emerson. We sang "Once to Every Heart and Nation." Four of us presented brief remembrances. I decided to begin mine by singing one of the many silly little ditties Margaret taught us – should it be "Ten men slept in a boarding house bed, roll over, roll over" or "I'm a Villain?" I selected "I'm a villain, a dirty little villain." (The style would be kin to the wonderful off-the-wall-humor of *Far Side* by Gary Larson.)

Following these remarks members of the congregation were invited to come forward and share happenings from her life. One shared that when they were learning to sing "They will know we are Christians by our love" Margaret challenged the content by remarking, "Well, we can also sing 'They will know we are Buddhists, or Muslims, or Hindus by our love.'" Hmm. Just when you had a bit of theology all wrapped up in a box, with pretty paper and a bow on top, Margaret would send you thinking again.

Another long-time member recalled when the church was considering placing memorial plaques with names of those who made major gifts – Margaret was requesting that *all* should be listed regardless of amounts given. To the question, "What criteria should we establish for those who are listed?" Margaret responded, "First, you have to be dead." Eight others shared, and by the end of the service, if you had never met Margaret, you now knew her.

We closed the service with a prayer, the Commendation, and sang the hymn "For All The Saints." I made it through the first two stanzas fine, but in the third stanza, when we came to: "O blest communion of the saints divine, We live and struggle, They in glory shine;" I found my eyesight becoming blurry and some moisture on the hymnal. So, I just looked at the lovely stained glass windows and tried to contemplate this event, and life, and death, and who we are, and Whose we are.

We formed a large circle and we all sang "The Lord Bless You and Keep You."

Then we went to the fellowship hall and had communion – the punch and cookie type. (One woman who was hosting informed me that the cookie recipe was Margaret's and reminded me that Margaret had been in the congregation for parts of six decades.) The daughters had used a large bulletin board to place numerous family pictures and letters relating to Margaret's life. Some from her school teaching days. We chatted, we laughed, we reflected. As we prepared to leave there were hugs all around and then – at the request of my two cousins – six family members sang again "I'm a Villain."

We made it back to rural Iowa and fell into bed about midnight. We were dead tired, yet with a fresh appreciation of life, and death, and relationships, and God.

Oh yes, the final section of the third stanza sings: "Yet all are one in thee, for all are thine. Alleluia, Alleluia!"

(The Disciple, November 1995)

Kings, Prophets and Yahweh

I Kings

In I Kings we find more "royal" individuals than we care to remember. We see the acting-out of good and evil, peace and violence; and boring evaluations of incompetent kings. A major question is: "What is the relationship of these kings to God?" Within Kings we note judgment and promise. Here we see Yahweh holding kings to high standards.

In the Hebrew Bible the term "prophet" can be used for both "true" and "false" prophets. Some prophets can be both, and can fluctuate to both extremes. Prophets may cause *us* to be uncomfortable.

Yahweh does not act alone, but works with what is available – human beings as they are – with all their weaknesses as well as their strengths. Yahweh can work through evil toward divine purposes (see Genesis 50:20). Humans are encouraged to act with the boldness and astuteness of a Nathan. This is not to suggest that the ends always justify the means. One must always be very careful in "seeing" precisely just how Yahweh acts in events.

In chapter nine the writer provides an image of Yahweh who is supportive and faithful, yet also judgmental. This two-facet theme is seen in the rest of both I and II Kings. How Israel responds (either positively or negatively) to Yahweh's ways will determine the future. In our time what we do and say determines our future. The future is not pre-determined; it is open to our activity. This is challenging and thrilling. As individuals, and as communities of believers, which direction do we choose for our journey: a road toward, or a road away from God? Am I saying, "Even God does not know the future?" Yes I am. We are not robots, simply role-playing a drama. Humans are *the* element in *the* story. The conclusion of *the* play is yet to be acted-out; with God, of course, as the Director.

Browsing I Kings we note that justice and righteousness find expression for those who are poor. Christians please note Jesus' juxtaposition of Solomon's glory as seen in Matthew 6:25-33. In doing research I found few, if any reflections/comments concerning Elijah's miraculous resuscitation of the "dead" son in Chapter 17; nor insights to Elijah's killing the 450 prophets of Baal in chapter 18. My own observation is that we need "the rest of the story" yet to be played-out in the New Testament. Lawrence Bash, former pastor of the Country Club Christian Church in Kansas City, reflected on the helpful and not-so-helpful sections of the Bible: "When you eat fish, you eat the meat of the fish, and place the bones to one side."

The difference that a strong leader can have on the history of a group or nation can not be under-estimated. In the end, the reign of Solomon, is tragic. Though there were many elements causing the division of the kingdom, the central issue for Israel was a spiritual illness that finally consumed the nation.

If you find I Kings full of difficult events and detours, wait until you travel through II Kings! That trip is a bumpy road; but remember it is not the end of the journey. Readers will need to go to other places in the Bible for a more understanding picture of God. Like most "books" of the Bible, Kings is experienced as part of the whole. Eat the meat; place the bones to one side.

(DisciplesWorld, May, 2004)

Beauty Becomes A Beast

From my third floor retreat I look out upon the lazy Des Moines River. Natives call it "lazy" because for most of the time the river calmly, quietly, and slowly flows from southern Minnesota into the Mississippi River at Keokuk. Too often canoeists complain they have to carry their canoe through, rather than float in, because the river is too shallow. Yet the river is a beauty to behold within our lovely valley.

The Des Moines River flows 100 yards south of the front door of our Mason House Inn at Bentonsport, Iowa. The Inn was built as a steamboat stop for travelers in 1846 – the same year that Iowa became a state. It was built by Mormon craftsmen who stayed and worked for a year on their famous trek to Utah. The Mason House Inn abounds with history. Abraham Lincoln, Mark Twain, George McGovern and Iowa governors have slept within the 26 room Inn. It is home to many unique antique items including a wonderful three feet by four feet memorial hair wreath, 1870 pump organ, nine foot headboards and a "murphy" fold-down copper bathtub. Many items have been within the Inn for decades.

My wife, Sheral, and I, purchased the Inn in June of 1989. I had served Disciple congregations as pastor for 29 years. We added a second vocation. We run the Inn as a Bed & Breakfast and host about 800 individuals per year. At times our innkeeping becomes a ministry – but that can be the subject of another article.

Our life was full and busy, yet peaceful until July 13, 1993, when the beautiful river became an ugly beast.

Prior to that April we had never had a water problem in our cellar. In the late spring we found water coming in through the old stone steps. For the first time in five summers we needed to use a sump pump. The rains continued and we added a second pump. We became very concerned during the first week in July. The river was running full, and I began to take some antiques to our second and third floors. In May we had just completed our third, and hopefully final, refurbishing project: a new hot water heater in the cellar, new first floor baths, new paint, new carpeting. I began to wonder: "Had we made the right choice by putting our savings into this historic piece of property?"

As those July rains increased, so did our anxiety. One area resident reported that during a 46 day period, some rain fell on 42 of those days. We wondered if this was Genesis 7:12 revisited.

Our destiny was in the hands of those who controlled the flow of water from Saylorville and Red Rock dams. Normal July flow from Red Rock is 5,500 cfs (cubic feet per second.) Now it had increased to 70,000 then 75,000 then 80,000 then 90,000 then 100,000 then 104,000. The water began to come across the road in front of the Inn, Joe Munford — the young carpenter who had done some of our renovation, appeared early one morning, and together we carried the large priceless antiques up to the second floor.

When the ordeal began we agreed we would move the major appliances to the old Presbyterian Church – and wait and see. Bill Printy, the local blacksmith and neighbor, came to us and said, "We need to try to save the Mason House, it's so rich in history, and it's important to the economy of the county. Let's sand bag." The following day Dave Paulek arrived ready to start the process of sand-bagging. He is chair of the county disaster program, and with our approval, he called in the National Guard, more helpers, and pumps.

On July 12 and 13 more than 200 volunteers, along with six National Guardsmen arrived; and our village population increased sevenfold. Printy is a retired engineer, and some days later he would calculate that on July 13, 1993, water was moving past our Inn at the rate of 46,671,653 gallons per minute. You read that correctly – 46 million – more than the Mississippi River on a normal day.

The sand bagging continued for two days. Our Inn became an island. Printy would later figure we used 570 tons of sand, which filled about 31,000 sand bags. Another 10,000 bags were placed in the road to divert the powerful flow of the river.

People came to help from Keosauqua and Stockport, from Farmington and Cantril. Fire departments came from Fairfield and Packwood. Fifteen Amish men came from the western part of Van Buren County. Some workers I knew, most of them I had never seen. Volunteers, who were too old to carry the bags, helped by filling them and tying them shut. Farmers who we had never met came with their tractors. Thirty to fifty bags were loaded into frontend-loaders, driven into the water, and placed into a row boat. Then they were taken around the building and set in place. At one time nine pumps were removing water inside the "moat" and cellar. Another farmer from Hillsboro brought his tractor with an irrigation pump. It was so powerful that it drew a sand bag through it.

During one thirty-minute period on July 13 the water rose 10-11 inches. Paulek would later tell the Ottumwa Courier: "I thought we lost it, there was too much water, rising too quickly." Late in the night on July 13 the Des Moines River finally crested with part of it about 20 yards *behind* the Inn.

In all of this fear and confusion and anxiety and anger I wondered – where is God? I recall that when the water was about three inches deep in our lower bedroom and pressure was causing sewage to come into four baths through the toilets and showers, I stood for a moment transfixed, staring at a cellar full of water and mud, and wondering, "Is God trying to say something?" Earlier that day I had attempted to move a riding lawnmower to higher ground. For a few moments I actually could not figure out how to start it, I was so disorientated by the event.

If God continues to work through persons, then we did find God to be alive and active. Early in our ordeal Beth Dobyns arrived from Fort Madison. Beth is an Associate Minister of the Upper Midwest Regional Church for Disciples. Not only did she come to fill sand bags, but she brought homemade sandwiches and drinks. Later as she left she asked, "Is there anything else I can do?" I responded, "Yes, we have no mail service, please mail my yearly dues to our Pension Fund." She did.

What I learned from our flood experience is that the power of nature did not overcome the power and will of humans working together. Those persons were young and old and middle aged, male and female, Democrats and Republicans, United Methodist, Catholic, Independent Christian, UCC'ers, and non-believers. A local physician was handing bags to high schoolers, who in turn handed them to farmers, and then to county employees, etc. Farmers who had strongly opposed the development of tourism at Bentonsport were among the first to help. They were outside the Inn, ready to help each morning, for six consecutive days. When we left the Inn because of high water, (we were out for 31 days) one farmer volunteered his home as a shelter. Some involved in the saving effort began to feel a vested ownership in the Inn and village.

Difficult times bring out the best and worst in humans. With all the volunteers we needed portable toilets. A businessman in a neighboring community would supply one, but informed us that it would cost $65 for a week. In contrast, the farmer who brought his $85,000 tractor to assist in the pumping, would not even allow us to pay for his fuel. Farmer-friend Sam Warner was there for 21 days.

During one lull in the action I had a brief theological discussion with a retired Christian Reformed pastor who lives in the immediate area. He remarked that prayers had been offered for our situation. I replied that I had not prayed about our problem saying, "This is minor compared to the daily life-and-death ways of those in Sarajevo, Bosnia-Herzegovina, so I pray for them." My clergy friend reflected, "Someone is always in a worse situation, and thus we might not pray for anyone." Hmm, I'm still mulling-over his observation. I do know that Prairie Avenue Christian Church in Decatur, Illinois – a congregation we served in the late 1980's – prayed for us, as did others. It helped!

Help arrived in other ways. We received many letters. From a former B&B guest we received this note.

> Sheral,
>
> I hope all is okay with you and that you will use the enclosed check as you see fit. My priorities are:
>
> 1. Food & shelter for neighbors
> 2. Mason House restoration
> 3. Historical Society
>
> I will leave it to you and know you will spend it well. We aren't even going to spit in the creek till you are dry!
>
> Sandy Textor
> Jewell, Iowa

I recall a cold, dark, November Saturday afternoon when I was feeling even-a-bit-more depressed that usual. I brought in the mail and opened it in the kitchen. Among the bills was an envelope from Burlington, Iowa. It contained a check for $1,000 from the Eastern Iowa Presbytery. I stood there and wept. We discovered later that a woman from an area Presbyterian Church had made a trip through Bentonsport some weeks after the flood. She had seen our need, reported that need, and that check was the response. (I recant any snide comments I may have made about the followers of John Calvin.)

Our flood experience was costly – both financially and emotionally. It will be months until we are back to normal. However even with the abrupt change in our lives we have again been called to understand that we humans were not created to live in isolation, we were created to live in community. We have experienced community; and we are grateful beyond words, and we thank God. Whatever the world gives us, we do not need to live as victims.

(This article is expanded from The Disciple, November 1993)

In A Court Room During Lent

(This writing has taken three forms. Part of it was a sermon given under the title: "It Is Finished" at the 1995 Good Friday community worship service in First Lutheran (ELCA) Church in Ottumwa, Iowa. It was the guest editorial "Life or Death?" in the Sunday Des Moines Register, January 22, 1995. It "won" – a word hardly fitting within this context – the Peace Sermon Contest of the Disciples Peace Fellowship in 1999.)

A trial is not an unusual event during the Lenten season. Pilate held one – a media event of questionable proportions. In any reflection, it was a dismal scene. A Shawnee County (Topeka) Kansas court room was not my choice of places to spend two weeks in Lent. One found there some of the same activity found in the events preceding the death of the Nazarene: charges, counter-charges, testimony, cross-examination, denial, betrayal; all connected to death.

Court room #4 was my home-away-from-home because I was participating in the trial of the one charged with murdering my brother – James Turner McDermet. The details are even now incomplete – as in many homicide cases.

I vividly remember that November phone call from our Vermont brother. Following a brief greeting, Stewart said, "We think Jim is dead."

My response was, "What do you mean, you think?"

He related he had just received a call from the Topeka police that a body had been found in Jim's apartment, and they believed it was Jim, but had yet to do fingerprinting. I recall putting my head down on the desk and crying. Stewart could only say, "I know, I know."

Indeed it was Jim's body. Later the District Attorney's office contacted our family to inform us they would keep us up-to-date concerning the details and coming trial. During the first part of 1995, the Iowa legislature was debating a bill that would restore the death penalty, a practice I have always opposed. I found myself trying to contain my own grief, yet wanting to speak out on the issue. The Des Moines Register had already taken an editorial stand against restarting the practice of executions, and I finally decided to submit my feelings on capital punishment. My opinion piece was the lead article on the editorial page. Part of my reflection centered on my theological understanding at an earlier time. Quoting some of the narrative:

In the early 1960's, our family lived in Kalona, Iowa, where I was the pastor of the United Christian and Baptist Church. In October 1962, The International Convention of the Christian Church (Disciples of Christ) meeting in Los Angeles approved business Resolution No. 43, "Concerning the Abolition of Capital Punishment." The resolution had been submitted by the Kalona congregation. I wrote the text, and nine members of that Advisory Board signed their names.

WHEREAS the Christian gospel is a redemptive gospel and many of Christ's teachings lift up the ideal of forgiveness of individuals, and

WHEREAS, punishment, when meted out with justice and with concern for the welfare of the offender, as well as the protection of society, should be a means of discipline, reform, and rehabilitation, and

WHEREAS, the possibility of rehabilitation is eliminated by the death penalty, and

WHEREAS, there is evidence to show that the death penalty itself is unequally applied, falling mainly on the poor, the friendless, the mentally unstable, the ignorant, and minority groups, and there is always the possibility (as has been the case)

or executing the innocent, and
WHEREAS there is evidence to show that it is doubtful whether capital punishment serves as a deterrent to capital crimes,
THEREFORE BE IT RESOLVED; that we as the International Convention of Christian Churches (Disciples of Christ) go on record as favoring a program of rehabilitation for criminal offenders rather than capital punishment.

In 1962, I wrote from theory, not practice. For more than 30 years, I have maintained an attitude against capital punishment – a concept that says: "We kill people who kill people to prove that killing people is wrong!" We left Iowa in 1964, and returned in 1989.

Knowing my beliefs on the issue, and following Jim's murder, a relative asked me, "Now, what do you think about capital punishment?" I responded, "I'm still against it." And, I am. How do I feel toward the person who murdered my brother? Anger. Anger, with a capital "A" with the word underlined, and followed by a half-dozen exclamation marks. ANGER!!!!!! Yet, would I feel better, or satisfied, if Jim's murderer were killed? No. (In March of 1995, the Iowa House did pass capital punishment legislation;but the Iowa Senate defeated the bill 39-11.)

To put a face on this tragedy, you need to know something about my brother. James Turner McDermet was born on November 11, 1948, in Lincoln, Nebraska, the youngest of four sons. Jim grew up in a kind and loving family. He was happy, yet reserved. He participated in activities, but was not a leader. He lost the sight in one eye early in his life, yet he read everything, especially history books. Jim was the person you wanted on your side when you played Trivial Pursuit. What was King George III eating for lunch on March 10, 1819? Jim knew. Jim would never, never harm anyone. In fact, when I phoned two of our daughters to tell them their Uncle Jim had been murdered, they softly wept and said, "Why would anyone kill Jim? He was so kind."

After his college days, at Emporia State, Jim moved to Topeka, where he worked for the state of Kansas for 15 years. He was presented with a Certificate of Recognition for being the Messenger for the Governor 1979-1987, by John Carlin, Governor, presented at the Capital in Topeka on the 9th day of January, 1987. At the time of his death, he lived alone, kept mainly to himself, continued his reading, ate too many pizzas, enjoyed sports, collected stamps, and bothered no one. The New Testament would call him "meek," one of God's special people.

Our parents live at Foxwood Springs, a church-related retirement community in Raymore, Missouri. Our mother has had a stroke, so travel is very difficult. On November 12, 1994, the day after what would have been Jim's 45th birthday, we remembered him at a memorial service in Raymore. The following Monday, we buried his broken body in a small Kiowa County, Kansas cemetery in a lot next to our grandmother, Juda I McDermet, who had homesteaded at Mullenville, in the 1880s. The weekend was painful beyond what any words could describe.

Following delays and the accumulation of evidence, the trial began three weeks into Lent. The district attorney had strongly encouraged family members to be present. We wanted to be there for many reasons, and as some type of tribute to Jim, and to let the world know he had a family who loved him. We wanted to know the facts of the case, so in later years we would not wonder about what transpired. And, yes, we wanted to see the human being who was accused of murdering Jim.

I still find bewildering the statement from the District Attorney, "We want you at the trial because extensive studies show we have a much higher rate of conviction, *if* family members are present for the jury to see." I found this to be a depressing observation. I wondered what ever happened to "just the facts, ma'am, just the facts."

The family decision was that I and another brother, Staley from Massachusetts, would attend the trial. So, beginning on March 28, Staley and I could be seen in Court Room #4 in the first row, immediately behind the district attorney's desk, and we sat there for parts of nine sobering days. We had been told there would probably be long stretches with little to do, so "bring reading material." Staley, an architect, brought design magazines, and I decided to tackle The Five Gospels: What Did Jesus Really Say? by the Jesus Seminar; insightful reading for a trial during Lent?

Jury selection took two full days. Staley and I began to wonder who we would want to be in that decision-making box. Prospective jurors came and went. How many women? How many people of color? How many could sort out fact from fiction? The defendant was female and a person of another color than Jim – thus possible gender/racial elements were brought to the event.

The judge, presiding since 1977, within the Third Judicial District, remained pleasant, casual, and ready to compromise any differences. My quarrel with the judge was that he did not allow me to testify concerning one very pertinent aspect of information directly related to the case. The District Attorney's office, too, must share some of the responsibility for this oversight, as they could have seen that evidence was presented in some manner. I could testify to the fact that Jim was blind in one eye and had a detached retina in the other eye. Yet, the judge would not allow me to testify because I was "not qualified as a medical expert." I wondered if the court was more interested in technicalities than evidence. Staley and I wondered if this might be crucial to the case.

We attempted to place ourselves as members of the jury. Thus stationed, might we not wonder, "How can a 260 pound man be murdered by a woman?" (She was over 200 pounds). We believed that with my information, it would then be very understandable that, if she had struck Jim, knocking off his glasses and detaching his retina, he would then be blinded and at her mercy. As the trial progressed, we almost wanted to shout, "He probably could not see his attacker."

The jury was seated with seven women and five men. Two of the jurors were people of color. My reflection on the jury was one of appreciation. From my vantage point, they listened with intense attention to every witness (the prosecution called 47, the defense 3), and the jury approached their task with dedicated decorum. The trial did seem to take a toll on them. Each day, they were a bit more weathered than the day before.

The facts of this case were that on November 9, 1994, my brother was murdered in his Topeka apartment. The District Attorney's words were, "One of the most brutal murders ever in this county." The year 1994 was a difficult one for Shawnee County as there were 38 homicides committed. So much for the tranquility of the state that gave us the image of the Yellow Brick Road.

The motive was robbery. Jim had less that $200 in cash in his apartment. His money was gone, plus some foreign coins. Three coins were found in the defendant's apartment.

The defendant was in her middle 40's and lived with her twelve-year-old son, within the apartment complex. She did not have a telephone, so in a friendly, neighborly act, Jim had allowed her to use his phone. Jim had also shown her son his stamp collection. A few months before his death, Jim mentioned to me in a phone conversation that "a large woman living across from me has taken some money I had out on a desk, ready to pay my light bill. She had used the phone."

It was awkward sitting only 15 feet from the accused during the trial. The D.A. remarked that they (the D.A.'s office and the Topeka police) were convinced she had committed the murder. The county coroner was on the stand for three hours. He testified that Jim received 63 blows with a knife and iron tools, and that he was "still alive" when he received those blows. Listening to that God-awful account, something within me died that day.

During those days when I sat in that courtroom, I reflected many times on what life itself was all about. I'm a person who finds insightful meaning in some movies. One of my own "top ten films" is the 1984 movie "Places in the Heart." The setting was in the 1930's. Royce was the sheriff of Waxahachie, Texas. A pious man, he gave thanks to God before their Sunday meal and then was called away from the table on an emergency. A young black boy had gotten drunk and was shooting off a gun down by the railroad tracks. Just as the boy was about to hand the weapon over to the sheriff, it accidentally fired. Royce was hit and died immediately. His wife Edna, and her children's lives were upended and they learned to live with the difficult. The movie then evolves around Edna, a black itinerant farm hand, and a blind man forming a bond and tackling the forces of evil.

The closing scene takes place in the Christian Church. As the camera slowly pans the congregation receiving communion, we recognize all the characters – those living and dead, and departed for other places. It is a Christian image in which the lambs and wolves, the wronged and the wrongdoers, the betrayers and the betrayed are all together as one in the Kingdom of God. It is an unforgettable cinematic statement about hope. Only God knows how many times I have encouraged people to view this ending and then capture and claim this wonderful example.

Yet, sitting in that Topeka courtroom and recalling that meaningful movie image, I could not embrace any element of forgiveness. I still try to deal with the evil within God's world and the "why" of it. "Forgiveness" for this act of murder is not a part of my vocabulary, at least at this time. I do not believe that there are evil persons, but truly there are persons who do evil deeds.

The defense attorney posed some problems for Staley and me. Court-appointed, he was slight of stature but loud of mouth and seemed to use every courtroom tactic available. We did not view him with any sense of objectivity, of course. In one of his tirades, he ended his monologue with, "The defendant should not be found guilty and thus it would be a tribute to the victim and doing a favor to James McDermet." Hmm.

What really bothered me was his attempt to Christianize the testimony of the defendant's mother. This family matriarch had organized the plan to quickly relocate her grandson – who knew about the murder – to Virginia. After her testimony that her grandson was scheduled to leave *prior* to the murder, the defense attorney asked her, "Do you go to church? Do you believe in God?" and with a loud and emotional voice, "You wouldn't lie to us, as a Christian, would you?"

Of course, what was happening was an attempt to find one juror who would buy the defense's rationale, leading to acquittal. It seemed to us that the criminal justice system was boiling down to who can win. That was the bottom line. As the D.A. said to us, "We have to convince 12 people, beyond a reasonable doubt, that she is guilty. The defense has to convince just one juror that there is some reasonable doubt."

The District Attorney was pleasant and shared the questioning process with her assistant. In one of our discussions, she mentioned she strongly approved of the death penalty and she went on to say she had been a member of the Kansas Parole Board and had met a number of persons who had committed capital crimes. Some of those people had stated, "You let me out (of prison) and I'll kill again." I shared with her that no one in Jim's family, including our parents, wanted Jim's killer put to death; incarcerated, yes, and for a long time; but "no" to capital punishment.

The most incriminating evidence against the defendant was a luminal blood trail from Jim's apartment to, and inside, the defendant's apartment. This strong evidence was coupled with the statement of the defendant's son, who said to neighbors, "My mom's done something really bad; you will hear about it on the TV."

The jury was given four possible verdicts. (1) Guilty of murder in the first degree. (2) Guilty of murder in the second degree. (3) Guilty of manslaughter. (4) Not guilty. Staley and I truly felt the defendant to be guilty; however much of the evidence was circumstantial; it just inferred guilt, and some of the prosecution witnesses were unconvincing. So we felt there was a strong possibility of a hung jury or even a verdict of not guilty.

On the third day of their deliberations, the jury returned their decision: guilty of murder in the second degree. Members of the jury left the courthouse quickly. Most of them were stoic; they did not speak to television or newspaper reporters, or members of the D.A.'s staff.

During the ordeal, I repeatedly attempted to make some sense out of the event. I asked myself the usual "why" questions. Why did Jim have to suffer and die in this horrible way? Why do people act this way? Why does God – if there is a God – allow such suffering? God love him, Jim deserved a better life and fate. Theologically, I am helped somewhat in understanding the murder, remembering that Jesus of Nazareth too deserved better. That fact places Jim in good company, and Jim lives in our hearts.

This year, I identify with the Good Friday event in a different manner than I ever experienced before. To some extent, I can vicariously enter into the horror of the dying Jesus. I recall a story of the preacher who dramatically and vividly portrayed the agony of the death of the Nazarene. The pastor's pulpit language was so realistic that a young boy began to sob loudly at the tragic description of Christ's dying. An usher escorted the young boy to the narthex and then attempted to comfort him by saying, "You must not take it so personally."

How else does one take the death of a person you loved but personally? To John's New Testament statement, "It is finished," I say, "Yes, it is finished for Jesus of Nazareth, and for my brother Jim, but not for us!" If there is any homiletical insight from this passage, it is the encouragement that we saw love, and now we carry on that love. Love, and hope, and meekness, and insights, and Kingdom-building do not die with any one person. My challenge to other Christians (and myself?) is that we are an Easter people living in a Good Friday world. God is present even in our darkest hours.

Months after the murder, I find myself at times remorseful and cynical. Yet, I find I am more sensitive to those with needs, especially those whom I would term meek, like Jim. I find I continue to live in hope – a hope of God's yet-to-be-fully-experienced Kingdom. My taste for the mystery of God's silence and activity is compelling.

After the dismal event, one of our daughters, in a philosophical mood reflected, "Remember Buddha said, 'Life is not fair.'" Indeed; still I contemplate a saying I found in that Topeka court room as I read the Jesus Seminar translation of the Gospel of Thomas – Jesus said, "Those who seek should not stop seeking until they find." (2:1) The future is open, and I continue to seek with hope. Amen.

Dogs, Wasps and a Peace Pole

My wife, Sheral, and I live by the Des Moines River in a village of 31 persons, seven dogs, scores of rabbits, squirrels and wasps, a few deer, wonderful memories and one peace pole.

We enjoy our historic environment, and we do our share in maintaining the buildings built around the middle of the last century. One of our special buildings is the Presbyterian Church. The Calvinists built their structure in 1855. They worshipped in the building until the 1930's, and then left it to the elements.

We keep it open so tourists may experience the building and especially note the many Devil's Spikes placed on the outside walls. They are two foot pointed iron rods that are suppose to prevent the Devil from entering.

However a recent addition may be the most important aspect of our village. I became aware of our neighbor's peace pole when I walked by it twice a day during my month to open and close the Presbyterian Church. The real cutting edge is the actualization of the words found on our peace pole, which I hope keeps the Devil at bay. These four sentences read: East (in German) MOGE FRIEDE AUF ERDEN SEIN. South (in Spanish) PAZ A TODOS LOS HOMBRES. West (in French) PUISSE LA PAIX RE'GNER DAIS LE MONDE. North (in English) MAY PEACE PREVAIL ON EARTH.

I wish our peace pole were closer to our one paved road that runs through the community, so more could see it. Yet the crux of peace is not just seeing it spelled out in different languages, but how we humans respond to the call for peace, especially primary for Christians.

If you visit our village we'll be happy to show you where the steamboats docked, the wonderful historic homes, the Devils Spikes and our peace pole. Still, seeing and acting out peace are two separate activities.

We will do our part for a peaceful world, and pray that you will do the same in your location, even if you see the peace pole only in your mind. Living and working for peace keeps the Devil away.

(The Disciple, December, 1990)

Reflections from an Ole Ecumenic

It may have been my last hurrah, but it was filled with humbling joy. In fact the hurrah lasted over two and one-half hours. There I was on Sunday, January 20, 2002 in the next-to-the-last pew on the main floor in Mt. Olive Cathedral (CME) sanctuary in Memphis. I was one of about a thousand packed into that historic church to celebrate the National Act of Worship Inaugurating Churches Uniting in Christ.

It was a long way, and long time from Kalona, Iowa where I had preached my first sermon out of seminary as their called pastor on June 19, 1960. The Kalona church was the product of congregations from two denominations. Those saints and sinners had given me a taste of the ecumenical spirit at its best; effectively doing ministry together better than going it alone.

In October of 1961 I had spoken before the International Convention of Christian Churches in Kansas City, supporting a Resolution from the Kalona congregation on local church unity. In July of 2001 at the now General Assembly, again in Kansas City, I was able to speak in support of CUIC. In the intervening 40 years a priority for me has been encouraging ecumenical work, worship and witness.

On that special CUIC day in Memphis, I recalled Granville T. Walker's comment: "I hope I see us Disciples unite before I die." (Walker was the long-time senior pastor of University Christian Church in Fort Worth, and International Convention Moderator. He died many years ago.) Finally, after all those years, I was able to experience a "happening" that would express something tangible in Christian unity.

The colorful banners representing the nine CUIC denominations were processed down the center aisle. Then came the representatives. Richard Hamm, the Disciples General Minister and President was beaming. And, there was Jack Rogers, Moderator of the General Assembly of the Presbyterian Church, USA. (Earlier that day we had introduced ourselves, discovering we had grown up in Lincoln, Nebraska, he graduating Lincoln High in 1951 and I in 1953. I said to myself: "It can't get any better than this.")

There was a variety of music, and it was outstanding: a brass consort, gospel choir, handbell choir, a trumpeter from The Canadian Brass, a vocal choir of almost 100 that sang four anthems. There were numerous opportunities for participation from worshipers. Part of the Declaration of Purpose was:

> People: We come to ask God's Holy Spirit to be with us as we seek forgiveness for the sin of division. We come to pray for the full, visible unity of the one Body of Christ.
>
> Leader: Led by the Holy Spirit, we will become Churches Uniting in Christ. In this new relationship with one another, we can speak the Christian faith more clearly. With fresh courage, we can oppose the powers that divide our churches and oppress the people of our land.

The old hymn "To God Be the Glory" is not one of my favorites, but I found deep meaning in the fresh words and I lustily joined in:

You've called us together, O God, by your grace:
No longer divided, our churches embrace.
Our new common mission has only begun;
We're learning the blessings of serving as one.
Refrain
We are called! We are freed!
We are baptized as one.
In the Church, all we need
Can be found in your Son!
With Christ to unite us, and born from above,
We witness together your wondrous love.

In the section: Inaugurating a New Relationship, we said in unison: "God, we praise you for the vision, intelligence, and courage of leaders in the Consultation on Church Union who have brought us to this day." (Worshipers were encouraged to say aloud the names of persons they remembered.) Some two dozen were called-out, including Paul Crow and Michael Kinnamon. I spoke the name "Robert Welsh" and it blended with others.

In the Declarations parts of worship we were given the privilege to state:

Leader: With gratitude to God, we affirm:
People: The one baptism that makes our members one people in Jesus Christ.
Leader: As members of Churches Uniting in Christ, we will establish a new relationship that transcends our divisions imbedded in worship, doctrine, polity, language, race, and communion.
People: We promise; to welcome each another in our churches as Christ has welcomed us.
Leader: In a process of theological dialogue we will endeavor:
People: to clarify and deepen our witness to the unity of Christ's church.

It was a God-filled time of wonder and grace and joy. What a marvelous beginning. Yet, I'm not sure if the world took note of the event. In fact the *Memphis Commercial Appeal* did not mention the event in their Monday edition. Maybe the world will note CUIC *after* we have provided concrete acts of ministry that meet the needs of humans?

On our bus trip back to the hotel, my wife, Sheral, lovingly said to me: "Now, you can die happy." Indeed. Hopefully we who sang and prayed and listened and took communion did so vicariously focusing on all those who were not able to be present on that remarkable day. I was never able to see who was in the back balcony. Maybe Granville was there!

(Reflections from Participants in Mid-Stream, April/July, 2002)

About Wanderings and Wilderness

(Browsing the Bible)
Exodus 16-40

The most important aspect of living is to journey with a strong relationship to God (in this case Yahweh) and other humans. One reason we read and study the Bible is to learn how persons did, or did not, develop meaningful relationships.

For Israel the Exodus experience was the crisis of faith between bondage and well being. In the first part of this browsing we note Israel's anxiety over good distorts their memory of the recent Egyptian oppressive past. How quickly people of faith can forget their Source of freedom! The wilderness – then and now – is not a void, but within it there is the powerful presence of Yahweh. The people harvest just enough bread: everyone has enough and nobody is left out. This is community at its best. Communism? Socialism? Nope. Sounds like a true facet of Christianity.

On this special journey, God through Moses, presents the Ten Commandments to the Hebrews. They are presented as guidelines to help them make ethical decisions in their relationships to Yahweh and others. In our day we draw up battle lines as to where these 10 shall be placed. Rather than demand they be placed on specific walls, we would be better served to hang them on our hearts!

The writer of Exodus spends extensive time giving details for building the Tabernacle. Here the people obtain contact with Yahweh. This same longing is with us. Yet, emphasis must be given – not to the place of worship – but to what happens within that special place.

While aesthetics are helpful in presenting awe, there always needs to be a balance between building and benevolence. For Israel, and for us, the question is: "What is our relationship with Yahweh within the Tabernacle/Sanctuary?" For us – how do we live a religious life within 21st century confident secularism? Among the many technical directions for details in the Tabernacle, which are not relevant for our time – is the reflection that Yahweh cannot be approached carelessly.

Dealing with the Golden Calf event we are challenged to probe: "What, Whom and how do *we* worship?" Do we eat and drink and dance and revel in a self-centered manner for self-enjoyment (Aaron and "his" people around the Golden Calf); or Yahweh as expressed by Moses and acted-out obedience to the Decalogue. This scripture is an insightful example of sin, punishment, intercession, and forgiveness. A strong element in this reading is the on-going presence of Yahweh, even after the calf debacle. How do we see/feel that Presence in our day, or are we also a stiff-necked people?

The book of Exodus concludes with a finished Tabernacle. The Tabernacle is filled with its most important ingredient: the glory of Yahweh. (Television preachers take note.) Yahweh has not taken up residence in a colossal palace, but with a slave community in the wilderness; and Yahweh will continue to be with them as they travel together.

This same feeling is found in the final book of the Bible: "See, the tabernacle of God is among mortals. God will tabernacle with them as their God." Rev. 21:3

(DisciplesWorld, June 2003)

Advent Adventures

the christian MINISTRY

DisciplesWorld

Watch and Wait

An Advent Homily - Habakkuk 2:1-3

This passage was written during difficult times. So what's new? Habakkuk says people were stationed on watchtowers to spot messengers, enemies and even weather changes. Watchers waited in the towers for long periods, but that waiting was filled with expectation. In one sense, these watchers rose, at least temporarily, above the daily struggle. From those towers, they may have gained some objectivity, which gave them vision and purpose in their waiting.

For centuries the church of Jesus Christ has begun its year with Advent – four weeks of waiting and watching. Advent begins with the beginning: angels, shepherds, wise men, animals, Mary, Joseph and the baby. The musical *Godspell* opens with John's exultant song, "Prepare ye the way of the Lord." Likewise, the church each year hopes that the good news of Advent will burst into the world with the same joy, filling us with the wonderment experienced by little children. We anticipate a season when wombs, like Sarah's will stir with hope and life, and when old codgers like Abraham can exclaim, "Well, maybe I'm more alive that I thought!" Advent is the waiting and watching time that captures and claims us.

How much of our lives are spent in waiting? At a time of dying we wait. We wait at the hospital. We wait for elevators. We wait for doctors and dentists, and for the lunch line to move. We wait for traffic and payday and mail and the newspaper. We wait for spring and fall. We wait for changes in the legislature. We wait.

Advent is waiting. Too often we rush into Advent, when we should be reading and reflecting as we watch for the silent night. When Luke told the story, it was mostly one of people waiting – Elizabeth, Mary, Joseph, Anna. Luke's Gospel is full of songs: the Song of Mary, of Simeon and of Zechariah. Singing is a part of waiting at Advent. In fact, the English musicians who sing carols in the street during Christmas are known as "waits."

Do you ever go to worship without expectations, and, by God, something happens? At least some of those who watched and waited that day as Mary and Joseph presented Jesus at the temple must have experienced that serendipity. The people in the temple came for different reasons: buying, praying, hoping, wishing, and dreaming. And that day, by God, something unexpected happened.

That incident is worth remembering as we enter our own temple this Advent season. For us too, by God something can happen.

Watching and waiting help to give us proper perspective. We openly and receptively wait, assured that Jesus will come. Watching and waiting give time to contemplate the meaning of Christ's coming. In Advent you can again consider your perspective on life.

We wait and watch to be pointed in the right direction. We wait and watch for Jesus, who will surely come. He points us toward hope, meaning and purpose in life.

(The Christian Ministry, November, 1984)

Partners in Prayer

1985 Advent Season

Theme: "Sing with Joy"

A devotional booklet for the Christian Church (Disciples of Christ)
and the United Church of Christ

This is the fourth annual edition of this booklet, now widely used for daily devotions during Advent. The hymns of Advent provide Christians with endless resources for devotional meditation. William W. McDermet III has carefully selected phrases from these hymns as starting points for these meditations. The connecting theme is "Sing with Joy." Joy is desperately needed in these times when we need to hear:

> "Their heavenly music floats
> O'er all the weary world."
>
> ~ from "It Came Upon a Midnight Clear"

Herbert H. Lambert, Editor
CPB Press

December 1

Rejoice!

"Then on through life's long path,
Still chanting as ye go,
From youth to age, by night and day,
In gladness and in woe.
Rejoice, rejoice, rejoice, give thanks and sing."
~ from "Rejoice, Ye Pure in Heart"

This is a hymn of thanksgiving leading directly into Advent. When Edward Plumpte wrote this hymn he may well have been reflecting on the words found in the 35th chapter of Isaiah.

What is amazing about Isaiah 35 is that it follows the deep gloom of Isaiah 34, which speaks about rage, doom, slaughter, corpses, blood, rot, and vengeance. It is indeed a dark time, with little prospect of any guiding light. Out of that context, Isaiah 35 tells of confidence and joy, plus the final intervention of a loving God.

Now we picture a wonderful gathering of adults and children in a joyful return over a highway through the desert to a recreated world. The one writing about this traveling experience shows the believers have healed bodies and eyes to see the beauty God has fashioned. The exiles return to their homeland, singing strongly, tears forgotten. The joy of God is their strength.

In our own journey and pilgrimage – both as individuals and as communities of believers — we are the contemporary pilgrims who can learn to sing, "rejoice" in gladness and in woe.

Prayer: Thank you, God, for always being with us as we journey. As we journey into Advent guide our words, thoughts and actions that by what we say, think, and do are directed by your spirit. May our activity become an expression of the joyful faith we experience as we stand beside the manger baby. Amen.

(also The Secret Place – April 15, 1985)

December 2

Christmas More Often

"Child, for us sinners poor and in the manger,
We would embrace thee, with love and awe."
- from "O Come, All Ye Faithful"

Rex and Dorothy Bicks served as missionaries in Jabalpur, India, where they were members of the Rotary Club. The majority of the club members were orthodox Hindus, while others were Sikhs, Jains, and Mohammedans. Rex and Dorothy were the only Christians.

Each December the Bicks held a Christmas open house for the club. In fact, if the date had not been announced by December 1, members asked about the happy event. The Bicks' home was always decorated with lights, a tree, and a number of special edible goodies. At the center of all this was the manger scene.

One Advent, the eighty-five members were openly enjoying themselves. A member and his spouse – both physicians and Hindus – were looking at the crèche and remarking about God's coming to earth in this humble event. Then one of them said, "We ought to have Christmas more often!"

Yes, that's right. If we Christians will provide the proper setting, and if joy and happiness are present, people will recognize the presence of God – even in the form of a baby.

Every one of us is important, God says so. Yet in Advent we need not take ourselves too seriously. We are the presenters – the ones who point the way to Christ. "There, see him! He cries, he nurses from his mother, he sleeps. He is real!" These are our words to the world. We don't demand that everyone become a Christian; we simply want to show everyone that "The Word became flesh."

Christ can be the center of all events. Christ can be the center of our lives. We see this as more than a possibility, as a reality – through our Advent eyes.

Prayer: God, may we present Christ honestly and openly, so that others may find him attractive and worth their attention. Amen.

(also The Secret Place – December 2, 1981)

December 3

We All Have It!

"Now let all the heavens adore thee,
And men and angels sing before thee
With harp and cymbal's clearest tone"
~ from "Wake, Awake, for Night Is Flying"

The Chautauqua Symphony Orchestra was playing a pops concert. For one selection the conductor asked the audience to stand and sing a familiar song. I soon realized the woman immediately behind me was a better than average singer. At intermission I remarked to her, "I enjoyed listening to you sing." We engaged in a ten-minute chat. She had once sung with the New York Metropolitan Opera Company, but she felt she had lost some of her range, to which I replied: "You still have it!"

We all have *it*! I've been told by a music teacher that *everyone* can sing, unless there has been damage to one's throat. Of course some of us sing better than others, but we are all members of God's choir. I believe that. I believe you do too, although too often we are timid about it.

In the 84th Psalm the writer states: "Blessed are those who dwell in thy house, ever singing thy praise!" That choirmaster could recall times when those singers differed; maybe even violently disagreed. There were times when the singers were bored and angry and depressed; just like today, and at the time of Christ's birth. Yet they sang.

"Wake, Awake, for Night Is Flying" was written by Philipp Nicolai in 1598 at the time of a great plague. Despite that fact, it was first published in a series titled Mirror of Joy of Life Eternal. Even when night was flying, Christians could sing.

Regardless of what we once were, we each have a song. God help us if we don't sing it! God will help us if we do sing it! We too would sing this *prayer*:

"All of my heart this night rejoices,
As I hear, far and near, sweetest angel voices;
'Christ is born,' the choirs are singing,
'Till the air, everywhere, now with joy is ringing." Amen.

(also Disciplines August 19, 1986; Journal of Church Music June, 1987; The Secret Place February 19, 1989)

December 4

Seeing with Our Advent Eyes

"See Him in a manger laid,
whom the choirs of angels praise"
~ from "Angels We Have Heard On High"

We see what we are trained to see, or want to see. We may shut out what we do not want to see. When God's very angels praise, shout, and sing with joyous strains, we take notice.

Seeing with our Advent eyes means:

~ seeing the best in persons.

~ celebrating the birth of all children.

~ loving the shepherds and wise men we meet each day.

~ being prepared to receive the Christ child into the inn of our lives.

~ having hope.

~ sharing the hopes, joys, dreams, and sorrows of anyone who might come our way.

~ understanding that we are not controlled by anything but the love and power of God.

~ making trips to the "Bethlehems" of our contemporary world to see the not-so-nice conditions where many live.

~ appreciating the people in our world family who live in smelly stables, yet manage to remain together as families.

~ hearing the sparkling good news that Christ has come into our world, even in the cold nights of our darkness.

Seeing God's wonderful world with our Advent eyes is as important to each generation as it was for the first-century believers. It is a plea for being on the alert, living on tiptoe, with eyes, mind, and spirit turned toward God. Let us see with Advent eyes, lest we neglect the renewal of life in communion with God, lest our opportunities for service come and we do not see them.

Prayer: Wise God, who measures things in the light of eternity, help us to take the long look at our activities and priorities. Guide us. Amen.

December 5

Being a Better Innkeeper

"Christmas gift so holy
Born in stable lowly"
- from "On This Day Everywhere"

We know almost nothing about the innkeeper on duty that night. We do not know his name, or age, or political beliefs, or religious persuasion. We do know two important facts: (1) He *did* find a place for them. He did have feelings, he was really not a bad person. (2) However, he did *not* receive the Innkeeper-of-the-Month award! He could have done much better. He missed a great opportunity.

Why is it that we seem to improve in industry but not in innkeeping? For example, a symphony orchestra program notes: "Hourly signals on electronic watches should be turned off prior to the start of the performance." We make better watches, washers, and weapons, but seemingly we can't improve our reconciliation, reasoning, and relationships.

In the 1980s, good innkeeping is encouraged by Mennonite-Your-Way, a program of hosting travelers in private homes. Open to all, the program's Directory states: "May the Directory increase the joy of belonging to God's Family." That's what we must do in Advent – consider being better innkeepers. We must develop a concern for the well-being of all persons.

Jesus was born in a manger, but he spent his life innkeeping. *I* am a better innkeeper when I recognize and acknowledge the good qualities in others. I can say something like: "I cannot love acceptance, strength, and compassion. I admire them and I strive to possess them, but I do not love them. Yet when I see them in your face, I know I love you."

So it was, long ago, that God, knowing we cannot love ideas, decided, "Let love become a person."

Prayer: O God, when we help others as they journey, our own journey becomes enriched and blessed. In the process, we find meaning for living. Amen.

(also Herald & Review — December 3, 1988)

December 6

What Is Your Name?

"For unto us a child is born,
unto us, a son is given"

"and his name shall be
called, wonderful . . . "
~ from "Messiah"

Your name is perhaps your most important possession. It is the sound to which you will most quickly respond. Your parents gave you your name at the time of your birth. Your name was the result of much discussion, when many names were considered, or they simply selected a boy or girl name. Maybe your name carries on a name within the family; maybe you were named after a good friend, or even after a person from the Bible.

When my name is spoken in love, shivers of joy move through my whole body. When my name is spoken in anger, I feel as if someone has slapped my face.

We feel a very important kind of belonging when we are with people who know our name. When I speak another's name, I hope I do so with respect and love. The way we speak someone's name often tells whether we like that person, or not. What inflections do we use when we call another person's name?

In his marvelous "Messiah" George Fredrick Handel gives many names to the new born Jesus: wonderful, counselor, the mighty God, the everlasting father, the prince of peace. All of these descriptive words are captured in the name: Jesus.

What is your name? When someone speaks your name, what do you believe they will think about – a person tall, or kind, or talkative, or interesting to be with, or grumpy, or happy, or . . . Maybe this is a time when you can seriously consider what others think about when they speak your name? It can be an opportunity for contemplation and growth, as you consider how you want to be remembered in the future.

In this Advent season of birth consider those who you love and who have loved you. Remember them by name. Thank God for them, by name.

Prayer: We are thankful, God, that Jesus was born. I am glad for the births of all the members of my family. May I always speak their names with love. In Jesus' name we pray. Amen.

(expanded from The Home Altar — November 28, 1989)

December 7

Who, Me, a Sinner?

"God and sinners reconciled"
~ from "Hark! The Herald Angels Sing"

If you were asked to make a list of sinners, who would make the list: Judas, Pilate, Hitler, Khadafy, leaders of many foreign countries, leaders in our country, that no-good neighbor? Do you have enough paper? Would you put your own name of the list?

The classic definition of "sin" is "separation from God." Who has not felt that separation? Who has not done some act that has left division? You and I make the list. We have sinned, and God knows it is so. We will no doubt sin again.

Hear and receive the heralding good news of the Advent angels: "God and sinners reconciled." Reconciliation is found on almost every page of the Bible. Possibly the best phrasing of the theme is found in Paul's second letter to the Corinthians: "In Christ God was reconciling the world to himself, not counting their trespasses against them, and entrusting to us the message of reconciliation" (5:19).

Early in a friend's ministry, he went to a county seat town where the previous pastor had retired and stayed. A difficult pattern soon developed, with the "old" pastor officiating at weddings and funerals. Visiting the sick, the new pastor frequently found that the former pastor had beaten him there. The differences between the two were marked. Finally my friend moved to another state. Eight years later he received a letter from his former competitor, lovingly and hopefully asking forgiveness. Deeply moved by this honest compassion, my friend responded in kind.

The message to all of us is: Go and do likewise.

Prayer: In your light, O God, we are ashamed of sins that cause separation. They have harmed others and have darkened our own lives. We seek your presence, O God, not only for our joy, but to illuminate our ways, so that we are brought out of any darkness into your marvelous reconciling light. Amen.

December 8

Meaning from Christ's Crib

"I love Thee, Lord Jesus, look down from the sky,
And stay by my cradle till morning is nigh."
~ from "Away In A Manger"

Advent means birth
that life is important
that life continues
relationships are valid
Advent means laughing and loving through death
enjoying
being able to cry when you need to cry
being able to rejoice, even in dark moments
having good memories
having starlight hope
being able to love in many ways
Advent means making a gift for a friend
learning your child got a B+
being the child that got the B+
listening to your favorite carol
greeting someone you have never met
realizing that God is close
Advent means God is working
God is present when you are unhappy
God is present when you are happy
God loves all children, old and young
God is present when you hurt
God is present when you love
God is present when you die
God is

Advent means we should greet each day with the same excitement and enthusiasm we have at the news of a newborn life. Advent is knowing that the supreme happiness of life is the conviction that we are loved. Advent means that we are loved forever.

Prayer: Christ of the holy crib, a snowflake falls, the wind blows cold; but the love from your crib warms the world. Thank you for your parables, your ministry of healing, and your faithfulness to God. Thank you for your touch that warms my life. Thank you for giving meaning to my life. Stay by my cradle. Amen.

December 9

He Came, He Suffered, He Died

"I wonder as I wander out under the sky,
How Jesus the Savior did come for to die"
~ from "I Wonder As I Wander"

This Appalachian carol is one of the most beautiful and haunting of all American folk melodies. The beginning of the song is about Christmas. The celebration of the birth of Christ is a cause for much rejoicing. Yet unlike most songs we sing at Advent, this one carries us beyond the babe in Bethlehem's manger to the man who died at Golgotha.

He came, he suffered, he died. "Why?" While ours is a world of much joy and happiness, it is also a world of suffering. Suffering is a part of our lives. Nowhere is it promised that it will be different. Jesus was born just as we were, and he lived life, as all of us must, in the constant risk of suffering.

Jesus died on the cross, killed by the Roman Empire. Christians affirm that God was in Christ. So God was suffering also. Jesus was not just some lonely saint, some advanced pioneer, some reckless prophet who was simply dying at Golgotha; God was there. God was in Christ. God was in Christ from the beginning. As Jesus opened his life to the will of God in meditation and in prayer, God was revealed to others. We, too, can open our lives to God.

Thus comes the answer to our query about the exact nature of the heart of life and the universe. God is love, and love suffers. Christ is the one who understands and knows our every situation. What an answer to the question posed by the carol. While God does not promise life without suffering, God suffers with us and sustains us in love so that we can live without fear.

Prayer: God, in a world of fear and dread, you have blessed us with the wonderful event of the birth of your Son. No matter what happens to us, you can reveal the good in it. Help us to establish in our lives the fact of Christmas. Amen.

December 10

He Comes, We Act

"He comes! O Church, lift up thine eyes!"
~ from "Wake, Awake, for Night Is Flying"

In the cartoon *Peanuts,* Snoopy the dog brings his empty food dish to Linus and Charlie Brown. They pat him on his head, and leave. Then, remembering it *is* Christmas, they go back to Snoopy and say, "Merry Christmas, Snoopy, peace on earth." They leave the empty dish again.

Are we so busy doing *our* thing this Advent that we miss opportunities to act on the meaning of Christmas? A young woman came into the church office rather shyly. "Could I have some food?" she almost whispered. As we walked down the hall toward our food pantry she said, "I'm embarrassed." By her inflection, tone and manner, I could easily see her humiliation.

What is your church doing this Advent to meet the needs of our impoverished sisters and brothers in our world community? It's important to have a personal relationship to God, but that relationship must lead us as a church to build our relationships with others. If necessary, you must be the person – a fool for Christ – who says, "Because he comes, we must act."

Since churches tend to be cautious and conservative, they need the leaven of outreach ministry. A congregation is not a club where the minister is paid to serve just the members; it is the body of Christ, a community called to serve its neighborhood and world.

"He comes! O Church, lift up thine eyes!" When did we see him hungry or thirsty or a stranger or naked or sick? "As you did it to one of the least of these . . . you did it to me." (Matt. 25:40) Anything that adds to the enjoyment, growth, or appreciation of another person, and anything that eliminates the agony, despair, or suffering of another person, is ministry.

Prayer: O God, open our eyes to see the human needs around us. Then open our hearts to meet those needs. May we help in providing both food for the body, and food for the human spirit. Amen.

December 11

Beneath Life's Crushing Load

"And ye, beneath life's crushing load"
~ from "It Came Upon the Midnight Clear"

We do have crushing loads! They come in the form of heart disease, cancer, divorce, failing sight, missed job opportunities, broken relationships, and the knowledge that persons within our world family suffer from lack of human rights.

Edmund Sears, a pastor in Massachusetts, wrote this hymn in 1850. As a pastor he may have seen too many crushing loads. Indeed, in that same stanza he pictures those "Who toil along the climbing way, with painful steps and slow."

In 1985, painful and slow steps are seen on the oncology and rehabilitation wards in our hospitals. Slow steps are the common movement in nursing homes. Loads can crush.

What we feel in Advent is the fact that God comes to us in the form of that load-bearer, Jesus Christ. When our Christ-Child-King becomes an adult, he will say to us, "In the world you have tribulations; but be of good cheer, I have overcome the world" (John 16:33).

The overcoming appears in the concrete form of Jesus' loving relationships with so many people: Luke's account of the woman with the unceasing flow of blood; Mark's man with an unclean spirit; Matthew's paralyzed man. The list goes on and on, but so does Christ's caring. That caring carries over to our day. Within our journeys he helps carry, and his load-bearers are all those who help other persons.

Advent means hope. There is hope in the final words of Sears' fourth stanza: "O rest beside the weary road, and hear the angels sing!" To whom do they sing? They sing to you and to those for whom you are concerned: "born this day . . . a Savior, who is Christ the Lord" (Luke 2:11). Yes!

Prayer: O Great Carrier of Loads, I give you thanks for guiding and sustaining me on any weary road I may travel. Be with all who journey. Amen.

(also The Secret Place – December 12, 1983)

December 13

We Shall Not Be Afraid

"Disperse the gloomy clouds of night,
and death's dark shadows put to flight."
~ from "O Come, O Come, Emmanuel"

Christ is coming and what shall we do? We shall not be afraid. At the coming of Jesus, we read, "Jerusalem was troubled." Sure it was troubled! Anyone is troubled when change is called for. "And in that region there were shepherds out in the field . . . and the glory of the Lord shone around them, and they were filled with fear." (Luke 2:8-9) That's a rather strange account – the shepherds being filled with fear. But many people prefer the darkness to the light. Many persons, both then and now, were/are afraid. Job longed for death. Jeremiah cursed the day of his birth.

Often we are afraid of the glory and the light. It's true when we discover some new knowledge.

The same is true of freedom. There is glory in the statement: "We hold these truths to be self-evident, that all men are created equal." Yet we are afraid of that statement. We are afraid of "other" people. We are afraid to the extent that we sell our house and move to the next school district. We may meet new neighbors, not with glory, but with fear. We buy guns for protection from fear and install the most expensive burglar alarms.

Thank God, the story of the shepherds does not end in a paradox, and neither must our thoughts. For the shepherds *and for us,* the story continues: "And the angel said to them, be *not* afraid; for behold, I bring you good news of a great joy" (Luke 2:10).

That is the joyful Advent good news: news that disperses gloomy clouds and dark shadows – then, and now.

Prayer: Especially when the night clouds are gloomy we need you, O God. And there you are, coming to us like the trumpet blast of joy that puts to flight all dark shadows. Thank you. Amen.

December 12

Becoming a Wise Man

"And by the light of that same star
Three wise men came from country far;
To seek for a king was their intent,
And to follow the star wherever it went.:
~ from "The First Nowell"

Who were those first wise men? Babylonian astrologers, magicians, interpreters of dreams, sages? Whoever they were, they came with mystery, wonder, and reverence. They worshiped Christ, and we never hear from them again. They are like us – spending a brief time on the stage of life. Yet the amount of time is not the important factor, but how one spends that time.

We are the contemporary wise ones. We crave to participate in the birth event. We come with wonder and excitement. We will not be blocked by natural barriers of time or by the political systems of any Herod. We have a deep feeling that all who venture will find the road that leads to life.

Some of us become wise in a few years, but most of us stumble and hack away at this growing business of faith, belief, and action. Then one day we internalize the light that shines from the humble manger, and it is strong enough to light our way to the end of our days. Christmas comes to tell us we can go back to the manger and understand that God does care.

Those wise men saw the beckoning star while they were busy at their work. Then these "foreigners" journeyed with noble abandon. They came not to talk but to worship. Our Advent journey helps us in answering the supreme question: "Why were we born?" We shout with those first wise men: "To glorify God and enjoy God forever."

Prayer: We hear you, O God, summoning us to become more and more your own. We know you must be in our work, our play, our love. We know you must see and speak through us, so that you may touch and transform lives, including ours. May we be wise in all that we do. Amen.

December 14

On Being Alive

"Now ye need not fear the grave;
Jesus Christ was born to save!"
– from "Good Christian Men, Rejoice"

I was amused to read the following notice from my college alumni magazine.

> Correction – It was incorrectly reported in the June issue of the NWU Journal that Ruby June Johnson was deceased. The erroneous report was based on information received from the U.S. Postal Service. Ruby is alive and lives in Broken Bow, Nebraska. The editor apologizes.

I wonder what Ruby felt when she learned she had been listed as dead?

( ) found it amusing
( ) indeed, at times wished she were dead
( ) thought of persons who were alive but acted as if they were dead
( ) thought of persons who were dead but left a legacy of love
( ) considered it a wonderful opportunity really to live until her actual death
( ) used the opportunity to reflect upon her relationships with others
( ) contemplated the parable of the prodigal son (Luke 15:11-32), which twice states that the young man "was dead, and is alive."

To be alive to one another is the greatest experience of life. The early church was alive with the spirit of Christ. Some called the Christians: fanatics. Fanatically we, too, must believe that heaven and earth may pass away, but God's word will never die. This belief was born at Advent.

"Alive *Now*" ought to be Ruby's motto, and ours.

Prayer: O God, be with us as we push aside our fear of the grave, and live fully. Christmas joy is knowing that God never dies – and that we are God's. Amen.

(also Christian Church Worship Bulletin Service – March 13, 1983)

December 15

Dear Christ, Enter in

"No ear may hear his coming,
But in this world of sin,
Where meek souls will receive him, still
The dear Christ enters in."
~ from "O Little Town of Bethlehem"

By the catalog counter of a large department store, mother and son were waiting impatiently for their number to be called. The boy asked, "Why are there so many people here Mom? Is it a birthday party?" His irritated mother replied, "It's nobody's birthday Robbie, it's Christmas."

That incident kept alive the tradition expressed years ago in Saturday Review:

> A night watchman in one of New York's largest department stores discovered the body of an unidentified man in the bargain basement last night.
>
> The man appeared to have been in his middle thirties, was very thin, and shabbily dressed. Officials believe the man was trampled in the Christmas rush and crawled under the counter for shelter, where he died.
>
> Officials however, were unable to explain what appeared to nail marks in his hands and feet. Authorities are still investigating.

Where are the meek souls who will receive him? Will you? Will I? We need to cultivate the right attitude so Christ can enter in. Let's be bold "meek souls" and invite God's son into our hearts.

So what if we live in a world of sin? We are called, by Paul, to live "by the meekness and gentleness of Christ" (2 Cor. 10:1). In our meekness we understand that God cared enough to send his very best. Thus, our life is a quest for adequate response to the wonder and the grace of the Incarnation.

Prayer: O come, O come, Emmanuel, bid envy, strife and quarrels cease; fill the whole world with heaven's peace. Amen.

December 16

Joy and Joy and . . .

"Repeat the sounding joy."
~ from "Joy to the World! The Lord is Come"

Surprise. Miracle. Wonder. Laughter. Fantastic. The Creator is in the crib. The Lord is in my heart.

That sounds pleasant, but what about the hurt in people in our own community? What about the world's hungry people? What is happening in South Africa and Central America? And you call us to laugh and enjoy life? How is this possible?

Yes, even in the face of death. The president of my college died during my senior year. I recall that packed college church and the sorrow expressed for a good man who died in his early 50s. One of the presiding clergy told of a funny event that happened to the president, and we smiled and chuckled. I looked at his family, and even in the face of death they could smile.

Matthew says, "When they saw the star, they rejoiced exceedingly with great joy." How could they rejoice? He was born in a barn with smelly animals. A cold wind was blowing the dust. There was no doctor, no crib, no toy. There was no light, except the glow of a star that persisted to shine through an opening in the torn roof. It was discouraging. But how quickly Christ transformed that scene with new life! His presence made the difference and there was joy.

The church through the centuries has been a place for feasts and festivity. A festival is a special time in which we affirm all of life by saying a *joyous yes* to life. All too often, we of the church are viewed as colorless, overly formal, and bland. We of the church need to say to ourselves and others: "The world is there to be accepted and enjoyed. The world is to be encountered and recreated." Discipleship is costly, but discipleship is also joyful.

Prayer: Here we come, O God, filled with laughter and joy. Accept and multiply our joy as only you can, for we sing with joy about the wonders of your love. Amen.

December 17

Christmas Means No More Death

"Born that man no more may die."
- from "Hark! The Herald Angels Sing"

I was asked what I considered the greatest fear that a person might have. I replied that I thought our fear of death topped all other fears. This seemed to be a favorite question of this person, and I seemed to be one of the few who answered his question with the word "death." He thought others would like to say "death" but avoided the word.

"Born that man no more may die" is indeed the good news of the Christ Event. Jesus did not live out his life in fear of death but in fear that human beings would not come to know and love God.

"Born that man no more may die" are words which can give direction to our life. Charles Wesley used "man" but you may substitute a word of your choice —people, women, human beings, all. Whatever you select, during the days ahead many will be more concerned about beer, bowling, and boastfulness than about inner beauty, Bethlehem, and the birth of the Babe.

Yet regardless of what others do, we who are strong in the Christian faith can and do enjoy the Christmas season far beyond what words can describe. We will see beauty even in a crude, dirty stable. We will know that greatness can come from a small, obscure village. And we know the birth of the Babe is the greatest event ever.

This season we will cheat ourselves if we take only the husks of Christmas (colored lights, decorated trees, parties, gifts) and crowd out the Christ child. If we ignore the Christ of Christmas, we become like children eating the banana peelings and throwing away the banana.

May we realize that Christ is not an accident of history, but a purposeful act of God. May we also reflect that the person who is not busy being born is busy dying.

Prayer: "Thanks be to God, who gives us the victory through our Lord Jesus Christ." Amen.

(also The Secret Place — December 24, 1986)

December 18

The Best Gift: One's Heart

"What can I give him, Poor as I am?
If I were a shepherd, I would bring a lamb;
If I were a wise man, I would do my part;
Yet what I can, I give him – Give my heart."
~ from "In the Bleak Midwinter"

A furrier in our city makes his Advent pitch over FM radio. "When she puts in on [new fur coat] and she giggles, and even tears come to her eyes, it is then that I'm happy just to be a part of it." I become so irritated with this type of prostitution of giving that I want to shout: "Friends, remember when those wise men came to worship, they did *not* participate in a gift exchange!"

Why did those wise men bring gifts? Did they believe more in the child than in Herod? Did they wonder what Mary and Joseph would do with them? I'm led to believe that the very act of giving was more important than the gift.

Hymn writer Christina Rossetti, who wrote *In the Bleak Midwinter*, wrote from a strong faith. In 1871 she suffered an illness which left her an invalid for the remainder of her life. Out of her own bleak midwinter she wrote about the ultimate gift of stewardship.

A church friend is a sensitive person and a gifted musician. Of all the hymns of any season, this is his favorite. Michael says, "It contains a very simple, gentle, yet elegant harmonization. I like the words of this stanza the best and probably the last line is the most important to me. Love is more special than anything else we can give."

Yes it is. That is the center of Advent. No gift has ever been, or ever will be, greater than the gift of one's heart. It is the highest, the best.

Prayer: O Giver of perfect gifts, we give our love in packages wrapped, ribboned, and marked. But the first Christmas gift was a love that needed no covering. It was a love that wrapped itself around our lives forever. Now, in return, I give what I can – my heart. Amen.

December 19

The Christmas Star Brings Joy

"O star of wonder, star on night,
Star with royal beauty bright.
Westward leading, still proceeding,
Guide us to Thy perfect light."

- from "We Three Kings of Orient Are"

"When they saw the star, they rejoiced exceedingly with great joy." (Matt. 2:10.) The trouble with so many of us Christians is that we are afraid to let ourselves be joyous. We are depressed by the evil, the cruelty, the hunger, the injustice in our world.

The Christian faith has never been a stranger to troubled times. Indeed, the Christmas star first shone upon a bloody, calloused, and violent society. If the little group in the stable had looked at the ugliness and injustice that filled their world, they might have cried in despair, "Look what the world has come to!" Instead, they looked at the baby asleep in the manger and cried out, "Look what has come to the world!"

A little boy stood quietly in the snow in his backyard, looking at the stars as they came out in a cold December sky. His mother had never seen him so still. She slipped out the back door to be by his side. "All those stars," he said. "They shine so. But they don't make a sound." The mother saw in his honest little-boy eyes the miracle of an awakening soul. He stood awestruck for a moment. Then he whispered to her: "I thought I heard them singing – sort of."

The stars do sing at Advent for hearts that are hushed to hear. We are not atheists; we just don't recognize the divine in our midst. We are not cruel or hateful; we are just too preoccupied to hear the singing stars. Christ's birth puts a song in our hearts again.

Prayer: O God of stars and life, I don't need a great deal of love, but I do need a steady supply. Thank you for supplying love with the Christ Event. Amen.

December 20

Let's Hush the Sounds of War

"And man, at war with man, hears not
The love song which they bring:
O hush the noise, ye men of strife,
And hear the angels sing!"
- from "It Came Upon The Midnight Clear"

An historian has noted that we human beings have experienced 3,520 years of history. During those years there have been only 286 years of real peace, about 8 percent of all that time.

Still, in 1985 we are bold enough to sing the good news – the way of the Christ-child is still *the* Way. We sing the love song that is God's way. Each one of us has a role, major or minor, in expressing peace at Christmas.

Contemporary hymn writers Richard Avery and Donald Marsh challenge us with their jingle:

"Give a little thought about your Christmas.
Should you really give a plastic gun?
Real enough to play with,
Teach him how to slay with,
Till that awful day when he must
learn to aim and kill some mother's son."

When we think, and talk, and prepare for war, the odds are that we shall reap war. When we write, and pray, and create peace, we shall experience peace.

The way of peace means turning our sensitivity outward rather than inward, realizing that hostility is usually the other person's way of self-defense against anticipated rejection. It means having the courage to dig below the surface of our relationships to make possible the birth of real persons. Christian love means requiring nothing of others and everything of oneself.

As you practice this sensitivity and courage, make the words of William H. Draper your *prayer:*

"Hush, all ye sounds of war, ye nations all be still, A voice of heavenly joy steals over vale and hill, O hear the angels sing, the captive world's release. This day is born in Bethlehem the Prince of Peace." Amen.

December 21

On Becoming a Shepherd

"Ye shepherds, shrink not with affright,
But hear the angels' warning.
This child, now weak in infancy,
Our confidence and joy shall be."
~ from "Break Forth, O Beauteous Heavenly Light"

The job of shepherding can be thankless, boring, and dirty. Sheep are not clean, the nights are long, and the pay is poor. Shepherds are a part of the Christmas story.

A friend was driving his car on a back road in Colorado when he came upon a large flock of sheep. He stopped, turned off the engine, and waited for the sheep to pass. Instead, they encircled his car. He yelled, "Hey you sheep, let me through." Blowing the horn didn't work; the sheep just bleated back. He grew more and more frustrated and shouted, "Listen, I could starve here."

Finally their shepherd came. "Your mistake was in stopping," he said smiling at him. "Sheep are like troubles; show them you mean to go forward and they'll move aside." Driving away, my friend thought about the shepherd-philosopher. He had a point. All the yelling and honking and fretting hadn't impressed the sheep. Only his moving forward showed them he meant business.

Today we can be Christ's shepherds. Do the sheep have enough food and shelter? Is life meaningful for them? We shirk the pasturing role because the sheep are so many. They are rowdy and they don't seem to care. When we start serving as shepherds we find we have less time to worry about our own pains.

Prayer: God, Jesus came to shepherds, humble herdsmen of the hills, despised and neglected. He came to shepherd the scattered and the lost, and they in turn became his first flock – under a stable roof, around a crib throne, bathed in your star shine. Come again today, Lord Jesus, and shepherd us, that we may shepherd others. Amen.

(also Herald & Review – December 17, 1988)

December 22

Life in the Winter

"It came a flow'ret bright,
Amid the cold of winter"
~ from "Lo, How a Rose E'er Blooming"

It was a dreadfully dreary December afternoon, and I had had too much of hospitals. Hospitals are too much: too much white, and "Don't do this," and tubes going in, and tubes going out, and the question: "Is it malignant?" So I left. I went to the parking lot, got in my car and sat. Moisture appeared on the steering wheel. Either the roof was leaking or it came from my eyes.

As I left the hospital parking lot, I turned on the radio and heard the mystical harmony of "Lo, How a Rose E'er Blooming." Sung by angels? When that carol ended, I thanked God for music, for all who make music possible – even taped programs and canned commercials.

Christ came like a rose in winter. We cannot ignore or forget that beyond Christmas lies Good Friday. But this is not the time to let our knowledge of the death of Christ impinge upon our exultation at his birth. A mother who has just given birth should not weep because she knows that one day her child will mature and die. There are times when unfettered joy is the only appropriate response.

The Bible speaks more to winter times than summer times. That's because we get through the warm, bright times of summer; it's winter that chills us. In the winter, after months of waiting, after days of travel and weariness, Jesus is born. The child is all potential, promise, and possibility. And there is so much yet to come! Christ came like a bright flower. May we follow his example and bloom where we are planted.

Prayer: Lay upon us, O God, the responsibility, not only to find our place in life as Christians but to help others discover theirs. May we learn to talk without embarrassment to others about our own spiritual blunderings and discoveries, that together we may bloom and experience the growth which we seek. Amen.

December]23

We Too, Can Sing

"With the angels let us sing,
Alleluia to our King."
~ from "Silent Night, Holy Night"

Let's face it, for most of us, angels are a problem, but there they are, alive and active, in both testaments. Angels ascend, meet, make bread, protect, speak, warn, intervene, come in glory, roll away stones, proclaim, minister, and sing. They always sing.

The writer of Hebrews said that God has made us little less than angels, and crowned us with glory and honor (2:7). Every one of us is special. We can act and sing like angels. Angels come in all shapes, sizes, and ages.

They came last week to Good Shepherd Christian. There, in the Christmas play, a third-grade boy, with a single line to say to Joseph ["There's no room in the inn"] grew concerned, tearful, and anxious. He cried – quite unrehearsed – "Come back Joseph, you can have my room." He ruined the play! Or did he save it? All embarrassments aside, did he depart from, or return to, the old script which used to point to goodwill and earthly peace?

Everyone can sing. Right now, whether by yourself or with others, as an act of worship and faith, sing these words to the familiar Edelweiss tune.

"Now oh God, may we hear
Voices of angels from heaven,
'Peace on earth,' is their cheer
Calling on us to extend it.
'Peace on earth,' sing it loud and clear,
Loud and clear forever.
Peace on earth, earth with peace,
This is our Advent adventure."

Prayer: O God, Advent is the time when we hear the angels sing a song we have almost forgotten. They sing that we can love, we can be human. Let us help everyone to hear the angels' song. Amen.

December 24

On Hopes, Fears, and Years

"The hopes and fears of all the years
Are met in thee tonight."
- from "Silent Night, Holy Night"

Phillips Brooks, one of America's great preachers, visited the Holy Land in 1865 and spent Christmas Eve in Bethlehem, where he received the inspiration for this hymn. Through his years, Brooks experienced hopes and fears. We experience them in 1985.

We don't know what Caesar Augustus was doing that night. Whatever it was, he and everyone about him thought it very important. Suppose an angel had appeared and said, "Come, what you are doing is not important; nothing is important tonight except the fact that a humble woman had a baby in a stable." Augustus and his cronies would have thought a lunatic was playing a joke on them. Some joke!

With our spiritual eyes let us now go to Bethlehem, not simply to hear these quiet streets tell stories of hope and fear, heartbreak and joy; but to kneel in adoration with a host of worshipers before the Child who is the Bread of Life. Let us go to Bethlehem not simply to look, listen, and learn, but to speak, shout, and sing: "This is how God imparts to human hearts the blessings of his heaven."

Ready or not, Christ is coming. Ready or not, Christ comes seeking the hidden, lost, lonely, hopeful, and joyful. Christmas celebrates our being found. Rejoice! Hopes and fears *are met.* On this holy night reflect and pray –

Hello, God, It's Christmas Eve and here I am in your sanctuary. So many confusing events have happened during the year. A death last summer, my daughter flunked a class, our daughter-in-law and son made us grandparents, I didn't get a large enough raise, our neighbors' home burned, and terrorism seems rampant. My best friend Ann is down the pew from me, and she too had her problems and joys. God, bless my daughter, my son's family, my boss, our neighbors, the victims of terrorism, and Ann. Bless all people. Thank you for the gift of your Son. I hope I'll find room for him in the inn of my life. Amen.

(also Herald & Review — December 24, 1988)

December 25

Love Is Ageless

"Love came down at Christmas,
Love all lovely, Love divine;
Love was born at Christmas,
Star and angels gave the sign."
~ from "Love Came Down at Christmas"

Ten-year-old Kimberly came running into my office excitedly and said, I have a boyfriend!" "You do?" I said. "Tell me about him." Kimberly stated, "He's pretty quiet, but he's the cutest boy in our class, and he's been my boyfriend now for a day and a half."

Later that week I visited in the home of a 70-year-old church member. Before I could be seated, she blurted out, "Guess what? I have a gentleman friend! We've been doing things together now for six months, and he is the handsomest man you ever saw!"

The capacity to love is a human function unimpaired by aging. Eyesight dims, hearing fails, bones become brittle, and memory lapses. But our ability to love, and be loved, remains unchanged. It's God's eternal gift to us. Love comes from God. It is vividly seen in the Advent manger. No love or friendship can ever cross our path without affecting us in some way forever.

A few years ago, a song asked the question: "Do I love you because you're beautiful; or are you beautiful because I love you?" If the answer to the latter is yes, then maybe Christians should carry that to include anyone, at any place, at any time, with no exceptions. How it improves people when we begin to love them!

There is a snowball effect to love, expressed by e. e. cummings, "Love loves to love love." Love came down at Christmas. Love can go out all through the year. Love can be understood even at the cemetery. Once star and angels gave the sign. Now you and I give it each time we love others.

We sing our prayer using the words of Martin Luther:

"Be near me, Lord Jesus, I ask Thee to stay
Close by me forever, and love me, I pray." Amen.

A Pastoral Prayer During Advent

He will feed His flock like a shepherd; He will gather the lambs in his arms.

God, even in this Advent season, we must confess we are here for a variety of reasons. Some of us are here only because others said we had to come; some come because we think we ought to; some because we need to; some because we want to.

Our names are legion: we are Tom and Dick and Harry, also Doris, Dorothy and Donna. We are a mixed bag of lovely colors: brown, black and white. Some of us need to lose weight, some of us hurt. Some of us need to have our ego's deflated. Some of us need to be stroked back to life.

We are people with different interests: some read Good Housekeeping and Newsweek; some Readers Digest and Modern Romance; some have lost the art of reading and watch the TV culture casket. Some laugh, some cry, some don't understand. Yet we all enjoy and love and bleed and hurt – and that is probably why most of us are here.

Please tell us again that we are accepted. Let us hear about the Word becoming flesh, the baby Jesus. Sing to us about the star, the sheep, and the shepherds. Accept our desire to bring our gold, frankincense and myrrh even if it is only $25.

God, if the hairs on our head are numbered then you know us, each one, and we are important, more important than any Herod or Caesar. We are important because you love us. That matters, more than anything.

And God, help us not to be passive toward *The Event,* but in our unique ways, might we – Go, tell in on the mountains and in the valleys – that Jesus Christ is born. Amen.

(Prayers For Public Worship – Ziegler, 1986 and Master Sermon Series – December, 1983)

A Prayer for the Christmas Gift

In this season of giving may we comprehend what we have already received – *The* gift of all time – your son. O God, we pray that our minds and spirits might be open so that we can understand that within this gift the very meaning of life is explained. The weather may indeed be bleak, but your love for us is not. Stables that stink become places that are holy. Shepherds, who might seem simple, become the proclaimers of the event.

The roads are many and varied, that we, travelers of the Way have taken. Here sits a woman that has seen more than seventy Advents. Her husband is gone, her children live in other cities, yet she treasurers the past Christmas-times, and those memories warm her. Receive her prayer.

Here sits a man discouraged, because at age 49 he feels he will not achieve all he dreamed for some 20 years ago. Yet he has much to give. Receive his prayer.

Here sits a young woman of 17. She does not really know what she will do after high school. She wants to be somebody in your world. She worries about many things, needlessly. She wants to love and help and care, but at times she is so awkward. Receive her prayer.

Yes here we all sit waiting. Waiting for news, good or bad. Waiting for fame and fortune. Waiting for boredom to pass. Waiting for you God. And here you come right into our lives where we least expected it – in our backyard sheds, not our living rooms. And we see you surrounded by "foreigners" – the wise men; and the uneducated and poorly dressed – the shepherds. And there you are, so close, so real, so alive, so warm, so priceless. I must do something for your son. I want to do my part – yet what can I give him – why yes, I can give him my heart.
Amen.

(Prayers For Public Worship – Ziegler, 1986)

A Pastoral Prayer for Christmas Eve

God, it is a cloudy night, and we cannot see the star in the East except by faith. We smell Musk instead of the stable, and we feel radiator heat instead of a cool breeze. We have a difficult time pronouncing frankincense and myrrh; and we don't know anyone named Herod or Caesar. Still we profess to be believers, even with ups-and-downs in our witnessing.

We are thankful for these intimate moments with you. 'Tis more than the season to be jolly, 'Tis the season to be eternally grateful that we can know you in the flesh and blood of the Bethlehem baby.

Your son Jesus came to shepherds and wise men. May the migrant farmworkers and secretaries of state, know of his coming in our time. He came for all persons, even Jim – who sleeps at the Salvation Army's Harbor Mission – and a million thousand more. Some may not realize that Jesus came for them, and if any of us prevented that recognition, we ask your forgiveness.

He came for Staley and Beth and Itoka and Fredo, for those known and unknown; for the rich and the poor and for all of us in-between. Your son came for this evening, with its joys and frustrations. He can be with us at mealtime, or work time, or play time, or think time, or rest time, even death time. There is not a time or place he cannot come.

As we go home, single or in groups, help us to realize that you are as near to us as the steering wheel, the Christmas cookies or our pillow. We ask this in the name of a crying, cuddly, content Christmas baby. Amen.

(The Disciple – December 21, 1975 and Master Sermon Series – December, 1981)

A Prayer on the Sunday after Christmas

We offer a prayer to you, O God, because you created us, you love us and you hear us. On this Sunday after Christmas we offer a prayer for those who did not have a very merry Christmas:

- for the refugees of our world
- for those confined to nursing homes
- for the unemployed
- for those incarcerated because they verbalized their economic, political or religions beliefs
- for those embittered because they experienced a broken relationship
- for those who have yet to learn that it is more blessed to give than receive
- for those with empty stomachs
- for those who spend the day alone
- for those who have lost hope
- for those who live in pain

We pray that with your nudging, and our activity, these persons will experience a better life in this coming year.

As we look to a new year we offer a prayer for those persons and organizations who are dedicated to helping:

- those who work for Amnesty International
- those who listen at AA meetings
- those who minister at the Wheeler Mission
- those who provide ministry through the National and World Council of Churches
- those who offer compassion through Church World Service
- for all Shalom congregations
- the staff at Sojourners Shelter
- those who witness for peace and justice
- those who seek to abolish the death penalty

We pray for this congregation, O God. We pray for the times we experienced and will experience purpose in truly being the church. Yet, lest we become too comfortable, show us again the newspaper. Allow us not only to see, but somehow to *feel* the pain seen on the television news. Then call us again, and again, and again to discipleship – for that is exactly who we are – disciples of Christ – who participate in the cost and joy of following Jesus of Nazareth. Amen.

(Prayers For Public Worship – Ziegler, 1986)

Angels I Have Known

Have I deserved those many encounters – the spiritual and mystical moments when, by chance or by God, angels have enriched my life with acceptance, caring, and sharing? Only God knows if I deserved (or needed) those things when I was given the spiritual food of insight and vitality. Here is but a partial list of honest-to-God angels – messengers who have heralded the good news of God's grace and love.

W. S. Lowe, my grandfather, a pastor who lived with us after he was 85. By chance – or by God's grace – I saw him through the opening in his bedroom door. On his knees, he was asking God to "forgive my sins." Sins? What sins? He did say "O shaw" on some occasions. Did I, then a young teenager, infringe on his private prayer life? Or did God allow me to be an active participant in this spiritual journey – grandfathers and mine?

Mae Yoho Ward, missionary and church executive. She was an Elder where I was serving as pastor. I vividly recall the setting. I was with the Elders in their monthly meeting in the church parlor. In a circle we were considering a serious subject with intense discussion. Finally, I cautiously shared a personal happening relevant to the dialogue. There was an awkward silence. Then Mae responded, "What wonderful honesty. Thank you. Those words are helpful and give us guidance."

Mrs. Rock of Nichols, Iowa. I met her in 1963, when I held a week of preaching at the small congregation where she worshiped. She and her family lived below the poverty level – far below. Still, she was involved in the life of the church. Her stewardship consisted of three things: She always brought 25 cents to worship; she made the coffee for all fellowship events; and she prayed for the members of that congregation daily. Her humble home was filled with love.

E. Rosadel Albert of McPherson, Kansas. After receiving her RN she served as a missionary nurse in Honduras for a decade. Returning to her hometown she was the nurse for a local internist. She is a pillar in the McPherson congregation, at times serving as a bridge between individuals and groups who hold different opinions on many subjects. Rosy simply called me: "Friend," and I her. Her friendship to all is in the form of a perfect kinship.

My wife Sheral, who, when I get depressed, says, "You remember I love you" – and means it. She means it to a depth not really expressed by words. It is something felt – as if I am a plant in the desert about to burn dry, and her words are a life-giving spiritual shower.

Angels are a part of Advents, then and now. We just have to acknowledge their presence and their presents. We need to focus on them through our Christmas eyes.

(DisciplesWorld – December, 2003. The format included the heads of W. S. Lowe, Sheral, and Mae Yoho Ward each within crocheted angels.)

Christmas Comes to Caripito

The year was 1965, and my brother Stewart was faithfully serving in the U.S. Peace Corps in Venezuela. Following a quick orientation - on how to be the opposite of "The Ugly American" - and a crash course in Spanish; he was off to Caracas.

Stewart was assigned to LaPalancia de Caripito, a wretchedly impoverished rural village of about 75 people. This barrio (neighborhood) was the poorest in the area. Here Stewart lived life with the natives, as they attempted to scratch-out a living. Of course there were no comforts, and no indoor plumbing. One of Stewart's projects was to encourage each family to build a latrine, and to use them, thus improving sanitation. He helped in supervising the building of a community volleyball court.

Stewart helped in organizing the village into a community unit so they could responsibly request and receive support from Caracas for much needed services and programs.

In his first weeks at Caripito, Stewart was befriended by Catholic nuns who were serving on the staff of a nearby hospital. They invited him to visit them for a weekly shower (one of his few luxuries) and conversation.

As the weeks became months, and community life continued in a somewhat static routine, Stewart contemplated possible activities. For the Advent season, how about the youth presenting a Christmas program? He knew the Sisters had a copy of a Christmas pageant.

Stewart had acting and stage experience, and later appeared in off-Broadway plays; however, this production may have been his greatest challenge. Many residents did not know the Christmas story. They asked: "Where are the dragons, and the ships?"

Surprisingly the Christmas event had never been heard, or at least it made no lasting or significant impression. The villager's only contact with Christianity was a once-a-year visit from a Priest who came from another community.

Rehearsals began with eagerness. The children became enthusiastically involved. While being very poor, some children used their small amounts of money to buy feathers, which were attached to cardboard, becoming angel wings. One boy was to be a wise man, but he was reluctant, as he had no proper clothing. Discovering this need, Stewart had the wise man use his own shoes and bathrobe. An older man was to be the narrator, but had no shirt, so he used one of Stewart's. A young girl with an excellent voice was selected to sing the solos.

There was no shortage of animals, as many constantly ran through the houses and the village; and they continued to do so the night of the pageant. Music was provided by one youth who had a guitar, from many who would compose their own music, creatively using the pieces of broken glass and metal. Others used discarded brake drums from junk cars as percussion instruments.

Preparation for the pageant almost ended in tragedy. A man was "splicing into" the only power line for the sound system and special lights, and made a wrong connection, resulting in unplanned "Christmas" fireworks and a near fall.

Re-telling me about the whole action-filled experience Stewart reflected: "I became so concerned with the many details that I almost missed the meaning of the event!" The setting was in a real stable, with a real Joseph (Hose), Mary

(Maria), and Jesus (Jesus).

On the night of the pageant over 400 persons attended. "I have no idea where they came from," remarked Stewart. True, it was the only show in town, yet The Show went very much according to The Script. After the pageant the people simply stood around for an hour enjoying talking about the "Feliz navidad" story.

The event left an impact of wonder and awe. For some it was a whole new story. The Sisters joyfully stated: "It was amazing; it was great, just great, it was wonderful!"

Weeks later the people of the region were still talking about "The Christmas Play." Outsiders were surprised that this type of "event" could come from backward Caripito. (Can anything good come out of Caripito?)

Stewart corresponded for a few years with Venezuelan friends. In one letter Sergio Malpica recalled with appreciation: "that marvelous Christmas pageant." The Story was told, seeds for reflection and application were planted. Human birth took on new meaning that night in Caripito. People who needed hope found it; as they can in 2002, as people can forever find hope. It is The Story born every Advent which transcends time and place.

So it was that the Christmas story (without ships and dragons) came to a poor rural Venezuelan village, much as it did to a rural village in Judea twenty centuries before.

"Dios esta aqui." God is here.

(DisciplesWorld — December, 2002)

Christmas Eve Communion

Something very meaningful happened to me on Christmas Eve of 1962. As pastor of the United Christian & Baptist Church of Kalona, Iowa, I had led the early service of worship. I then drove to an Iowa City hospital to share communion with Ora Rogers. Ora was in his 80s, and his medical outlook was not good. He graciously asked the nurse to leave us alone. I poured the juice and broke the bread and prayed. Then Ora shared some deep thoughts about life and death and one's purpose for being. Then he asked if he could offer a prayer. He lovingly expressed his appreciation for my being there and sharing those important moments. As I drove home I asked a question that I would ask myself often: "Who really ministered to whom?"

(Minister's Bulletin — January/February, 1988)

To Mother, at Christmas

She stands by the tree, crying softly,
    Your daughter-in-law.
Advent holds mixed memories.
She fondles the white crocheted angel,
the one you made, years ago.
Lovingly she asks, "Why?"
I cannot muster a response.
"Why did she have that stroke?
She was so full of life.
Now she can't make angels."

She hangs your angel on the tree.
Against the green it seems to shine,
    as does your daughter-in-law
    as do you, mother,
    as did the angels who sang
    centuries ago.

(The Secret Place – Winter 1999-2000)

Escape to Egypt

Matthew 2:13-15, 19-23

Many events in life are not planned. The urgent call had come – "Herod's soldiers are out for blood, take what you can grab, and get going." It was not a planned trip, and the odds were strong there would be no room at Cairo's Holiday Inn, and Joseph remembered the lack of hospitality at the Bethlehem Inn.

It was the first of many roads and journeys Jesus would take. His journey took him to valleys and cities and gardens and upper rooms and hills. The last hill was Golgotha.

There was a purpose in Jesus' comings and goings; and there is a purpose in our journey. You may not travel the Interstates, and of course there will be detours. We are not alone as we travel, for we continually remember that promise from Jesus, "I am the way" (John 14:6)

We follow Christ, wherever the road may lead, and we travel with a hymn in our hearts:

Christ will make all things new,
by God's word we are led;
That inspiration is our cue,
it marks the road we tread.
His love is what we wear,
so put your doubts away;
Clasp hands with others then to share,
His radiance today. Amen.

(Christian Church Worship Service Bulletin – January 1, 1984)

Meditations for the Trip

the SECRET PLACE

POWER

THESE DAYS
Daily Devotions for Living by Faith

THE UPPER ROOM

World Call

THE WORD IN SEASON

DISCIPLINES

FAMILY DEVOTIONS

THE MENNONITE

Catalyst

The Home Altar

The Ottumwa Courier

On Being a Bruised Reed

Isaiah 42:1-7

Thought for today: A bruised reed (God) will not break. Isaiah 42:3

When you are bruised, the blood vessels immediately under your skin are broken. Your bruise hurts and often looks horrible, but with time it usually heals.

All of us have been or will be bruised. Bruises can appear in the form of the death of a loved one or a nagging problem such as growing old, separation, or missed opportunities.

Helen had a bruise. As I brought her home from the hospital we talked about our medical histories. She had been to a number of physicians, some giving her one diagnosis, some another. She had many health problems and this time her doctor had said: "I really won't know what's wrong with you until you die and we can perform an autopsy." She laughed. We both laughed. She was bruised physically but her spirit would not break.

Isaiah foresaw a prolonged and exhausting campaign for his people. Respect for human dignity and liberty of speech and religion seemed to encounter bruise after bruise. Isaiah – and Helen – understood God to be tender toward bruised reeds.

Prayer: Life is full of bumps and bruises. We offer a prayer of appreciation for all caregivers, and God, we thank you for being a part of the healing process. Amen.

(The Secret Place, October 31, 1986)

Saving on the First Chance

James 2:8-18

Thought for today: "Only a life lived for others is a life worthwhile." Albert Einstein

In The Fall by Albert Camus, French lawyer Jean Baptiste Clamence one evening heard the desperate cries of a drowning woman. His reaction was to stop and listen, but he did not get involved, and when the cries ceased, he continued on home.

Years later he verbalized his agony over the experience by talking to himself: *"Please tell me what happened to you one night on the quays of the Seine and how you managed never to risk your life. O young woman, throw yourself into the water again so that I may a second time have the chance of saving both of us."*

Loving one's neighbor includes the combination of works and faith. James 2:18 challenges us by saying: "I by my works will show you my faith." Jean Baptiste hesitated when his chance came to serve, so he pleaded for a second opportunity.

We may only get one chance, so with God's help we must be prepared to get into the swim for people.

Prayer: Be with me, God, when the water is cold and deep. Help me to respond immediately when the opportunity arises. Amen.

(The Secret Place, June 30, 1987)

TGIM

John 9:1-4

Thought for today: . . . busy yourselves in the Lord's work. Be sure that nothing you do for him is ever lost or ever wasted. I Corinthians 15:58 (Phillips)

TGIM! What's that? It stands for "*Thank God; it's Monday!*" Enough of the emphasis on Friday: TGIF. Is Friday more important than Monday? For most persons, the answer is "yes." because their work week is over, and too many feel their work is boring and dull. They believe their labor is wasted. They want to escape into the weekend; so Friday is a day of anticipation. Friday is the prelude to two days of freedom from the job.

What's needed is a fresh attitude toward what we do Monday through Friday or anytime; an attitude and approach that finds a holy appreciation for vocation. Hardly anyone works in isolation; we work for and with people; and thus our attitude toward and enthusiasm (or lack of it) for work can be contagious. A word, a gesture, a suggestion, a smile, a "thank you" – all of these, when given lovingly and sincerely, affirm life, both our own and others.

Why not start the TGIM philosophy toward work in your own life? Thank God for Monday. Thank God you are alive, for the alternative to being alive is not too exciting!

Prayer: God, rainy days and Mondays may get some persons down, but help me to get them up. Amen.

(The Secret Place, January 12, 1981)

A Razor-Sharp Tongue

Psalm 52

Thought for today: May the words of my mouth be acceptable to God.

A friend was sharing his recent experience of traveling to a large but unfamiliar city. While driving in heavy traffic, he tried to make a left turn at a "no left turn" intersection. A driver in the next lane yelled: "Where in the (expletive deleted) do you think you're going?!" The driver was evidently not employed as the public relations representative for the chamber of commerce, but was an example of the "razor-sharp tongue."

Razor-sharp tongues can come in all shapes and colors and ages. Tongues can harm and hurt. One's tongue can build up or tear down. Tongues can help and support and care and love.

Hopefully our tongues are encircled with love – for as Paul says: "If I speak in the tongues of men and of angels, but have not love, I am a noisy gong or a clanging cymbal" (I Corinthians 13:1).

Prayer: God, help take the edge from my tongue; allow it to speak words of love. Amen.

(The Secret Place, August 2, 1981)

Show Hospitality to Strangers

Hebrews 13:1-6

Thought for today: "Practice hospitality ungrudgingly to one another." I Peter 4:9

When our Midwest family was in Boston visiting relatives, we decided to tour the city by ourselves. At the subway station we stood confused, map in hand. Should we take the blue line or the red line? Three strangers offered to help us, and their instructions were perfect.

Later that day, at a busy intersection, one family member started across the street. A stranger caught her by the arm and quickly pulled her out of the path of a car. We were grateful beyond words. On our subway trip back to our relatives' home at the end of the day, a local man initiated a delightful conversation.

Among indifference, selfishness, and the "me generation," we discovered that many people still show hospitality to strangers. In response, we try to be hospitable, showing Christ's love to all we meet.

Prayer: Friendly and loving God, you who call no one stranger, help us to go beyond passing "hellos" to genuine hospitality. Amen.

(The Secret Place, February 14, 1993)

Following Directions

Exodus 13:17-22

Thought for today: Neither the pillar of cloud by day nor the pillar of fire by night left its place in front of the people. Exodus 13:22

It was a hot and dusty day on that Iowa highway. I was forced to stop by the young flagman because of road construction ahead. The next few minutes were long, boring, and wasted. Finally I was permitted to restart my journey. Leading the procession was a pickup truck bearing a large sign that read "Pilot Car, Follow Me." Although irritated by the delay, I was intrigued by the term *pilot* and began to focus on the pilgrimage hymn that goes: "Chart and compass come from Thee – Jesus, Savior, pilot me!"

God is always giving us directions. For the children of Israel, God took the form of a pillar of cloud by day and a pillar of fire by night. In the wilderness the Hebrews did not travel alone. Today Christians find guidance in the words of Jesus: "I am the way."

The road ahead may be under construction, but we can travel through dust, dirt, and darkness, and even on dangerous curves, with the assurance of the guidance of God.

Prayer: Guiding God, I do not know what roads are ahead, but this I do know: I am not alone, for you are always with me. Thank you. Amen.

(The Secret Place, August 11, 1997)

We Too Are Chosen

Luke 9:28-36

Bob and Barbara are a lovely couple. They happen to be white. In their early thirties they decided to adopt a young boy, who happens to be black. They chose him. They named him Michael. Michael's social worker reported that Michael had some very tough times as a young baby. Bob and Barbara hope Michael's most difficult days are past, for they have chosen to love and care for him.

Luke's transfiguration scripture notes the voice came out of a cloud, saying, "This is my Son, my Chosen; listen to him." This is a significant passage as it tells us what the real meaning of Christ's life was. In this event the true meaning of Jesus the Christ was for a moment glimpsed by his disciples. Peter and John and James saw a new and glorious aspect of Jesus. Jesus was chosen. He chose others. Indeed he has chosen us. Hopefully we will choose to follow him; and follow him with a hymn in our hearts.

In Christ we find new hope,
that fills all human space,
His Spirit fresh, it does invoke;
a glimpse of God's own grace.
Away with scorn and fears,
our Brother sheds new light,
That's music to our hearts and ears,
which makes the future bright. Amen.

(Christian Church Worship Bulletin Service, February 27, 1983)

Your Strength Is From God

I Corinthians 10:1-13

Japanese horticulturists have learned the art of raising dwarf trees by cutting off the tap root. Thus those trees grow to only 12-18 inches. Some of us have cut off the tap root of our spiritual growth and we lose our source of strength. And Paul reflects (in Ephesians) we never obtain "the measure of the stature of the fullness of Christ."

In today's Corinthian text Paul states that temptation is very common to all. Nothing has changed! If we are honest we too can testify we have been tempted to gossip, hate, renege, cheat, be lazy, over eat, and ignore the hurts and needs in God's world. Paul notes that some of our fathers (and mothers) allowed their temptations to overtake them; but he calls on the Christians at Corinth (and us?) to believe God's faithful strength will allow us to overcome temptations.

Finding our strength in a faithful God allows us to put into practice faithful discipleship. Dietrich Bonhoeffer, another Christian who found strength in God, assures us: "And if we answer the call to discipleship where will it lead? What decisions will it demand? Only Jesus knows the answer, only he knows the journey's end. But we know it will be a road of boundless mercy. Discipleship means joy."

(Christian Church Worship Bulletin Service, March 6, 1983)

On Winning and Losing

II Samuel 18:24-33

Thought for today: If we learn to accept losing as a necessary part of living and growing, we acquire a keen insight.

In the scripture story of father against son we are told that Absalom lost his life, David lost a son, and the nation was divided and bloodstained with the lives of many.

Losing gives us the opportunity to reexamine our goals and dreams. Perhaps, like Absalom, we have been expending energy in false battles and are endangering our lives. Perhaps, like David, we have tossed aside precious relationships. Losing can be an occasion for reflection.

Our worth is measured by the quality of our relationships with God and each other. From the biblical perspective, any victory at the price of a broken relationship is really a loss.

We are all called to grow. From the biblical standpoint there are no winners, only redeemed sinners.

Prayer: O God, when we understand that we no longer need to prove ourselves as winners, we find our release to care openly, lovingly, and genuinely for others.

(The Secret Place, November 11, 1982)

Hold Fast to the Faith

I Corinthians 15:1-11

Thought for today: Since then we have a great high priest . . . Jesus, the Son of God, let us hold fast our confession. Hebrews 4:14

The local high school had set aside one day for special interest-study groups with leadership coming from the community. A professor of religion from the nearby college and me, a resident pastor, were given the topic "Christianity vs. Atheism." I drew the role of being "for" atheism.

I played my part to the hilt and was an aggressive devil's advocate. "There is no God. Jesus was a fake, and the resurrection is a joke; prove Christianity to me!" Despite the fact that the students knew we were role-playing, a girl stood and shouted at me, through tears, "You're wrong. Stop saying those awful things."

As we grow in faith, we need not be afraid to ask, question, doubt, challenge, and dialogue over issues of belief. In so doing we remain firm that God is God and Christ gives meaning regardless of what any human might say.

Prayer: I believe, O God. Help Thou my unbelief. Amen.

(The Secret Place, November 27, 1982)

Thoughts

(A series of five meditations, each on a page, with a picture. Written for high school youth)

— You Need Someone Else –

It takes two to: Tango
Tangle
Tennis
Talk
Fight
Love

Oh, I might try to do these things myself, but I'd be kidding myself – I can't. I guess I could love my car or clothes or stereo, but that's not real love. It takes two to have a really complete life.

It takes two to make three – to produce life. Noah put two of each kind on the Ark so nothing would be lost. God has said that when two persons are together he is there with them. That's real power – to have God there in any situation.

God, I am beginning to realize that I need someone else. By myself I am incomplete. With another person or with you I am whole. I wish I were holy too. Forgive me for thinking that I could be self-sufficient.

All my relationships with persons now help me to build properly for my future life together with a marriage partner. I hope that I and that someone else may make a complete oneness.

— Love is Being a Part of God –

Most adults I know think of their purpose in life is to make money. They think you fulfill the purpose of life by having a large house in the proper residential neighborhood and at least two cars. You must have a cabin on a lake and a fistful of mutual funds.

Is this what life is all about?

From the beginning of time God has tried to instill in humans the fact that one four-letter word is the purpose of life. That word is love.

Love is a gift.

Love is from God.

Love as a noun is receiving.

Love as a verb is giving.

You can love another in many ways: supporting, listening, understanding, touching, sharing, caring, bearing, and giving. This then is the real purpose of one's life.

If loving is from God, you might ask yourself: "Am I apart from God or a part of God?"

— King Told Us His Dream – What's Yours? –

Youth in the sixties just seem to be more concerned about the real issues of life than were we youth of the fifties. We played basketball, went to the movies, and sang in the church choir. In the early sixties youth marched for civil rights; and now they discuss and demonstrate, and they disagree that military might is right in places like Vietnam. I admire many of the youth of today. They make me wish I were a youth of the sixties.

I strongly believe that youth will do their part to fulfill that good dream of a good man – Martin Luther King. He said his dream was to have little black and white children live, learn, and love together. Why do so many fear and hate this dream? King wanted open schools, housing, churches, and equal opportunities in Mississippi, Maryland and Massachusetts.

The Bible reports that "it shall come to pass" that "your old men shall dream dreams, and your young men shall see visions" (Joel 2:28). Don't you think it's about time somebody put that scripture into practice? For God's sake, how much longer shall we wait for good dreams to become realities?

King's dream was about reconciliation. The Bible places high priority on the subject. In fact, being in the right relationship with others takes precedent over gift-giving. Jesus said, "first be reconciled to your brother, and then come and offer your gift" (Matt. 5:24).

Carl Sandburg wrote that "nothing happens unless first a dream." Do you have any dreams? King died for his. Would your dream be worth dying for?

— Linus: Is More Than Thumb and Blanket –

There he sits, sucking his thumb and holding his blanket. A psychologist would have a field day delving into his makeup. The thumb and blanket are psychological crutches. But with characters like Lucy, Snoopy, Pig Pen, Charlie Brown, and Schroder, with their own neurotic problems, that thumb and blanket seem a necessity for our friend Linus.

Now, I'm not saying he shouldn't grow to the place where he can rid himself of the crutches; but what is important is to overlook these unbecoming attributes and accept Linus for his good characteristics. They are many.

Consider his reading of the Christmas scriptures (Luke 2:1-20) and then saying, "with a story like that, who needs Santa Claus?" Or his warm, childish concern for persons, even those who tease him.

It's difficult to overlook the thumb-sucking and blanket pseudo-security in people and see their good qualities. Youth are like Linus, aren't they? They hold onto the security of the home and yearn for the adult life. I strongly believe that God wants us to overlook the idiosyncrasies of individuals, accept them for what they are and where they are; and notice all their worthwhile qualities.

If we look for the insecure feelings in persons, we will find them; but if we look for the childlike warmth of kindness and love, we fill find that instead.

How do persons react around you? Do you bring out their best or worst?

— Please, Mrs. Robinson –

Wo, wo, wo, Mrs. Robinson. Can you possibly comprehend that "Jesus loves you more than you will know?" After all you have done. You have prostituted the true meaning of love. Think of your son-in-law, your daughter, your husband, yourself.

Yet, Jesus loves you. He has revealed it in his own life. His love "bears all things." "Jesus loves you more that you will know." My pastor says it is good theology.

As your teenage neighbor, I ponder my own future. Is your type of life the kind into which I will graduate? Or can I feel and know that Jesus will love me also, more than I will know, by just living a normal life.

You've tried to hide your affair from the kids. But we have learned from your affair.

Please Mrs. Robinson, Jesus will not stone you, allow Jesus to love you. Heaven does hold a place for those who pray. Hey, hey, hey.

P.S. Read John 8:1-11

(Catalyst, January, 1970)

I Just Became Thirty-Three

I just celebrated my thirty-third birthday. It was much like the ones before. Then I fell into serious meditation about the fact that with each day I am now living longer that Jesus of Nazareth. I am starting to live the days and years not afforded him.

It is food for thought. Jesus never celebrated his thirty-fourth birthday. We worldly people saw to that. The great question now is one of the stewardship of my life. Can I live out days in his stead?

"It what 'some career':
He was a flop at thirty-three!
His whole career was one of failure and of loss;
But the thing that's so distressful
Is he could have been successful,
But instead of climbing 'up', he climbed a cross!" 1

That cross stood between his thirty-third and thirty-fourth year. That cross is a stumbling block for many. But right now I'm not concerned about those many, I'm concerned about me. Can my days ahead be substituted for those he never saw? Why not? Be they days of wine and roses; days of death, defeat and despair; or days of dedication and devotion, they shall be days full of living.

Living for Jesus.

Yet one need not wait until one is "old" to live a Christ-like life. The "living for Jesus" motif may be woven into one's life pattern at any age – 13, 33 or 73.

It's never too late or too early to start witnessing and living.

(1 From For Heaven's Sake! by Helen Kromer, (c) 1961)

(World Call, March 1970. This item appeared in both English and Spanish.)

Hannah, One who Prayed for Years

(Senior Citizens in the Household of God)
I Samuel 1:12-20

"Go in peace, and the God of Israel grant your petition which you have made." I Samuel 1:17

This is a fascinating episode. The priest Eli believed Hannah to be drunk because of her unorthodox manner of praying. (My, how we can be hung-up on tradition and custom!) Then, through dialogue, Eli understood Hannah to be praying in and from her heart. Her prayer was simple and honest.

However, Hannah seemed to feel, erroneously, that by offering a child to God, God would fill her womb. Her reasons for prayer were selfish. Yet it is from such elemental beginnings that the life of devotion develops. Hannah's prayer brought her peace; it did not sharpen her ethical insights. Maybe our prayer life can be better – and indeed it can!

We do need to pray, though, as did Hannah, with persistence. Prayer often must become a tireless asking before God can richly reward it.

When we plead in prayer our patience is perfected, our humility deepened, our purposes clarified. Our prayers must be freed of insincerity and selfishness. God cares for us, listens to our prayers, and rejoices to give us what we really need.

O God, may we like Hannah pray at all times. Teach us also to pray not only for our own families, but for all in our world family. Amen.

(These Days, April 13, 1986)

Enoch, 365 Years Old

(Senior Citizens in the Household of God)
Genesis 5:21-24; Hebrews 11:5-6

Enoch walked with God. Genesis 5:24

Before [Enoch] was taken he was attested as having pleased God. Hebrews 11:5

What would one do for 365 years? There would be so many trips to the in-laws, and lawns to mow, and garbage to take out! You would hear so many problems, and you would face a great many more temptations. Enoch lived a long life, but while he lived he walked with and pleased God. That is the testimony of both Genesis and Hebrews.

The two key words are *walked* and *pleased.* They refer to a very close relationship with God. Walking together has much to say about one's life of prayer. When we walk with a friend it provides us with insights and applications for walking with God.

When we walk with God we have a happy sense of companionship. There is the opportunity to experience unforced, spontaneous conversation as the two of us journey together. Sometimes we keep silent and simply feel God's presence; sometimes we listen to what God will tell us along the road.

None of us expects to live 365 years. Length, however, does not matter, but quality in living does.

O God, here we come: sprinting, stumbling, shuffling, slipping, and sliding. Receive us, and walk with us, until the end of our days. Amen.

(These Days, April 14, 1986)

Huldah, Faithful Prophetess

(Senior Citizens in the Household of God)
II Chronicles 34:22-28

"Your Heart was penitent and you humbled yourself before God when you heard his words." II Chronicles 34:27

It was the sixth century BCE, and religion was at a low ebb. A priest found a scroll in the temple at Jerusalem. Huldah was selected to interpret it.

Only a deeply devout woman would have been sought. Huldah confirmed the scroll's authenticity, but she said evil would eventually come because the people had forsaken God. However, the doom could be postponed.

Huldah thus served as a channel for God's word. Her prophecy gave King Josiah courage to put into action the scroll's laws. The result was the most thorough reformation Judah had ever known.

The role of this prophet was to call the people into a right relationship with God. Huldah is noted not as a great lover or mother, but for her relationship to God. She lived close to God, and that is how we too should live.

Prophets were not so much concerned about the events of the future as they were about the sins of the present, calling the people to repent. Prophets, women and men, are needed today. Can you be one?

God of all prophets, we thank you for your daughter Huldah, who loved you will all her heart and dared to speak your word of truth. Amen.

(These Days, April 16, 1986. Also appeared in
The Secret Place and The Word in Season.)

Joshua, 110 Years Old

(Senior Citizens in the Household of God)
Joshua 23:1-3; 24:14-15

And the people said to Joshua, "The Lord our God we will serve, and his voice we will obey." Joshua 24:24

This is not a "devotional" type of meditation. The subject matter of the book of Joshua forces us to deal with hard issues. Enemies, fighting, war, peace is in our daily news, and they were very much a part of Joshua's Israel.

Although there is much praise of Joshua, the glory for the conquest belonged to God alone, for the conquest was not Israel's but God's. With God's support, Israel drove out the previous owners. Yet this raises a piercing question for the Christian conscience. Can a God of justice, mercy, compassion and peace support a bloody conquest? We cannot, indeed we must not, pass on this important question lightly.

Of course Joshua did not have the benefit of Jesus of Nazareth. That makes all the difference – or how much difference does it make to us who are called Christians? Does God "choose" a side in battle? Does God endorse killing? What does Jesus say about enemies, and killing, and revenge, and hating, and reconciliation?

I told you this wasn't a tranquil meditation! After 110 years of living, Joshua encouraged the people to respond to God, and they responded, "We will serve God." How do *we* serve God today?

O God, may we be bold to do only your will. Amen.

(These Days, April 17, 1986)

Abraham, "An Old Man and Full of Years"

(Senior Citizens in the Household of God)
Genesis 22:1-19

"Now I know that you fear (love) God." Genesis 22:12

This is a difficult story. At age 100 Abraham had fathered Isaac. Then, just as a loving relationship began between the two, God told Abraham to take this only son, "whom you love," and offer him as a burnt offering. The agony and anguish of it!

How could a good God act in this manner? Or is this just a portrayal of how God was seen, experienced, and understood centuries before Christ? I believe I have an insight that will help. Consider: Abraham was not blessed because he had a correct concept of God; he was blessed because when he *thought* he knew God's will he obeyed it to the limit. Ponder that thought.

This friend of God provides us with an example of how to live. Abraham's generosity was seen when he offered his nephew, Lot, first choice of the new land. (Canaan) His courage was shown when he accepted without fear the challenge of a new and strange land. His patience was revealed as he waited without doubt for the fulfillment of God's will.

Abraham's faith in God is the hard-won result of a difficult human struggle over recurring doubt, a victory gained through God's forgiving grace.

Abraham died "full of years." Ah, that is the way to die. God, fill us too. Amen.

(These Days, April 18, 1986)

Sarah, 127 Years Old

(Senior Citizens in the Household of God)
Genesis 21:1-7

The Lord did to Sarah as he had promised. Genesis 21:1

How do you "see" others? How do you view older persons – those, say, over 65? Do you feel sorry for them (perhaps for yourself) because you believe their best years are past? Or can you look at older people and ask, "What are their possibilities, their potentials, regardless of age?"

Abraham found Sarah when she was 65. He also found her attractive. They became husband and wife, and at age 90 Sarah gave birth to Isaac. That's living up to your potential (not disregarding that God had a hand in it.) Sarah greeted this monumental event with joyous laughter. Thank God for laughter, for it carries us through the journey of life.

In her time (19 centuries before Christ) a woman was of little importance until she produced a son for her husband; for it was through his son that a man lived on. (Talk about male chauvinism!)

Sarah's life was one continuous trial of her faith in God's promise that she was to be "a mother of nations" (Genesis 17:16). She overcame trials; she was that mother. Found among the Dead Sea Scrolls is this inscription to Sarah: "Above all women is she, lovely and higher in her beauty than them all."

"God who touches earth with beauty, make us lovely too." Amen.

(These Days, April 19, 1986)

(The next five devotionals are a series based on: "Extraordinary persons from the Old Testament.")

Hosea: Lover Extraordinary

Hosea 1:2-3; 2:14-15; 3:1-5; 14:9

Thought for today: So I am going to take her into the desert again; there I will win her back with words of love. Hosea 2:14 (*Good News Bible*)

The story of Hosea and Gomer plays like a TV soap opera. Hosea married and loved Gomer though she was a wild one. They conceived a son and a daughter, but Gomer's next son was named "No Kin of Mine." Although Hosea was not the father, and despite Gomer's being "talked about" in the community, Hosea would not divorce her. Gomer left the home and became a prostitute-slave. Hosea still did not renounce her, and he wept over her. Finally Gomer was sold again, and Hosea bought her freedom. We do not know if they lived "happily ever after."

Hosea was the first person to see clearly the central place of love in religion. In his own sufferings he entered into the deep fellowship of God's suffering.

Because of his deep relationship with God, Hosea made his tragedy a source of spiritual illumination.

Prayer: God, help us to second-mile-it in our living and loving. May we love as you love us. Amen.

(The Secret Place, October 25, 1980)

Jonah: Traveler Extraordinary

Jonah 1:1-4, 17; 3:1-3, 10

Thought for today: Those in the Nineveh's of our day need our word of love.

God's call for Jonah was to go to Nineveh (enemy of Israel), but he responded by traveling to Tarshish. Yet for Jonah there was, and for us there is, a second call to ministry.

When calls come from God, our main preoccupation is with ourselves, family, job – what do we care about others, let alone enemies? Yet on the ship Jonah saw hated foreigners as persons and was willing to be sacrificed for them.

The emphasis in this parable-story is not on Nineveh or the whale or the ship; rather, it is on the traveler Jonah. He might have mused, "It's not *how* you get there, but what you *do* when there."

We might ask, "Have I bought a ticket to Tarshish, when the call is to Nineveh?" The contemporary application of the Jonah event is: can anyone withstand the call of God?

Prayer: God, the trouble is that you insist on entering our lives just where we least want you. But don't stop; try us a second time. Amen.

(The Secret Place, October 26, 1980)

Habakkuk: Struggler Extraordinary

Habakkuk 2:1-4, 18-20; 3:16-19

Thought for today: God is very willing to support the sufferer, the doubter, in their honest questioning.

The prophet Habakkuk has been depicted as a man who debated and doubted God; yet he is also pictured as a person of faith. He seeks God's help and guidance and finds the adventure a difficult yet rewarding experience. His spiritual struggle was worth the insights gained.

Through the struggle of doubt and questioning, Habakkuk understands that if God were to force persons into a right relationship by punishment, they would serve him through fear, not love.

The prophet declares a vital insight to religious truth: "The righteous shall live by [their] faith" (Habakkuk 2:4). Faith is a living companion for all of God's children, in Habakkuk's time, and ours.

In his relationship with God, Habakkuk found that nothing matters except that relationship.

Prayer: God, be the center of our struggling and growing. May we feel your guiding Spirit in our lives. Amen.

(The Secret Place, October 27, 1980)

Nehemiah: Layman Extraordinary

Nehemiah 2:1-6; 6:15-16; 8:9-12

Thought for today: . . . and the people were full of joy because God had made them very happy. Nehemiah 12:43 (*Good News Bible*)

Nehemiah is a twenty-five-year-old wine steward for the king of Persia when he hears of the sorrowful conditions in Jerusalem. He considers and prays about his response, which results in asking the king to let him go to Jerusalem.

This layman deliberately abandons a position of honor and security, making sacrifices and facing difficulty and death, that he might be helpful to Israel and to God. His organizing and administrative ability leads to community stability and the completion of the work begun by religious leaders.

Nehemiah's life and work provide an example for all because: (1) he heard the need, (2) he found a cause, (3) he was faithful to that cause, (4) he used his abilities, (5) he knew him limitations, and (6) he was deeply dependent on God and made frequent prayers to God.

Prayer: God, please bless the laity of your church as they find joy in giving their talents in ministry. Amen.

(The Secret Place, October 29, 1980)

Elijah: "Mooder" Extraordinary

I Kings 18:36-40; 19:1-4

Thought for today: Elijah was the same kind of person as we are. James 5:17 *(Good News Bible)*

Amazing, the two Scriptures you just read are about the same person. Elijah goes from the mood of saying, "The Lord is God!" to "I might as well be dead!" After his tremendous victory over the prophets of Baal, he feels that he stands alone. Has he been a failure? No one congratulated him; so he broods. All have felt like Elijah. We are on first-name speaking terms with disappointment and insecurity.

Elijah desperately needed the support of individuals and a religious community. So do we. We also need to understand the constant presence of God. If necessary, we need to force ourselves into the caring ministry of individuals and community. As one believer said, "Black despair will scarcely clutch and hold for long if one can talk it out with a friend who understands." Elijah needed to understand that God was not absent. May we so understand.

Prayer: God, if we feel you are not as close as you once were, help us to understand which one has moved. Let's get together. Amen.

(The Secret Place, October 31, 1980)

(This series of seven carried the theme:" Friends of Paul", however they were published as individual devotions.)

Onesimus/Slave Becomes Son

Philemon 1:8-14

Thought for today: The greatest experience you will ever have is that of your individual relationship to God.

Onesimus was the slave of either Philemon or Archippus and not only had he run away from his owner but also had robbed to do so. After becoming acquainted with Paul and converted to the Christian faith, he grew very close to Paul. The new relationship between them was more than a friendship; it was like that of a father and son. Paul wrote to Philemon requesting that Onesimus be freed to work with him.

Onesimus in Greek means "useful," and was a common name for slaves. Paul evidently found him very useful in promoting the gospel. His past did not handicap his new relationships or his service to others.

The important elements in life for Onesimus were his friendship with Paul, his conversion, his relationship to God, and his continuing ministry. These elements are *important* to every life!

Prayer: A friend is someone who knows all about you and still calls you friend. Thank you, God, for being our Friend. Amen.

(The Secret Place, June 15, 1982)

Demas/Wanted This World

I Timothy 4:6-10

Thought for today: For Demas, in love with this present world, has deserted me and gone . . . II Timothy 4:10

Demas had been Paul's friend. Indeed, in Colossians Paul wrote with great feeling: "Luke the beloved physician and Demas greet you." However, later he was compelled to write the words that are our "Thought for today."

We believe Paul regretted having to write such a sad message. In his service to Christ, Demas had gone as far as he would. He refused to pay the price that Paul and his true friends were constantly paying. Demas was in love with present worldly things. He no longer loved the things of the spirit.

Except for persons like Paul, most people draw up limits as to how far they will go for Christ Jesus. What is your limit? What are your loves? Will you take the road that leads to adventurous service and find real life? You can, with Christ!

Prayer: "In the hour of trial, Jesus, plead for me, lest by base denial I depart from thee . . ." Amen.

(The Secret Place, October 9, 1982)

Titus/Comforted by Coming

II Corinthians 7:5-16

Thought for today: But God, who comforts the downcast, comforted us by the coming of Titus . . . II Corinthians 7:6

Untrue rumors are very damaging. They can destroy relationships, cause disunity, and cripple friendships.

Paul had heard the rumor that the Corinthian Christians had defied his instructions and were hostile toward him. So Paul sent Titus to see if the reports were true. After an anxious period of waiting, the two met at Macedonia where Titus said the reports were not true; the Corinthian church was still reconciled to Paul.

Rumors know not time nor place. They occur in our day as well. What is the Christian response to the spreading of rumors? No answer need be stated. We know how we should act. When we participate in meaningful dialogue, even miracles happen. We, too, can comfort by our coming, by our serving, by our friendship.

Prayer: Use my tongue to spread your word of love, O God. May my comings and goings be an act of ministry. Amen.

(The Secret Place, August 11, 1982)

Erastus/Treasurer and Traveler

Romans 16:21-27

Thought for today: To dream of the person you would like to be is to waste the person you are.

Erastus was the city treasurer of Corinth. We are not sure if this was an honorary title or if he was a full-time city official. Such officials were usually slaves or of servile origin, though often wealthy. In Acts 19:22 we note that Paul sent Erastus and Timothy into Macedonia. At other times Erastus was in service to Paul at Corinth. We believe that regardless of his station in society, Erastus used his talents faithfully in his service to Christ as a friend of Paul.

Today many of us feel: "If only I were an important person in government, or an outstanding sports figure, or a media star, then people would notice me and I could be a great witness for Christ." That attitude causes us to waste the person we are. Erastus used what he had for ministry, and so must we.

Prayer: "Take thou ourselves, O Lord, heart, mind, and will. Through our surrendered souls thy plans fulfill." Amen.

(The Secret Place, April 20, 1985)

Epaphroditus/Sick but Spared

Philippians 2:25-30

Thought for today: . . . he risked his life and nearly died for the sake of the work of Christ . . . Philippians 2:30 (*Good News Bible)*

Can you pronounce Epaphroditus? On a test could you spell this man's name correctly? No matter. His actions and exemplary faith are what matter.

His name was common in the first century. What was uncommon was the fact that he was a friend and co-worker of Paul. Epaphroditus served as messenger and bearer of a gift from the church at Philippi to Paul when Paul was in prison. He wanted to stay and help Paul but had become so seriously ill that Paul wrote that Epaphroditus "was sick and almost died." But Paul felt that God spared him.

This incident requires us to consider our attitude toward those in prison and those who are sick. Jesus himself called for such ministry. What can we do individually as Christians, and collectively as the church?

Prayer: O God, receive our prayer of thanks for all who have risked their lives for the work of Christ. May we, too, risk when the need occurs. Amen.

(The Secret Place, July 8, 1985)

Euodia and Syntyche/Sisters in Serving
Philippians 4:1-9

Thought for today: Euodia and Syntyche, please, I beg you, try to agree as sisters in the Lord. Philippians 4:2 *(Today's English Version)*

These two Christian women were members of the church at Philippi, a congregation in which women were prominent from the beginning. Evidently they had disagreed, and Paul realized this would hinder them in their gospel work. Paul encouraged the two to resolve their differences and live in harmony with each other.

Euodia and Syntyche were important friends of Paul, and he states that their "names are in God's book of the living." In this same letter Paul gave rules for living, themes for thought, and a message of victory over anxiety, causing the Philippians to understand there was no time for bickering.

In our day we who bear the name Christian, too, must pull together and become united in spirit and service if we are to serve our God effectively.

Prayer: O God, may I look upon all Christians, regardless of denomination or country, as my sisters and brothers in Christ. Amen.

(The Secret Place, January 29, 1983)

Phoebe/Friendly and Faithful
Romans 16:1-16

Thought for today: . . . for she herself has been a good friend to many people and also to me. Romans 16:2 (*Today's English Version*)

In this personal greetings section of *Romans*, Paul listed twenty-five persons by name, but Phoebe was listed first. She was a trusted friend of Paul's. To be a Christian at Cenchreae was no easy matter; for seaports during this period were extremely evil places. She was the only woman listed at that place. She was a woman with great and good influence.

Paul seems to have indicated that Phoebe devoted herself unselfishly to the ministry of the church. Indeed her industry and trustworthiness, her goodness and sympathy, her loyalty and kindness marked her as a woman whose ministry inspired all.

Just who are the Phoebes of our day? Who are the friends of Paul for Christ's sake? They are all of the sisters and brothers who live the Christ like life by their acts of friendship for others.

Prayer: O God, help me to be a good friend to many people. Amen.

(The Secret Place, February 24, 1983)

Zacchaeus, Tall in Belief

(Friends of Jesus)
Luke 19:1-10

Jesus said to him, "Today salvation has come to this house." Luke 19:9

It's no "piece of cake" being adult and short. You buy clothes in the junior department. You hope to get the front seat for events. You need a stepstool.

Yet Zacchaeus' size was not his major problem. He was a hated tax collector. Jesus was coming to town, and Zacchaeus wanted to see him. Thus, Zacchaeus sat waiting in a sycamore tree.

Imagine a conversation between a group of the Jericho women as they consider where Jesus might eat. "We want it to be a nice event. Shall we take him to the Jordan Inn or Sarah's Tea Room? Would he mind a pot-luck meal, but let's use the nice china!" Then someone sarcastically says, "If we really want a nice place we might ask Zacchaeus." The chances of Jesus and Zacchaeus breaking bread were practically zero . . . but Christ's call was: "Zacchaeus . . . come down."

This is a story of God's search for us. It demonstrates the relationship between Jesus and one who would become his friend. The powerful acceptance of Jesus was met by the honesty of Zacchaeus. We can identify with Zacchaeus – for this is our story, with God's grace as the ending.

God of the tall, the small, and the in-between, may we be alert to your constant seeking and saving. Amen.

(These Days, September 12, 1982)

The Bleeding Woman

(Friends of Jesus)
Luke 8:42-48

And he said to her, "Daughter, your faith has made you well; go in peace."
Luke 8:48

The New Testament records forty-one occasions of healing by Jesus. He performed them by touching, by working, through a friend's prayer and a friend's faith, through compassion and preaching.

This occasion reveals God as good and caring, seen in Jesus' sensitivity to human suffering. Within the crowd he feels the touch-of-need on the fringe of his robe. Jesus says persistent faith caused her to become well. He then supports his new friend with: "Go in peace."

Part of Jesus' central purpose was to bring the power and healing of God's creative, loving spirit to bear upon the moral, mental, and physical illnesses of those around him. The methods Jesus used accomplished two effects: (1) They awakened the spirit that lay deep within each one, waiting to be touched .(2) They brought contact with God, who recreates minds and bodies, and makes them whole.

We continue Christ's healing ministry today as we (a) use every medical and psychological resource available; (b) allow family and friends to share in the healing process; and (c) develop our own inner strength, as we feel Christ's touch.

"What a Friend we have in Jesus,
All our sins and griefs to bear!
What a privilege to carry
Everything to God in prayer!" Amen.

(These Days, September 14, 1982)

The Man with an Unclean Spirit

(Friends of Jesus)
Mark 5:1-20

"Go home to your friends, and tell them how much the Lord has done for you, and how he has had mercy on you." Mark 5:19

Mark does not describe a nice, clinical setting. Jesus was met by a shouting, emotionally disturbed man, whose home was a cemetery. Yet Jesus provided an example of how to deal with a distraught person.

Jesus greeted the man as a friend. He asked for his name. He accepted the man as he was, then took the necessary action. The primary feature of the story is the calm confidence and courage of Jesus. Understanding, treating the distressed man as a person, reaching into the heart of the problem, and bringing with him God's power to expel the unclean spirit within, Jesus brought healing. So does Jesus deal with all his friends.

However, Jesus would not let the man (now restored to emotional health) go with him. "Go home to your friends." That refusal has much to say to us as we help in channeling religious emotion into duty and service. Often we are blocked by a desire to stay with the original religious experience. Must we simply go back to familiar surroundings? Yes, "Go home to your friends." Tell them about the accepting love of Jesus.

"Friends, friends, friends, I have some friends I love. I love my friends and they love me; I help my friends and they help me. Friends, friends, friends, I have some friends I know." Amen.

(These Days, September 16, 1982)

Joseph of Arimathea, "Undertaker"

(Friends of Jesus)
Luke 23:44-53

"I have called you friends, for all that I have heard from my Father I have made known to you." John 15:15

Today we are followers of Jesus mainly because of the resurrection. No resurrection generally means no turned-on followers of Jesus, little witnessing, and not much "clout" in Christianity. Seen in this context, the attention given to the body of Jesus immediately following his death, by Joseph of Arimathea, is astounding.

Where were the disciples? The sons of thunder: James and John made not even a whimper. Peter, the rock, had turned to sand. The others had denied, betrayed, and fled the scene. But not Joseph. He boldly asked for the body of Jesus. That was risky. Then Joseph himself played the role of undertaker.

One of the most loving, caring acts of ministry of all times was that of Joseph taking the sweaty, dirty, beaten, bruised, and bloody, dead body of Jesus down from the cross. There was nothing romantic about it. Then Joseph relinquished his own tomb as a "last resting place" for Jesus.

I don't need to tell you the ending. We now understand that God is the giver of life on both sides of death. Yet Joseph found something unique in Jesus *before* the resurrection. He found a friend. This example stimulates us to risk and serve and to be an example of kindness, wherever we may journey.

". . . Jesus, I have promised to serve Thee to the end; O give me grace to follow, my Master and my Friend!"

(These Days, September 13, 1982)

The Mute Man Speaks

(Friends of Jesus)
Matthew 12:22-28

Then a blind and [mute] demoniac was brought to him, and he healed him, so that the [mute] man spoke and saw. Matthew 12:22

How would you feel if Jesus healed you? Let's say the man in this scripture was without speech and sight for thirty years, and then Jesus healed him. It's logical that he became a witness for Jesus.

Picture this man, formerly unable to speak, telling his story to a group in the marketplace. "Look at me! I'm a new person because Jesus of Nazareth befriended me. In Jesus I saw and felt God. I seemed to be a walking dead man; now I am alive. Now I enjoy life. Every event is an opportunity to serve. Yes, at times life still does become very routine; and I still have sorrows and joys. But now there is an inner strength because of my friendship with Jesus."

One finds insights from this event.

— The healed man's experience is tied together by the ever-present, ongoing activity of God; coupled with the man's acceptance and appreciation of the event.

— Jesus can cause radical changes in human lives.

— If a person digs into scripture they can meet Jesus and share in a religious experience.

— This same Jesus is presented to us. The same power that transformed the mute man can be felt in the here and now.

Amen!

(These Days, September 17, 1982)

The About-to-be-Stoned Woman

(Friends of Jesus)
John 8:1-11

And Jesus said, "Neither do I condemn you; go, and do not sin again."
John 8:1-11

The Pharisees were not interested in what insight Jesus might have as to how to interpret the relationship between love and justice. In this context the reality of guilt in the lives of *every* person is the most relevant issue.

After the accusers left, Jesus looked up at the woman with what can only have been a face full of mock surprise, and said, "I was sure there were some men here making accusations against you; are there none?" The woman caught the irony and presumably the profundity of Jesus' wry remark and joined in, "None sir." Then Jesus in effect said, "Me neither. Let's drop the whole thing; only friend, you should rethink your sexual activity."

We don't know about her future. Maybe she: (1) reorganized the priorities in her life, becoming a witness to God's forgiveness and love; (2) continued as before for a while, then decided to change her lifestyle; (3) continued as before and never changed. (Could anyone coming into direct contact with Jesus continue on as before?)

In a way Jesus was talking to each of us: "I forgive you for past sins, but don't repeat them."

O Jesus, who forgave the woman, who would have forgiven her lover, and who forgives me, thank you for your love. Amen.

(These Days, September 18, 1982)

God's Presence in Peacemaking

(A Present God)
Jeremiah 26:1-9

Jeremiah spoke about war, famine, and pestilence. The world knows these evils all too well. He spoke of a true prophet "who prophesies peace." However the world knows too little about peace. For Jeremiah, and for us, we focus on certainty: constant thinking and talking *about* peace lead to actions *for* peace.

As we consider Jeremiah's hope, for those living in exile now, and the Holy Land as it is today, I offer a true story.

During the Israeli-Egyptian Six Day War, at a checkpoint set up by the Israeli army, an old Jewish man came with a basket of fruit. The guards were going to stop his crossing, but the sergeant in charge let him through. Why? The officer said, "During the war the enemy raped and killed his daughter. For the past year he daily takes a basket of fruit to Bedouin shepherds in the nearby hills. He says war and killing didn't work, so he is trying another way."

We are not called to be peace-thinkers, or peace-prayers or peace-hopers; we are called to be peacemakers.

World peace and the survival of humankind may well depend on those who are willing to be peacemakers. And certainly if we profess to follow Jesus Christ, that task must become ours.

Prayer: O God of peace, let peace come to earth, and let that peace begin with my peacemaking. Amen and Shalom.

(Disciplines, August 18, 1986)

God's Presence when Journeying

(A Present God)
Luke 13:22-24

Luke says that Jesus went "journeying toward Jerusalem." Jerusalem was not a pleasant destination. For Jesus, the so-called "Holy City" represented the power and oppression of Rome, the hard legalism of traditional religion, a city for which Jesus wept. Yet he journeyed.

We journey. In our journeying, Jesus encourages us to "enter by the narrow door." His tone is one calling for discipline, stressing that time is short and that there is no favoritism. He calls upon us to enter through struggle and self-denial.

As we journey and as we encourage others in their journey, let us notice the resources Jesus provides.

1. The Story. The stories are endless, stories of insight and hope and encouragement: tree-dweller Zacchaeus, the boy with his five-loaf, two-fish lunch, the prodigal son, the widow who put in two coins, etc.
2. Water. Jesus said, "The water that I will give . . . will . . . give . . . eternal life" (John 4:14).
3. Bread. Jesus said, "I am the bread of life" (John 6:35).
4. Friendship. Jesus said, "I have called you friends" (John 15:15). His

friendship crosses time and space. Call it spirit and love; call it the presence felt in Holy Communion; whatever, it is real – a friendship that doubles our joy and divides our grief.

We must learn to be goal-spirited in our journeying. We are helped by Jesus. Let us press on.

Devotional exercise: Every time you are stopped by a red traffic light, think about God's presence with you.

(Disciplines, August 20, 1986)

God's Presence in Kingdom Building

(A Present God)
Luke 13:25-30

In today's scripture, Luke speaks of the kingdom of God as universal fellowship. Jesus emphasized kingdom building, and he insisted it was not a private matter. Kingdom building means taking an active role in transforming our society. Through the words of Jesus, we learn that the kingdom of God means:

- economic parity
- equal manna
- harmony
- sitting at the same table
- no regionalism
- lambs and lions together

Each believer must find a place in helping to build that kind of kingdom. When we are actively working, God is indeed present. The model for God's kingdom is not behind us but before us. The kingdom is both present and future. God acts through what we do with the opportunities given to us.

In the seventeenth century a European king made a visit to a small school. Speaking to the children, he held up a rock and said, "To what kingdom does this belong?" The class replied, "Mineral." He held up a flower and said, "To what kingdom does this belong?" The class replied, "Vegetable." He pointed to a window and said, "To what kingdom does a bird belong?" The class replied, "Animal."

Then the king pointed to himself and asked, "To what kingdom do I belong?" After a pause, a young girl replied, "The kingdom of God." The king said, "That's right, and each one of you also belongs to the kingdom of God." No kingdom ever has been nor ever will be as important as the kingdom of God. With God's help, let us undertake to build the kingdom.

Prayer: Dear God, "*Thy kingdom come, Thy will be done.*" Amen.

(Disciplines, August 21, 1986

God's Presence in Worship

(A Present God)
Hebrews 12:18-29

At times God must be amused, even disappointed at what we allow to pass as worship. We have all endured worship experiences which were shoddy and shallow. The writer of Hebrews challenges, "Let us offer to God acceptable worship, with reverence and awe." Consider these offerings from our congregation:

* From a call to worship:

In the midst of starvation, we dare this day
to celebrate the bread.
In the midst of frantic, laughing death,
we dare this day to celebrate life.

* From a call to Communion:

Partaking of the bread,
we know our strength from thee derives.
And as we take the cup,
we go to witness with our lives.

* From a prayer:

In an age of cold steel and towering buildings,
we thank you for warm havens of human love.

* From a hymn:

Christ's power is from God,
It truly can disturb;
The church must always push and prod,
Till love becomes a verb.

* From an Easter call to stewardship:

On that first Easter the stone was moved and light shone into the tomb. We need to open our wallets and our lives and let light shine upon our check book, our cash, our words and our actions. Seen in this light, blessed in this light, given in this light, our stewardship becomes holy.

* From a unison benediction

Our faith is like a staff of oak,
a traveler's sturdy aid;
It gives us hope and strength to walk
through shadows unafraid.
We'll journey on, and still be stirred
by vision bright and Gospel word.
Amen and Shalom.

Suggested activity: When asked to lead worship, I will make it more than acceptable; I will make it awe-full.

(Disciplines, August 22, 1986)

God's Presence in Suffering

(A Present God)
Mark 5:1-20

"What Is Your Name?"

My God, I've heard of
    nondirective counseling
    but that was absurd.
Any guy who wanders among
    the graves screaming
    and cutting himself
    isn't worth wasting time on.
Now, what will the
    Gerasene Psychiatric Unit do?
Since when does
    just matter-of-fact
    faith and belief count?
And I ask,
    what about all those dead pigs?
    Remember farmers vote.
    (Let the welfare mothers have them!)
Jesus, leave us alone.

Prayer: O God, Jesus healed that tomb dweller, and his action assures us that even in times of despair your presence is real. We are grateful for this event, for it reveals how you choose to deal with us and the confusion that is within us. As this man was accepted and loved, so we are loved.

Now direct our thinking toward those who are troubled. May we, too, reach and touch with gentle kindness and compassion. May we not mouth any unkind comments about those who are disturbed. May your presence reach us and all who need your calming touch. You do not leave us alone. Thank you. Amen.

(Disciplines, August 23, 1986)

God's Presence in Our Joy

(A Present God)
John 16:16-20

I associate this day, August 24, with joy. On August 24, 1957, I was married to Sheral Adene Yates in the Bethany Christian Church of Lincoln, Nebraska. On August 24, 1960 I was ordained to the Christian Ministry in the Tabernacle Christian Church of Lincoln. Remembering the events of this day in my history allows me to recall the presence of family and friends, saints and sinners, and God. It all adds up to joy.

Need I spell out the times when there were a few difficulties in our marriage? Shall I bore you with a listing of church events when the sisters and brothers proved they were more sinful than saintly? So? So, joy is still a powerful gift from God, and welcome after vanquished difficulties.

The Bible relates more winter times than summer times. This is because we can easily handle the summer times, when joy and happiness and understanding are paramount. It is in the winter times when we especially need God's presence and assurance.

This passage from John also cites winter and summer times. Jesus speaks of the disciples' sorrow when they will no longer see him, and of the travail of a woman in labor. Yet within five verses he speaks of rejoicing twice and joy four times.

This week we have considered God's presence in peacemaking, journeying, kingdom building, worship, suffering, and now joy. In all these events God is present. As God shares in and carries us through our winter times, God also participates in our joy. May every day – every day – of your life be special as you continue to experience the presence of God.

Prayer: O God of night and day, seedtime and harvest, thank you for being with us at all times. We ask you to be present at our times of sorrow, but somehow we forget you also share our times of joy. Receive our song of joy: "Joy to the world, all the boys and girls, joy to the fishes in the deep blue sea, joy to you and me." Amen.

(Disciplines, August 24, 1986)

The Rainbow Connection

(Relationships with God)
Genesis 9:8-17

Critical scholarship recognizes the Genesis flood story as probably based upon the Babylonian story, the *Gilgamish Epic*. The story contains a keen insight: "How do we treat God's creation?"

This ancient story may be partly myth; yet it is also a parable of what is not myth but terrible reality. There comes a point when evil and sin are so heavy that something has to break. When that time comes, the forces of decency on earth are not strong enough to hold back the deluge. For Noah it was 40 days. For the first and second world wars it was four years; for other wars even longer.

But after the rain, the flood, the waiting, the weariness, the stink and filth of the ark – came the loving word of hope: "I set my bow in the cloud, and it shall be a sign of the covenant between me and the earth."

The powerful word from Genesis is that we are not left alone to face the seemingly impossible conditions of flood, fatigue, and failure. The writer said, "God remembered Noah." Humankind was not forgotten!

The rainbow given by God is not an accident or a fleeting hope. It is the sign of the covenant establishing a permanent relationship between God and humankind.

Prayer: God, thank you for being the rainbow in the storms of my life. Amen.

(Disciplines, February 15, 1988)

Remember Not My Sins

(Relationships with God)
Psalm 25:1-10

A story from the 1940s provides an insight concerning our relationship with God. A family of sharecroppers lived in Georgia. Each year their meager income just covered the necessities. But one year the crops were exceptionally good and they had a little extra money to spend. They decided to order a small mirror from a catalogue.

The mirror arrived, and some family members saw their own image for the first time. It was especially emotional for young Willie, whose face was disfigured by a fire early in his life. After looking in the mirror, Willie was silent. Then he turned to his mother and said, "Ma, all these years you knew I looked ugly, and you still loved me."

God is like that where our spiritual lives are concerned. Regardless of an "ugly" past, even in a relationship apart from God; or the sin and subsequent sinful behavior of our lives, we are loved by a God who is steadfast and forgiving.

A meaningful covenant relationship with God is created when we open ourselves completely to God, even if that opening is painful. Suppose you receive a phone call from a friend you have not seen in several years. She says she is about thirty minutes from your house and is stopping. The house is a mess. You quickly pick up everything and throw it in a closet, praying that if your friend asks for a tour, she will not want to look in *that* closet.

There are times when we must open that closet and acknowledge our junk, trash, and non biodegradable garbage – indeed, sins. God can help in cleaning out *that* closet.

Prayer: Remember not the sins of my youth, nor my transgressions; according to thy steadfast love, remember thou me, for thy goodness' sake, O Lord! Amen.

(Disciplines, February 16, 1988)

Now Hear This!

(Relationships with God)
Mark 1:9-11

Today is Ash Wednesday. The Mark passage is timely because it serves as a beginning. The baptism of Jesus was his beginning in ministry. Ash Wednesday is our entry into the Lenten season and a unique opportunity for a hard, disciple-like look at our relationship to God's beloved Son. This is a day for rededication.

Reflecting on these three verses, I think it appropriate to color the scene blue and green. The water of the Jordan is cool and refreshing. The heavens open and God's dove-like Spirit proclaims, "Thou art my beloved Son."

God was claiming Jesus and calling him to ministry. As we begin our Lenten pilgrimage, we, too, are again called to Christian ministry and discipleship. Where will it lead? What decisions will it demand? Only Christ knows the journey's end, but we know it will be a road of endless mercy and grace. Discipleship means joy and fulfillment.

The baptized Christ is our model. So we also need to model the Christian faith. In fact, most of those who are Christians are so not because they have hacked a slow, laborious way to a hard-won faith through a jungle of doubts and intellectual perplexities. No, they saw and believed in others who trusted, believed in, and modeled Christ. Thus they, too, believed in the Baptized One and his call to be a part of and work for the kingdom of God.

Devotional exercise: Many of you may not have had the sign of the cross placed on your forehead with ashes. Nevertheless, I invite you to make a cross – out of any material handy – or use one you have. Hold it, look at it, and think passionately about what it symbolizes – a relationship to God, not the worldly power of humans. Put it in your pocket or purse, and look at it daily from now until Easter.

(Disciplines, February 17, 1988, Ash Wednesday)

Satan Comes up Empty

(Relationships with God)
Mark 1:12-13

If yesterday's scripture reading was colored by a backdrop of blue and green, today's verses would be in hues of gray and brown. A 40-day period in the wilderness does not translate into fun and fellowship. This was not a joyful picnic.

Once again Jesus models a true relationship with God. Jesus spent this time "tempted by Satan; and he was with wild beasts." Our Lenten "sacrifice" may be to do without television once a week, skip desserts every other evening, and make at least one nice comment to someone we don't like. We can do better!

The wilderness experience was a testing time for Jesus. Our Lenten experience is an opportunity for growth in our spiritual life. In our times of temptation we learn that God is not a rich uncle. God is more like an earthquake. God does not simply sit back and let the world exist but comes into our world as a disturbing force, stirring people to action.

As Jesus went from his baptism into the wilderness, we experience him as a man for every season. After taking all that Satan could dish out, Jesus said, "Begone, Satan!" (Matthew 4:10) The final insightful words from today's reading are: "And the angels ministered to him."

Suggestion for meditation:

And though this world, with devils filled,
Should threaten to undo us,
We will not fear, for God hath willed
His truth to triumph through us.
The Prince of Darkness grim, we tremble not for him;
His rage we can endure, for lo, his doom is sure:
One little word ["Begone"] shall fell him.
— "A Mighty Fortress Is Our God" – Martin Luther

(Disciplines, February 18, 1988)

The Kingdom, Oh so Close!

(Relationships with God)
Mark 1:14-15

Barton Hunter was out doing his usual thing – helping those who need help. The refugee family our congregation was sponsoring needed a set of used tires for their car. He approached the manager of a local service station, who sorted through his supply. Then the manager pointed across the street to a competing station, "They really have a better selection and can sell you used tires at a cheaper rate." In our cutthroat, get-ahead-at-any-cost competitive age, this incident, Barton felt, was at least a glimpse of the kingdom!

Pointing people toward the kingdom of God is the work of Jesus – the reason for his being. The Kingdom of God is peace and joy, but this joy is not reached by living on the edge of life. Kingdom living is breaking through the surface of shallow relationships to penetrate the very depths of our reason for being. When we reach that depth we can experience a joy that is eternal and can never be destroyed. In the process of seeking the kingdom, we find truth, hope, and joy.

The pastor was making the rounds of the church school classes and he stopped to visit with those in the fourth grade class. He asked the group, "Can you tell me, what the Kingdom of God is?" Following a long pause a young boy said, "I think its God's tomorrow, sir." There was another pause, and the young student added, "But I guess it's kind of here today already." Sounds good to me.

Prayer: O God, help me to do my part in kingdom building: by my acts of love and compassion, by my service to humankind, by what I say and do. Amen.

(Disciplines, February 19,1988)

Baptism, More Than Lava

(Relationships with God)
I Peter 3:18-22

Our scripture on Monday was about Noah and the ark. Wednesday's was about the baptism of Jesus. Today's scripture combines the two and helps to clarify the purpose of baptism.

The writer of First Peter states, "Baptism . . . saves you, not as a removal of dirt from the body but as an appeal to God . . ." This is a keen insight. Baptism is not a scrubbing of one's body; it is a participation in the life and ministry of Jesus.

Baptism should cause one to see life and all life's relationships in a Christ-like light. Unfortunately, this is not always the case.

Ivan the Great of Russia (1440-1505) freed his country from the Tartars. That was accomplished by a lot of fighting. Following this event Ivan desired to take as his wife, Sophia, the daughter of the king of Greece. The king requested only that Ivan become a member of the Greek Orthodox Church.

Ivan agreed, but then he discovered he must be baptized and cease to participate in warfare. Ivan felt this would be too great a change in his lifestyle.

On the day of his baptism, Ivan came to the water with 500 of his soldiers. Five hundred priests were ready to baptize them all. But as Ivan and his soldiers were immersed, each held his arm and sword above the water. The fighting arms and the swords were not baptized.

Thus Ivan the Great became a member of the Christian church, married the princess of Greece, and kept right on fighting!

Devotional exercise: Recall your baptism/confirmation. What did it mean to you then? What should it mean to you now? What does it mean for your future? Is there a change in you, or do you keep right on "fighting?"

(Disciplines, February 20, 1988)

On Being Born

(Relationships with God)
Jeremiah 20:14-18
I John 4:7-8

Today is *my* birthday. I was born on February 21, 1936 at York, Nebraska. You know my age. As for my spiritual age, I may not be 52, but I pray my relationship with God is growing and maturing.

For our scripture readings I selected two passages with very different concepts of birth. In a fit of utter despair Jeremiah laments: "Cursed be the day on which I was born!" How devastating! What a contrasting view of birth we receive from the writer of First John: "He [she] who loves is born of God."

What matters in our relationship with God is not when we were born, nor when we die. It is that *dash* between our birth and death. We had nothing to do with our birth, and we can do nothing on earth after our death. How we use the time that the dash represents is vital because we can use that time only once.

At a recent wedding reception I was trying to hold a conversation with the grandfather of the bride. Twice, in a loud voice, I said, "What do you enjoy doing?" He finally said, "I'm 93. I'm just trying to stay alive – that's what I'm doing."

In contrast there is that delightful story of Chief Justice Oliver Wendell Holmes being visited on his birthday by President Franklin D. Roosevelt. When Roosevelt found him reading, he asked, "What are you reading, Mr. Chief Justice?"

"I am reading Plato, Mr. President," he replied.

"Why are you reading Plato?" Roosevelt asked.

"To improve my mind, Mr. President."

The Lenten season provides the proper backdrop for viewing life. In his season of suffering, Jesus rather than cursing the day of his birth, loved people. He was born of God.

Prayer: Loving God, may we be born daily, to love. Thank you for gifts, the gift of meaningful relationships with family and friends; and for the gift of being able to give and receive. Amen.

(Disciplines, February 21, 1988)

I Pant for Understanding

(Acting with Understanding)
Psalm 119:129-136

Upon the death of her child, a mother asked a holy man to restore her child to life. The holy man replied, "If you can bring me a bowlful of rice from a home that has known no sorrow, I will restore your child to life." At the end of the day the grieving mother returned with an empty bowl, but with a mind full of understanding.

In this longest of all psalms, the psalmist stresses the importance of God's understanding. The writer has comprehended that God's testimonies are wonderful; so wonderful that the believer pants and longs for "thy commandments."

This understanding is not difficult nor is it complex. Even the keenest minds in the world are challenged by God's ways. Yet "the unfolding of thy words gives light; it imparts understanding to the simple." Applied to daily living, that simply translates that you don't need a university degree to know how to give and to receive love.

The world needs more persons who act out of their knowledge of the commandments. Maybe we will even "shed streams of tears, because men do not keep thy law." When we become emotionally involved in God's work, then we are a great asset for God.

Prayer: O God, I pant for you with my whole being. In response to your ongoing support of me, help me to always be understanding in my relationships with all who come my way. Amen.

(Disciplines, July 29, 1984)

An Understanding Mind

(Acting with Understanding)
I Kings 3:5-12

Solomon's prayer is a model for any person in a position of leadership. This prayer speaks of humility, and he offers it not-withstanding his own personal imperfections. Would that all leaders might pray as Solomon!

Even though he is not yet twenty, Solomon displays a keen understanding of his relationship both to God and with those he is to govern. In this context, understanding is more than simply processing information; it is intellectual apprehension. And when understanding is applied to human values, it includes imaginative comprehension. An understanding person is one who can empathize with others.

Is this not what all leaders need to do? Is this not what we need to do? We pray with an understanding mind when we consider the feelings and needs of those in our community, or nation, and our world. Solomon looked to God first. He did not ask for "long life or riches or the life of [his] enemies," but for understanding. Thus God gives Solomon a "wise and discerning mind."

Ah, that we might pray in that model! How many still have a difficult time praying for the lives of enemies? The ultimate – praying for enemies – is the model that Jesus would have us consider. All of this takes an understanding mind. Solomon had one and, of course, so did Jesus. Now it is our turn. Will we pray with an understanding mind?

Prayer: God, our prayer is for all leaders – those in the United Nations, those who lead denominations, those in our Congress, our governors, our mayors, and our local church leaders. May they lead with understanding. Amen.

(Disciplines, July 30, 1984)

Understanding That Which Is of Value

(Acting with Understanding)
Matthew 13:44-46

Are we mature disciples – ready to sacrifice everything for the kingdom? That is truly what Jesus is asking his disciples in these two parables. The kingdom of heaven is that desirable.

More questions: Was the man a fool to sell everything for the single field? Was the merchant acting irrationally in liquidating all his assets to buy a single pearl? Many would say yes. But to know when to risk all makes for a successful financier. You must always be sure of the value of the property you are buying.

Giving-everything discipleship is seemingly not for the multitudes, only the faithful few. Indeed, very few will understand that which is really of value. One day the poor plowman found the treasure, of all places, in his dull and weary field. But he knew he had uncovered the treasure of all times. Then he went, he sold, and he bought. The gospel is treasure, and Christ is the supreme jewel.

The Man of Nazareth calls for twentieth-century merchants, merchants who will understand that the kingdom is the supreme good. He says to us, The pearl can be found by those who seek. "If with all your heart you truly seek me, you shall surely find me" (see Jeremiah 29:13-14).

Each follower of Jesus must come to treasure his or her own discipleship. Then, and only then, will we come to understand what is of eternal value.

Prayer: O great Giver of jewels – even your Son, and the kingdom of heaven — help me to so desire your kingdom that I will seek it with my whole being. In a time when values are distorted, may I understand what is of real value – my relationship to you. Amen.

(Disciplines, July 31, 1984)

Understanding the Kingdom of Heaven

(Acting with Understanding)
Matthew 13:47-52

The point of this scripture is that when you fish with a dragnet you cannot expect to select your fish – your catch will be mixed. Similarly, those who fish for human beings must understand they need to be prepared to cast their net widely over the whole extent of human society. These words are an exhortation to understand disciples, then and now.

The allegory of the last judgment used here should not be overlooked. Judgment is not ours to administer; rather our job is to be "trained for the kingdom of heaven" and its new connotations. Day by day the dragnet is being drawn, for the kingdom is an event. The appeal must go to everyone. The worthy are separated from the unworthy by their own reaction to the demands of the kingdom.

When New Testament scholars talk about the Kingdom of God they understand the Kingdom to be in one of four categories: (1) The Kingdom is in the here-and-now; you can experience it daily; (2) the Kingdom is in the future, start preparing now; (3) the Kingdom is *both* now and in the future; (4) the Kingdom is "within" you. Can you blend all four together? Why not?

To accept God's new kingdom and to enter it brings blessedness, because we should all be in obedience to the will of God. Such blessedness may be enjoyed here and now, but it is never exhausted in any experience that falls within the bounds of time and space. Thus in Christ we find new hope, hope that makes the future bright.

Prayer: O God, I offer a prayer for all who have thrown out the net – pastors, teachers, missionaries – yes, even me. Amen.

(Disciplines, August 1, 1984)

Understanding Our Calling

(Acting with Understanding)
Romans 8:28-30

This epitaph is from a tombstone found in a New England cemetery:

> Here lies the body of John Leonard.
> In his lifetime he killed 97 Indians.
> He was living in the blessed hope of
> making it 100, when he fell asleep in
> the arms of Jesus.

John Leonard evidently never understood that those in Jesus' arms are "called according to his purpose." Many within the church do not understand their calling to responsible Christian discipleship. Christians don't kill; they love.

Gilbert Scott, one of England's greatest architects, designed a telephone booth and a cathedral and both were buildings of genius. Architect Scott did the best he could with every assignment. Many can easily find their calling within the comfortable framework of the church, but in Romans, Paul calls us to faithfulness in everything.

A certain eighteenth-century prince's activity, language, and demeanor belied his royal calling. So his governess pinned a piece of royal purple on his lapel. She then said to the prince, "Whenever I find you not acting properly, as a prince should, I will point to the purple, and appeal to your royal attire." God appeals to us, through Paul, asking us to believe that "everything . . . works for good with those who love [God]."

John Leonard missed his calling, Gilbert Scott understood his, and the young prince may finally respond to his.

Prayer: O God, you have called, justified, and glorified us. As you work in our lives, may we understand that faith is really a verb, not a noun. Amen.

(Disciplines, August 2, 1984)

Understanding Leads to Justice

(Acting with Understanding)
Proverbs 2:1-15

Understanding is our theme for this week, and the writer of Proverbs plays that melody in the second chapter. After equating understanding with wisdom and knowledge, the writer urges us to realize that understanding leads to "justice and equity, every good path."

The company of those committed to God ought to lead the way to justice. However, I found this comment in a metropolitan newspaper:

I don't understand my church anymore. They talk about politics, social issues, and world problems. I'm not against all this, but I've got some real problems of my own. I feel alone in a church that has moved away from me.

Understanding calls us to make the journey of faith in two directions: inward *and* outward. Both areas of Christian living are necessary for the complete Christian experience. Therefore, the inward development of our devotional life and our outward ministry and service to others is vital.

Justice, fairness, rightfulness don't just happen. Justice happens when we – individuals, congregations, nations – apply God's equity to all circumstances. Proverbs reminds us to guard "the paths of justice" and preserve "the way of [God's] saints." We must see that justice is part of our daily living.

An older man took his nephew to a silent Quaker meeting. After sitting quietly for about ten minutes, the nephew whispered, "When does the service begin?" Responded his uncle lovingly, "When we leave here!"

Prayer: Justice and peace, may they bloom and grow, bloom and grow, forever. Amen and Shalom.

(Disciplines, August 3, 1984)

Understanding God's Judgment

(Acting with Understanding)
Obadiah 1:5-15

When was the last time you did a Bible study from Obadiah? Ten years ago? Never? Obadiah is not the capstone of the Bible, but it is a prophetic book that helps us understand God's judgment.

The writer reminds us that there is no such thing as national security. Obadiah states that it is the responsibility of leaders to take action for the safety of all their people, but not to exploit the weakness of another nation.

The idea of national invulnerability is a dream. In Edom's case she tried to place her strength in military force, taking advantage of a weak nation. This is not God's way. The outstanding thought of this small book is God's moral judgment on nations throughout history. Obadiah has a prophetic message that every powerful and wealthy nation ought to heed.

What was needed were seekers of understanding. But there were none. Are there seekers of understanding in our time? Can we stand aside and let others suffer? Ought we to capitalize on another's misfortunes? We need to seek understanding.

Prayer: We cannot merely pray to you, O God, to end starvation; for you have already given us the resources with which to feed the entire world. We cannot merely pray to you, O God, to end despair; for you have already given us the power to clear away slums and to give hope. Therefore we pray to you, O God, for understanding, strength, and will, to do, instead of just to pray; to become, instead of merely to wish. Send us forth. Amen.

(Disciplines, August 4, 1984)

Gracious Words of Support

II Kings 1-3

"I will not leave you." II Kings 2:2

Reading II Kings is a challenge in one's Christian pilgrimage. This is more than a friendly stroll in the park, ending with a happy climax. We will have to search through a lot of blood, fighting, human sacrifice, and treachery, to find a verse, here and there, to develop our faith.

Today's verse was spoken by Elisha to Elijah the prophet. It was a statement of loyalty to a common cause, a belief in the one God of Israel. It was a loving, supportive word between two persons who shared in the heritage of faith.

We all have heard those gracious words, "I will not leave you," from family, friends, pastors, members in our Christian community, and those in other churches. They are words of life.

Can *we* form the same words with our lips? Can we develop a faith, a "tie that binds" through thick and thin, winter and summer, depression and joy? Yes, we can, and yes, we must.

The mantle that passed from Elijah to Elisha was one of righteousness. We would wear it too.

Loving God, help us to become strong links, in the chain of righteousness. Amen.

(The Word in Season, April 8, 1989)

About Killing and Living

II Kings 4-4

"Shall I slay them?" He answered, "You shall not slay them." II Kings 6:21-22

A few years ago, on the evening television newscast, I observed the unveiling of the first Super B-1 Bomber. About 1,000 people had been invited to the Seattle event. They all stood and applauded as the plane was rolled into view. I felt strange, as if I were viewing a potential execution for which tickets had been issued.

The answer to today's question was: "You shall *not* slay them."

In biblical times, and in our time, there are those who continue to support the slogan that "might is right." A man from the Pentagon recently made a public relations presentation. He was pleasant and suave. A husband, father and grandfather, he started his talk with an amusing story. Then, in a matter-of-fact manner, noted, "We have 8,000 fewer missiles than we did 10 years ago." However, he did not state the fact that some of today's missiles are 30 times more powerful. Another interesting quote was, "New weapons are safer." Colleagues in the Pentagon refer to him as the "Prince of Darkness."

As we reflect on the Prince of Peace, which motto should we follow: "Peace through strength" or "Strength through peace?" Thinking and talking and praying and acting for and about peace leads to peace.

God, take the word *slay* from our vocabulary. Amen.

(The Word in Season, April 9, 1989)

A Representative of God

II Kings 8-10

"The man of God has come here." II Kings 8:7

Did you make it through II Kings, chapter 10? You must have a strong stomach! A natural question follows this reading: why is this in the Bible? It is full of unimaginable atrocity and merciless butchery, a nightmare that drips with blood. Maybe its purpose is to portray the dark side of human activity, and the desperate need of people for God.

In the middle of any difficult situation, I cannot think of more helpful and supportive words than "the man of God has come here." Within the context of this scripture, that man was Elisha. Yet I believe we can apply those words to our day. Do you agree? Can you, can I, be that man or woman of God who comes bearing some hope and promise?

People of God can be laity or clergy. We can be old or young, or in-between. We can be liberal or conservative or moderate in our thinking. We can drive Fords or Buicks or Hondas. We can come with cookies or a Bible or with a hug, or we can simply sit with those in need and hold their hand. We *are* the Elishas of 1989.

God, be with us in our comings and goings. Use us in your ministry of love and guidance and hope. Amen.

(The Word in Season, April 10, 1989)

Covenant

II Kings 11-13

The Lord . . . turned toward them, because of his covenant with Abraham, Isaac, and Jacob . . . II Kings 13:23

Covenant is one of the most important words in the Bible. Early in scripture, God established a covenant with Noah, giving the rainbow as its sign (Genesis 9). *Covenant* means "strong relationship."

God's covenant with us is not like recordings we hear when we make some phone calls: "We're sorry; we cannot come to the phone right now. At the sound of the beep please leave your name and number, and we will get back to you as soon as possible."

God does not respond in that manner. God is present to speak with us at any time. Covenant between God and humankind means that God has an ongoing relationship with us, any time, any place.

Harry Chapin in his *Cotton Patch Gospel* says it this way: "There ain't no busy signals on the hot line to God."

In II Kings, chapters 11-13 we find theft, treason, slaying, and conspiracy. Then the writer recalls God's covenant. Covenant was needed then, and now.

Thank you God, for your covenantal relationship. Amen.

(The Word in Season, April 11, 1989)

Stubborn and Turn

II Kings 14-17

They would not listen, but were stubborn. II Kings 17:14

Today we consider two words: *stubborn* and *turn.* My dictionary defines stubborn as "fixed in purpose or opinion; unreasonably obstinate," with *unyielding, perverse*, and *headstrong* as synonyms. *Turn* means, "to change the position of something; to take a new direction."

They in today's verse are the people of Israel (17:11). They were stubborn and would not turn from evil ways. Stubbornness, however, is not a trait of only Old Testament people. You and I can be stubborn in many ways. We rationalize that we inherited the trait, or developed it because of our childhood environment, or claim "That's just the way I am."

We can change. This is the heart of the gospel. We can turn from any evil thoughts or actions. God's grace is the loving power that helps us in turning from stubbornness to understanding and creative living. It is never too late to turn. Believe that fact, and act accordingly.

Loving God, some of us need to turn slightly, some 180 degrees. Be with all as we turn. Amen.

(The Word in Season, April 12, 1989)

Relying Completely on God

II Kings 18-21

"We rely on the Lord our God." II Kings 18:22

Reading II Kings does not cultivate a happy attitude. In today's chapters we note the slaying of 185,000 people. A king burns his child as an offering, and consults mediums and wizards. Evil reigns.

What we need is a ray of hope, and we find it in today's verse. Relying on God is a faith issue, placing one's whole trust in God.

Jackson did a neat job of mowing lawns in a town in Georgia; working on them like an accomplished artist would approach a canvas. He did such fine work that the county hired him to manicure the courthouse lawns. When Jackson retired, his friends decided to treat him to an airplane ride, to observe his lawn work from above. He had never been in an airplane, and hesitated, but finally agreed.

Following Jackson's ride a group of friends met him at the small airport and asked, "Did you enjoy the ride?" He replied, "Yes, but I never put all my weight down on the seat." He lacked complete trust.

God of the Hebrew Bible, New Testament, and our God, be patient with us as we learn to rely on you. Help us to put down all of our weight. Amen.

(The Word in Season, April 13, 1989)

God is with Us

Isaiah 7:14

"The Lord himself will give you a sign. Behold, a young woman shall conceive and bear a son, and shall call his name Immanuel." Isaiah 7:14

Six-year-old Julia lives next door to us and often visits with us when we are in the yard. During one of these chats, Julia said to me, "If I saw a big, orange monster coming down the street, do you know what I would do?" I replied, "What would you do?"

Julia smiled and said, "I would tell him funny jokes until he laughed himself silly, and I would laugh with him, and we would both laugh, and then we would be friends."

I think Julia knows a good way to get along with people – and even with make-believe monsters. Throughout his life Jesus, too, was good at getting along with people. Some people hated him, but he loved even those people. In 1989 Jesus still loves all people – children and grandchildren and parents and teachers and school bus drivers and everyone else.

The word *Immanuel* means "God is with us." God is like Jesus.

Thank you God, for all of the loving things Jesus has done. Amen.

(The Home Altar, November 27, 1989)

We Are Branches

Isaiah 11:1-2

There shall come forth a shoot from the stump of Jesse, and a branch shall grow out of his roots. Isaiah 11:1

Have you ever seen a new shoot grow out of a tree stump; in your yard, perhaps; or down the street, or in a park? New shoots often grow out of tree stumps. Our Bible reading today talks about a shoot and a branch; that branch can be Jesus.

Jesus is a branch, and so are we. Children are like the new growth that comes out of a tree, out of a family tree.

Our special friend Jesus has said to us, "I am the vine. You are the branches." We are all part of the same family, and we are connected to each other.

Dear Jesus, we are thankful that you always stay so close to us and that we are part of your family. Make us the family you hope we will be. Amen.

(The Home Altar, November 29, 1989)

The Good Judge

Isaiah 11:3b-5

He shall not judge by what his eyes see, or decide by what his ears hear; but with righteousness he shall judge the poor. Isaiah 11:3b-4a

Have you ever noticed that some of the most wonderful things in this would are things you cannot hear or see? You cannot hear kindness. You cannot see love. Yet you can feel kindness and love.

Can you tell me what the wind is? You might have a hard time explaining the wind. Yet when you are outside, you know that the wind is very real. You feel the wind. There may even be times when the wind can push you over. You cannot see the wind, but it blows cold in winter and warm in summer.

Today's Bible reading talks about a good king who judges people with wisdom, and not on the basis of what he sees or hears about them. How do you judge people? Just because a person is big, do you think that person is mean? Just because you hear that your friend told a lie, do you believe that your friend did? We must not think that our eyes or ears enable us to make fair judgments about other people. Only God is a good and perfect judge.

Dear God, even though we cannot see you or hear you, we know that you are real. Thank you for judging all people with love and kindness. Teach us not to make judgments about others on the basis of what we see or hear. Amen.

(The Home Altar, November 30, 1989)

God Shares Our Hopes and Fears

Micah 5:2

But you, O Bethlehem . . . , from you shall come forth for me one who is to be ruler in Israel, whose origin is from of old, from ancient days. Micah 5:2

I once took a water safety class in life saving. In the class we learned this motto: "Throw, row, go." If you see someone in trouble in the water, you first throw something to the person – anything that will help the person float. If it's not possible for you to throw something, you next try rowing in a boat to the person. If it's not possible to throw anything or to row, then you must swim.

If you ever try to save someone – in the water or anywhere – you are likely to find yourself feeling fearful and hopeful at the same time. Many things in life contain both hope and fear.

During the Advent season, one of the hymns we will sing is "O Little Town of Bethlehem," written by Phillips Brooks. In this hymn we sing: "The hopes and fears of all the years are met in thee tonight." From Bethlehem came Jesus, to handle all of our hopes and fears.

Dear God, thank you for staying close to us when we are filled with hopes and fears. Amen.

(The Home Altar, December 1, 1989)

Strength is Sharing

Micah 5:3-4a

He shall stand and feed his flock in the strength of the Lord. Micah 5:4a

We were in line, waiting to place our order for ice cream cones. Immediately ahead of us, a mother was directing her three young children through the important process of choosing and ordering their ice cream treats. When the youngest got his cone, he graciously suggested that each of the older two take a bite. The second child also shared his with the other two. Then the oldest child said, "When I get mine, you both get bites." And, indeed they did.

What a great family, I thought to myself. The three showed they cared about each other and they were willing to share. Those children had probably learned from the parents that real strength is found in sharing both pleasures and problems.

The prophet who wrote our Bible reading for today was a man who loved God and who appreciated a leader whose strength came from God. Micah believed that a person who takes care of other people is a strong person.

Dear God, help us to understand that your strength is seen and felt in caring and sharing, in loving and understanding, in helping and praying. Amen.

(The Home Altar, December 2, 1989

Around the Manger

Micah 5:4b

They shall dwell secure . . . Micah 5:4b

This is the First Sunday in Advent. It is a very special day for the church and for the family. For hundreds of years, the church of Jesus Christ has begun its year with Advent – four weeks of waiting and watching for the celebration of Christ's birth. During Advent, we read about Mary and Joseph, about angels and shepherds, and most of all, about a baby.

Almost every Christian home displays a manger scene during Advent. You probably have one.

Last year my wife gave me a special manger scene made of stained glass. In the scene, a pig, a rhinoceros, a butterfly, and a hippopotamus with a bird on its back, all gather around the manger. I think its fun to look at these animals, because they tell me that every animal and every person is invited to come to the manger. All of us are invited to welcome Jesus into the world.

Dear God, let the light of the first Advent candle, the one we light today, remind us of Jesus' coming into the world. Amen.

(The Home Altar, December 3, 1989)

Joyful Stewardship

The Sunday worship service was over and I was standing on a sagging porch at the battered front door of a house very much in need of paint. Homebound communion had been requested, so I was fulfilling my pastoral duties.

Once inside I quickly realized I was in the midst of illness and poverty. The husband was on a respirator that made a constant, disturbing "shu-shu-shu" sound.

After we shared the Lord's Supper we visited briefly: "No, his health will not improve – yes, it is not easy to keep going, but we survive – he will have to go into a care facility in a few months because I can't handle him."

As I prepared to leave, she handed me a $20 bill, saying, "This is for Ollie (the church treasurer)." I almost replied, "My goodness no, you keep it." I took it and expressed thanks.

Back in my car I reflected on the incident. Truly it was not my place to refuse her gift for the church, however impractical her stewardship. Maybe they found joy in the act of sacrificial giving.

Once again I had been privileged to experience a joyful faith: theirs, then mine, and now yours.

(The Disciple, April, 1990)

Just Being There

Psalm 25:8-18

Thought for today: The friendship of the Lord is for those who fear [love] him.
Psalm 25:14

My clinical pastoral education was at a state mental health institution. We were each assigned a client to whom we related on a weekly basis. Following each session we shared our observations as a group with a psychiatric social worker.

Another student spent each session with his client in silence. At each forty-five minute period he introduced himself and then simply sat with the patient in a small room. Following one of those times, he shared with us: "There are 1,645 tiles on the walls in that room." Still the staff encouraged him to be with this man every week.

At the end of the fourteenth week, my colleague in training burst into our room and said: "When I left today, my friend said, 'I enjoy our times together; thanks for your friendship.'"

Ministry can come from every person. At times the most important aspect of any journey is just being there.

Prayer: Thank you God, for being there – at the hospital, at the cemetery, in the classroom, and in my life. Amen.

(The Secret Place, May 8, 1990)

Winning the Race – Together

Ecclesiastes 9:7-12

Thought for today: Again I saw that under the sun the race is not to the swift.
Ecclesiastes 9:11

The event was the hundred-meter dash. It was part of the Special Olympics for the disabled. The starter shouted: "Runners to your mark! Set!" and then fired his gun. The runners lunged forward and sprinted down the track. Thirty meters from the finish, one runner tripped and sprawled on the track. She lay in the dirt, in pain, with disappointment and embarrassment on her face.

Then the race became special in another way. Without a word among them, the other contestants slowed and stopped. They turned and jogged back to the girl on the ground. Then they picked her up, brushed her off, and, arm in arm, they all crossed the finish line together.

Races are not always to the swift, but they are "won" by those who persevere – and frequently with the help of others.

Prayer: O God, may Hebrews 12:1-2 become our prayer, in word and in deed: "Let us run with perseverance the race that is set before us, looking to Jesus the pioneer and perfecter of our faith." Amen.

(The Secret Place, January 13, 1996)

Dying Gloriously

Luke 18:18-27

Thought for today: "I want to be thoroughly used up before I die, and I want to die gloriously spent . . ." George Bernard Shaw

"What shall I do to inherit eternal life?" This was the question the rich ruler put to Jesus. The Nazarene's instant reply was, "Sell all that you have and distribute to the poor . . . and come, follow me" (Luke 18:22). What a wonderful one-line, complete lesson in stewardship.

Can we die gloriously, thoroughly used up? Using, or losing, one's life for Christ's sake is the best way to go. After your family is financially cared for, why not see that much of your estate goes for continuing Christian ministry and service or for medical research? Why not use your time for volunteer work at the hospital or in visiting with shut-ins? Consider being used up by frequently going the second mile. You will thus be tired, exhausted, and spent.

What a great way to die!

Prayer: Take my life, and let it be consecrated, Lord for thee. Amen.

(The Secret Place, February 10, 1981)

We Are That Junkpile Vase

Romans 9:19-24

Thought for today: Suppose he has a vase that's already marked for the junkpile and he works it over . . . Romans 9:22 (The Cotton Patch Version of Paul's Epistle)

In Romans, Paul says we are vessels of clay and God is the potter. In Clarence Jordan's version of Romans, Jordan says ". . . we are that junkpile vase . . ." Jordan continues, ". . . doesn't the potter have the right to make his lump of clay into either an expensive vase or an everyday pot? . . . he works it over very carefully just to show his marvelous skill to a favorite vase he made earlier for display. Isn't that OK?"

We are immersed in junk. We see junk cars and we attend junk sales (often disguised as flea markets and garage sales). We receive junk mail addressed to "occupant or current resident." However there is no junk when it comes to people. We notice a poster with a picture of a boy that reads: "I know I'm somebody 'cause God don't make no junk."

Indeed we are junkpile vases, and God is continuing to shape and form and remake us.

Prayer: God, as you work in our lives, may we remember that you are a verb, not a noun. Amen.

(The Secret Place, September 26, 1982)

Honoring with the Heart

Matthew 15:1-11

Thought for today: "Honor your father and your mother, that your days may be long in the land which the Lord your God gives you." Exodus 20:12

Our family had made plans for more than three years. The weekend was filled with special events to celebrate the fiftieth wedding anniversary of our parents, Grace Eleta and Mac. One meal was just for our family where we presented a gift and expressed our love.

Brother Stewart had written and was to give a reading about Mom and Dad. Stewart had acted in major roles in high school and college plays. He had gone to acting school in New York City and had performed off-Broadway. Still, he was nervous, and his wife, Kris, remarked, "He has given it (the reading) to me three times." It was perfect.

In sharp contrast to today's scripture reading, Stewart honored our father and mother with both his lips and heart.

We all have the choice to defile or to honor with our words.

Prayer: O God, may we honor with our heart through our lips. May our vocabulary be stocked with words of praise. Amen.

(The Secret Place, May 25, 1989)

Seeing in the Dark

Psalm 139:1-12

Thought for today: When I sit in darkness, the Lord will be a light to me. Micah 7:8

The physics teacher asked the class: "Can you see farther during the day or during the night?" Many quickly replied: "In the day, or course." They were wrong. The teacher then noted that the most distant object we can see in the daytime is the sun, but that at night we can see stars millions of light years away.

In the darkness of disappointment, despair, and even death, we are surrounded by God's light. Within desperate periods we may see more clearly the place of the Christian faith in our lives.

In today's reading – a period of doom and gloom for the psalmist – he depressingly says, "Let only darkness cover me." Yet, by experience, he learned that "even the darkness is not dark to thee" (Psalm 139:11-12).

With God, we can "see" at the funeral, in the hospital, on the job, during retirement, even into the tunnel of doubt – with a vision of hope.

Prayer: May David's prayer in II Samuel (22:29) be our prayer. "Yea, thou art my lamp, O Lord, and my God lightens my darkness." Amen.

(The Secret Place, May 22, 1989)

A Grateful Hymn Writer

Deuteronomy 28:1-6

Thought for today: All these blessings shall come upon you and overtake you, if you obey the Lord your God. Deuteronomy 28:2

When I once encouraged members of the congregation to write new words to hymn tunes, a number met the challenge. One hymn by a woman named Nancy was submitted as "a hymn of praise and thanksgiving."

What made the hymn special for those of us who knew Nancy is that she wrote those words while her body was being destroyed by cancer. She knew she was dying; so did her family and friends. Still she wrote: "Thank thee, Lord for all the blessings I've received." Nancy was also not one to lose sight of others – and expressed a world vision: "Also for the needs of others." That type of faith is the kind you can build your life on!

You might sing this hymn for your family or personal devotions and remember Nancy, as well as those in your congregation with health problems – and all those "others."

Prayer: Loving God, may we live – and die – trusting you; our hearts filled with praise and thanksgiving. Amen.

(The Secret Place, Thanksgiving, November 23, 1995)

"Thank Thee, Lord, for All the Blessings"
(Sung to the tune of "God of Grace and God of Glory")

Thank thee, Lord, for all the blessings
I've received from thy great hand.
For thy care in times of need and
For the beauty of our land.
Grant us health of mind and body;
May we live as thou hast planned,

Also for the needs of others
May we ever mindful be.
Show us ways to help each person
Have a life that's full and free.
Grant to each the strength and courage
To bring each one dignity. Amen.

— Nancy Jane Wilson

Your Place at the Table
Luke 14:7-14

Thought for today: Christian humility is concerned with an attitude toward others that excludes pride and arrogance.

The parable, "The choice of places at the table," in our scripture reading for today has humility as its central theme. Christian humility means a lack of concern for one's own prestige. It is the reverse of frequent, sought-after social desires such as prestige and power.

Some years ago my family attended the wedding of a cousin in Mexico, Missouri. The bride's father, my uncle, was the president of the largest firebrick company in the world and would later become president of the U.S. Chamber of Commerce. We were warmly greeted, and then we took a seat in a back pew. Before the ceremony began, my uncle noticed this and had an usher escort us to the front, immediately behind the bride's parents. I recall the mixed feeling of humbleness and prominence we felt. These feelings may be contained in this parable.

Prayer: Thank you, God, for providing a place for me in your world, in your kingdom, and at Christ's table. Amen.

(The Secret Place, August 11, 1983)

Reflections on Earlier Commitments
Isaiah 6:1-8

Thought for today: Once a year – you pick the time – each one of us ought to make time to renew our commitment to the Church of Jesus Christ.

Each year I reread statements that I wrote and used when I was installed as pastor – my statement of commitment.

And each time I ask, *I wrote that? I affirmed that*? Yes, and it is good that I reflect on my commitment at least yearly.

All Christians have made commitments. You made one when you said, "Jesus is the Christ, the Son of the living God." You made one when you were baptized. Reflect on those commitments. What should they mean now and for your future?

The commitment made in the sixth chapter of Isaiah came at a time of national bereavement when the people had "unclean lips." Even then, as now, our commitment can be, "Send me."

Prayer: Use even me, O God, as I attempt to model your image seen most vividly in Jesus of Nazareth. Amen.

(The Secret Place, September 13, 1983)

A Letter For 2020

II Corinthians 10:7-12

Thought for today: "What we say by letter when absent, we do when present." II Corinthians 10:11b

In 1970 the community of McPherson, Kansas celebrated their Centennial. During ceremonies a large capsule was buried which contained letters. The capsule is to be raised in fifty years – 2020, and the letters mailed. We participated and wrote to the youngest family member, feeling our son, Bill, then five, had the best odds at being alive in 2020.

How would you write such a letter? We selected our words carefully, and expressed our love for him. We wondered what God's world would be like in 2020. We enclosed a picture of our family and our home.

This was one of endless opportunities to think about relationships. Relationships are developed in person, and in letters. In his letter to the Christian community at Corinth, Paul gives us a guideline for all relationships: "We are Christ's."

Someday family and friends will have only letters to recall our love – for the present let us exhibit love in our living.

Prayer: God of the Corinthians, and our God, guide our hands as we write, for letter writing can be a loving ministry. Amen.

I See God's Face

II Corinthians 4:1-6

Thought for today: Filtered through Christ's holy sight
We become children of Light.

There would be no sermon that Sunday morning. A college choir from a neighboring town was presenting "the Word" in song. Besides meaningful music from the total choir there were quartets, duets and solos. Toward the end of the concert two students came to the chancel, one leading the other – who happened to be blind. They sang: "I see God's face shining on me."

At first I thought this was an oxymoron, as the blind singer could not see. Yet he sung with an obvious smile, and his voice resonated with joy and hope. He communicated that spiritually he did "see God's face."

In his second letter to the church at Corinth, Paul says, "God lets light shine out of darkness." Earlier in today's passage, Paul notes "cunning and falseness" has "blinded the minds" of some people but Christ's followers "see the light of the gospel."

Seeing God's face was a real happening in Paul's time, as it can be today, in our time.

Prayer: Open our spiritual eyes, loving God, that we might see your face in both the uncommon and common events of our daily lives. Amen.

On the Other Side
Galatians 2:15-21

Thought for today: "Let him who boasts, boast of the Lord." 1 Corinthians 1:31

We were overnight guests of a family friend, Ruth Spies. She had graciously given us her bedroom. Preparing for bed, I noticed the nameplate her deceased husband had placed on his office desk. The front side said simply "Lew Spies." On the other side, where only Lew could see them, were the words:

My life is committed to God through Jesus Christ and therefore, Christ lives within me. If Christ lives within me , my decisions must reflect his presence.

What an unpretentious and proper manner to remind himself of his Christian discipleship! Lew's slogan captured completely Paul's words in Galatians, "It is no longer I who live, but Christ who lives in me. . ." (2:20).

What slogan describes your life?

Prayer: God of the living and the dead, claim us more fully as we write "Christ lives in me" on our hearts. Amen.

(The Secret Place, April 5, 1988)

A Smile of Confidence
Job 29:15-25

Thought for today: "I smiled on them when they had no confidence." Job 29:24a

In my mind's eye I can still see him – the pastor's son, Russell Bythewood Jr. I was a young teenager in that Lincoln, Nebraska congregation, where he greeted us warmly every Sunday. Russell Jr. was physically impaired from birth, and spent most of his life in his wheelchair.

Every Sunday four men carried him to our second floor sanctuary. A few times I helped. I remember Russell Jr. with a smile on his face. What was it that caused him to smile through his pain and his confined life?

The word "smile" is used only once in the Bible – in the 29th chapter of Job. Job (through much anguish) learned (after debating God) to smile at his problems. He found his strength in God. I believe that's where Russell Jr. found his strength to smile.

I'm sure Russell Jr. did not smile all the time; and neither can we. Not everything that life gives us deserves a smile; yet we live in the confidence that as God was with Russell Jr., God is with us.

Prayer: God, help me to understand that – if my life had been easier to live, I might already have finished living it. Help me as I turn my frowns upside down. Amen.

That "Clergy" Cadillac

We had just purchased our new family car — a two-year old Plymouth wagon – and I was on my way to make a pastoral call. Another car came along side, and then passed me. It was the longest Cadillac I think I ever saw. Even longer than those at the funeral homes. It was new, dark blue, vinyl top with all the extras. Nice! Wouldn't it be neat to drive one, let alone own one? It probably belongs to a banker. Then, as it went by I noticed the prominent sign on the trunk: CLERGY. The word "CLERGY" was bordered by two crosses.

You've got to be kidding! One of my brother pastors owns that boat? How? What's he got that I haven't? Finally I told myself that it doesn't matter, I've got a good used car, wonderful wife, family, dog, etc.

Then I began to guess how he acquired a Cadillac. My first suggestion was that he won it. He got that dream $100,000 from those mail-in sweepstakes! I keep sending in those cards with all my "five special numbers." And he bingoed. Darn, now I'll have to save my stamps.

Next I got a thought that really grabbed me: He did such a wonderful job as a pastor that his grateful congregation gave him this gift. Some pastoral work. Some gift! Maybe I should get up earlier, and stay out later. I might be worth a Honda Mini Bike.

I considered other possibilities. He probably has a second job. He does something on the side. Is it legal? Does he play the stock market? Maybe his Aunt Ina left him a bundle from her will.

He drove on leaving me second-guessing. I thought of that passage in I Timothy, "Set the believers an example in speech and conduct." If we who are clergy are going to parade that fact, I hope we can back-up our label with activity, service and a life-style which sets an example and honors our calling.

(Concerning honesty in reporting, some years after writing this piece, I bought a Cadillac, used of course. It is maroon, with a very nice ride, I enjoy it. If a Cadillac dealer reads this, maybe he would give me a trade in?)

A Cadillac Is Not A Henhouse!

Mom made me go to church. It was dark and raining and it sure would have been great to stay under the covers; but there I was in worship. At least I got to sit in the balcony with Stephen and Kent. We usually drew pictures and tick-tack-toe games on the back of the worship bulletin.

The minister had just started his sermon, and we three had just started a game when the minister said, "A Cadillac is not a henhouse!" What? What did he mean by that? Then he followed by saying, "The church is not a social club!" We stopped playing. (At least for the moment.) He kept talking, that someone might believe a Cadillac would make an excellent henhouse. Why, with all the padding there would be very few broken eggs. When it was hot you could turn on the air-conditioning and the hens could be nice and cool. When it was cold you could turn on the heater. If you wanted it moved, you simply drove it to a new location. "A Cadillac would make an excellent henhouse! But, that's not the *purpose* of a Cadillac."

Then he said a church was not a place where you have garage sales or bingo or card parties; but it ought to be the place where lives are patched-up and put back together. The church was another name for the body of Christ. It was the place where you "rescue the perishing, care for the dying" as an old hymn puts it.

He said the ministry of Jesus Christ was one of preaching, teaching, healing, praying and caring. That was the *purpose* of the church. The church today needs to undertake this ministry in our world on His behalf, and thus act on Christ's Gospel message.

Well, he kept talking and we went back to playing; but it's now been five weeks since he said that and I still remember it. We even discussed it one night at our youth meeting. Now I think I understand the difference between a hen-house and a Cadillac; and I have even thought a bit about what the church ought not, and ought, to be.

We Live With A Questing Faith

I had the privilege of hearing scholar Joseph Sittler once when we lived in Indianapolis. I arrived at the setting at CTS early and took a front row seat. Within his comments he strongly stated: "When the gospel says 'Jesus healed the man' why can't we believe that fact – Jesus healed him!"

In my reading of Lamentations (3:19-25) I appreciated the writer's insight: "The steadfast love of the Lord never ceases, his mercies never come to an end." 3:22

Those words of faith are echoed in our time by Sittler, who lived his faith within the Lutheran tradition, and who gave an insightful interview shortly before he died. He said in part:

> "I was thinking . . . here I am in my eighty-third year . . .dangling, unresolved . . . about how many things I'm still uncertain. I have not in my lifetime solved the problem of God. I only know that to try to escape is unfaith. How does one end life in enormous uncertainty and still remain with a religious center? I'm going to wrap it up in the chorale of the *St John Passion,* hand it to God, saying, 'You take it from here.'"

Sittler knew that life is not all joy and laughter. Yet he deeply believed, as did the writer of Lamentations, that, "The Lord is my portion, therefore I will hope in him." (3:34) The one who wrote Lamentations experienced the siege and fall of Jerusalem, and all the miseries that followed. Yet the book was written, not to simply recall the destruction of that city, but to provide interpretation of God's dealing with God's people, even in the face of disaster. There is deep sorrow over the past, yet there is deep hope for the future, particularly in chapter three.

The one who laments, and Sittler, both believed: "The Lord is good to those who wait for him, to the soul that seeks him." (3:25)

Arrested for being Honest

I wonder what it is like – to be arrested having committed no crime. That's the case with Jesus.

Were his teachings a criminal act? He told people to go a second mile, to love those who were unloving, and to bless those who swore at them. He went against social custom. He told the Romans that his kingdom had nothing to do with their rule. He told the religious leaders to be less concerned with the law and more concerned with compassion for persons.

Yet because he called himself a king, and son of God, he was arrested.

Have you ever been arrested – not for a traffic violation but for a major crime? Think what it would be like to be arrested; to go through a "trial" in which witnesses lied about you, with all of this culminating in a sentence of death.

Have your close friends betrayed you? Remember Judas? Have *you* ever betrayed God? Come now – ever?

Ever had your intimate friends deny knowing you? What a terrible feeling! Have *you* ever denied God, ever said in essence: "I don't know God – God is not for me?"

If Jesus had been a little more tactful, if he had hedged a bit, been vague about who he was, chosen different friends, toned down his prophetic message – he might have lived to an old age.

But Christianity wouldn't be worth much, would it?

(World Call, March, 1972)

In Jesus Death Died

Death may come, but God is the giver of life before and after death. In the event of Jesus of Nazareth, death died.

Death is not an unforeseen accident; not something left out of the total scheme of our God. Rather, God must see it as necessary in his design. It is an appointment for each of us. Death is a birthday, with God.

Some persons are already spiritually dead. They are dead to new ideas; they don't give a tinker's damn about anyone. Oh, they eat and sleep and move. Physically they are alive, but spiritually they are dead. I hope I don't get that way.

I'm still young, but Death, if you were to come tomorrow, I hope that you'd find me doing something of worth.

(Power, July-September, 1969)

Friends of God

Job 19:14-21

There are friends who pretend to be friends, but there is a friend who sticks closer than a brother. Proverbs 18:24

Our church youth were discussing what it means to be a Christian community. Richard, an older, pillar-of-the-church type, was asked to attend the next meeting and give his concept of church. Richard talked about being "friends of God."

He told of the time his son, then eight, had to be in a body cast for eighteen months. During this period, members of the church family made the boy feel they were his friends. One man gave him a dog for a pet. The boys' Sunday school class came to his home and met in his room once a month. Others brought his favorite foods. They showed they cared.

The story of Job offers a sharp contrast to this. Job said, "My kinsfolk and my close friends have failed me," and, "All my intimate friends abhor me." They could hardly be called friends; they were acquainted with Job, yes; but true friends – no.

We can be friends of God and friends for God. This is our vocation and our ministry. People yearn for friendship every day, and we can fill that yearning.

Prayer: As I am thankful for the friendship Jesus shared with so many in the Gospels; I too would share friendship with those I meet, each day. Amen.

Thought for the Day
A friend is one who knows your faults and still calls you friend.

(The Upper Room, November 19, 1982)

Hearing God Speak

Deuteronomy 5:22-27

Go near, and hear all that the Lord our God will say. Deuteronomy 5:27

The mother of a young boy told him that the family went to worship to hear God speak. Following worship, the boy said, "I heard the choir sing and the pastor speak, but I didn't hear God!"

His mother replied by telling a story about an unemployed telegraph operator who went to a railroad station in response to a help-wanted advertisement. He found the room full of applicants, yet in the midst of the noise of trains and the voices of commuters, he heard a message being tapped out in Morse code. The message was: "The first person who hears this message and comes into the office will get the job." He heard, he went, and he was hired.

Today's reading immediately follows the listing of the Ten Commandments. The commandments were given in the midst of fire, a cloud, and darkness. Yet Moses heard God speak, and then gave God's commandments to the children of Israel.

People of the 1980s are surrounded by noise and confusion, yet God's voice continues to be strong. We must train ourselves to listen for it.

Prayer: Unclog our ears, O God, that we may hear You as we worship – in the scripture, in the hymns, in the sermons, and in the prayers. Amen.

Thought for the Day
Those who have ears to hear, let them hear.

(The Upper Room, August 12, 1984)

Help Carry Burdens

Galatians 6:1-10

Help carry one another's burdens, and in this way you will obey the law of Christ. Galatians 6:2 (TEV)

October of 1981 was my worst month ever! I had three eye operations and faced the unknown with pain and boredom. I felt useless and depressed.

However, during that month and after, I felt the support of family and friends helping to carry my burdens. I was carried by prayers, touches, notes, food. One note read: "I guess you have joined me in the Disaster-may-strike-again-at-any-time-but-maybe-it-won't – so-go-lead-a-normal-life club!" Every note, phone call, and gesture of concern helped to carry me.

In writing to the Galatian Christians, Paul asked them to carry one another's burdens. Caring, sharing, helping, supporting is at the heart of the whole Bible. Sharing experiences keeps life fresh, strong, and useful. Paul always got down to where we hurt and feel. And then he had helpful insights for meeting our needs.

When we make a phone call, send a card, give a simple gift, or make a visit, we not only help in carrying someone's burden; we find a purpose for living.

Prayer: Dear God, may I understand that anything that adds to the enjoyment, growth, and appreciation of any person is ministry. Amen.

Thought for the Day
When we help carry another's burden, we find purpose in living.

(The Upper Room, March 17, 1983)

On Being Rejected

Isaiah 53:1-9

He was despised and rejected. Isaiah 53:3

We regret that your submission for publication in our magazine does not meet our present editorial needs. Accordingly, we are returning it to you. Please accept our thanks for having given us the opportunity to consider your work.

— The Editors

Some rejection slips even conclude with: "May God bless your work." Regardless of how nice the words are, any rejection slip is discouraging.

Rejection hurts. *Rejected* is an active, personal, cruel word, a word with which all of us can identify. Social groups and clubs reject. Persons are rejected because of physical and educational standards.

Isaiah speaks of a suffering servant who was despised and rejected, even wounded and bruised. It reminded me of the passage in I Peter that describes Jesus as the living stone, chosen and precious in God's sight even though people rejected Him.

That is the key. The servant was rejected, but was chosen and precious in God's sight. So are we. We are never rejected by God. We can live in that confidence.

Prayer: Thank You, God, for accepting us as we are. May we accept others in that same light. Amen.

Thought for the Day

We are accepted by God; all we need do is accept the fact that we are accepted!

(The Upper Room, June 18, 1984)

A Permanent Mark

Isaiah 49:13-18

Thus says the Lord: . . . See, I have inscribed you on the palms of my hands. Isaiah 49:8, 16

With or without permission to do so, did you ever carve your initials in wet cement? Were you a romantic who inscribed your initials, along with those of another, within a heart on the bark of a tree? If so, you have made your mark in the world – until the cement crumbles or the tree falls.

Any inscribing we do is temporary. What we write today, we may want to erase tomorrow. Some relationships last only as long as those involved can see benefit for themselves in the relationship and no demands are made.

Isaiah 49 talks about a far more lasting relationship between God and God's people. Picturesque language tells us that we are a part of God – inscribed "on the palms of [God's] hands." This description of a unique closeness follows a passage that acknowledges human joy, singing, suffering, and compassion. God's relationship with us encompasses all of life, the good as well as the not-so-good. That relationship is loving and strong and permanent, for we are written forever on the palms of God's hands!

Prayer: Loving God, help us to see that we are yours, this day and forever. Amen.

Thought for the Day
God's commitment to us is not a short-term romance.

(The Upper Room, August 13, 1995)

The Strike-Out King

II Corinthians 13:5-10

Examine yourselves, to see whether you are holding to your faith.
I Corinthians 13:5

The baseball game is in the bottom of the last inning. The bases are loaded, and there are two outs. League rules for children's teams state that all team members *have* to play. But one child has not yet played – one who usually strikes out. The coach puts in that player, who then drives in the winning run, and the team wins the championship. That's how we usually hear the story.

But suppose the young player strikes out and the team loses the game and the championship. Then there is the opportunity to put real love into action. Then the coaches, the players, and the parents have the true opportunity to support the mediocre player with a relationship that is faithful to real, honest-to-God, through-thick-and-thin love.

Most of us know more about striking-out than about being a hero. In today's Bible reading, even Paul states: "We may seem to have failed." But Paul also gives this great encouragement to each of us: "Do you not realize that Jesus Christ is in you?"

Prayer: Dear God, may we appreciate the fact that You care for us and love us in all situations. Thank You. Amen.

Thought for the Day
God loves us; nothing we do will change that fact.

(The Upper Room, September 17, 1984)

What's in a Name?

Acts 11:19-26

In Antioch the disciples were for the first time called Christians.

Acts 11:26

When our son was nine he was a member of a children's baseball team. One team practice was held at a neighborhood park named: Christian Reformed Park. When our son returned home after that practice, his mother asked him, "Where's your jacket?" He looked puzzled, and then said he must have left it in the park. We were hopeful, but doubtful it would be found.

To our inquiry he replied, "You won't have to worry about it; after all, it's in a *Christian* park!" We went to the park, but his jacket was gone. Though his name and address were clearly marked in it, the jacket was never returned. Apparently, the name of the park did not affect what went on there.

What does it mean to bear the name *Christian?* Do we act and react and think and speak in a manner that will bring honor to Christ's name?

According to today's scripture reading, Barnabas went to Antioch and saw that the believers there were faithful to the Lord Jesus. Then he "exhorted them all to remain faithful to the Lord with steadfast purpose."

We are not perfect, yet like the early believers we can live so that people will call us Christian, because we are like Christ.

Prayer: God, may our actions and words remind others of the Christ we love and serve. Amen.

Thought for the Day

What does it mean to bear the name *Christian?*

(The Upper Room, June 22, 1982)

You are More than a Number

How often have you had the feeling that in today's machine-business age you are just a number?

When you stop at the gas station you become credit card number 578 634 809 4. At the department store you are 538-8532-21. Or you are phone number 251-1632, area code 816; and you live at 10425 West 73rd Terrace, zip code 64570.

You are given a social security number; you must use checks with special bank identification numbers. Even at the worship hour you may become offering envelope number 135. I once forgot to put my given number on my monthly life insurance payment, and received the letter: "Would you please record 147983-20 on all your checks."

Have we become just numbers?

A Scripture passage found in the Psalms and repeated in the New Testament says: "What is man but thou art mindful of him? . . . thou hast made him little less than God . . . thou hast crowned him with glory and honor, putting everything in subjection under his feet." This description of humans says we are valuable creatures.

Surely we have learned that God does not consider us as numbers. However, the manner in which some of us mistreat our bodies betrays the fact that we are created by God.

You do not treat other persons as numbers, or do you? Have you been concerned about others this past week? Have you been "other directed?" Have you listened to others? Have you been concerned about the feelings of others? Or do you see others as nameless numbers?

What you see in humans shapes your attitude toward them. The degradation of humans begins in the mind. Some people may think that humans are numbers and that a person's labor is a commodity to be purchased in the open market at the lowest price. A man is a number on an identification tag, so that when he has been blown to bits the military record may be kept straight. A woman is often only an object of lust.

What is man? He is more than a number. He has been made by God to be little lower than the angels. So you may only be 506-41-4902 on an income-tax form, but to God you are priceless. Treat yourself as such. And may your relationship to other persons reflect an attitude that they also are "little less than God."

So may it be!

(World Call, December 1970)

Fifty Years of Singing

Psalm 71:17-24

Thought for today: "Happy are those who live in your house ever singing your praise." Psalm 84:4

For 50 years Russell Huff sang in the church choir. More than 2,000 times (not counting summers) he put on a robe, processed, sang and recessed. He sang after busy Saturdays. He sang when it was too hot and too cold in the sanctuary. He sang anthems old and new. He sang loud and softly. He sang for eleven choir directors. He sang with the organ, piano, other instruments, and he sang a cappella. He sang for half a century.

The Judeo-Christian faith is a singing faith. Songs of the faith have guided us through the good and the not-so-good times. Singing surrounds us in Advent and Lent and throughout all the year. Singing helps give meaning to belief. Singing helps to keep-us-going.

The writer of Psalm 71 remarks that God has been close from youth to old age. The writer has seen many troubles and calamities from the depths of the earth. Yet God brings comfort and is faithful.

The response to this reviving and rescuing is to shout for joy, and to sing praises to God. This, too, was the response of Russell, a life of singing for, and with, God.

Every time we worship – in a small chapel or large sanctuary; in a special season, or in ordinary times; we can participate in a singing faith. From "Jesus Love Me" to Handel's "Messiah" singers blend their voices in celebration and thanksgiving for a God of forgiveness, understanding and love.

Prayer: O God, with the Psalmist we "proclaim your wondrous deeds . . . from youth . . . even to old age and gray hairs." Amen.

For Reflection
If you hear the music, join the singing

Dressing Properly

Colossians 3:12-17

Thought for today: "Clothe yourselves with . . . kindness." Colossians 3:12

Some bumper stickers are humorous, some are humorless, some are crude, some puzzling, some selfish, some are helpful and thoughtful. I am at an intersection where the red light seems to be breaking a record for not changing. Of course I am in a hurry; yes I know I should have left sooner. Can I come up with a good excuse why I am late? Then, in the midst of my fretting and agitation I spot it. It is a bumper sticker that reads: "Today I will commit a random act of kindness — will you?"

That's my kind of bumper sticker. That's my kind or philosophy for living. The opportunities for putting kindness into action are endless.

Making a trip into Nebraska we stopped briefly to say "Hi" to a friend we had not seen in more than 30 years. In the conversation Carlyle mentioned: "I remember when we were together at a summer youth conference. I had recently undergone surgery, and you carried my suitcases for me." I would hardly consider that a major contribution to one's life, but to Carlyle it was a remembered random act of kindness.

In his letter to the Colossians, Paul recommends how Christians ought to dress: "Clothe yourselves with compassion, kindness, humility, meekness and patience." This dress can come in many styles – a phone call, a letter, a hug, a statement of support, a dozen home made cookies given, letting someone be in front of you in line, etc. and etc. Each one of us can be creative in performing random acts of kindness.

Prayer: O God, if it is more blessed to give than to receive, then keep us alert to recognize and act upon the daily opportunities to extend kindness. In giving we do receive; we receive insights for our very reason for being. Amen.

Through Bitter Tears to Joy

Luke 22:52-62

When Peter "went out and wept bitterly," he started on a new road of Christian discipleship. Through tears he began to put his life in proper perspective. After Easter Peter will understand there is a cost and a joy to discipleship. Where will it lead? What decisions will it demand? Only God knows the answer, only God knows the final outcome. But we know it will be a road of boundless mercy. Discipleship means joy.

Yes, Peter, weep for past mistakes, as indeed we all must. Then dry those tears, for God is always understanding and forgiving.

In 1980 Harold Hughes is in full time Christian service. That is a dramatic change, for in 1955 Hughes was a truck driver with an uncontrollable alcoholic problem. He abused his wife and was obnoxious to all. He reports that one night he had an intimate session with God, on his knees, next to the bathtub. Through tears he acknowledged his failure as a decent and caring person. He vowed to quit denying Jesus and to accept him as the inspiration of his life.

Years later Harold Hughes became Iowa Governor Hughes, then U.S. Senator Hughes, and now, servant Hughes.

"Jesus is the Christ, the son of the Living God," is a confession of faith not reserved only for Peter or Harold Hughes. Each of us makes it daily in our joy of living, even through tears.

Prayer: Spirit of the living God, fall afresh on me. Melt me, mold me, fill me, use me. Amen.

(Family Devotions, July 14, 1980

Stewards of the Message

Tender and compassionate God, whose strength is made perfect even in weakness, help us to believe that You receive us as we are. In our human journey, give us hope for what we can yet become. Help us, imperfect though we are, to be stewards of the message of Your love; like earthen vessels which carry treasures through Your loving grace. Amen.

(The Gifts We Bring, 1987)

Decisions, Decisions

Luke 23:13-25

At Passover time it was the custom of the governor to release a political prisoner. One such person was Barabbas, a robber and a murdered. Early manuscripts state that Barabbas and Christ had the same first name.

The crowd had to decide between the two. Jesus Barabbas appealed to the eye and ear, to hate and to force. Jesus the Christ appealed to the conscience and the spirit, to reconciliation and love. The same choice is always before us.

Luke says, "And their voice [the crowd] prevailed." The people were disappointed that Christ was not ruling like an earthly king. So the crowd prevailed. Any support for Christ would be like going to a home basketball game and cheering for the visiting team.

Is this the way we continue to make decisions today? Are we intimidated by the crowd? Where are the voices, the youth and adults, who will call out for our Lord?

Prayer: God, may I speak the supportive word for your son even in difficult moments; even when the crowd yells loudly: "Crucify!" Amen.

(Family Devotions, July 17, 1980)

Remembered into Paradise

Luke 23:32-43

Our Scripture readings for the past few days have been very "heavy." They can create a sullen mood. Maybe they are okay for Holy Week, but it's the middle of July, when we are enjoying vacation, swimming, and picnics. Yet we must be reminded of the real and awful events of the passion of our Lord.

Jesus did not die alone. There were three crosses that day at Golgotha, two were reserved for criminals. One criminal was sarcastic to the end. But he was rebuked by the other, who admitted his flaws and then asked Jesus to "Remember me when you come into your kingly power."

That second criminal gives us some very meaty food for thought. If a criminal, during the agony of dying, can see God's son in the flogged, bleeding body of the one dying next to him – then we can.

And, what of Christ's response: "Today you will be with me in paradise." Is that simply a one-time comment for one person, or is it to be applied to all who ask to be remembered. For Christ also said: "Well done, good and faithful servant; . . . enter into the joys of your master." (Matthew 25:21)

Joy and paradise may wait for those who believe.

Prayer: O Christ of all times, remember me. Amen.

(Family Devotions, July 19, 1980)

A Gift of Love

Isaiah 58:6-12

Thought for today: Take my blood, and let it be
A gift of love, to you from me.

At least six times a year we gather in a church fellowship hall. We are farmers and carpenters, teachers and innkeepers and clergy. We are female and male. Some of us are retired, some just beginning careers, some are in-between. Four Amish farmers are always there. I once counted persons from eleven different churches. We cover the spectrum of religious and political beliefs. We participate in a breaking-of-bread of sorts; as we eat sandwiches, cookies, and juice. What draws us together, like a congregation, is our common mission: we are all blood donors. I believe most of us feel this is a silent act of love.

The Bible is full of stories relating tales of shedding innocent blood. Against this, Isaiah calls for a caring ministry: "Offer your food to the hungry and satisfy the needs of the afflicted" (Isaiah 58:10). That is in effect what blood donors are doing: fulfilling Isaiah's call to share and satisfy.

Blood is the gift of life.

Prayer: O God, we are thankful for those who give blood. We are thankful for all gifts: hugs, words, time, and prayers. Amen.

(The Secret Place, February 22, 1996)

A Community Sympathy Card

Galatians 6:2-10

Thought for today: Let each of you look not to your own interests, but to the interests of others. Philippians 2:4

As I was paying for a gallon of milk at the Dutchman's Grocery in a small neighboring community, I noticed a woman signing something on the counter. When I asked what it was, the clerk said that there had been a death in the town, and this was a sympathy card to the family.

I was impressed. The only grocery store in this small Iowa town was enabling the whole town to be a caring community for that family. Denominational and ethnic ties did not matter; what counted was a shared concern.

Paul calls on both the Galatians and the Philippians to bear one another's burdens, to do good to all, and to look to the interests of others. May we continue that tradition, wherever we live.

Prayer: O God, help me to treat everyone in my community as neighbors who both need and give your love. Amen.

(The Secret Place, January 29, 1993)

Body Broken, Spirit Okay

II Corinthians 1:3-7

Thought for today: Suffering produces endurance, and endurance produces character, and character produces hope. Romans 5:3b-4

As I walked into the hospital, I searched for what I could say to Margaret. She had fallen on the ice and broken some bones. This eighty-year-old widow had already experienced too much suffering.

When I walked into her room, I was greeted with a cheerful smile. Instructing me to pull up a chair next to her bed, she said, "Good to see you, my friend. Let me share my good news. I've broken my elbow, but I'm thankful for two things. First, it's an elbow and not a hip. Second, it's my left elbow, and I'm right-handed." Margaret had learned to turn adversity into blessing and to be grateful.

Paul, writing a follow-up letter to the Corinthians, boldly stated that God "consoles us in all our affliction, so that we may be able to console those who are in any affliction" (II Corinthians 1:4). Margaret's body was broken, Paul's body was beaten, yet their spirits were strong. What fine examples to follow!

Prayer: God, as you were always with Jesus of Nazareth, so you are always with us – in the hospital, in jail, at the cemetery. Thank you for your gift of presence. Amen.

(The Secret Place, July 4, 1999)

When Sirens Call

Ephesians 4:25-32

Thought for today: "Remind them . . . , to avoid quarreling, to be gentle, and to show every courtesy to everyone." Titus 3:1-2

The children were seated on the chancel steps ready for "their time" in worship. This Sundays' leader shared that her family had long practiced the habit – whenever they heard a siren – they always stopped whatever they were doing, and prayed. They prayed for ambulance drivers and those who were ill; for victims of accidents and fires; for police and firefighters.

The children listened intently while the woman said: "A few years ago my high school daughter and I were driving to a neighboring city while having a heated argument. The conversation was intense; the mood was one of anger."

She continued: "As we were quarreling we heard a siren. I was speaking harshly, when my daughter said: 'Mom, a siren, we need to pray.' I pulled over to the side of the road, we prayed, we hugged, and we cried. The siren had called us back into a meaningful relationship."

In Ephesians Paul gives a number of insightful guidelines: ". . . do not let the sun go down on your anger." (26b). "May your words give grace to those who hear." (29b). ". . . and be kind to one another." (32a)

Prayer: Amen.

(The Secret Place, November 14, 2000)

Differences Demolished

Ruth 1:8-18

Thought for today: There is no longer Jew or Greek, there is no longer slave or free, there is no longer male and female; for all of you are one in Christ Jesus.
Galatians 3:26

The television news story happed years ago, yet it remains vivid in my mind. We were taken inside a blacksmith shop. The reporter interviewed the smith, a German-born Jew who had escaped during World War II and resettled in Chicago. He was a senior citizen, single, and had no living relatives.

We were then introduced to two African American men in their twenties. The older one had been with the smith for six years, the other for four. Both men came from difficult backgrounds: crime, drugs, violence, and broken families. The smith had been the major factor in a positive change in their lifestyles, and he had taught them the craft of blacksmithing. The final revelation was that the smith had willed his entire business to these two – the sons he never had.

The Hebrew Bible story of Ruth and Naomi is a tale of human love that transcends our ethnic differences. Ruth was a Moabite who had married a Hebrew. Although he died, she chose to go with her Hebrew mother-in-law, Naomi, back to Naomi's people.

Such are stories of human kindness that know no boundary of time or place. Do you have a story to tell as well?

Prayer: O God, you set before us many stories of your continuing love in creation. Help us to appreciate them – and to live them. Amen.

(The Secret Place, September 5, 1998)

"My, that was refreshing!"

Luke 22:14-23

Thought for today: "Sir, give me this water, . . ." John 4:15

Family and friends were gathered for a memorial service for our younger brother. At the age of forty-eight, Jim had met a tragic death. After brothers Staley and Stewart had shared insightful reflections about Jim, I told this story: When Jim was young, he sat with Mom and Dad at the front of the sanctuary. Jim usually felt free to express himself. When the offering was received, for instance, he would dive-bomb his coins into the plate. When Jim was old enough to receive Communion, he once drank from the cup, beat on his chest, and said, "My, that was refreshing!" That's when the three of them began sitting in a back pew!

In response to my story, our mother, who had had a stroke several years earlier, quietly but clearly mused, "Yes, that did happen. And yes, Jesus is refreshing. He refreshes us to go into the world and help others. He is to be taken internally. He is inside us as we live for others." The moment was electrifying.

Luke reports Jesus as saying, "I have eagerly desired to eat this Passover with you" (Luke 22:15). "This is my body, which is given for you" (22:19). Every time we participate in the Lord's Supper, we are refreshed.

Prayer: Loving God, you have refreshed us with the gift of Jesus. In response, we will serve you. Amen.

(The Secret Place, November 6, 1998)

Raised in the Church

Psalm 71:17-19

Thought for today: Let no one despise your youth. I Timothy 4:12

I am a product of the church, and I thank God for the many persons who accepted me as a youth. As a young boy I had a tweed suit that scratched something awful. To make it bearable during worship, under the pants I wore pajamas. All was okay until one Sunday when my pj's showed below my cuffs. Yet no one made fun of me.

When I was in the junior high youth group, our leaders (Ralph and Mary Virginia Edwards) treated us to a meal. I ate seven hot dogs; yet they said nothing as I "pigged-out." As a teen I was given a set of offering envelopes. My giving amounted to only twenty-five cents a month. Yet at the end of each quarter, there was a written note on my financial statement from Belle McKim: "Thank you, Bill, for your support." As a college sophomore I gave my first sermon, which lasted all of seven minutes; still, there came approval.

Today I am a pastor, mainly because of those of my home church (Tabernacle Christian of Lincoln, Nebraska) who nurtured and loved me from my youth.

Prayer: O God, let us never despise our youth. Let us share our faith so that together we may all grow. Amen.

(The Secret Place, September 13, 1989)

Kindness Begins Early

Zechariah 7:8-14

Thought for today: A lovely deed was in my heart/ I never set it free;/ it died from lack of exercise/ And made its tomb in me.

Our daughter, Stephanie, was in the second grade when the incident happened. Her mother and I learned about it only because Stephanie's teacher told us at a parents' conference.

One day after school, Stephanie and a group of students were walking home. The group began to make snide remarks about Bob, who was overweight. By the time they reached our home, Bob was in tears because of the unkind comments. As he headed for his home, Stephanie said: " I'm sorry they called you 'fat.' I'll be your friend." Bob's parents were so grateful and impressed by this kindness that they told the teacher, who relayed the event to us.

The prophet Zechariah points the way: "Show kindness and mercy" (7:9). It is hoped children will catch his vision and practice kindness throughout their lives. Can we help by our examples?

Prayer: Dear God, what deeds of kindness can I exercise today, and every day, for your sake and mine? Keep me active. Amen.

(The Secret Place, March 8, 1990)

Letter Writing is Ministry

III John

Thought for today: Our lives are shaped by those who love us and those who refuse to love us.

We were greeting friends at the reception following a special worship service. It was our first visit back to the old church since leaving the area many years before. Lee approached me and warmly said, "You'll never know how much your letter meant to Arkie when Edna died. It really helped." Afterward I admitted to myself that I had forgotten about my letter of support at the time of Edna's death seven years previous.

Letter writing is a great New Testament tradition that needs to be continued in our day. In his third letter John writes to Gaius, "I pray that all may go well with you. . . . I know that it is well with your soul. . . . Peace be to you."

Prayer: God, as I write letters of support, may your Spirit guide my hand and shape my words with care and love. Amen.

(The Secret Place, January 8, 1985)

The Right Light

Luke 24:1-9

Thought for today: We can appreciate the miracle of a sunrise only if we have waited in darkness.

I'm a person who likes neither flowers nor funerals. If I were to bring my wife some flowers, it would be a dead giveaway that something was very wrong.

In a two-week period I presided over five funerals, the last held in the sanctuary on the Saturday before Easter. At about 5:30 on that afternoon I received a phone call: "Would you please see if we closed the windows in the parlor?"

Coming back from the parlor, I glanced into the sanctuary and noticed the "left-over" funeral flowers mixed with new ones ready for Easter worship. They were gorgeous! The late afternoon sunlight was just at the right angle coming through our stained-glass windows, making the flowers sparkle. I said to myself, "You just have to see things in the right light – the light created and recreated by God."

Prayer: God, deliver us from our dead selves and feeble faith, and help us to see life in the light of Christ's ongoing life. Amen.

(The Secret Place, October 30, 1985)

On Love and Friendship
John 15:12-17

Thought for today: No love or friendship can cross our path without forever affecting us in some way.

The adult church school class was discussing the qualities that bind persons to- gether. With some emotion Mary said of her husband, Bryan, "He not only loves me, but he is my very good friend." Her face was flushed as she surprised herself and others with her unrehearsed words about Bryan.

Jesus saw his disciples as friends, not servants. They had grown in love. Love and friendship are two sides of the same coin. We need to accept friendship; we need to be a friend. Being a friend is one of the best gifts that life can bring to an individual.

Lovers may be good friends, and friendship may bring people closer than kinship. God is the cement in this kind of relationship, which results in the activity where, "friends always show their love" (Proverbs 17:17, *Good News Bible*).

Prayer: God, I thank you for friends I can love and help, and for the friends that can love and help me. Amen.

(The Secret Place, March 12, 1986)

The Days of Weeping Are Past
Genesis 49:33—50:14

Thought for today: The bird of sorrow may fly close, but it need not build a nest.

Jacob died and his son Joseph mourned. There was weeping for the fifty days required for embalming, and then there was weeping for seventy days. Then the writer of Genesis states, " . . . the days of weeping for him were past . . ." (50:4). Not quite. Joseph took his father's body to Atad in Canaan, and there was sorrowful lamentation and mourning for seven more days.

We all have had or will have days of sorrow, depression, and separation; these type of days are a part of every person's journey through life. "If only we had not moved;" "If only my spouse had stayed with me;" "If only they had discovered that medicine sooner," are comments often made by those experiencing sorrow. No one is denying the need to mourn. However, you do not need to live in sorrow for the rest of your life. It's one thing to be nostalgic and recall the past – even unpleasant events – but you need not pitch your tent among the sorrowful ruins. There is a time to let go. The days of weeping are past.

Prayer: God, there is a time to weep and a time to laugh. Help me in organizing my time so I expend more of my time laughing. Amen.

(The Secret Place, June 30, 1986 – also
Devotions Day by Day, 1988)

We Declare in Our Day

Isaiah 43:16-21

For many centuries women kept silent in worship and sat in "reserved" sections. But (thank God) in our day women are declaring the same thing Second Isaiah declared: "Remember not the former things, . . . Behold, I am doing a new thing."

Eunice Miller is a woman who was an active member of our congregation for many years. When our church celebrated its centennial in 1975, we published our history. One section contained "Letters of Appreciation." Eunice's letter was a declaration:

"It has been 10 years since I chose Downey as my church home. Through the years the church has given me many opportunities to serve my Lord through service to others. I have enjoyed serving as a Sunday school teacher, a worship committee member, a helper in the summer program, a member of CWF, a deacon and presently as an elder. Through the love and concern of my fellow Christians at Downey, my life has been enriched. My faith has grown to the point that I have been able to face my loneliness and problems."

For Second Isaiah, Israel is the praising and worshiping community. Today we are that community. Declare it!

The greatest days for the church are in the future.

(Christian Church Worship Bulletin Service, March 20, 1983)

"I Go, Sir"

Matthew 21:23-32

Charlotte (that's not her real name) was a warm, supportive leader in the church. She was kind and gracious and loving. I was her pastor and a bit stunned when she shared her earlier years saying, "At one time I was the town's bad girl." She revealed that she had lived on the wrong side of the tracks, both literally and spiritually. But in her early twenties she became deeply involved in the life and work of the church. She changed her lifestyle and continues to live within a religious journey – even among many who can recall the days when she was "not-too-nice."

I never asked Charlotte if she identified with the tax collectors and harlots that Jesus speaks about in Matthew. There, the one son said: "I go, sir," but he did not go. What Jesus wanted was repentance and actual obedience, not lip service. What counts with God is actual righteous conduct; and yes, even those who do not know they are working for God will be rewarded.

The Matthew account is not for the past but for the present. We fall victim to thinking we will do something about change – tomorrow. Why is it that we are not greatly ashamed to sin, but are greatly ashamed to confess our sin?

The story holds promise: we need not be slaves to an unfortunate past. It is not too late for us! It is never too late to start over.

Prayer: God, be with us in our comings and goings and push us in new directions. Amen.

(Family Devotions, July 12, 1980)

The Power of God
Luke 22:63-71

One summer Saturday I was pulling crabgrass from our front yard. Between pulls I noticed that Russell (a neighborhood boy, eight years old) was bullying another boy about five inches shorter and twenty pounds lighter. Russell finally hit the smaller boy, but the younger child returned the blow. Surprised, Russell began to cry and returned to his house.

Russell's father then appeared and asked him why he was crying. Russell told his father that the other boy had hit him, hearing this the father yelled: "Well, hit him back a good one!"

What a contrast with the way Jesus lived! Today's Scripture reports that the men who held Jesus mocked, beat, blind-folded, and reviled him. Might not an all-powerful God intercede and pay back those who struck his son? But that is not the way God acts; nor did his son act; nor should we act.

Jesus speaks of power; a power that breaks the bonds of death; a power that ultimately causes love to win over hate and peace to win over war.

If we are parents or grandparents or friends or neighbors, we need to tell the Russell's of the world (and their dads) that power is not hitting and hurting, but real power is acknowledging Jesus as the Son of God, and living within that knowledge.

Prayer: God, I hope I never inflict pain on any person. Help me to live by your loving power, seen in Jesus of Nazareth. Amen.

(Family Devotions, July 15, 1980)

One Simon of Cyrene
Luke 23:26-31

Roman law required the condemned to carry his crossbeam to the place of crucifixion. There was nothing romantic about it. The weight must have been unbearable on the back of one recently flogged.

At one point along the way to Golgotha, Jesus either fell or became so weak that he could not carry the crossbeam. So, "They seized one Simon of Cyrene, and laid on him the cross."

Simon met Jesus at the Cross. This is where we will meet him in our journey to find God! Simon might have felt strong resentment at this strange twist of events. He just happened to be in this place at this time. One moment he is standing at the edge watching; then he is a character in the drama.

Simon of Cyrene carried the crossbeam of Christ. That beam could be carried only once. However, we can act on the words of Jesus: "Whoever does not bear their cross and come after me, cannot be my disciple." (Luke 14:27)

There may be only two directions open to us – to crucify Jesus, by ignoring his teachings; or to carry his cross by following him into discipleship. Carry or crucify?

Prayer: "Must Jesus bear the cross alone, and all the world go free? No, there's a cross for every one, and there's a cross for me." Amen.

(Family Devotions, July 18, 1980)

Walk Across My Swimming Pool
Luke 23:1-12

Herod and Pilate are treating Jesus like a political hot potato. Luke says "When Herod saw Jesus, he was very glad." However his happy mood was brief for later "Herod treated Jesus with contempt."

Webber and Rice in their rock opera, *Jesus Christ Superstar,* use this passage for their "King Herod's Song." Herod sings:

> Prove to me that you're divine
> change my water into wine.
> Prove to me that you're no fool
> walk across my swimming pool.
> Feed my household with this bread
> you can do it on your head.

Herod missed the point, as did Pilate, as did most of those in Jesus' day not to mention our day. People are always looking for a cheap trick, a meaningless miracle. And please do one now, for our entertainment.

That is not how God acts. God did not call Jesus his son as one who would simply amuse us. God comes into human lives so we might have life and have it more abundantly. Others can act in the sideshows.

Another view of this scene is the hymn of Martin Luther: "A Mighty Fortress Is Our God."

> And though this world, with devils filled
> should threaten to undo us,
> We will not fear, for God hath willed
> His truth to triumph through us.

Pilate and Herod acted like devils. Yet the final triumph would soon be coming – and in all places – from the borrowed tomb of Joseph of Arimathea. God always has the final world.

Prayer: God of mercy and love, at times our spirits are cluttered and sadly neglected. They are so crowded with "necessary" items that many times there is little room for You. The living rooms of our souls are messed with the debris of self-indulgence. Our efforts seem to go toward the satisfaction of self.

God of mercy and love, we confess that when we have what we wanted, then we do not really want what we have. Speak to us concerning the losing of life, the giving of life, the using of life. Then by Your mercy guide us on our journey that we may be found faithful in all of our living. Amen.

(Family Devotions, July 16, 1980)

Your Name in Scripture

Matthew 28:16-20

David and Mary Luo are Disciples of Christ missionaries serving in Thailand. Prior to their commissioning service, they were asked to share some of their motives as to why they wanted to be missionaries. David Luo responded strongly, "One reason was that one day, while reading the Bible, I found my name in Scripture." He was very serious, and went on to say, "Reading the final sentence of the gospel according to Matthew, I found my name." The words from that closing sentence of the 28th chapter are, ". . . and *lo*, I am with you always, . . ."

Years after this incident I talked with a close friend of the Luos, and the friend stated, "Yes, that is a true story. David felt a personal call to participate in Christ's great commission to 'Go therefore and make disciples of all nations.'"

Yet each of us can also participate in the Christian missionary movement. For today's passage says ". . . and lo, I am with *you* always, . . ." That pronoun *you* stands for every Muriel, Don, Velma and John who believe in and support the Christian faith.

Go, therefore, by sending your dollars to places where you may never be able literally to go. Go, therefore, by sending your prayers to those in need. Go, therefore, by acting out the role of a disciple wherever you live. Go, therefore, by being a loving Christian servant, strengthened by God's love.

Prayer: "Go, make of all disciples," we at thy feet would stay. Until each life's vocation, accents thy holy way. Amen.

(Family Devotions, April 23, 1981)

Looking Out the Wrong Window

Luke 24:1-12

An older woman recalled an incident from her early childhood. Her family had a favorite dog that was closest to her older brother, then about twelve. The dog died, and the woman remembers watching out a back window as her father and brother dug a hole to bury the dog. In great sorrow she recalls the scene of her bereaved brother digging a small grave.

Some years before this event, the girl had planted a small tree in the front yard, and it was just starting to leaf. Her grandfather lived with the family, and he was observing the sorrow of his granddaughter as she stood at the back window. He called to her and asked her to come and look out the front window at the new green leaves on the budding tree. Then he lovingly said to her: "You're just looking out the wrong window."

That may be another way of saying, "Why do you seek the living among the dead?" As a pastor I frequently use this prayer at the grave as we conclude the committal service. – Almighty God, grant as we come here that the voice eternal which spoke long ago, may also speak to us at this moment: "He whom you seek is not here; he is risen and goes before you."

Prayer: "No more we doubt thee, Glorious Prince of life! Life is naught without thee; aid us in our strife." Amen.

(Family Devotions, April 24, 1981)

Raising Sounds of Joy

I Chronicles 15:16-28

Thought for today: Joy can be expressed at any time, at any place, by anyone who has hope and understanding.

I was on my way to the intensive care unit to visit when I happened to enter a lobby where a volunteer was playing a "mean" grand piano. That instrument was making sounds of joy! I stopped for a few minutes and soaked up the happy atmosphere. After my visit I returned by the same route. Now there was a vocalist and pianist giving a miniconcert of Broadway tunes mixed with operatic selections.

As I leaned against the wall and listened for about fifteen minutes, I observed the comings and goings of many – nurses, physicians, custodians, and patients. Some were in their pajamas; some were in wheelchairs; some used crutches. Their faces pictured both hope and anxiety. Many passed through quickly, while others stayed and allowed the music to capture and claim them.

In I Chronicles the writer states that David appointed the singers to play musical instruments. Their purpose was to "raise loud sounds of joy" as they carried the Ark of the Covenant. We, too, can raise sounds of joy wherever we are. The Hebrews experienced joy as they entered the City of David. For me, it was music in the midst of medicine. Where will it be for you?

Prayer: Joyful God, make us music makers today. May our sounds be raised with joy. Amen.

(The Secret Place, January 15, 1997)

At Any Age

Psalm 71:9-19

Thought for today: And I thought the dead, who have already died, more fortunate than the living. Ecclesiastes 4:2

We were on the Gettysburg, Pennsylvania, battlefield for the first time. Through the various presentations and extensive displays, we were reliving that defining four-day Civil War battle.

It also happened to be my sixtieth birthday. In jest (and some seriousness) I was moaning to my wife, that her old-man husband was entering his seventh decade. I was listing the things I could no longer do because of my senior years. Sheral responded by pointing out that almost all of those who died at Gettysburg never saw their sixtieth birthday. Her insight put my age into the proper perspective.

In Psalm 71:9 the writer asks God to "not cast me off in the time of old age; do not forsake me when my strength is spent." Later he pleads, "Even to old age and gray hairs, O God, do not forsake me" (18a). The reason for not becoming forsaken is the writers' conclusion: "Until I proclaim your might" (18b). That challenge is also for me; and you.

Prayer: God of all times, regardless of our age, we proclaim your might, as long as we live. Amen.

(The Secret Place, September 12, 1997)

Each of us is a Seeker

We live in an Inn, built in 1846 by Mormon craftsmen who stopped to work here one year before continuing their famous trek to Utah. Those travelers had been forced to leave their community of Nauvoo, Illinois. They had created some of the problems that caused them to "move-on." Still they traveled in hope. Some rode horses or in wagons, some walked, some pulled hand carts. It was a 2,400 mile trip. Many sang hymns as they trekked. Most of them made it to their "Promised" land. Many died along the way, and are buried in Iowa, Nebraska and Wyoming.

Recently, the Mormon Tabernacle Choir made their first-ever appearance at Nauvoo, and our family attended their performance. One selection was their theme-hymn: "Come, Come Ye Saints," which was written in Wayne County. It was in Southern Iowa where many of those pilgrims died. They were buried by the hundreds in unmarked graves.

At that concert the choir sang these words as a tribute to their sisters and brothers: ". . . and should we die before our journey's end, safely rest, all is well." I do not buy into most elements of the Mormon beliefs; yet those words from that hymn form a faith to live by. We, too, can embrace a belief that at the start, middle and end of our journey: "All is well," for God is our guide.

In the form of a pillar of fire by night, and a pillar of smoke by day, God was with the children of Israel as they trekked in their Exodus experience.

God was with Martin Luther King Jr. as he – with many others – trekked the streets of America. God is our guide as we journey through life.

Might this be our prayer: Loving God, we are both saints and sinners; but we all are seekers. Be with us in our travels. Amen.

(The Ottumwa Courier, July 1, 1995)

Hands are for Holding

Psalm 63:1-8

I am the Lord, I have called you in righteousness. I have taken you by the hand and kept you. – Isaiah 42:6a (NRSV)

One of our families had come from Massachusetts to Iowa for a visit. There was not much to do in our rural county. The males decided to take-in the county seat 4th of July fireworks display.

So Bill III, Bill IV, and Bill V (who we call Will) took folding chairs and went to town. Following an hour of stars, sparklers, sirens and screams we three headed for home. As we walked along the way, Will (age 7) came beside me, took hold of my hand, and for a few minutes we walked silently to our car.

Why he wanted to hold my hand, he did not say. Was he tired? Did it seem too dark? Did I, his grandpa seem to need support? I do not know. I do know his touch was deeply meaningful to me.

When he was in the wilderness of Judah, the Psalmist states that God's love is "better than life" and that "your right hand upholds me."

We humans can do many things with our hands: hit, hurt, harm; but we can also help, heal and hold. The response of the Psalmist to God's power and glory is: "I will lift up my hands and call on your name," with songs of joy. May it be so with us.

Prayer: Use even my hands, O God, to pass your peace of hope and understanding in all who stand in need. Amen.

Thought for the Day

May my mouth praise God, may my hands uphold those who stumble, so they do not fall.

Prayer focus: Persons who need a hug.

(The Upper Room, July 4, 2003)

The Perfect Kinship

Isaiah 41:6-10

Some friends play at friendship but a true friend sticks closer than one's nearest kin. Proverbs 18:24

In an Indianapolis hospital, a social worker was visiting 93-year-old Frank, who was about to be dismissed. Frank was anxious to get home, and the social worker asked him why. He explained that he wanted to get back to Ralph, who is 78 and lives on the same block with him.

Frank and Ralph are both widowers. Ralph enjoyed cooking for Frank and made him a special meal once a week. Frank had wanted to do something in return, and he asked Ralph how he could express his gratitude. Finally, Ralph had said, "Yes, Frank, you might be able to help me. I cannot read, and I would like to learn." So they began reading lessons for Ralph. Now Frank wanted to get home so the lessons could continue.

Proverbs talks about the nature of friendship and how closely true friends are joined. Isaiah reminds us of an even more enduring and powerful friendship, God's friendship. God says, "I will uphold you with my victorious right hand" (Isaiah 41:10).

Our best friendships can be reminders of the wonderful friendship that God offers to each of us.

Thought for the Day
Friendship lubricates the rough edges of life.

(The Upper Room, June 5, 1998)

With Harmonica and Piano

Psalm 150

Thought for today: Let everything that breathes praise the Lord! Psalm 150:6a

There was no reference to "special music" in the worship bulletin. It was my final Sunday as interim pastor; and two "saints" in the congregation had prepared a surprise duet. Both women were past the age of 70 and both had been loving, faithful, servants of the church for decades.

Martha stepped to the piano and Evelyn stood next to it, harmonica in hand. Harmonica? In my 63 years, I had never heard, nor heard of, a harmonica played in worship.

Their presentation was marvelous! I might not have picked their selection: "Love Lifted Me." That hymn begins with the words: "I was sinking deep in sin." I remember as a teenager our youth group had sung those words; then, we added our own, not-so-reverent, exclamation – "Whee!"

Thus reflecting, sitting only a few feet from the duo, I startled myself with tears of laughter, fulfillment, farewell and praise.

The Psalmist wanted everything to be used to praise the Lord: trumpet, lute, harp, tambourine, dance, strings, pipes and cymbals.

I would add: harmonica and piano.

Prayer: Praise the Lord. Amen.

(The Secret Place, October 14, 2000)

Wisdom Leads to Understanding

Proverbs 3:13-18

A devastating fire wiped out all earthly belongings of Reuel Howe's family when he was a boy. He and his father returned to the charred remains, to find his mother had arranged a meager lunch on a log in the middle of which she had set a rusty tin can filled with wild flowers. In the midst of sadness and loss, joy can be found. Reflecting on the wisdom of his mother Howe asked, "Do you have any wild flowers in a rusty tin can close to *your* smoking ruins?"

My own mother's wisdom and grace were evident at my 7th birthday party. A neighborhood boy gave me a small red rubber ball that probably cost about five cents. I made fun of the seemingly insignificant gift, in front of the giver. Following the party mother and I had "a little session" where she shared the background of the boy's family – that he gave what he could. More wisdom gathered about neighbors and relationships and values and feelings.

The profit gained from wisdom is better than that gained from silver. Wisdom is the source of life and happiness. The person who has found wisdom and gained understanding is happy because that person has found the insight into life that is above everything else.

Wisdom is to know that love is the biggest word in the Bible no matter how many words are longer.

(Christian Church Worship Bulletin Service, October 24, 1982)

"Do You Want to Be Healed?"

John 5:2-9

Thought for today: Even in pain or difficulty we may be content to stay in our ruts. Do we want to be made whole?

The man in this Gospel story had been ill for thirty-eight years; closer to death than life, resigned to the role of victim. However, we were not brought into this world to be victims. He didn't need the water from the pool. Indeed, he never got into the water. He needed the presence of Christ and a change in attitude.

Choosing life means engagement and commitment. The difference between existing and living is one step. The man didn't negate his pain and suffering, but he did pick up his bed and take a step. He didn't walk the whole distance at first, but he did begin to move in the right direction.

Looking to Christ, we find we can do what we before failed to do alone. We can be what we could never be. We can master what had baffled us. Encouraged by Christ, we move to what seemed impossible.

Prayer: To encounter the God who is in Jesus is to know that whatever the world has given to us, we can be more than victims. Amen.

(The Secret Place, October 4, 1986)

Floundering, Fishing, and Following

John 21:1-19

Thought for today: Followers of Jesus feed sheep in his name

As a disciple of Jesus, how would you have felt following his death if you did not yet know of his resurrection? You spent three years in comradeship. Then you went through the final days filled with confusion, questions, the trial, the crucifixion, and Jesus' death.

Now you are floundering – sleep is difficult; food tasteless. There is no purpose to your being. Finally you fill the void by responding to Peter's "I am going fishing," with, " I will go with you."

Then it happened. "Just as day was breaking, Jesus stood on the beach" (John 21:4). Then the responses: The insight of John: "It is the Lord" (21:7). The action of Peter: "[He] sprang into the sea" (21:7). The faithfulness of the others: "dragging the net full of fish" (21:8).

How many times will we be floundering and fishing to eventually understand the presence of Jesus on the beach of our lives?

When it was least expected there was a reunion/communion time. Jesus said: "Come and have breakfast," (21:12) and concluded the event with the call for continued discipleship, "Follow me" (21:19).

Prayer: God, the next time I am floundering, may I read John 21 and understand it was written for me. Amen.

(The Secret Place, November 20, 1986)

That Old Auburn Car

I Timothy 5:1-8

Thought for today: Do not rebuke an older man but exhort him as you would a father. I Timothy 5:1

My grandparents were lovely persons. One thing I learned from them, and other older people, is that they are often lonely and that they need to share their past with others. My grandmother, Juda I. McDermet, and Elmer Yates, my father-in-law, lived in the same community years ago. After she moved to a new location, Elmer visited her once or twice a year. At every visit my grandmother would retell how Elmer helped push her old Auburn car out of the mud. She repeated the story often as if it were a fresh experience.

What a valuable service Elmer rendered by sharing the experience with her. He himself was enriched by the sharing. We all need to accept older people where they are, for what they are, and can yet be. Contemplate the thought of Robert Browning:

> Grow old along with me!
> The best is yet to be,
> The last of life,
>   for which the first was made:
> Our times are in his hand
> Who saith, "A whole I planned,
> Youth shows but half; trust God:
>   see all, nor be afraid!"

Prayer: God, as you love people, may we also be in love with persons. When we share with others, we too are blessed. May we help to enrich their lives. We thank you for the gift of life. Amen.

(The Secret Place, June 11, 1968)

A Labor of Love

II Thessalonians 3:6-13

"Brothers and sisters, do not be weary in doing what is right."
II Thessalonians 3:13

I was in the church sanctuary becoming acquainted with the meaningful symbolism. The chancel area had been tastefully refurbished while retaining the older colorful stained glass windows.

At the bottom of each window were the words: "Given in memory/honor of" then a name. I inquired about each name and the reason they were honored. When I asked, "Who was Muriel Conroy?" I was told to see Luzon who was considered to be the church historian.

Visiting Luzon I asked about Muriel. Luzon said Muriel was the church custodian for thirty years during the first part of the century. She kept the building spotless and was always cheerful – even when church members tracked mud into the building. To honor her labor of love, a window in her name, was placed in the sanctuary.

In his second letter to the church at Thessalonica, Paul challenges them, "we were not idle" (v7) and "we . . . give you an example to imitate." (v9)

Muriel was an example of what Paul wanted: one not living in idleness, but quietly working for the Lord. Who are the Muriel's of our times? Can you be one?

Prayer: Use our hands, heads and hearts O God, as we grow faithfully in working for and serving you. Amen.

Thought for the Day
What have I done lately to honor God?
What can I do to do so this week?

Prayer Focus: That I may be a cheerful willing worker for God.

September 11

Romans 14:5-9

Thought for today: "For everything there is a season . . . a time to be born, and a time to die." Ecclesiastes 3:1-2a

September 11, 2001, was the day the twin-towers were destroyed.

For me, September 11, has a special meaning. For on September 11, 1910 my father was born. William Wallace McDermet II ("Mac" to mother and his friends,) was born at Hope, Kansas. What a marvelous name for a birthplace!

Mac was a social worker. He worked at the county, state and federal levels to help eliminate suffering. He remarked: "For some individuals the only friend they have is their case worker." He did not use religious jargon to define the role of social workers; yet he captured the heart of the Gospel – caring for others. So, September 11 has significance for me; yet it is a time for grieving for those who died on this day.

Today's scripture from Paul's letter to the congregation at Rome is both haunting and helpful within the context of September 11, 2001. Paul notes: "Some judge one day to be better than another, while others judge all days to be alike." Indeed as we reflect on September 11, 2001 we would of course say that September 10 and 12 were the better days. Paul then challenges the reader: "Those who observe the day, observe it in honor of the Lord."

A passage from the Hebrew Bible also helps us on this day. "Do not fret because of evildoers. Do not envy the wicked; for the evil have no future; the lamp of the wicked will go out." (Proverbs 24:19-20)

Assurance comes from Paul in the Romans reading: "Whether we live or whether we die, we are the Lord's." Yes.

Prayer: O God, it is very difficult to even attempt to find any meaning in days of anguish. Yet help us to regard every defeat as an opportunity; an opportunity to love more and hate less. We do not know what a day may bring, but we live in hope, a hope that acknowledges that you are our God, and we are your people. Amen.

A Meaningful Meal

John 20:24-29

Thomas, . . . said to his fellow disciples, "Let us go, that we may die with him." John 11:16

Meal times are special times. Family members, who may be going in many different directions, are often able to be together at least for the evening meal. Meals become very special during holiday seasons, reunions, birthdays and summer picnics.

Jesus was always the gracious host for meals. No one was ever excluded: "sinners" of all kinds, tax-collectors, prostitutes; all were warmly welcomed to break bread together.

Our congregation was planning their Maundy Thursday communion service. The event would be a "Living Lord's Supper" styled after Leonardo daVinci's "Last Supper." Twelve men were needed, would I be a disciple? I agreed to be Thomas, knows as the "doubting" follower. I even grew a scraggly beard for the event.

Thomas (the twin) was an intriguing individual. He was courageous: "Let us go, that we may die with him" when Jesus set his face toward possible stoning. He was skeptical: "Unless I . . . put my hand in his side, I will not believe." (20:25)

Thomas, the at-times-doubter, may have taken the gospel message to India; and he may have written the Gospel of Thomas, a collection of 114 sayings of Jesus. On that special evening he took his place at the Passover table.

I thought about Thomas as I took my place at the table. Indeed, we all have a place at the Lord's Table.

Prayer: Thank you God that we are included among the "Blessed are those who have not seen and yet have come to believe." (20:29) Amen.

Thought for the Day
We can grow from doubt to belief.

Still Enjoying Life
Isaiah 12:1-6

The Lord God is my strength and my might. Isaiah 12:2

My wife and I owned a B&B which allowed us to host a variety of interesting guests. One gentleman visited us frequently He was a graduate of Harvard University, a retired newspaper editor, who acted in and directed plays, into his 80's. He and his wife had no children. Ten years ago his wife needed to be placed in an Alzheimer's care center. She did not recognize him for years – yet daily he visited her taking her a cut flower. A few years ago she died.

One evening our guest and I were sitting on our front porch when he reflected: "Every night I get some cheese and crackers, and my drink, and I sit in my living room and turn off the lights. Then I thank God for what I have: my art, music from Mozart, and my books. I thank God that I can still enjoy life."

In his 12th chapter we find Isaiah saying: "Give thanks to the Lord, call on his name; . . ." (verse 3). Isaiah also knew of difficult times, yet he gave thanks for comfort, trust, strength, salvation, deeds, and the greatness of "the Holy One of Israel."

Isaiah and our friend both made time to thank God for the joy of living. We would be wise to do the same, daily.

Prayer: O God, even if life at times seems busy, and then at times boring; direct our lives at loving and enjoying you forever. Amen.

Thought for the Day
May we live each day growing toward a loving God who helps us enjoy all of life's wonders.

Prayer Focus: Those who provide support.

A Minor Role

Philippians 2:12-18

He must increase, but I must decrease. John 3:30

His name is ellis. His name is not misspelled. He uses lower-case letters when his name appears in public. He is a pastor. In the worship bulletin; on the sign outside the church; in newspaper articles, he always uses small letters to designate his name.

I asked him why he used small letters? He replied that he believed he was not the important being in God's world. He felt this was a way to remain humble before God. God was *the* important Person, Element, Being, Creator, Sustainer, Lover in his, and all lives. Being ellis, and not Ellis, was one way of constantly reminding himself, Who was the important Thing in the universe. This belief is expressed also in an old YMCA slogan: "God is first, other people are second, and I'm third."

The NRSV heading for today's scripture is, "Shining as Lights in the World." In writing to the church at Philippi Paul reminds the "beloved" that "it is *God* who is at work in you." Paul wants the Philippians to always remember that God is the Cause which allows us to "shine like stars in the world."

You and I may not choose to start writing our name in lower-case letters; however to always practice humility should be given priority. Even though we do not play the major role in the drama of life, we can give-our-best in supportive roles.

Prayer: Always present God, thank you for your constant support and grace. May You always be first in our lives. Amen.

For Reflection
To God be the glory

Prayer Focus: That God is the center of our lives

A Time to Remember

II Timothy 1:3-7

. . . I remember you constantly in my prayers night and day. . . . I am reminded of your sincere faith. II Timothy 1:3, 5

The memorial service was a regular part of the Women's Fellowship meeting I attended as their interim pastor. Their custom was to provide a time to remember members who had gone-to-be-with-God.

The worship leader spoke the name of the deceased member, and invited us to share memories and happenings about that person. Following these reflections there was a time of silence. Another practice was the placing of an amount from their general fund into their mission/outreach fund in memory of departed sisters.

In Paul's second letter to Timothy he notes he remembers in prayers not only Timothy, but his grandmother Lois and mother Eunice. Then he reminds Timothy to "rekindle the gift of God . . . a spirit of power and love and self-discipline."

We are grateful for memory. Of course within memory we could recall the not-so-good along with the good. At that Fellowship meeting, those women could have dwelt on the death of friends; or given their energy to remembering past meaningful moments. May we concentrate on living, and leave dying to God – who will do all things well.

Prayer: O God of hope and love, we thank you for memory, for with it others live within us. Amen.

For Reflection

How can I best be remembered?

Prayer Focus: May we remember that God is a part of our remembering

We Are the Noisemakers
Psalm 98

Thought for today: "Make a joyful noise to the Lord, all the earth." Psalm 98:4a

The Massey organ at Chautauqua Institution in southwest New York is the largest outdoor organ in the world. It weighs 40 tons, has 93 ranks and consists of 5,628 pipes. One pipe is 34 feet in length. It is powerful; it is magnificent; played in the correct manor it sounds like a voice from God.

The organ was recently refurbished. We were privileged to be on a guided tour by the man who helped re-furbish the instrument and then he took us into the two story organ chamber. Following our journey through the chambers we were invited to a concert. We were introduced to a young man who played Bach's "Toccatta & Fugue in D Minor."

The Psalmist uses the word "noise" as a synonym for the word "sound." He encourages us to "announce" or "proclaim" the steadfast love and faithfulness of our God. We are called upon to do this with our singing and instruments. We are to become the noisemakers for God. This is a joyful activity. The writer requests us to be front and center in our noisemaking.

I recall that simple yet memorable line from The Sound of Music: "A bell is no bell 'less you ring it, a song is no song, 'less you sing it." As massive as the Massy organ is; regardless of how inspiring it can be; it is of no use unless it is played. In like manner our faith is useless unless we live it.

The 98th Psalm is a classified for those who will play the lyre, for trumpeters, for noisemakers. Will we respond to the ad?

Prayer: O God, we are the noisemakers in the 21st century. Be with us as we play and sing a new and joyous song of praise to You. Amen.

For Reflection
May our "noise" be in harmony with others

Was God There?

It's a tiny room
about 9 x 9.
There are no pictures
and the air is heavy.
The pink-lady hostess
ushers you in
where the doctor waits.
(He's explained surgery
to so many he could
not tell you the color
of the walls.)

It's a tiny room
and it cannot begin
to hold the emotions:
often —-
    "We won't know
    until pathology reports."
sometimes —-
    "It wasn't malignant,
    she'll be okay."
for us —-
    "We couldn't do anything
    I'm sorry."
We thanked him for being
honest.

It was long after
we left the tiny room
that I wondered
"Was God There?"
If God can:
    embody love
    roll stones and
    practice resurrection
Then, of course
God was there.   Yes!
Amen.

(The Mennonite, January 14, 1986)

The Lover

He keeps smiling
 his gentle-loving smile.
She keeps making
 her gurgling noise.
They sit together
 in the lounge of
 her "nursing" home.
It is sing-along time,
 residents and their families
 moan the old favorites.
He holds the book for her and says,
 "You know this one Georgia."
She is unresponsive and
 only makes her sound –
 "ugh-ugh-ugh-ugh."
 Her eyes are open, but
 she does not see.
His gaze is full of joyful
 memories and tender support.
 He is pleased being next to her
 (a closeness of decades)
 and continues speaking quietly
 as if she really does understand.
She continues her steady,
 sickening grunts as
 her saliva slides down her neck.
 The straps hold her tightly
 in her wheelchair.
They sing the final hymn.
 He says, "You like this song
 Georgia, remember?"
 He holds her hand
 as if this was a special outing.
 She does not reply.
Their time together is over.
 He pats her shoulder and
 wheels her chair away;
 his queen on parade.

PRAYERS FOR
PUBLIC WORSHIP

Kansas Messenger

THE UPPER ROOM

CLERGY JOURNAL

CHRISTIAN
LEADERSHIP

the christian MINISTRY

A Pastoral Prayer for Easter Sunday

God, Easter has come late this year – or are we simply celebrating it late? According to your clock, all things happen at the right time; for there is not a time or place where you cannot come.

Easter time is anytime when those who believe in you celebrate the resurrection of Jesus the Christ. We associate it with color: dogwood-white, budding-red, leaf-green, even dandelion-yellow. We marvel at life seen in all colors.

On this day you so lovingly created, we bask in the colors of hope, joy, happiness, peace and resurrection; and those colors speak to us about a second life, eternal hope and a purpose in living.

God, there is color in your world, by Your creation. The children sing, "Red and yellow, black and white, they are precious in His sight." As you have given us the covenant of the rainbow you have given us a rainbow of people – all precious in your sight.

We have passed through the color of Holy Week:

the green of Palm Sunday,
the red of the Last Supper,
the black of Gethsemane,
the gray of Good Friday, the blue and white of Easter.

In all these colors you were present.

What's ahead for us? Depressing grays and sunshine yellows will come to all of us. And yet because of Easter all events now take on a different hew. For indeed your act of resurrection shows us a bright light at the end of any dark tunnel. Thus, receive our Easter prayer of thanksgiving. Halleluiah God. Thank you for your gift of life on both sides of death. AMEN!

(Master Sermon Series, April, 1983)

A Prayer in Assembly

(Prayer offered at the Sunday morning Worship service for the State Assembly of the Kansas Christian Churches, Hays, April 12, 1970; and appeared in the *Kansas Messenger*.)

God, come, be a part of our worship and breathe Your spirit and strength into us. Come and cast out the many devils that divide and distract us. You have called us to labor with You. Labor then we must. With the gift of Christ Jesus, a carpenter-shop drop-out who loved the world, you have given us a vision of victories to be won. Inspire us with a child-like faith, the reformer's zeal, the prophet's fire and the saint's devotion.

God, as your disciples in Kansas we know that with Your guidance the mission of Your church is possible. Hear our prayer of Thanksgiving for our ministers: Lloyd Cox, Bill Harris, Glenn Johnson, Bettie Griffith and Glenn Warner. We covet their leadership. Thanks be to you O God, for the gift of our state minister Gilford Olmsted. He continues to set before us the nitty-gritty-gut issues of our day. He shows us the difference between life and death and challenges us to choose life. We pray that indeed we do choose life.

God, we need you to turn our minds from their distractions, to release our souls from their tensions, to lift us out of unworthy habits and to set our will upon Your purpose. Grant Your ministry to us. As the branch abides in the vine so may our spirits abide in you, bringing forth rich and abundant fruit. To that end deal with us as the vinedresser cares for the vine, and may Your expectancy be fulfilled in us, as we bring forth not wild and bitter grapes, but grapes that are good and satisfying to You.

Some of the bitter grapes among us are those of segregation, sown by our forefathers, and we continue to cultivate them. How shall we respond to this issue? Shall we buy watchdogs and guns and build still bigger barriers? We pray not. We pray that we might be Agents of Reconciliation. We must confess that at times we have looked down on hippies and black panthers and those who drive motorcycles or wear mini-shirts. We must confess that we look with hate upon those awful persons who bear the name Roman Catholic or Republican or Rotarian or Russian. Make the mind of Christ ours – who loved persons whether they were male or female, young or old, healthy or sick, prostitute, tax-collector, robber, white, black, green or polka dot – he loved them completely – even to the end. God, make us agents of reconciliation.

God, surely You are not dead – for Your spirit is alive – calling us together into tangible Christian Unity; a unity not just of convenience – but a unity of Christian strength and witness. Your son prayed for unity – Alexander Campbell pointed us that direction – it is long overdue – but it may come in the 70's. God, may we recognize that the things that unite us are far more important than the things that divide us! Use us to help bring about a United Church.

God, you have called us to witness. Christian witness is often what we do, sometimes what we say and always what we are. May we be found faithful in our witnessing.

God, bless us that we shall give less consideration to ourselves and more to Your Kingdom. Help us as we accept the cost and joy of discipleship. Amen.

A Prayer for Christian Unity

God, be the unifying spirit that makes us one in your name. Our earnest prayer is that ecumenical is more than an old Greek word. Others may find delight in pointing out differences; but our prayer is that we might be agents of reconciliation, understanding and openness.

This night we come together aware of our common heritage. Our traditions are meaningful and important. We are part of the One Body that includes the devotion of Martin Luther who wrote: "The body they may kill, God's truth abideth still." We acknowledge the common sense, devotion to principle, courage, faith and sacrifice of Joan of Arc. We admire the missionary spirit of Adoniram Judson; the belief of Mary Baker Eddy who said, "God is all-in-all; God is spirit;" the evangelistic-preaching zeal of John Wesley. We marvel at the unique honesty and integrity of Thomas More who died for the belief in the supremacy of God, not king. We understand the faith of John Calvin who believed in absolute sovereignty of God; in whom he believed all honor and glory were due. We acknowledge with George Fox the call for simple life and love of peace. We too are dreamers, along with our brother Martin Luther King, Jr.

Our prayer embraces the thought of Thomas Campbell who over 150 years ago said, "The church of Christ upon earth is essentially, intentionally, and constitutionally one." Surely we are indebted to a great soul, John XXIII, who called the ecumenical spirit into being in our time, who opened the windows of the church, and allowed the fresh breath of Your Holy Spirit to breathe upon us.

Our prayer includes the thoughts of our Lord Jesus, "I pray that they may all be one, O Father. May they be one in us, just as you are in me and I am in you. May they be one, so that the world will believe."

God, every person here tonight must assume their responsibility and opportunity to give what they can to Christian unity. Our Lord's prayer for oneness must be our prayer. Our Lord's spirit must be our spirit. It is within that framework we come, and it is within your passion for unity that we live and move and have our being. May we ever be faithful to the high calling of Christian unity and service as sisters and brother of the faith. Amen.

(This prayer offered at the Week of Prayer for Christian Unity service in the Irvington area of Indianapolis. Personalities mentioned represent those groups whose congregations are a part of the Irvington Association of Ministers.)

(The Disciple, March 17, 1974)

A Prayer for Church Secretaries

God, we pay tribute to those servants who serve in the position of church secretaries. They may bear the name Phyllis, Willetta, Nita Floe or Shirley, but we who are pastors call them blessed.

We have beheld them trying to wash off the ink on their hands from the uncooperative mimeograph, as they consoled a church member who did not like an event that took place in the church. They answer the phone, they type the letters, they serve as receptionist, file clerk, social director, and at times, assistant custodian and associate pastor. They have been understanding and helpful to both the sinners and saints of the parish. Having seen our clay-feet they still respect us with dignity. They may even damage a friendship to speak a supporting word for their boss, and they too have ministered.

We have used them as a sounding-board, and found their advice of great value. They are a vital part of the work of the church, indeed they are a part of the team ministry. Therefore God, we are thankful not only for their work, but for their personality. May we, as pastors, and our congregations, remember to show appreciation to them. May we be mindful that our task is one of communicating Your love. To this end we pray that we would be faithful in our jobs. Amen.

(This prayer offered for the meeting of church secretaries and pastors at the State Assembly of Kansas Christian Churches in Hays, 1970)

(The Clergy Journal, February, 1980; and Church Administration, February, 1982)

A Prayer at a Senior Citizen's Meeting

God, we are getting old in age, and we pray older and wiser in Thy ways. Steps are difficult, faces are not as clear, we wish people would talk louder, our knees hurt and we can't eat what we want. Some of our family is gone and friends have moved. God, we know old age is not a punishment, but we do have our problems.

God, keep us going. What we pray for is an understanding attitude; an attitude that calls up our best. Give us a second wind. Instead of living in the good old days; call us to this present time that we may live and be active in these good *now* days.

We may have retired from a job; but not from life. Might not we stimulate each other to look around and see what service we can do. We do not have to look far to see someone in a more difficult condition than we find ourselves – and there is where ministry can begin. God, make our minds clear to understand that we can visit and talk and read and share and care and pray and laugh and enjoy, regardless of our age.

May our understanding attitude see that *all* of life is a stewardship; a time to be appreciated and enjoyed. May each new day bring us an opportunity to share with someone, Thy love for us; a love which is as close as our hands and feet and as real as our breathing.

We offer our prayer in the name of Jesus the Christ who loved all: the healthy and sick, the blind and lame, the greedy and the timid, the young and the old. Amen.

(Christian Leadership, June, 1982)

A Prayer for New Nurses

Come God and share our joy, satisfaction, and happiness. In a time when wholeness is being emphasized, we are pleased to recognize sixty persons who will participate in a vocation that assists in keeping persons whole. Receive our prayer of appreciation for all who served as instructors: both physicians and nurses. We are grateful for every insight, technique, suggestion, encouragement, even admonishment they gave that will allow for good nursing to be practiced.

May each person being recognized this evening feel a joy of accomplishment. As family and friends we share that joy.

Now as these persons nurse, may they do so with dignity and compassion. May they labor for more than a paycheck, may they join with you God – The Great Physician – in serving, in caring, yes indeed in ministering, to those who are sick and suffer. May they always know and feel they have helped. That alone makes life a joy. Amen.

(Invocation offered at the February, 1981, Completion-Pinning Exercises for the Practical Nursing Program of Indiana Vocational Technical College, Indianapolis.)

A Prayer for High School Graduates

Eternal Spirit, the God of Abraham, Issac and Jacob, and our God – we are grateful for all learning and growing experiences.

We recognize and honor this class who has spent the past years as students of Howe High School. May they be grateful for all those opportunities to: sing, read, play, understand, draw, paint, write, make friends, think, reason, and grow in wisdom and stature and hopefully in Your favor.

We express appreciation for those we have called teachers; especially those who gave far more than their contract called for; who opened young minds to new ideas. May we also appreciate the custodians who cleaned up the messes we made; and the cooks who prepared the food we complained about.

If we are wise, we will have learned from the mistakes and satisfactions we experienced in high school. Indeed maybe in future years we will look back at our high school experiences and be thankful for new thoughts, ideas and relationships.

God, continue to be with us in our growing and learning. If the future is to vocational school or to find a job, or to college, may we desire to be useful and not destructive persons in Your world. May we understand we are your children – you created us – you continue to love us always.

God, high school has been a good happening, so please share our joy, satisfaction and achievement. Amen.

(Offered at the graduation exercises of Thomas Carr Howe High School, Indianapolis, Indiana, 1979)

A Prayer on Mother's Day

This is a sentimental day for many, O God. A day marked as special for mothers, old and new. So we are filled with many thoughts, some charged with emotion, as we consider our present state – and recall memories from the past. For all memories that satisfy, uplift and challenge, we are grateful. Make them holy.

Receive our prayer for mothers with special needs:

- For the mothers who out of frustration encourage violence, please come to them in some concrete manner that they may change and direct their children in a different direction – taking the path of reconciling peace.
- For the mothers in many countries who do promote peace within an atmosphere of violence, give them your special love.
- For the mothers whose children are retarded, touch them with your holy care, relieve any guilt feelings, and make beautiful the relationship they have with their child.
- For the mothers who simply want to get through the day, or who are anxious for children to succeed – calm them with your patient understanding.
- For the mothers of the world who grieve because they cannot give their children the essentials of life – may your nudging word of love be spoken by us and others, who might and can, help to provide those essentials.

O God, for all those who wanted so much to be mothers, but could not become such for many reasons – may they somehow know the importance of simply being who they are – your children – called not to consider what they might have been, but called to live to the fullest of being who they are, and yet can be.

God what really matters in life is not that we are male or female, parent or child, single or married, but what really matters is our ongoing relationship to you and to others. May our ears be clear so we can once again hear your two greatest commandments: Love the Lord your God with all your heart, soul, mind and strength; and your neighbor as yourself. Encourage us to be busy in finding our neighbors – and thus live as your true sons and daughters – within the love of Jesus of Nazareth. Amen.

(Master Sermon Series, May, 1983; The Disciple, May, 1986)

A Prayer for a Community Meeting with the Mayor

God, we come as persons concerned about our community and about a quality of life.

We are persons within the framework of the Jewish and Christian faith, uniting with others who are concerned about our city.

Our prayer is first that we see the uniqueness of every person that lives in our city. We hope those who are elected and selected to run our city government do so with such a purpose that they are people-oriented. It is right that we say "thank you" for all city personnel who provide services for us: those who fight fires, those who pick up trash, those who police our city, those who fill chuck holes, those who do paper work and those who make administrative decisions.

Our prayer is for our mayor and all persons associated with city government. Our prayer is for our immediate community of Irvington, for all that is has been, and all that it can yet become.

Thank you for food – when some persons starve; for community when some persons live in isolation; and for life itself. May we live wisely. Amen.

(Offered at an Irvington area community meeting ,with Mayor William Hudnut of Indianapolis; and with administrative associates, 1983.)

The Dedication and Prayer for a Cross

The cross we dedicate today is *the* symbol of the Christian faith. The hymn writer captures the meaning of the cross in the words: "In the cross of Christ I glory, towering o'er the wrecks of time." One must ask the question: "What does the cross mean?" To those in Roman times the sight of a cross meant cruelty and oppression. Jesus of Nazareth gave meaning to the cross. Paul notes that the cross is a stumbling-block to some; but to believers it is "the power of God and the wisdom of God."

Jesus directly challenges us to "take up your cross and follow me." He asks us to do this by our life-style of loving persons in his name. There is a sense of actual enjoyment in our call to discipleship.

The cross is placed above the baptistery. The symbolism of the cross and one's baptismal experience come together in the Romans passage: "Do you not know that all of us who have been baptized into Christ Jesus were baptized into his death? We were buried therefore with him by baptism into death, so that as Christ was raised from the dead by the glory of the Father, we too might walk in newness of life."

The dictionary says a symbol is "a material object representing something immaterial." Christians have used symbols to express the Faith for centuries. The very presence of this church building is a symbol that we care. We care about God and Jesus. This cross will remind us to "be about our Father's business." A piece of wood is just a piece of material until a craftsman makes something from it. When he makes a Christian symbol it has deep meaning for us.

This cross is dedicated to the clergy of Christ's church, past, present and future. Clergy are those persons *called-out* to be God's vehicles for Christian ministry. Some clergy of the past were named Andrew, Thomas, Martha, Mary, W.S. and Austin. Those of the present are Clark, William and Kris. Those of the future may be Warren and Linda; we are not sure who they will be; however we are sure that they will be, because God will always be.

The Prayer of Dedication

God, you loved us completely in the Christ Event that we might have life and have it abundantly. We see not only death and suffering when we see the cross, we see purpose in living as your children; and we also see resurrection.

Whenever we come into this room, be it for weekly worship, or private prayer; in times of joy or grief; may we look upon the cross and see and sing: "The strife is o'er, the battle done; the victory of life is won; the song of triumph has begun. Alleluia!" Amen.

(Dedication and prayer offered on February 12, 1978 at the Community Christian Church of Camdenton, Missouri. The cross is a gift to the church by William "Mac" and Grace Eleta McDermet. It was crafted by Wayne Selsor.)

Prayer at the Ground-breaking of a Business

God of all life and new opportunities, acknowledge our presence at this time of a new undertaking.

We are grateful for this construction of a new N&W Credit Union building, for it symbolizes jobs, growth and vitality in our city.

We pray for the welfare of all whose talents will construct this building. We acknowledge the skills of carpenters, plumbers, electricians and all whose efforts will make this building possible. We pray that they work free from injury.

We also pray for those who will work within these walls. We pray that as they provide services, and as they receive and loan money, they do so with the highest ethical standards.

Help all employees to see customers as persons; persons with needs who may be helped with courtesy and kindness.

May all who work within this structure find satisfaction in their work; and may their interactions with each other be positive.

We pray for your presence today, during construction, and when this building is occupied. Amen.

(Offered at the ground-breaking of the N&W Credit Union building in Decatur, Illinois; across the street from Prairie Avenue Christian Church, 1988.)

A Prayer for Peace in Nicaragua

God of love and hope and compassion; God of Abraham, Isaac and Jacob; God of Jesus of Nazareth, and God of us all – whether we realize it or not – receive our prayer.

Within this very special time – a time of Passover for some, and a time of Lent for others – we gather in the heart of our community to offer a prayer of hope and peace.

We pray boldly because we believe we live within a world family. We feel we have a relationship with all people. Our love and concern does not stop at any natural or national boundary.

We pray specifically for our sisters and brothers who live in Nicaragua. They have suffered so much from shootings and bombings and interventions from other countries. Their economy and life-style and freedom has been disrupted so often that many live in despair.

But thanks be to you O God, now we have a ray of hope. Our prayer is that peace in Nicaragua is not just a word, but an activity. We are grateful that foreign troops have been withdrawn, prisoners have been released, and proposals for peace are in actual process. For this receive our prayer of thanksgiving.

Now we hope in the future. We hope that first world countries will refrain from activity in Nicaragua, and all Central American nations. May they work out their own problems and opportunities in peace.

Our prayer is not only for President Danial Ortaga, but for every person in that country.

Our prayer is offered in the spirit of Shalom, for you have created us – all of us – to live and dwell in peace. Amen.

(Offered in Central Park, Decatur, Illinois on April 2, 1988.)

A Prayer "By" Children

God we are thankful for:
grass and trees,
baseballs and teddy bears,
picnics and swimming pools,
flowers and rainbow butterflies,
grandpa with his big laugh and grandma with her warm hand,
peanut-butter and jelly sandwiches,
parents who help with homework,
the lady down the street who gives us candy and UNICEF quarters at Halloween,
bright colors,
the Muppets,
dogs and bikes,
radios and stereos
fluffy animal clouds,
teachers who really love us even though we may not think so,
our hands and eyes,
chocolate chip cookies,
3:15 on Fridays,
our pastor,
the Bible,
Jesus, who lets us come to him without being hindered.
Amen.

(JED Share, Fall, 1983)

A Prayer for the Right Attitude

O God, we admit that we cannot change much of what happens in the world, or even to us. Yet we pray for a proper attitude; an attitude that takes us through the ups and downs and all the plateaus. Some of us notice only the office drudgery, the floor that needs cleaning, the boring routine, or the "dumb" school. We seem to have so many plateaus they need not be listed; or we would need to sharpen our pencil too frequently to list our hurts, and our downs, and our boredom.

So, we come to you praying for an attitude that sustains us between our own Bethlehem to our own Golgotha. An attitude that finds meaning and purpose through both the pleasant peaceful days beside our Sea of Galilee, and our gloomy final days of darkness of our Jerusalem.

In all of our days we would be filled with a child-like attitude which says: "Yea, it's another day!"

We pray for an attitude of understanding. An attitude that understands the neighbor who complains about and hates, the next door children; for he was an only child, and he fathered no children, and he simply does not enjoy people. We pray for understanding as we live by him.

We pray for the fellow employee who is always loud, always is critical and who always interrupts the conversation. He is afraid he will not be noticed. He feels he must let you know he is present. We pray for understanding as we go beyond enduring him, to accepting him.

We pray for the older sister who always got better grades, always participated in more activities, and always had more friends. Many times she simply wanted to help, and we mistook her action for an — I'm-older-and-better-than-you attitude. It's not too late to have a great relationship and friendship with her and we pray for just that.

We pray for the proper attitude toward our bodies. As we grow older the Temple of God seems to have lost its zip; we get slower and awkward and clumsy. Someone tells us to stop complaining: "See that man, he has no arms. See that woman; her home is a wheel chair. See that child, she cannot see. You don't have those problems, so stop complaining." That helps, but we still have our needs.

God, what we pray for is an attitude that claims the spirit of Jesus; an attitude that sees us through thick and thin. That attitude is ours for the asking. We ask God, hear our prayer, and sustain us in our journey through life with a Christ-like understanding and attitude, of others and ourselves. So may it be. Amen.

(Master Sermon Series, May, 1984)

A Pastoral Prayer

God, our sisters and brothers of the past vigorously sang that they loved to tell the story of Jesus and his love. However when we are honest most of us have known times when we have not even whispered about your love. Yet we need to tell the story, because it did so much for us. Countless persons are hungering and thirsting for ministry of the gospel.

O God, move within us so that we may feel that what we do in relationship to others is true ministry. Some of us may never preach sermons, or serve at our Lord's Table; or never teach a class in religion – but we all can learn to give, and receive love. We can hug and hold. We can talk and listen. We can read and write, and learn to grown in your love. Every one of us is able to share with others.

God, help us to see all our acts of serving and kindness as ministry for you and your son. Nothing done in your name is worthless or forgotten. No task is mean or low. No person is unworthy of interest and support. Even those we do not like, need our care.

We reflect on the ministry of our Lord. He moved in places that were not holy. He associated with many who were sick, lonely, sinful and unwanted. Not only did he love them, he risked much for their sakes.

When we take ministry seriously, we know that we are called to go a second mile in service.

Ministry is sometimes what we say, and how we say it to others in need, in trouble, in joy, in sorrow. Ministry is sometimes what we do – with our time, our mind, our money, and our actions. Ministry is always what we are, for we are Yours, O God.

In our generation we too would sing:

I love to tell the story
To tell the old, old story
Of Jesus and His love.

Amen.

(The Christian Ministry, September, 1979;
Master Sermon Series, May, 1984)

A Prayer for the First Sunday in July

Let us silently consider what it means to be a Christian and an American. (A half minute of silence.)

God, our prayer takes the form of the words Samuel F. Smith penned in 1831:

> My country, 'tis of thee, sweet land of liberty, of thee I sing;
> Land where my (mothers and) fathers died, Land of the pilgrims pride, From every mountain side let freedom ring.

We treasure freedom, yet we know not all are free. People within our own city are confined to live in certain areas and work particular jobs and live within limited life-styles. Let these facts concern us as they ought to concern us – because we are yours, O God. When we acknowledge our relationship to you, we also acknowledge our relationship with all people.

We thank you for our country's unique history. We even glory in it. As we express our gratitude for strength to overcome oppression – we find it difficult to hear other nations' cry for freedom.

As a nation we have progressed and we are thankful for that progress. Minorities, women, youth, the aged do have better opportunities – although everything is not perfect, we are still thankful for gains made.

We pray for the best from our public schools, from our judicial system, from our legislative bodies.

Finally we pray that our prayers and visions and actions may never become narrowly nationalistic. Teach us that there is no distinction between "Greek and Jew, slave, free man, but Christ is in all."

Correct our priorities – set them within the framework of the Gospel of Jesus Christ so that we may again offer this our prayer:

Our faithful God to thee, author of liberty,
To thee we sing;
Long may our land be bright
with freedom's holy light'
Protect us by thy might,
Great God, our King. Amen.

(Master Sermon Series, July, 1984)

A Pastoral Prayer Following a Sermon on Suffering

God, on this day when we have considered suffering, we pray first that we separate suffering from simply inconvenience. Not being able to go on a trip, or the rain spoiling an outing, or our favorite sports team being defeated, or losing our hair because we are growing older – is not suffering.

Still after serious consideration we do have some suffering. Our prayer is that you, O God, will help us in dealing with it. We ask forgiveness for any unnecessary suffering we have caused others, yes, we ask forgiveness of the times we have supported a national policy that caused others to suffer.

Deal with us gently as we work through any personal suffering. Only you can know and understand the depth – and therefore only you can ultimately give us support.

God, we may never know the "why" of suffering. Instill us with the wisdom that it is foolish to attempt to debate with you as an equal. You are God, we are humans. It is helpful to understand that others have suffered at greater depths than we have – and yet they have lived meaningful lives.

Still we have our own sufferings – and they are real. Then at that bottom-line-time we humbly, honestly and openly ask you to minister to us.

Your unique ministry comes to us by:

- the support of family and friends
- the support of a caring congregation
- the examples in scripture
- your Spirit which surrounds us, holds us and loves us.

You are aware of suffering and you are aware of us. Help us to move even deeper into your presence and grace to the extent that we find meaning through your love and compassion – even in suffering.

In the person of Jesus who suffered, your final comment was not suffering and death, but resurrection and life. This too shall come to us. Amen.

(Prayers For Public Worship, Ziegler, 1986)

A Pastoral Prayer for Sunday Morning

God, our prayer is for every person in every hospital in this world. May they feel care and love through nurses and physicians and cleaning ladies and aids and relatives and friends. Be as near to them as the sheets on their bed.

God, our prayer is for every person in every institution in this world. For those who committed crimes against property and persons. For those who are disturbed. For those who sit on death rows. For those who are political prisoners and are unjustly detained. For all those who are behind closed doors and locked gates we pray that somehow your presence may be felt. If some need to ask for forgiveness, move them in that direction. Our prayer is also for all persons who have been wronged by individuals or systems or groups or nations.

God, our prayer is for every person in every benevolent home. To those whose step falters, whose eyes see faintly, whose life is but memories of yesterdays, who have no family. May they all know that you are family to them.

God, our prayer is for every person in this sanctuary. For those just starting life's journey; for those who are in the middle years; and for those who are nearing the end, we pray for all of us – knowing that ultimately nothing matters unless it is blessed by you. Regardless of our condition we seek and feel your love, a love of caring and sharing. Amen.

(Prayers For Public Worship, Ziegler, 1986)

A Prayer During Lent

God, source of all that is, receive us, challenge us, and believe in us for as long as we live.

In this holy Lenten season, speak to us again about complete obedience and commitment. We recall the vivid impression of a loving-giving person dying on a barbaric cross. Maybe we even feel that: despair, hopelessness, denial, betrayal and death have the final word. We wonder if: going the second mile, obedience unto death; helping the unloving; forgiveness and sharing are really useless activities.

O God, we must confess that at times we live as if we were Good Friday people, and not Easter people. We must also confess that at times we live lives that seem to say: Golgotha, death, darkness, greed, self-centeredness, and the spirit of Judas, Pilate and Caesar control us.

Yet, we are Easter people. We are beginning to believe, hope, act and respond to the Christ Event. In this Lenten time might we develop a spirit of responsible discipleship where we can pray at our Gethsemane's and not sleep; say we know Jesus before the cock cries; believe he is worth more than 30 pieces of silver – we pray the seemingly impossible – to go beyond the belief and actions of the first disciples.

Our prayer also embraces the desire – that with your activity, and our belief – the element of joy may be as much a part of our being as eating and sleeping. Joy that works through, frustration, anxiety, bereavement and meaninglessness to – singing, laughter, embracing, living and loving.

May the tree of faith put down deep roots during this Lenten season, and may those roots find us to be good soil. Amen.

(Prayers For Public Worship, Ziegler, 1986)

Pray for Everyone in a Year

Churches can pray for every member once a year at weekly worship. In my ministry as an interim pastor I have helped congregations do just that. We list in the bulletin, right after the Pastoral Prayer, the names of those we will specifically mention that day ("It is our joy to remember in prayer: Chuck, Stephanie and Brian Malancuk, John Henry and Mildred Cain," etc.). I read the names out loud.

If you list 15 names each Sunday you can cover 390 in six months; 20 a week for 520 members. Names are not listed alphabetically, so members do not know when they will be remembered. All family members are listed, whether they are church members or not.

Those congregations that keep accurate attendance records or have a small membership can assign someone to send to those not present the day they were remembered, the bulletin with their name circled.

At one church I secured from the denominational headquarters the names and addresses of overseas church staff. We prayed for one or two of these individuals every week. Each Sunday a member circled those names, sent the bulletin and wrote a one-page letter of appreciation to the staff person. The sender also told him or her about our congregation and community. (A Sunday school class or other church group can take on this project.) Many of these missionaries have written us back and thanked us for our prayer, and given us a brief description of their ministry.

This praying project has helped to bring members close together, shown the churches' appreciation for every member, strengthened the churches' outreach/mission connection and more than once elicited this kind of comment from a prayed-for member: "You did not know that I needed prayer this week but you surely lifted my spirits!"

("Tricks of the Trade" section in The Christian Ministry,
July – August, 1997)

Which Blow Caused the Tree to Fall?

Suppose you needed to cut down that old tree in the back yard. You did the chore and counted the number of blows it took to fell the tree – in fact it was one hundred and thirty-six. Suppose in your reflection afterward you posed the question: which blow caused the tree to fall? The last one, of course; but the tree would still be standing if you did not strike the first blow, and what about blows two to one hundred thirty-five?

In the eleventh chapter of Luke we find the Parable of the Friend at Midnight. This parable follows Jesus' giving to his disciples the Lord's Prayer. The parable deals with our prayer life. The Revised Standard Version says the man was heard, "Because of his importunity." Today's English Version states the passage, "You are not ashamed to keep on asking," yet the Jerusalem Bible may say it best, "Persistence will be enough . . . the door will be opened."

Getting out of bed at midnight to give the man some bread was not an easy event for the friend in this parable. In New Testament times the family all slept in the same room – no split-level three-bedroom home then. To unbolt the door meant all sleepers would be roused by the noise. This is a vivid illustration with a keen insight as to how we need to pray: with persistence.

The central figure is not the petitioner, but the *Friend* who is roused. There is a certainty that the petition will be granted. So, if persistence achieves its end in everyday human relationships, how much more we will achieve in our relationship with God! According to Luke, Jesus' assertion that prayer will be answered was absolute. Jesus encourages prayer even when it is an experience of desperate struggle. For the struggle is not with God but with us.

A mother reports that during a family vacation a daughter asked her to join in climbing a mountain. The mother offered a brief prayer, "God, please give me the stamina to make it to the top." But the mother made it less than half-way. She then reflected she needed more than a "help me" prayer. She further noted that in her "climbing through life" she could not expect to rise above life's problems without a spiritual exercise program. If she wanted mountaintop experiences, she needed to develop spiritual muscles through a disciplined prayer life.

To Jesus prayer was the simple outpouring of human need. Maybe Jesus, himself, one night experienced the same parabolic event. A neighbor came at midnight asking his father Joseph for some bread. He may have begun to understand what the writer of Hebrews later put into words, "Now faith is the assurance of things hoped for, the conviction of things not seen." (Hebrews 11:1) Prayer must become a tireless asking, before God can richly reward it.

Religious history is marked with experiences where prayer had to be persistent. Jacob wrestled with his "angel" until he said, "I will not let you go, unless you bless me." (Genesis 32:26b) Paul asked God three times for his "thorn" to be removed; yet Paul came to know God at a deeper level, "My grace is sufficient for you, for my power is made perfect in weakness." (II Corinthians 12:9)

Jesus himself prayed earnestly until, "His sweat became like great drops of blood." (Luke 22:44) While we plead in prayer our patience is perfected, our humility deepened, our purposes clarified. Our prayers must be freed of insincerity and the trivial. Then for the really necessary we must beat with bruised hands until the door is opened!

The main point of this parable is not that we will get whatever we ask (although that seems to be said, and we must deal with it), but an understanding that we are not placed in the position of having to plead with God, as with an uncaring neighbor, when we ask for what is necessary, whether it is bread, or justice or human rights.

God does not meet our every need just because we are persistent toward God. God is ready and indeed eager to do for us in response to a simple request. In other words, God is *not* like the uncaring neighbor; God is a loving God, only infinitely more loving. God cares for us, God listens to our prayers, and God rejoices to give us what we need.

Which blow caused the tree to fall? Why the last one, of course. But was not the first one necessary? Of course. And what of blows two to one hundred thirty-five? Every blow was necessary! So it is and will be with us, Sisters and Brothers of the Christian Pilgrimage. We see old trees that need to fall now, and we know there will be many other trees in our future – so get out your axe and start chopping – with persistence.

(The Upper Room, "Prayer Workshop" – September/October, 1983)

Maps for Traveling

THE CHRISTIAN

YOUR CHURCH

Crusader

THE CHURCH MUSICIAN

Vanguard

the christian MINISTRY

Suggestions For Christian Funerals

(This was my first published article. It appeared in the May 24, 1964 issue o The Christian, while I was the pastor of the United Christian and Baptis Church of Kalona, Iowa. At that time their circulation was 135,000 and received $6. The follow-up article appeared in the April, 1985 The Disciple There was an abbreviated form of my [1964] 1-7 suggestions, then suggestion 8-14. I received $35, whee.)

"We do just what the family wants."

This is the statement generally made by undertakers when it comes to th elements of a funeral service. Today's churches have often failed to provide ade quate guidance for its membership on vital matters, and the preparation for th Christian funeral service is certainly no exception.

Eighteen months before the publication of Jessica Mitford's Th American Way of Death (the book was excellent), the congregation which I serv as pastor published a set of "Suggestions for the Christian Funeral Service."

Months of preparation resulted in our final statement. Three members o our Advisory Board worked with me to its completion.

I feel that there is no need for the open casket even for members of th immediate family; and that a memorial service of worship might even be con ducted without the casket present. But this was not the place for radical changes these may come in the days ahead.

We do not have a suggestion in regard to casket prices. Maybe we should Good stewardship should be the guide. Instead of a $1,500 casket, maybe on of $1,000 could be selected and $500 given to one of the many worthy causes o the church. Or, the family might select a $500 casket, giving $500 to th church.

Failure to take action or give guidance often stems from fear of hurtin someone's feelings. In this case, funeral directors, especially if they are in th membership, may produce a problem. If a congregation were to make sugges tions for the service, the funeral men might imply that you are stepping on thei toes – often stomping.

The church does not need to "square-off" against the funeral men. Le the church go to the families, providing them with guidance for the service.

My statement to the congregation as a preface to the suggestions was: "A you study and think about the area of death, I feel sure that God wants you to embrace the Christian view of death and the resurrection of the spirit Remember the words of Jesus as they echo through the centuries, 'I am the res urrection and the life, he who believes in me shall never die.'"

The comments preceding the specific suggestions were: Death is, even to the best of us, a mystery to which we shy away. Edgar N. Jackson in his book Understanding Grief, says: "Although grief comes close to being a universa emotion and few escape it, it has not received the attention it deserves on th part of careful researchers. Like the common cold, it has been taken for grant ed by most people. But like the common cold, it may be the source of other and more acute reactions that cannot be overlooked."

From the beginning the church has felt a responsibility to minister to the ief-stricken, to provide aid and comfort for them in their bereavement. The rly church fathers wrote letters of consolation to those in the fellowship who d suffered the loss of a loved one. They attempted to give comfort by assur- g the mourners and reminding them of the Christian view of death and resur- ction. The Christian religion can open doors to involving the mind, emotions, d social impulses. The Christian faith can lead even the sorely bereaved to iderstanding and emotional health.

As the Church of Jesus Christ on earth takes the leadership in such areas : stewardship, prayer, worship, education, social concerns and world outreach, also should give guidance in the area of death and the Christian attitude ward death and the funeral service.

Because death is often not a part of our everyday conversation; and cause the family is often not prepared to deal adequately with the problem of e funeral service when death comes; the church is making the following sug- stions. (Please note that these are suggestions; they are not by any means "hard d fast" rules. But as the church should be able to give help in all areas of life, certainly should be helpful in the area of death.)

++++++++++

Our specific suggestions are:

1. That the pastor be informed and consulted so that an early and effec- ve ministry to the family might begin as soon as possible. Your pastor is anx- us to minister to the needs of the whole family at the time of death. He is par- cularly concerned with the spouse and with minor children. Details of the neral service itself are not the major concern. While the pastor is helpful with e details, he is much more concerned about bringing strength and faith into e situation.

2. That any public viewing of the open casket be completed before the hristian service begins. While the body should be respectfully prepared for urial, undue emphasis upon "viewing the remains" and any compulsory filing ast the casket are offensive practices which do not do credit to our belief that e soul has left the body and dwells with God.

Let us repeat that last sentence, as it brings out the heart of the Christian ith: *the soul has left the body and dwells with God.* Most of the time there will e no need to open the casket after it has left the funeral home, as those who ant to view the body may do so there. Conditions may exist when the casket never open.

3. That many types of memorial tributes are considered as appropriate, cluding floral tributes at the time of the service, and gifts to permanent memo- al funds of churches and charities which are meaningful to the family. The ractice of memorials in place of an overabundance of flowers as a tribute to the eceased is rapidly gaining favor in many areas. In some cases the flowers pro- ided by the family are sufficient for the service, and other tributes could well ke more permanent forms.

A Memorial Fund was established in our church in 1960 so that membe and friends could make a "living gift" in memory of those who were a part of o congregation.

4. That the role of music as a source of strength, consolation, and dign ty in the service be carefully considered at all times. Here your pastor can helpful in suggesting music. Great hymns and music providing strength ar comfort are recommended. The intensely personal hymns which magnify t grief of the family should be avoided. Sometimes just organ music is appropr ate.

5. That obituaries are generally not educational or helpful and therefo are not included in the service. Such facts as those given in an obituary a already known by the family and friends. The elimination of an obituary elin inates any undue emotion.

6. That small children and others who do not wish to go to the funer home to "view the body" should not be overly encouraged to do so. Emotion disturbance, not only in the area of death, but in many areas, is often caused b forcing the individual to do something which is not necessary, and which t individual does not want to do.

7. That the use of the church building where feasible and appropriate b encouraged. The church funeral brings with it the associations of the who Christian life of the family: dedication, communion, baptism, marriage ar many occasions of strength and inspiration. For the one who was a member the church we would encourage the service to be at the church.

++++++++++

Attached to these suggestions was a carefully selected list of hymns, boo and scripture passages that we felt would prove helpful

I will not soon forget a conversation with a funeral director in Fort Wort Texas. I was securing information for a semester paper on the subject: "Pastor Ministry to the Bereaved" and I asked the man about music. He replie "Anything goes; even 'Meet Me Tonight in Dream-Land' is okay." More than few congregations have weathered through: "Going Down the Valley One b One," and "Goin' Home."

Our list of hymns were in the area of hope and assurance, e.g., "O Jesu I Have Promised," "This Is My Father's World," "Eternal Spirit, Evermo Creating," "God of Grace and God of Glory," and "O God, Our Help in Ag Past." We also listed a number of books that are in our church library. Finall thirty-one scripture passages on the subject of eternal life were given.

What was the response to the suggestions? Some months later our churc put before the congregation a questionnaire concerning our church's life an work. They were asked to check either, "suggestions were helpful," or "did care for them." Five out of six checked these as helpful, and six out of seven sa that they saved them for future reference.

After twenty years I feel this remains a helpful list. Congregations ought to be creative concerning memorial funds. One congregation established a learning-experience fund where gifts enable members to participate in workshops, retreats, assemblies, lectureships, seminars – thus gifts in memory of deceased members – provide experiences so living members can grow.

When music is considered, one should keep in mind the possibility of congregational singing. This allows another avenue for family and congregational participation.

In 1985 my seven additional suggestions are:

8. That congregations provide Funeral Arrangement Forms. A Patient Representative at a local hospital, who deals with scores of bereaved families every week, states that any preparations done in advance of death are of great relief to the family. Forms should indicate if arrangements have been made with a funeral home, and if body organs are to be donated; preferences for the place of the service; who is to participate; music to be used; scriptures to be read; recipients of memorial gifts; and adequate space for other preferences. Completing the form when death is not eminent allows for a relaxed atmosphere when family is not pressed into decision making. Copies of the completed form should be given to: (1) next of kin (2) church office (3) funeral home or memorial society, if selected (4) one's own file for yearly review.

9. That the congregation provides a meal for the family. This courtesy allows the church to be at its best. Preparing and serving a meal to the immediate family, relatives and close friends, either immediately before or following the service is very helpful. The meal may be served at the church or in a home. This could be a ministry of the Diaconate or another church group. A frequent comment from the family of the deceased is – "Providing us with a meal eliminated all that hassle, allowed the family to be together with plenty of room, and was an expression that our church cared for us."

10. That Christians take the lead in "cleaning-up" the camouflaging terminology of death. There is something special in the way Christians ought to view death. We acknowledge death, but for Paul, and us, the "last enemy death" is not victorious, Christ is.

We do a dis-service to those who grieve, indeed all of us when we use artificial language. "The departed" or "entered into rest" when we really mean "died." "The resting place" when we really mean "buried." "Passed away, expired, or succumbed" when we really mean "died." And just what are "visiting hours" in a "slumber room" at the funeral home? The more honest and open and natural and matter-of-fact we are in dealing with death, the better for all.

11. That thought is given to the sequence of final rites. Consider this sequence: have family members go with the clergy to the cemetery. There have a brief committal, and then have the service in the church, followed by the family greeting their friends in an appropriate room. Thus, the final act is not at a cemetery, but within a place of worship, where we are surrounded by the sym-

bols of faith. This also eliminates a long funeral procession, at times in dreary weather. Families who have gone this route have expressed strong satisfaction.

12. That cremation is recommended as one option. Creation has gained wide-spread approval in our society. Many within the church are calling cremation "good stewardship." Good stewardship of the resources of the family, good stewardship because less land is used, good stewardship of our theological belief concerning death.

13. That cremated remains be disposed on church property. The congregation of Downey Avenue recently approved this possibility. We voted that ashes may be spread in a designated area of our enclosed patio; and that urns may be placed in another designated area. Many state statutes allow this practice. As one member said, "I was dedicated in the church, married in the church, shared concerns and joys in the church, worshiped in the church, and, I would like to have my ashes on the church property."

14. That clergy provide for personal sharing during funeral/memorial services. We have allowed this to happen in our sanctuary with excellent success. This is not appropriate for all situations, but when it is I use the following procedure. I ask the spouse and/or immediate family if they would like to have an informal sharing time during the service. If they agree, I provide a time when I come to the center aisle of the nave and invite persons to stand and make a comment about the deceased, or to share an event or happening. I always come prepared to share the first anecdote myself. Yes, some of the sharing is accompanied with tears, but that is a natural expression and has not been a detriment to the service. At one service a relative stood and tired to speak, but could not. I simply suggested we come back to her later, which we did, and then she was able to share a meaningful story. The clergy in charge have to have a feel for when it is time to stop. Every time we have tried this, between five and ten persons have shared, and the families of the deceased have been appreciative of this sharing.

Death can be struggle, yet peace. We should not privatize death. In community Christians ought to be able to do more than simply acknowledge death; they can acknowledge that the dead one has just participated in the victory-event of their Lord, Jesus Christ. Amen.

Church Union That Works!

(This was the lead article in Crusader, the American Baptist monthly ws-magazine published for all American Baptist homes, December, 1965. The nt cover and 12 other pictures accompanied the story. The same basic article der the title: "A Tangible Expression in Unity" appeared in the January 23, '66 issue of The Christian national weekly of the Christian Churches.)

lona Iowa:

"Large enough to serve you; small enough to know you; population 235." So says the sign on the outskirts of Kalona, Iowa, a farming communi- 17 miles southwest of Iowa City. Here is the horse and buggy of the Amish; e conservatism and thrift of the Mennonites; the friendliness of the small town d the open country. And here, too, is one of the most successful accomplish- ents in church union to be found in America. In the accompanying article, 'illiam W. McDermet, a former pastor now serving the Blue Ridge Boulevard hristian Church in Independence, Missouri, tells you how it was accomplished d how it is implemented. This is a "grass roots" union – the kind all will plaud – and is not intended as argument pro or con participation in the onsultation on Church Union discussed elsewhere in this issue. – The Editors

"Does it really work?" "Which side is stronger, the Baptists or Disciples?" Where do you send your missionary money?" "Do you have one or two mem- rship rolls?" "Where do you get your church school materials?"

For four and one-half years, as the pastor of the United Christian & ptist Church at Kalona, Iowa, I was besieged with questions such as these.

The American Baptists and the Disciples of Christ are working together three ways on a national level by publishing: *The Secret Place*, *Hearthstone* and hristian Worship, A Hymnal. But a real test of Christian community comes hen churches of different ways and backgrounds become one.

*****

Kalona is a small farm-orientated community. In the 1890's the Baptist d Disciple bodies established churches at Kalona. During the next 50-60 years e two churches each maintained a minimum witness in the community. The o congregations were guided by semi-retired or student-minister pastoral lead- ship. At the close of each church year membership remained about the same. ttle witness or leadership development was carried on outside of the weekly urch school and worship services.

Now and then members of the two congregations considered the possibil- y of a stronger, united witness. An example is a sentence in the Sunday wor- ip bulletin from the Christian church in 1951: "Would you be interested in aring a minister with the Baptist church?" Nothing was done in 1951, but in 956 the opportunity for unity arrived quite accidentally.

The pastor of the Baptist church, who was also pastor of a Baptist church a neighboring community, resigned. In attempting to hire new leadership, the o Baptist churches could not agree on a pastor, so the neighboring Baptist urch hired a pastor for them, leaving the Kalona Baptist church without pas- ral guidance. At the same time the Christian church pastor retired. A new era dawned for the two small congregations; due mainly to a few in each churc who said, "Why can't we call one person to serve us?" Eventually the first fu time minister to serve both churches was called.

Those first months together were not easy. Some people always associa a church with a building. Thus, the first of many organizational problems aros For many weeks the two congregations held separate meetings. Identical servi es were held at 9:30 a.m. at the Baptist building and at 10:30 a.m. at t Disciples building. Then church school was held in one building and worsh at the other. Finally, the decision was made to sell the old Baptist building another church group and call the old Christian church building "home."

The Christian Church had an old parsonage and with the money receiv from the sale of it, plus that received from the old Baptist building, a ne $17,000 parsonage was erected in 1957. Still a few of the old Baptist grou could not agree to give up "their church;" so they did not participate in t union. (With some loving cultivation – with the exception of three people this small group is again a vital and cooperative part of the fellowship.) If t shoe had been on the other foot, would a few of the Disciples been able to ca the Baptist building home?

The majority, however, would not be overcome by the small things th could divide. As to the problem of church organization, the governing body called the Advisory Board, and the congregational leader is called the Moderatc Both are Baptist terms, and they are good terms.

Graded church school materials are purchased from the Judson Pres Take home papers, e.g., *Storyland, Junior World* are from the Bethany Press. *Th Secret Place* and Christian Worship were naturals for the congregation, and a used. Those in junior high attend Baptist summer camps. Those in high scho are expected to participate in the Christian Church summer conference exper ence.

What about mission money? This is an issue which has caused divisio before. The decision was to make an equal disbursement. Fifty percent of a special missionary offerings go to the mission concerns of the American Bapti Convention and the other fifty percent to mission concerns of the Disciples Christ.

How would they take communion? The Baptist custom was to hold bot the bread and cup until all were served and then partake. The Disciples custo was to partake individually when served. Today in the United Church all pa take of the bread individually and hold the cup and take it at the same momen

At one of the early congregational meetings an individual of the Christia church background suddenly made a motion that the official name of the cor gregation be "The United Christian and Baptist Church." There are a few cor gregations of similar background and they are called the Baptist and Christia Church. (The letter "B" does come before "C" in our alphabet.) This coul have become a dividing issue. Yet many thought it was too small to argue ove Thus the name today reads: The United Christian and Baptist Church." B need it be pointed out that the first word is the word "United."

At first the letter "B" (for Baptist) and "C" (for Christian) followed each nam on the membership roll. There was also a breakdown between a regular men ber and an associate member. I suggested, "Wasn't it time we could drop thes letters?" The response was, "Yes, we believe so." Today there is one membershi roll, with no divisions and no letters following the names.

Enough of the members were dedicated to the purpose of a strong united witness, that the minor details would not, and did not, overcome their vision.

Has it been worth the trouble? Is the one church more effective than two? What have been the advantages in creating a united church? A letter to members of the old Baptist Church in 1956 lists seven advantages in having a united church. The first advantage on this list is of value: "More people working together in one program would be more efficient and more effective than having a few people struggling in two programs."

The advantages today of a united church are seen in every area of the life and work of the Kalona congregation. The first five years of the 1960's have been thrilling ones. In the fall of 1960 a two fold program of (1) entering into a needed church building remodeling and (2) establishing the Every Member Canvass was launched. Not all the problems were solved with the union. Some members said, "I've never pledge before, and I'm not going to now." "I've never put my offering in an envelope before and I don't plan to do so now." "I'm not going to sign a pledge card; what I give is between God and me."

To this last statement we said, "That's right; what you do give is between God and you. But please be sure that God does have a part."

With encouragement from both denominational state offices we moved into the EMC. In 1960, the last year before our first EMC, the $11,500 church budget was $1,117, in the red. When members began yearly pledging, larger annual budgets — $13,800 in 1961; $15,462 in 1962; $16,632 in 1963, and $18,080 in 1964 – were successively topped.

The complete remodeling program was also successful and on October 22, 1961, the $50,000 project was dedicated. The late Paul Smith, then executive secretary of the Iowa Baptist Convention, was the morning speaker, and Loren Lair of the Iowa Society of Christian Churches was the afternoon speaker. This building now gives the congregation a place that is aesthetic and functional.

Probably the finest expression of a cooperative effort is in the area of missionary giving. Since 1958 the Kalona Church has been among the top 100 churches reporting to the Year Book of the Christian Church for per capita giving to missions. In 1963 the figure was $44.47; for 1964 it was $41.53. In 1964 the church gave $6,354 for world mission causes, divided equally between the two communions.

Because Disciples and American Baptists each have several missionary offerings a year, the Kalona congregation observes special fall and spring offerings. These two offerings now amount to more that $1,600 a year. The church may well meet a 1970 goal of "as much for others as ourselves." The church has adopted the objective that 50% be given to missions starting January 1, 1970. To this end the congregation has put into practice (a) that each yearly budget take into consideration the goal of 50-50 giving by 1970 and (b) that when the payments on the remodeling loan are completed, this amount be applied to outreach. Payments on this loan will be completed before 1970.

Even in uniting, the membership is small. There were 95 resident members in 1959 and about 140 resident members now. Yet because of unity there has been a marked increase in program and the life and work of the church. Various study-discussion groups are held. There are membership classes and schools of missions, and every church home receives Crusader and The

Christian. There is an expanding library of about 500 volumes. A calling group for evangelism and membership cultivation is active. The church is now able to have vital worship services e.g. Maundy-Thursday and Christmas Eve communion, special Advent and Lenten services, a 24-hour prayer vigil. There are two choirs.

Any dividing walls that denominational hostility might erect have been broken down. The congregation has adopted the Disciples conceived "Code of Ethics for Local Congregations." In January of 1963 all women of the church helped in preparing 14,000 program packets to be used by the American Baptist women all across the United States. In a three-day period three tons of material (598,798 items) were assembled, packed and shipped from the church.

Twice in the past four years, the church has received the "Award of Merit – Honorable Mention" at the Iowa Christian Rural Institute. The program of the church was judged as "distinctly above average" for 1961 and 1963. The merit citations are presented "to recognize and encourage the development of vital religious programs that have a bearing upon leadership, service and cooperative endeavors contributing to better living in Iowa communities."

A good idea which has succeeded should be shared. Therefore the church submitted a resolution to the 1964 Detroit Assembly of the International Convention of Christian Churches: "Concerning Local Church Union." It said in part, "Whereas, Christian unity in the form of local united congregations has proved successful, has often provided one strong congregation where there were two or more weaker ones, and has made possible adequate physical facilities, qualified ministerial leadership, and a vital church program; therefore, be it resolved that the Council on Christian Unity of Christian Churches publish a booklet containing information on successful examples of local church union, how differences were met, and provide guide-lines and suggestions to facilitate steps to be taken in uniting two or more congregations." Though the Council on Christian Unity says the idea is a good one, it does not have the necessary funds to carry out the project.

Yet it is a story that needs telling. A few years ago I delivered to the Kalona church a sermon titled: "United, and That Starts with U." Today I feel that the membership, which includes persons from 18 denominational backgrounds, points with pride to the one congregation.

One of the state secretaries has called the church: "A tangible expression in unity," and without doubt, it is.

The Adult Class – Friend or Foe?

George Hamilton Combs, founding pastor of the Country Club Christian Church in Kansas City, Missouri (today one of the largest Disciples congregations) often watched with longing sadness, the recession of many adults who left the church building after attending Sunday School. Those adults felt they had had enough "church" for the day, and thus, they neglected worship. Too bad!

The clergy are not the only ones yearning for a full Sunday experience for adults, with the proper balance between study and worship. Those responsible for the congregation's education program also want participants to have a well-balanced diet of religion.

Church leaders, teachers, and adult class participants need to take inventory, now and then, to see just what is happening in the adult class experience. Indeed, is that adult class a friend or a foe of the total church program?

Within this article is a check list of possible indicators that may start discussion to discern if an adult class is *a part of* or *apart from* the rest of the church program. If you are a church school superintendent or the teacher or a member of an adult class, see how your group scores.

How many items in the *foe* area must you check? Does the list seem too unkind? How many items in the *friend* column are appropriate for your situation? This is for you to decide. These observations may help you in future planning and leadership with the congregation's education program. No church leader wants to see a "hatchet job" done on existing adult classes. But teachers and leaders should find ways to help them claim full partnership with the church.

This kind of soul-searching about the adult class leads to a closer look at what the unique roles are of both the church school class, and the service of worship. Each can provide opportunities that the other cannot. The class can be a place where discussion comes to grips with the purpose of being a Christian. A class provides a place for *koinonia* – fellowship – to develop. Often sharing occurs more easily in small groups. There is a necessary place for the adult class. Yet the class should be a part of the whole.

Worship is an activity in which the entire congregation can gather together – young, old, middle-aged – to proclaim the mighty acts of God. Here we sing, pray, listen to the Word witnessed. Here the choir helps us in our experience. Here we participate in Christ's baptism and eat at his table. Here we begin to feel the strength of Christ's whole church.

Worship and study are two activities that can complement each other. But friendship between the two is necessary. Are you a part of an adult church school class? If so, is that class a friend or a foe of the total church?

Where Does Your Class Stand?

___The teacher always uses the lecture style.
The lecture style of presentation does not allow for questions, or discussion of other points of view. The lecture is a substitute for a sermon. The teacher becomes a substitute for the pastor.

___The teacher's attitude toward issues dominates.
This is tied closely to the preceding possibility. Educators tell us that if we are told something often enough we will start to believe it. If no one is allowed to present alternative positions it may be assumed that the views of the teacher are correct. Not even the clergy should be given this kind of arbitrary authority.

___The classroom is arranged in a formal lecture manner.
This does not allow for discussion and sharing of ideas.

___The same kind of material has been used for years.
The class does not participate in edu-
cational planning with the rest of the church school, and is not interested in exploring the various resources offered by the denomination.

___The class operates as an organization unto itself.
The group constantly looks inward and feeds upon the question, "How can we be satisfied?" The class may have its own membership and officers distinct from the rest of the church. The organization becomes all important. Service and ministry run a distant second.

___The class uses discussion, and encourages dialogue.
Isn't this the way by which we all grow? The give and take of ideas and opinions can be an exciting adventure.

___The class appreciates various points of view.
This grows out of dialogue. Is there more than one understanding of a parable? Are there two sides of an issue? Should the church "rescue the perishing and care for the dying?" Can there be disagreement in an atmos-phere of mutual acceptance? Yes, it has been done in other places, and it can work for you.

___The class uses an informal setting.
The group sits in a circle or around a table, or in small groups. This encourages dialogue and exchange of ideas.

___The class uses a variety of resources.
Teachers and leaders participate in educational planning for the whole church. They explore many kinds of resources offered by the denomination.

___The class sees itself as a part of the whole.
Class members do enjoy the fellowship of other class members, but they enjoy the life and work of the total church as well. They appreciate all aspects of the church.

__The class has its own schedule f events.
'his helps to make the class self-suffi- ient. Often events may be planned nilaterally with no class member hecking the church calendar. This an cause unnecessary strife.

__The class is locked into tradi- ions.
ìverything is done as it has been one. For example: the YOMACLS 'lass (YO-young; MA-married; CLS- lass) was formed in the 1940's. Today ew members are young; many are ingle. But the name and the format tay the same. One need not even read he church newsletter to know that he class Christmas party will be at he same restaurant, with the same andle-light installation-of–the-same- fficers-ceremony, conducted by the ame man.

__The class is wary of anything new.
'his is of course a problem for any nstitution. They feel secure when hings stay the same. Any suggested hange in lifestyle is greeted with sus- icion.

__The class has become a substi- ute for worship.
The trappings include room arrange- nent, with chairs in straight rows. 'ews are even better. There is a piano r a small organ, so that the class can ing hymns. An offering is received, usually for causes selected by the class. 'rayers are prayed, announcements re given. The morning lesson is a ubstitute for the sermon. Some kind f organization and functioning is mportant, but structure and activities re not sacred.

___The class is informal, with shared leadership.
Leadership is shared by many. The group may be asking: "What application can we find for the gospel in our time and place?"

___The class doesn't take itself too seriously.
If there is to be a special program in the Fellowship Hall during the church school hour, the class can be set aside so the members can support the special event. The prevailing attitude is: "We can pick up our discussion next week. Let's join the special event."

___The class is willing to consider new approaches.
New ideas, new methods, new materials are welcomed.

___The class nurtures the spiritual life.
The class may sing hymns and discuss their meaning. The class may study prayer and may pray informally together. But it recognizes the importance of worship within the corporate body of Christ.

JED Share, Summer, 1980)

1,500 at First Biennial Assembly of Kansas Disciples

McPherson, Kan. – The first Biennial Assembly of Kansas Christian Churches (KCC) was held here April 14-16, with over 1,500 persons in attendance. The theme of the Assembly was: "Celebrate the Good News." Special speakers included Thomas J. Liggett, Fred B. Craddock and William E. Pannell.

Dr. Liggett, president of the United Christian Missionary Society, spoke on the subjects: "The Issues of Survival" and "Christian Unity – in Our Time." He called on Christians to plan now for dealing with the issues of overpopulation, starvation and technology. He also asked for a rereading and action on *The Last Will and Testament of the Springfield Presbytery.* That document called for the death of the Disciples of Christ by uniting with other Christians.

Dr. Craddock, professor of preaching in the Graduate Seminary of Phillips University, make three presentations, using as biblical resources the Book of Romans. He encouraged those in attendance to make "Doxology" a permanent partner in one's life style.

Pannell, associated with the Tom Skinner Crusades, said, "For too long we have used a toilet-bowl philosophy in dealing with problems, as we try to flush away the real issues." He called for "real reconciliation by having suburbanites bring their guns to the inner cities, and burning them."

Mrs. Walter A. Meyers, outgoing president of KCC, spoke at the Friday evening Achievement Dinner. She asked diners to look into mirrors that had been placed at each place, and then remarked; "Now you are looking at part of the problem in the church today."

Honored at the dinner was Wesley S. Sims, who for the past 47 years has served as pastor of the Second Christian Church in Lawrence. Sims was cited for early support of NAACP and CORE. For many years, he served without salary and also ministered to blacks in the hospitals and jails. During depression years, he alone made the monthly building payment.

Ten congregations were recognized for having made significant ministries. After-session Espresso Groups were held on topics including world order, justice and peace, welfare, ecology, COCU, Christian symbolism and outreach programs.

Resolutions approved by the Assembly delegates included the renaming of the Department of Church Development to the Department of Ecumenical Involvement and Church Development, so that "ecumenical involvement will be the first business of the department."

Lewis A. McPherren, of Arkansas City, served as Assembly program chairman. William W. McDermet III oversaw all local arrangements.

(The Christian, May, 1972)

Minister's Forum: Use Caution

In the July, 1979 issue of the *Christian Ministry,* Lyle E. Schaller provides helpful insights in his "Twelve Tips for Church Growth." He suggests congregations plan for a Lay Witness Mission. I would like to provide input from my own experience with a LWM, which might provide constructive caution in planning such an event.

"Expect a Miracle, Come to LWM;" the sign was in the church narthex. It was one of many methods being used to get members to attend our Lay Witness Mission. Some who did attend the week-end event felt they had received a "spiritual high," others felt they needed Alka-Seltzer, still others felt indifferent.

The Lay Witness Mission program is billed as a renewal experience and the inception of Ben Johnson; a United Methodist pastor, head of The Institute of Church Renewal at Atlanta, Georgia. Promotional information from that Institute states that eight major denominations support the LWM. The main thrust is to have laypersons, called Witnesses, come and communicate their faith.

Missions are held over one week-end with the format always the same. On Friday evening a fellowship supper is held for members, friends and the visiting guest Witnesses. Following the meal there is singing, with emphasis on the good old Gospel hymns. Next, Witnesses are asked to "Share what Jesus is doing now in your life." Then participants are divided into sharing groups. On Saturday morning at 10:00 coffees are held in homes. At noon separate luncheons are held for men, women and youth. The Friday evening format is again followed Saturday evening. On Sunday morning the Witnesses teach the church school classes and the weekend Coordinator (also a layperson) speaks at the worship service.

We found the LWM to be a mixed bag. On paper it reads well. Indeed some of the methods used are of value. However, some of the "witnessing" done by our visitors left me breathless.

The prime problem for our people was being able to sift the wheat from the chaff. There was some of both, but seemingly more chaff. One did not have to get too far into the event to start hearing a number of clichés. "Give it over to the Lord." "The Lord led me to this." "God loves you and I love you." In the youth sessions, one of the leaders would periodically say, "Attitude check," to which all were to reply, "Praise the Lord."

At the men's luncheon the witnessing ran the gamut. A retired Witness from southeast Kansas reported that his life was, "Turned around for Christ following a wonderful experience for laymen at Oral Roberts University." Since that time he witnessed that the Lord was able to give him directions to churches in strange towns when he called on the Lord. At the other end was a university professor who stated that he felt his relationship with God allowed him to have a deeper appreciation for students. Earlier in his life he had disregarded students he did not understand; now he was working hard to show compassion to all. He was the *only* witness that I heard who mentioned God during the event. Most comments were on the Christ-and-me-as-pals level. Some of the presentations were accompanied with tears.

I did appreciate the questions presented at the small sharing groups. In the one I attended, the lead Witness started the session with, "What do you want to see happen in your church?" This was followed up later with, "What are you willing to give and do to see it happen?" However at the same time in another group a Witness was saying with forceful authority, "God punishes you for your sins, with sickness!"

I dropped in on one of the youth sessions in the Sanctuary. They were having a catacomb service with the lights dimmed. Again, some of the comments were helpful. I especially appreciated the constructive appeal from one boy, to show love for parents. Yet there seemed to be much unnecessary sobbing; to the extent that our own eighth grade daughter found it convenient to babysit on Saturday night rather than to return.

Even the literature for sale in the narthex was a mixed bag. The Institute supplied books ranging from the Swiss physician, Paul Tournier to ex-cowgirl Dale Evans. One could also buy 25 cent aluminum crosses with "Jesus Christ is Lord." (An Institute staff person had earlier informed us that if you could not verbalize your faith you could shake hands and leave a cross.)

The weekend found me bearing two crosses: the Adult and Youth Coordinators. The air of sanctity was heavy around both, and through their surgically implanted smiles the words, "Precious Lord," came frequently in stained-glass tones. I guess we did not hit it off from the start. I had been asked to arrange for a song leader. I did, but the Adult Coordinator had brought his own. Our established order of worship would also not work. The Adult Coordinator said, "I feel that the Spirit moves me to change it." As I had agreed to let the weekend be theirs, we scratched "Renew Thy Church, Her Ministries Restore" and "Praise to the Lord, the Almighty" in favor of a solo from a Witness, "He Touched Me," and that old sawdust trail favorite, "Just As I Am."

The Youth Coordinator spoke first during the sermon time. She was a good-looking ex-sorority twenty-year-old who had "Taken out a semester to sort out her life" and soon was going to a Bible College. Her witness centered on "Precious Jesus" directing her to the right airplane and thus witnessing to her seat mate.

Yet it was left to the Adult Coordinator to drop the theological bomb of the weekend: "If God wants me to have an accident, that's fine!" Later that day my fifth grade daughter told me quietly that she was confused about that statement. We attempted to work it through. During worship she had asked, "What's going on?"

At the conclusion of the service, during "Just As I Am," about one-third of the congregation did come forward to "rededicate their life to Christ."

The Adult Coordinator mentioned that he went forward frequently. Some were primed to come forward, others were caught up in the emotion of the moment; still others felt that it might help in their searching along the Christian Pilgrimage. Some who remained in their seats were irritated by the whole show.

At a prior meeting, Melvin Chuning, a staff member of the Institute, responding to a question I posed, said that the LWM was *a* way, and not *the* way. Following the event we found that for some it was a way, but for others it simply was not their bag. Elton Trueblood says that a "Fragmented gospel is better than none." Some found the weekend uplifting, others feared that the Gospel had not been fragmented but alas butchered.

I have my own reflections on that mixed bag of wheat and chaff. The wheat comes in the form of an acceptable weekend format. The strategy of laity speaking to laity is excellent. The Witnesses come at their own expense and some do try to share on a low key level from common daily events. They do bring enthusiasm and can be helpful in small sharing groups.

The chaff is also present. There is no good screening process of the Witnesses, or what or how they witness. A method of evaluating the Witnesses themselves is needed. Surely a total Gospel needs to be presented. Not once during the event was mention made of social gospel concerns. All comments were directed toward one's relationship with Christ.

The LWM also has the problem of forming its own denomination. Although the Atlanta office suggests that those who do become Witnesses remember that they have a local congregation to serve, many Witnesses are frequently gone, thus creating a void in their own congregation.

Another sign in the narthex read, "LWM – Try it you'll like it." It will be more likeable and tasty if there is more wheat and less chaff.

(Christian Ministry, November 1979)

(After 43 years in ministry, I reflect that this event was *the* most disgusting and distorting event I experienced. It may be a prime example of how sad and shallow the real Gospel is presented in contemporary America. God help us if we cannot do a better job.)

Getting to Know Everyone in Church

When I started at a new congregation, the search committee and I agreed that in my first year I would visit in every home. This is not easy, especially in a larger congregation, but it can lay a solid foundation for pastoral ministry.

First, the church secretary phoned each member to make appointments. This was easiest with the homebound and the retired members. The secretary then organized the names of those who worked outside the home and those with children into geographical sections. She told them that I'd like to visit their homes between 7 and 9 p.m. the following week, and asked what dates would fit their schedules. (An alternative for large congregations would be for host families to invite four or five neighboring families to their homes for a group visit with the pastor.)

The purpose of my visits was simply to get to know members on their own turf. I brought no hidden agenda. I started the conversation: "As your new pastor I would like to learn about your family, schooling, vocation, interests, hobbies, etc."

Sometimes members would ask the same about me. On some visits, if it seemed appropriate, I also asked: "What do you like best about our church?" This gave folks an opportunity to talk about the positive aspects of the congregation.

Following my visits, I wrote on note cards the information I'd gathered. These became valuable tools for future reference.

("Tricks of the trade" in The Christian Ministry, July-August, 1999)

The Church Choir: Koinonia Fellowship

The church choir is one of the most vital parts of any congregation. Any church choir can be a workshop in koinonia fellowship. This kind of fellowship is more than sharing a cup of coffee and mutually agreeing that it's too hot or too cold. In her book Beyond Our Selves, Catherine Marshall describes real koinonia as follows:

"Christianity was never meant to be a lone-sheep experience. One reason the first Christians received so much guidance was that they had the koinonia, a corporate fellowship which made them 'of one heart and soul.' It was in this setting that illumination, inspiration, and guidance flourish." (1)

Indeed, today, everyone needs as much of the koinonia as they can find. Of course, the reason we have church choirs is to praise God in song. Yet, is that all? Is there no interaction between choir members?

My introduction to a church choir was while I was a junior in high school. The choir director was searching for high schoolers who would fill the choir loft. I sang in that choir for the next six years until I left to go to seminary. I will always believe that being a part of that choir and being a participant in their koinonia fellowship was a major factor in my decision to go into the ministry.

I also need to be honest and state that there were some non-theological reasons for my going to those Thursday evening choir practices. I was allowed to drive the family car and there were high-school girls in the choir. It wasn't long, however, until I developed a feeling that I was wanted, needed, and accepted, even though my baritone voice did not quite fit into either the tenor or bass sections.

One of the happiest times in choir happened during the summer of 1955, when I was a sophomore in college. I was asked to sing in the summer quartet, but I felt that I would have little in common with the other three members. The soprano was over sixty-five – a quiet grandma-type. The alto was twice my age and shared none of my social, political, or religious beliefs, and she said so. The bass was the alto's husband, who I later learned was between stays in our state reformatory. Yet, we found ourselves blending not only our voices, but our lives. We practiced together, sang together, made ice cream together, and shared the summer together. We never called it koinonia fellowship. Those words may not have been in our vocabulary. I do recall, however, that the summer of '55 was a great experience.

Was it an isolated happening? I think not. Today, I'm the pastor of a congregation, and I note a close koinonia fellowship in our sanctuary choir. I feel this should and can be present in any church choir.

One necessary ingredient for choir koinonia fellowship is a caring choir director. In our case, this person is well qualified.

1. He has a knowledge of, and experience in, music. He keeps active in music circles.
2. He provides for flexibility without embracing an "anything goes" attitude. The choir may sing a Bach selection one week, followed by a contemporary anthem the next.
3. He is concerned for the choir members. Is a member absent? Why? The director checks on that person by phone or sends him or her a card.
4. Once a month he provides light refreshments after choir practice. And

few members miss the annual picnic at his home.

The choir members still share in the koinonia. They constantly care for and support each other. This concern, openly expressed, quickly becomes contagious. Casual relationships begun at a choir rehearsal often become lasting friendships.

I'm grateful for my college and seminary days, and for the growing experiences I've shared with many congregations. I'm also grateful for a church choir experience where I learned about God through music and a caring fellowship.

How about your church choir? Is it a koinonia fellowship? What can you do to see that it is one?

(1) Beyond Our Selves by Catherine Marshall, Copyright © 1971, published by Chosen Books Publishing Co. Ltd., Lincoln, Virginia 22078. Used by permission.

(The Church Musician, January, 1980)

Hear Our Voices Singing

Hear our voices singing,
Dear God we bring our praise.
Like clear bells when ringing,
Our hymn to you we raise.
Our joy turns into song,
As we feel love and grace.
Your music is so strong,
It fills all human space.

In rainbow harmony,
We echo Christ's great love.
With crystal melody,
Like angels from above.
Receive glad sounds of hope,
Emerging from within.
Of universal scope,
Our gift is genuine.

Each one must sing a part,
Then blend in unison.
Our tune comes from the heart,
Reflecting on Your son.
Sisters and brothers true,
We sing as one great choir.
We celebrate anew,
Your gift that does inspire.

Give Your Choir Warm Fuzzies

We all want and need recognition. All of us thrive on being stroked. Provide us with some warm fuzzies, and watch us perform! Yet too often we may simply take our choir for granted. Yes, their purpose is to praise God collectively. Yes, for many it is an honor simply to be a member of a choir. Yes, they may feel they often receive more than they give. But nothing beats tangible expressions of praise and appreciation.

Following are six simple, yet basic models of putting recognition into concrete form; they have been tried and found effective. You can apply some to your situation, or use them with modification; or maybe these suggestions can spark other ways to highlight those saints and sinners who sit in the choir pews.

1. *Spotlight choir members in your church newsletter.* Have this approved by the one who edits the newsletter. Then provide forms for each choir member to fill out and spotlight one each issue until all have been recognized.

Here is the one page form we found effective:

Choir Spotlight on

____

Place of birth ______________________

Places lived ______________________

____

Education ______________________

____

Family ______________________

____

Joined our church in ______________________

Occupation ______________________

Hobbies and interests ______________________

____

Favorite hymn ______________________

Favorite anthem ______________________

Favorite place to be ______________________

Favorite food ______________________

Favorite quote ______________________

Anything else you would like to share

____

2. *Hold an annual choir retreat.* This builds community and camaraderie that pays dividends through the year. The event could be on a Saturday, or a Sunday afternoon. Hopefully the church could provide part of the expenses, with choir members helping with the cost of meals. At one choir retreat the director secured the services of a college vocal professor. This person shared insights on how to breathe properly, which proved helpful both to the experienced and the neophyte.

. *Present a Hymnal when a choir member moves.* Our choir has done this for ıany years and it has become a very meaningful gift. Prior to the presentation, ave every choir member sign their name on the page of their favorite hymn.

. *Recognize the choir annually on a designated Sunday.* Announce to the congre-ation that choir members will be recognized on that Sunday after the service. 'his is an opportunity to present some special music during worship. Following ıe service allow adequate time for choir members to move to the place of fel-›wship. Encourage choir members to leave their robes on as they can be easily lentified. Special eatable treats, provided by the membership, are appropriate. 'his annual event provides church members an opportunity to say "thank you" n a face to face basis.

. *Allow your pastor(s) the privilege of providing a meal for you choir.* Many pas-›rs have a discretionary fund that could be used. This does not need to be an laborate event. The pastor could provide the main dish and others bring side ishes. A back yard picnic is adequate. Following the meal the pastor could xpress his/her appreciation to the choir for their ministry of music.

. *Provide certification for those who have sung ten years.* How many choir ehearsals are there in ten years? How many services? Even in our mobile soci-ty there are many within the choir who have sung faithfully for ten years. Those vho have sung for a decade are deserving of recognition. A simple certificate ould be designed easily and printed in your community. Certificates might be igned by the choir director, a member of the music committee, and the pastor. Certificates could be presented during worship; or a special meal, or _______.

There are too many times when we simply take the choir for granted. 'hey deserve to be recognized. Their ministry of music is important. Blessed re those who give of their time and talent as choir members. They deserve a pat n the back, and some warm fuzzies. So, let's give them.

(Vanguard, O/N/D, 1983)

Let the Congregation Compose

Our congregation has discovered and participated in something creativ that we find exciting – there are hymn-writers in our membership. The first sug gestion to allow this to happen came from our worship committee. "Let' encourage our own members to write hymns; and then use them in our wor ship," one member said with positive forcefulness. "But what if we get stuff tha really isn't sing able, that's junk, what then," responded another. Okay, so w needed some guidelines, but we put out the word that Harry Emerson Fosdick Charles Wesley, Georgia Harkness and R. Vaughn Williams wrote in their day what about our day, let us hear from you writers.

From the pulpit, and in the church newsletter, it was announced tha members were invited and encouraged to submit hymns for use in worship. W asked them to consider how God speaks to us today, and to share those feeling by writing words to hymns. We provided ourselves with an "out" by stating w might not be able to use all submitted selections. We asked members to take look at our worship service and consider writing material that would fit int weekly or seasonal worship.

All but one of the submissions has words to already written tunes. Tha single composition was "really bad" said our organist and our choir director, an because we stated we would not be able to use all submissions, we were no forced to use it.

I spent three hours working with one member until her words fit th music of the tune she selected. Her satisfying smile when we finished proved th time had been well spent. One member from our choir received encouragemen from this process, and he wrote the words and music to an anthem we used a the building dedication service.

Too frequently local congregations have encouraged members to be goo stewards by giving their time, talent, and money; but seldom providing oppor tunities to produce and use that talent. Our members responded to our call t compose. Selections came from women and men, young and old, from thos with college degrees and those with no higher education.

As soon as possible we included their offering of hymn-writing. Thei words were printed on an insert for the Sunday worship bulletin. Most wer used with hymn tunes our members knew. Here are some samples.

A Hymn of Prayer

"Lord I thank Thee"

(Tune: Pleyel's Hymn, 7.7.7 or Innocents, 7.7.7.7.)

Lord I thank thee thou are nigh,
Hearing when to thee I sigh,
For thy mercies aye endure
Ever faithful, ever sure.

Even when I fail thee sore,
Hateful, slamming shut thy door,
Yet thy mercies aye endure
Ever faithful, ever sure.

When I next seek thee in prayer,
Wonder that I find thee there —
Yes, thy mercies still endure
Ever faithful, ever sure.

— Mabel Metze

A Hymn of Invitation and Dedication

"We Yield Ourselves to God."
(Tune: St. Anne or Serenity, C.M.)

Amid life's tumult, strife and grief
And anguish of man's pain,
We hear the challenge of God's word,
That we be whole again.

From shatt'ring hatreds, hearts of stone,
We pray we may be free,
As with contrition, Father God,
We yield ourselves to thee.

Help us reveal forgiving love
Toward all, both friend and foe;
On men of every race and creed
Thy Spirit's grace bestow.

So with humility and hope,
Delivered from despair,
Our yielding spirits triumph know
In Thy enfolding care.

— Ruth Fillmore Lentz

A Hymn of Joy and Love

"Dear God We Trust in Thee"
(Tune: St Thomas, S.M.)

Dear God we trust in thee
Open our hearts today
Help us to see thy beauty, Lord
Let us rejoice with thee.

Praise, joy and love be ours
Hearts full of joy and peace,
That in our lives the love of Christ
Will cause all hate to cease.

— Nancy Schoen

A Hymn of Stewardship

"The Gifts of God are Great Indeed"
(Tune: St. Anne, C.M.)

The gifts of God are great indeed;
They're more than we can know
They awe us with their magnitude
Until our lives o'erflow.

When nature shows her moon and stars,
Her forests and her seas,
And sunsets glow in western skies,
We share God's mysteries.

When children run and laugh and play,
And parents join their fun,
God's priceless gift of family
Is seen by everyone.

The gifts of God continue on,
And all are underpriced;
O God, we thank thee for them all,
But most for Jesus Christ. Amen.

— Samuel F. Pugh

A Processional or Recessional Hymn

"God of Faith, Hope and Love"
(Tune: Tidings, 11.10.11.10. with refrain)

O God of *Faith*, who daily gives life meaning,
Help us to know and feel your presence near.
When we are weak, expand that faith within us,
So we may know that we need have no fear.
Give us your blessing, use us each day,
Serving and witnessing, that *we* might find our way.

O God of *Hope*, who makes tomorrow brighter,
When days are dim, let hope come shining through.
Lift up our eyes and hearts to all before us,
Fill days to come with hope that comes from you.
Give us your blessing, use us each day,
Serving and witnessing that *all* might find your way.

O God of *Love,* whose son you gave as Savior,
So fill our lives, that this same love may shine
Out from our lives, to touch the lives of others,
That they might know that they are also thine.
Give us your blessing, use us each day,
Serving and witnessing that *each* might find your way.

—Russell F. Harriso

The benefits of this "in-house" hymn writing have been many. Eac member who has written has found an avenue to express and witness th Christian faith. They have found satisfaction in sharing the faith.

Another benefit is the personal touch the hymns give our worship. W are able to experience, as a body of believers, the feelings, beliefs and joys of "on of our own."

Not every member can write hymns, so our congregation has provide other ways to be creative in worship. Some write prayers: invocations, interces sions, benedictions, prayers for communion and offering. Still others have mad banners used in worship. Who knows what might come next?

Our congregation has enjoyed hymn writing and singing the hymns o members. We do not know if any will become as famous as Samuel Longfellov or Isaac Watts, but the hymns by members have enriched our lives, and we rec ommend this practice to others. We found that the pews are alive with th hymns of worship.

(The Hymn, January, 1981; also The Church Musician, September, 1981)

$10,000 For Compassion

On Sunday, November 7 1982 at about 11:00 a.m. some person's giving allowed Downey Avenue Christian Church of Indianapolis to go over their $10,000 goal for Week of Compassion. The congregation thus achieved a goal they had set one year earlier.

Downey Avenue followed some simple guidelines which helped them achieve their highest gift ever for Week of Compassion. Those guidelines, listed following, might be helpful for other congregations.

1- *We set a goal that was a challenge, yet achievable.* Downey (with 453 participating members) had a strong interest in Week of Compassion, with giving in the last few years ranging between $5,000 and $8,000. The goal needed to be reasonably realistic yet stimulating. Thus a $10,000 goal.

2- *Our goal was for the entire year of 1982.* The main thrust continued to be in February, yet offerings were received throughout the year. However offerings were sent to Church Finance Council regularly not held until December.

3- *Special commitment cards were used.* The World Outreach committee devised a card solely for Week of Compassion giving.

WEEK OF COMPASSION

During 1982, I (we) hope to support the
Week of Compassion through
Downey Avenue in the
following manner:

$ ________ Per Week $ ________ Per Month
Name ______________________________
- Downey's 1982 Goal is $10,000 -

The commitments resulted in $1,875 of the total.

4- *We reported on our progress frequently.* On the first week of every month we printed a United-Way-type thermometer-graph in our church newsletter. For example at the end of August we were able to say, "We need only $656.57 before December 31." Then we stated, "We have rounded the final turn and are in the home stretch. Victory is within our grasp. We can smell it, we can feel it. Friends, keep those Week of Compassion gifts coming and we may be able to say 'We did it!' even before Advent."

5- *We encouraged all members and groups to get involved.* One family volunteered to make special posters depicting compassion needs. The Chi Rho held a leaf raking project, with money received designated for the goal. Our CWF, having met their already high Basic Mission Finance goal, made an extra gift.

6- *We reminded our people that every gift was important.* Students away at college sent money. Dozens of children learned about human suffering in church school and extended sessions. Then they responded by bringing special Week of Compassion coin boxes as an act or worship. We acknowledged them in the Sunday service, noting that many were heavy with coins given in love.

7- *We kept our people well informed about human needs.* We had a special mailing to our people. We used Week of Compassion material in our Sunday worship bulletins and in numerous articles in our weekly newsletter. We sent every member the *Week of Compassion Reports.*

8- *We built upon the enthusiasm created within.* We shared with the membership comments like this one from a retired couple who made a pledge and then wrote on the back of their card – "We want to help those in need in the Third World. Thanks to Bob and Nita Floe (Outreach chairpersons) for their lovely letter asking us to support the Week of Compassion." Throughout the year people kept asking, "How are we coming on our goal?" The membership created their own enthusiasm.

On Sunday, November 14, 1982 we devoted a few minutes of our worship service to celebration, for being able to provide compassion to those who suffer. We quickly reviewed the year. Some shared their thoughts from the pew. Then we stood and sang the Doxology. It was a moment of joy.

However our Outreach committee will not let us rest on past achievements. Even though we are now engaged in a special fund for a new roof, the Week of Compassion goal for 1983 has again been set at $10,000. And we plan to hold another celebration some Sunday in 1983.

(The Disciple, February 6, 1983)

Who Can Eat?

Beth was ecstatic, "Isn't it wonderful to have new families with young chil-
en in worship! We've hoped and prayed for this, and now they are coming."

"Amen to that," responded Jack, "but we've got our old problem again. ne of those new parents asked me if their young son – who has not been bap- ed – could take communion. What should I tell him?"

The "rule" that often governs this question among Disciple congregations – you do not partake of the Lord's Supper until you have received Christian ptism. End of discussion. Yet for many that "rule" does not satisfy, and they uld counter with this concrete example.

Lucille is a grandmother and a member of Prince of Peace Christian iurch. Yet she attends worship only once or twice a year, never gives more than a visit, and is not involved in the life and work of the congregation at any vel. Participating member?

Lucille's grandson, Robby, is a ten year old. He attends Sunday School d worship almost every week. He looks forward to the opportunity to wor- ip each Sunday. Robby enjoys singing the hymns, he faithfully brings fifty nts each week for the offering, and he even brings a Bible and follows the scrip- re readings. He feels he has a relationship with Jesus and His disciples at ince of Peace. But Robby is never invited to partake of Christ's meal; grand- other Lucille of course is.

In 1981 our congregation dealt with this concern. Two church families, th young children, requested guidance. They brought their concern to our ders who referred the matter to the Church Board, who referred it back to the ders. The Elders finally asked the Christian Education Committee to provide ritten guidelines. (Congregations love to refer issues rather than deal with em.) After reading, research, special meetings, consultation and refinement, e committee did provide guidelines.

In every pew in our sanctuary worshipers may read the following.

— Children and Communion –

The Christian Education Committee, in response to parental concern about children receiving communion and after documented study, presented the following guideline which has been adopted by both the Elders and the General Board of Downey Avenue Christian Church:

By belief and practice the congregation does not withhold communion from anyone experiencing or affirming a belonging to Jesus and the Church Family. Children, as unbaptized members of the Family of faith, and with parental consent and preparation, may respond to God's call at Christ's Communion Table to partake of the bread and the cup with baptized members of the Faith. This should be based on the child's own sincere desire to remember and love Jesus as he asked, "Do this in remembrance of me," and that the child wants to be loving, fair, and kind like Jesus.

It is Christ who invites (not the church) and urges all to become as a little child in loving trust of God and God's Son, Jesus Christ.

The flip side of this card states:

Suggested helps for parents in
preparing their children for communion

Communion has a special meaning for each person who participates according to one's own understanding and experience.

No one can claim that he or she fully understands Communion. Certainly the first disciples had little idea of the event which went on at the last supper. It was only after they had shared the bread and wine with Jesus, and after his death and resurrection that their experience became clear to them. And so it is with us whether we are young or old, we need to be continually growing in our experience and understanding of communion.

Communion has as much meaning for a young child at his/her level as it does for an older person at his/her level. Mutual sharing and careful guidance can help each of us grow into a richer experience of communion.

For us, Communion is an act of remembrance. Children can participate meaningfully in remembering Jesus and his love for them.

What results have we had? Some members still feel no one should tak communion before they are baptized. Some may frown when children and the parents partake. Many are grateful for the guidelines, *and* raising the concer which has allowed us all the opportunity to consider our place at Christ's Tabl and *who* does the inviting.

(Vanguard, Autumn 1984)

A World Wide Experience

The largest supper-event in the world takes place on the first Sunday in :tober, and all Christians are invited to attend. On that Sunday millions of ıristians will celebrate together the Lord's Supper. On October 5 more ıristians will receive communion than on any other Sunday of the year.

World Communion Sunday, observed internationally since 1938, stresses e world fellowship and unity of all Christians, and the oneness of Christ's folvers at his table. On this Sunday we are particularly aware of all believers who ake up the world-wide Christian family. We rejoice in the knowledge that as gather for this observance we join those of differing tongue, dress and lifele, to give thanks to God for the gift of Jesus Christ. We remember that in e church there is "Neither Jew nor Greek, slave nor free, male nor female; for u are all one in Christ Jesus." (Galatians 3:28)

This special Sunday provides an opportunity to become intentional conrning the world aspect of Christ's open table. This is an excellent time to come creative and to use the resources available in your community. llowing is a list of suggestions that can enrich and highlight the day – tried and oven successful in Disciple congregations.

+ Use a special format. Worshippers receive the elements at the front of e chancel area. Instruct them to go forward using the center aisle and return the side aisles. Special music related to communion might be sung by the oir.

+ Read the scripture in a foreign language. Select a familiar passage, plain it, and then have it read by a member who speaks another language, a ıdent studying a foreign language, or a language teacher. The search for those ho know another language(s) can be rewarding in itself.

+ Sing part of the service using another language. Jim Strathdee wrote n Loving Partnership" as the theme song for the 1982 ICWF Quadrennial. he first stanza can be used in both English and Spanish as a congregational oral call to prayer.

In loving partnership we come
Seeking, O God your will to do.
Our prayers and actions now receive,
We freely offer them to you.

Tus companeros de Amor,
somos Senor paro servir,
Accepta nuestros he, chos,
Las oraciones recibir.

+ Invite a foreign language teacher from your school system (or your conegation) to teach you the words of the Doxology in French or Spanish or erman or another language.

+ Use breads from other countries. Ask the CWF or another group to cure recipes and bake breads native to various countries. Suggest those comuning, sample more than one as they partake. Label the breads.

+ Use a juice other than grape. We might assume that grape juice is used all parts of the world as the symbol of Christ's blood. This is not so. For

example, in many areas of Africa grapes are not grown. These Christians u
grapefruit juice. Pineapple juice is used in other places.

+ Give the words of institution for communion in another language. La
October our congregation had nine members dressed in clothing native to lan
where they had lived. As worshipers received the bread they heard: "This
Christ's body, take and eat," in Arabic, English, French and Indonesian. As th
took the cup they heard, "The blood of the new covenant," in German, Japanes
Lonkundo, Spanish and Tagalog. You may be able to use just one or two la
guages, but the effect will be significant.

+ During the greeting/sharing period ask all who have lived in anoth
country to stand, giving their name and the country.

+ Use many places within worship to emphasize the world aspect of t
day. Here is a sampling.

An Invocation – Eternal God, creator of this world and all its beau
create in us the beauty of your true faith; that we might behold a vision of wh
our world should be, and become bearers of its rebirth. Amen.

A Call to Prayer — O come, desire of nations, bind
All peoples in one heart and mind;
Bid envy, strife and quarrels cease;
Fill the whole world with heaven's peace.

A Silent Meditation — A modest proposal for peace: Let tl
Christians of the world agree that they will not kill each other.

A Call to Stewardship — "And he said to them, 'Go into all the wor
and preach the gospel to the whole creation.'" Jesus spoke the words of this te
in the imperative mood. The command is "Go . . . preach" everywher
Through the world outreach of the church, it is possible for all of us to obey th
command. All of us can have a share in the work both here and abroad throug
the giving of our money.

A Call to Communion – Loving Jesus, remember your scattered churc
around the earth; gather it in unity and preserve it in truth. In communion wit
the saints and sinners, and with all creation, we worship and glorify you alway

A Unison Benediction — As the earth keeps turning, hurtling throug
space, and night falls and day breaks from land to land, let us remember *peop*
— walking, hurting, loving, sleeping, being born and dying. One world, o
humanity, living together within God's love. Amen and Shalom.

As we seize the great opportunity to expand our Lord's Table on the fir
Sunday in October may we center our thoughts on this hope: O Risen Chris
who made yourself known to disciples in the breaking of the bread at Emmau
the bread we break at your table is a sign of the brokenness of the world; throug
our sharing in the Bread of Life, open our eyes and hands to the needs of all peo
ple. May our hearts burn to share your gifts, and help us go into your worl
feeding one another with bread. You are the Bread of Hope, Life and Peace.

(Vanguard, O/N/D, 1986)

A Litany of Solidarity
With God's People in South Africa

eader: Twenty nine million people live in South Africa. Yet only the 4.5 million whites have full rights of citizenship.

eople of God: ***Twenty-one million Africans are treated as foreigners without rights.***

: The Africans were born in South Africa, work in South Africa, and will die in South Africa.

: ***But they are black, and under South African law, the color of their skin makes them non-citizens.***

: We once considered Africa to be the "Dark" continent, full of the unknown, mystery and danger.

: ***In the face of the darkness of apartheid, we claim the witness of the fourth Gospel: "The light shines in the darkness, and the darkness has not overcome it."***

: Apartheid is a huge, ugly, violent machine which ensures the supremacy of South Africa's white minority while brutally repressing the black majority. It is a system of legalized racism.

: ***We stand in solidarity with those who suffer in South Africa. We lift our voices using the powerful words of the prophet Ezekiel: "Thus says the Lord God: Enough. . . . Put away violence and oppression, and execute justice and righteousness; cease your evictions of my people, says the Lord God."***

: The Church has a scriptural mandate to ". . . preach good news to the poor, proclaim release to the captives."

: ***Nudge us O God, to urge our governments in the United States and Canada, to bring pressure on the government of South Africa, to take speedy action to end the system of apartheid.***

: The Church has a scriptural mandate to "set at liberty those who are oppressed."

: ***Be with us O God, as we lift up in prayer South African sisters and brothers in this struggle for liberty, even if we cannot call them by name. We affirm support for all religious leaders in South Africa and throughout the world, who are working for reconciliation.***

: We are grateful for those who have set this issue squarely before us seeking our aid and support.

: ***We commend the Division of Overseas Ministries for sending persons to South Africa to monitor the situation, to act as agents of reconciliation, and to further the cause of peace.***

: Our Christian brother Desmond Tutu has said: "The liberation of blacks involves the liberation of whites in our beloved country, because white people can never be really free until black people are free. There is no such thing as separate freedom – freedom is, and will always be, indivisible. It is a universal law that when a people decide to become free nothing will eventually prevent them from reaching their goal."

: ***We are grateful for those persons, white and black, who have labored for liberation, both in the past and in the present.***

: In our youth we may have sung a conference song: "We are marching to Pretoria." It was a fun song to sing, but we sang it not knowing that it was the capital city of a racist government.

P: ***We now sing a different tune, as we harmonize with those who are lite ally marching to Pretoria singing their anthem: "Let my people go."***

L: Paul said to those at Galatia: "There is neither Jew nor Greek, there is ne ther slave nor free, there is neither male nor female; for you are all one i Christ Jesus."

P: ***We say to those in South Africa: "There is neither African nor White nc Coloured nor Indian nor Afrikaner, for you are all one in Christ Jesus.***

L: Black and some white South Africans will continue to struggle again apartheid until it is eliminated. They are prepared to sacrifice much, t stand firm under the torture and violence of apartheid.

P: ***We stand with them. We know a change in lifestyle is a Christian prir ciple — witnessed in the Bible, practiced in the church, and hoped fc in contemporary society.***

L: "God so loved the world."

P: ***We live in God's world family, and we reach out to our sisters and broth ers in every land; but on this day especially to those oppressed in Sout Africa.***

L: "God so loved the world."

Unison: ***We believe that God created and is still creating; and that we ar called to join in this creation. We believe that God's loving spirit sti sets people free, and that God calls us to help in this task of liberatior Amen and Shalom.***

(Dan Hoffman, DOM Executive Secretary for Africa asked me to prepare thi Litany. In was used in Disciples congregations on the Sunday designated as a time of special concern for South Africa; 55,000 bulletin inserts were printed. Division of Overseas Ministries, June 15, 1986)

Church Boards Can Do Better!

The issue was – flowers or books? The custom was to have a florist send a planter to all hospitalized church members. Now, in the Church Board meeting, someone had made the suggestion that a book be sent instead of flowers. The reasoning was that paperback religious books would cost less if purchased in quantity; and they would be more "Christian" than flowers. Thus ensued a thirty-five minute (I timed it) hassle over this provocative issue; with no decision being reached.

That event happened over fifteen years ago, but was it an isolated example? I believe not. I'm afraid both you and I have experienced, or heard about too many occasions when the Sisters and Brothers did not act like a loving Christian family, to say nothing of becoming the Body of Christ.

We have gloried that our Disciples heritage allows for broad open freedom within our congregational lifestyle. But, is the Church Board meeting simply a place where people are allowed to air their petty concerns; a place to grind axes; to make the pastor uncomfortable; or an open forum to whine for those days past when things *seemed* to be "spiritual?"

I know of a congregation where Church Board time was used to sign petitions – both "for" and "against" the preacher; and where decisions were attempted to be made by fist-fights.

Friends we can do better! I share some suggestions/guidelines which might prove helpful as we Disciples do the business of Christ's Church.

+ Give careful consideration to the selection of your Board leader. In the congregation I now serve we call this person our Moderator. It is a good title. The dictionary defines moderate as, "with in reasonable limits; avoiding excess or extremes; temperate; mild; calm." If you can find such a person, and you can, elect her to lead the Board.

+ Start the Board meeting at the appointed time and end on time! Few Board meetings need be longer than an hour and a half. Congregations usually range from lackadaisical to down-right rude when it comes to starting and stopping on time. Get serious about this, and then do it.

+ Begin and conclude the Board meeting with prayer. Have this assigned long before each meeting. These prayers can be short and crisp, calling Board members together to seriously consider the life and work of the congregation.

+ Leaders and pastors should not go into the meeting and "wing-it." Plan an agenda and share it with the Board at the start of each meeting. Allow members to add agenda items.

+ Place the important items on the agenda first. This allows adequate time to consider those items, leaving the less important items for the last.

+ Be alert for possible "explosive" issues. The Church Board should not ignore the many contemporary concerns. Indeed when the church rules all controversial issues off its agenda, it has ceased to be the church. But leadership needs to be prepared to deal with these issues so they can be handled creatively, not destructively.

+ Have Cabinet/Functional Committee reports given in condense form by one person. In our situation our Cabinet meets the week prior to the Board. Our Vice-Moderator highlights this report for the Board; thus eliminating lengthy reports from a dozen individuals.

+ Allow for flexibility. One congregation had a clause in their

Constitution that the Annual Meeting (to elect and organize the Board) be held on the first Wednesday in July. One year the first Wednesday happened to be July 4rh. A few members were insisting the meeting *had* to take place on the 4th. In the discussion one Board member finally remarked, "I guess it would be easier to change the 4th of July than our church meeting!"

+ Are those at Board meetings usually bored? Are the same items disgustingly discussed meeting after meeting? Does one always hear, "We're not making our budget again this month." Controversial issues – if handled creatively – make for lively meetings. But also consider a variety of ways to make the meeting come alive. Seek out a Board member who can give a stimulating devotional. At the end of the meeting ask everyone to share *briefly* some "happening" from their life. Or have each one reflect on "one thing I like about our church is . . ." Or ask the pastor or a committee chairperson to relate future hopes and dreams.

Church Board meetings can be a time for Christ-centered creative contemplation and action. Too many times they have not been so. Board members need to remember that they are all on the same team. They are going in the same direction, on a collective journey, hopefully carrying out the ministry of Jesus. And, when votes are taken, and some members are on the "losing" side, let us remember that ideas are defeated, *not* persons.

If we work at it our Church Board meetings can become important events for the life and work of our congregations. They might become so meaningful and productive that Board members would rather come to those Monday evening Church Board meetings than watch the football game on TV!

(The Disciple, September 19, 1982)

That Valuable Honored Minister Pin

A funny thing happened on our way to give the Honored Minister pin to llow member Spencer P. Austin. It was stolen! I was first aware that something as wrong when Jennifer, our associate pastor, phoned and said I had better ɔme to the church. We had a break in. Late Thursday evening some person ad broken into the church office. The intruder had tramped through the main ffice, taken out the public-address microphones, and then went into my office.

A detailed look showed the person had taken only two things – a cassette pe-recorder and Spencer's pin. I had placed the pin on a cabinet next to my esk in a small envelope. The torn envelope was on the floor. We later found ıe recorder in another room.

The thief had passed by electronic equipment, electric typewriters, radios, ɔose change in a desk drawer, and took only one item – the Honored Minister in. Someone thought it of great value.

Because our congregation is in Indianapolis, we were able to secure from ıe Pension Fund another pin the next day, and presented that one to Spencer n Sunday. No doubt the thief thought he had something of value, and would y to sell it. But he would find it of no intrinsic value.

We too value the Honored Minister pin, but in a different light. Spencer ustin found that the pin represented another type of value – a symbol for the ords, "Well done good and faithful servant."

Pension Fund Bulletin, March, 1977. For many years this story was included with every pin presented to ministers who retired, provided by the Pension Fund.)

Twenty Things Every Church Should Try

Are things a bit stale around the church? Do events seem to be the sam
week after week? Are the words boring, and monotonous, synonymous with th
present state of the church? Then it is time to launch into new waters and ste
the church in a new direction. Following are twenty proven (tried in at least on
congregation with positive results) minor and major programs of ministry you
church should try.

1) Share ministry with another congregation. Seek out a congregation i
your community and then explore possible areas of joint ministry. This migh
be joint sponsorship of a community ministry, i.e., telephone ministry, foo
pantry, clothing supply. It might be a joint work project, or united worship serv
ice. Your two youth groups might plan a joint Christian heritage trip. The tw
congregations could hold their Vacation Church School experience togethe
This can become a lasting venture where both congregations learn to apprecia
and share Christian ministry together.

2) Allow members the opportunity to volunteer. Do you need someon
to arrange bulletin boards? Is someone needed to sit one hour in the churc
office on Sundays answering the phone and assisting in the Sunday morning rou
tine? Provide members with the opportunity to volunteer. A member might b
willing to turn the heat up on Saturday evenings; or wash the towels from th
kitchen; or help in the church library; or assist in home visitations, or ??? Bu
members must know the needs. Ask in the church newsletter, in meetings, etc

3) Give a symbolic gift to those who worship on Christmas Eve. Begi
a tradition that seizes the opportunity to make gift-giving significant. Thes
need not be costly. Have the worship committee plan the surprise gift, the
present one to each worshiper following a story/information time that reflects o
the symbolism of the gift. Possibilities are: a Christmas cookie, sharing the tal
ent-cooking of members; a flower bulb representing birth; a small Christma
ornament.

4) Start all events on time. Are services, meetings, and programs impo
tant or not? Does the organ prelude start at 10:30 or 10:35? Do you start whe
the majority gets there? Churches usually range from lackadaisical to downrigh
rude when it comes to starting on time. Initiate a policy of starting on time, an
then do it! The things the church does are important. We are about the mos
important "business" in the world. Then let's get serious about it. Start th
event on time.

5) Sponsor a refugee family. Every congregation ought to do this at leas
once. This is a wonderful way to become involved in some of the real hurts i
God's world. Your denominational offices can help, or contact Church Worl
Service. Sponsorship will take time and planning and money and energy. Yo
will experience the frustrations of dealing with endless local, nation, and inter
national red tape. You will participate in the agony of relocation. But you ma
be a part of seeing firsthand the ministry of Jesus in action; of helping those i
desperate need within our world family.

6) Once a year share what you would like to see happen in the comin
year. This probably needs to be done with a group appointed by your officia
governing body. Some guidelines need to be established before such a session
This might prove fruitful for both pastor and people. Have a group of four t

‹ spend an evening with the pastor(s) and brainstorm the dreams you have for e church. Some of those dreams might turn out to be held by the congrega- on.

7) Exchange choir music. How can you secure new music for your choir, id yet stay within the music budget. This is an annual question asked in con- egations, large and small. An excellent way to deal with this concern is to enter to a program of sharing choir music with neighboring churches. Make a list ' all music in your choir library, or have a volunteer make a list; then approach cluster of churches and suggest you begin sharing music. Most choirs use an ıthem only once a year. Why not share your anthems with other congregations ıd have them reciprocate? Depending upon how many congregations join the ogram you have increased "your" music library many fold, at no cost.

8) Participate in the New Testament example of letter writing. Paul and hers wrote letters of encouragement, guidance and hope to congregations and dividuals in New Testament times. Have your church join in the ministry by riting letters. Select a Sunday, preach on "Letter Writing as Ministry," and then ovide worshipers with a sheet of paper and an envelope. Ask them to use these aterials to write: a much loved friend not seen for some time; someone who ıce helped (them, or others); someone facing a difficult event, etc.

9) Begin a Name-on-a-door program. Congregations can begin a pro- am of sensitizing members to persons incarcerated for political or religious onvictions. On the first Sunday of each month worshipers are presented with name printed in large letters, conspicuously placed on a door at the front of the nctuary. (The church that did this had a large door at the front. Other situa- ons may call for the name to be placed on the Lectern or Pulpit, or next to a ecial window – any place of prominence.) The name represents a child of God ho is incarcerated for no "real" reason, with her/his imprisonment being ques- onable. Members are asked to pray for this person when they enter the sanc- ıary and to remember the individual in their private devotional life. When vis- ors ask: "What's that on the door?" members are encouraged to respond: That's the name of a person who has unjustifiably been placed in prison and we e praying for her/him." Those interested in adopting this program of solidar- y may write to their denominational office on Human Rights, or the United lations, for names and information on persons incarcerated. Another good ontact is Amnesty International, 322 Eighth Avenue, New York, NY 10001.

10) Encourage the people to say "Amen." Maybe your church is already oing this but too many Christian congregations are afraid of that four-letter ord: "Amen." We use it at the end of our private and public prayers. We often ng it at the end of our hymns. We say it at the end of The Lord's Prayer, but hy do we shy away from it at other times? We seem to be afraid to vocalize our ith. "Amen" is a good word and we ought to use it often. Encourage the con- regation to affirm the spoken prayer by saying "Amen" following prayers in the ervice of worship. Try this habit with in your committees and boards and small roups. It often becomes contagious. Let the people of God say "Amen."

11) Install a thermostat with no connections. It happens all too frequent- . One worshiper says, "I enjoyed the service, but it was too hot in there for ıe." The next person remarks, "Great sermon pastor, but why don't we turn up ıe heat!"

Solve this problem permanently. Have the property committee install a ıermostat in a conspicuous place at the back of the sanctuary. But do not connect it! This will allow *all* worshipers to turn the dial to whatever setting th desire.

12) Provide a "Put and Take Table." In a main areaway or narthex, pla a table and designate it as the "Put and Take Table." Have members bring ma azines, books, and other items they no longer want, so others may use ther This has proved to be helpful for older members on fixed incomes, who mig not be able to afford the cost of new books and magazines. Members have al found it a way to share excess vegetables from their gardens. Others may pla items they no longer want. Someone can be designated to periodically "clea up the table, and discard items that have served their time.

13) Have informal sharing within the worship service. Some congreg tions call it, "The Time for Sharing" or "Opportunity for Concerns," still ot ers, "Moment of Fellowship." This needs to be approved by the worship con mittee and the pastor. Done with the *proper* attitude it can be an effective w to provide support, sharing and caring within the church.

Prior to the Prelude, have the pastor go "into the congregation" and a for sharing. These might be happy or sad events, but they are enlarged an enriched when they are shared – special anniversaries, persons or groups to b prayed for, visitors introduced, special opportunities. This is *not* the time announce the weekly choir rehearsal or sewing session.

14) Allow for prayers from persons in the pews. This could be a bit risk But have the worship committee consider providing a time in worship – say f one month – when those in the pews are invited to stand and give a *senten* prayer. Don't worry about two persons speaking at once; or if all cannot hea Allow it to happen. It's been done with positive results.

15) Make the organ prelude meaningful. The organist hates it, churc members really don't know what to do with it, and pastors are frequently caug in the middle over it. "It" is the organ prelude which ought to start the servi of worship. What often happens is that half the congregation want a time f silent mediation, while the other half want to greet their friends and catch-up o the latest news. One congregation has solved this perennial problem by usin the following format.

The Time of Informal Greeting
The Chimes – 11:00
The Time of Community Sharing (see #13)
The Organ Prelude

Within this arrangement members are invited, even encouraged, to gre each other and welcome visitors prior to the chimes. (A few notes on the orga could suffice.) Next, sharing takes place under the direction or the pastor c worship leader. Then, the one leading the sharing invites all worshipers to pr pare for worship by being silent while listening to the organ prelude.

16) Have open discussion on the sermon topic following worshi Announce the sermon topic, along with discussion questions at least a week pri to the sermon. Select a respected member to moderate the discussion. Do n you this yourself as pastor. Have the moderator keep the discussion on the se mon topic. This opportunity allows parishioners to express their feelings co cerning the subject.

17) Provide a list of disciplines for Lent. Print a check list of opportun ties for growth during the Lenten season. Place the emphasis on positive poss bilities. These could be placed within the Sunday worship bulletin or maile

within the church newsletter. These might include:

_____ I will pray at least once a day.

_____ I will be conscious of a hungry world by eating more simple meals than is my custom.

_____ I will spend at least fifteen minutes a day in Bible study.

_____ I will contact some person each day either by note, phone or visit to express appreciation, friendship or concern.

_____ I will read one religious book during Lent, preferably one on the life of Jesus.

Each congregation can provide a list that has meaning for their location.

18) Form a Membership-Celebration Committee. Appoint, elect, delegate a group of six to eight to plan large and small events throughout the year that provide opportunities to affirm life. Hold a birthday party where members sit at tables according to the month of their birth. Sponsor a church picnic. Form koinonia-growth groups. Provide a fellowship time every Sunday after or before worship – inside in winter, outside in summer. Turn the group loose and allow them to plan fun events for the membership.

19) Have your Evangelism Committee visit other churches. Send those in charge of evangelism out to see what it's like to be a visitor. How did they feel? Were they welcomed and included, or not? What insights could they apply to the home congregation? Getting the "feel" of a visitor will help to program for adequately receiving visitors.

20) Make an Event Banner for the year. In January unveil a large banner with only the date of the year. Display it prominently and encourage groups and individuals to make and attach symbols that relate to happenings in the life and work of the church. Refer to the banner throughout the year.

(Your Church, March/April, 1983)

Twenty More Things to Try

"Jesus Christ is the same yesterday, today, and tomorrow." We know this often quoted statement is true. Yet too many congregations allow the life and work of the church to continue along the same old all-too-familiar path with most church happenings being classified as "boring-routine." It need not be so. Let us take a look at new twists to church activity.

21) Provide a time for silent meditation within the Sunday service. We live in a world of noise. When, where, how, does one find time to commune silently with God? One congregation structured into their worship a time for meaningful silence. That church ended their worship in this manner. – They placed in their worship bulletin a section: "The Time for Meditation and Reflection. First, they collectively sang "Teach Me To Stop" by Ken Medema. It is from his musical, "Jesus, the Story Tellin' Man." That church titled it, The Choral Call to Reflection.

Teach me to stop and listen,
teach me to center down

Teach me to be collected,
teach me to be in tune

Teach me the use of silence,
teach me where peace is found.
Teach me to hear your calling,
teach me to search your word
Teach me to hear in silence,
things I have never heard.

Teach me to be directed,
silence will end so soon.
Then when it's time for moving,
grant it that I may bring
To every day and moment,
peace from a silent spring.

(For permission to use, contact Word Music Inc .P. O. Box 1790 Waco, TX 76703)

Following this musical introduction there was a printed meditation to be read in silence. One was ("Quiet before God is all too rare. These moments of contemplation, while we listen to the organ, are for considering what has transpired this morning in – hymns, prayers, scripture, the spoken word, communion and other elements. It is also an opportunity to consider the week ahead and our place in God's world.") Then the organist played a 2-3 minute selection. Appropriate ones could be "Largo" and "Arioso" by Handel or "Jesus, Joy of Man's Desiring" by Bach. The service ended with a quiet choral benediction.

22) Have family members stand during a baptism. This exercise is especially meaningful for communions that practice baptism by immersion, where family members cannot be at the immediate area of the baptistery. But the practice could be used in all faiths. Immediately before the candidate is baptized, ask the candidate's family/friends to stand, and remain standing while the baptismal statement is given and the act of baptism performed. Although this time may last only a few moments, families who have participated in this event state it was one of the most meaningful acts of family participation they have experienced.

23) Select round tables for your fellowship hall. The next time your church buys tables for your church dinners give that selection special consideration. Most churches now have the traditional 36" by 96" rectangle tables. They are serviceable, but does fellowship take place around them? Those sitting at the ends usually have to shout to be heard. Instead, consider buying round tables. Those who do use them are high with praise: "Round tables allow those eight or nine sitting at the table to enter into conversation without yelling. Every person has a feeling of being a part of the group. You don't feel you are at an institutional event."

24) Hold a Worship-Through-the-Arts month. One church held this event during the Lenten season. They formed a small task group to organize and coordinate the events. The time was divided into two sections. The first part was an open invitation to church members, and members of the community, to share their works of art. People were invited to bring pictures, prints, needlework, banners, stained-glass or sculpture, and display them in a designated area in the building. Items shared were to have a religious theme.

The second part was a series of programs presented as worship on Sunday evenings. These were concerts by the vocal and hand bell choirs; concerts by choirs from colleges in the area; drama and organ concerts, or puppet ministry. Offerings may be received at the evening presentations to off-set any costs. This program allows the artistic creativity of those within the congregation, and of friends in the community, to be appreciated as the arts are used to worship God.

25) Have the wedding couple face the congregation. How uninspiring it is for wedding relatives and guests to look at the back of the heads of the bride

nd groom. During the preparations for the wedding ceremony suggest that the ride and groom face the congregation during the service so the congregation ees their faces and the back of the clergyperson's head. Who is being married? Who is important? Yes the couple will be nervous. But they are surrounded by amily and friends who love them, and who want to see them. Clergy can learn o station themselves so they are not the center of attention. Let it truly be the ouple's moment.

26) Practice the universal aspect of Christ's Church. Christians need to lways remember that the Church of Jesus Christ was one before it was many! There are ways a church can act upon the words of Jesus found in the Fourth Gospel, "I pray . . . that they may all be one . . . that the world believe." (John 17:20-21)

Invite a pastor from another denomination to preach during times of acation, illness or special days.

Invite a pastor from another denomination to read the Scripture when nembers are baptized.

Help in organizing a pulpit exchange among neighboring congregations.

Help in organizing a choir exchange.

Help in organizing a Sunday afternoon where members from a number of hurches may go to other church buildings to see and hear how and why churches worship and do ministry. This can be a "Journey in Understanding."

Use your imagination for ways where your congregation can symbolize he universality of the church.

27) Use the phone more. Most churches and members pay the same nonthly phone bill regardless if the phone is used 10 times or 1,000 times. Why not take advantage of this service? Yes, nothing beats a face-to-face encounter. But, often a phone call to support, or speak words of kindness, can mean almost as much as a visit. When members receive promotions, or celebrate anniversaries, or at anytime, why not simply use the phone, "I'm calling some members oday, and thought I'd phone you." Ask Deacons or Elders or a women's group o make weekly phone calls on behalf of the church. They can make these mportant contacts without even leaving home.

28) Organize a movie discussion group. One church used some special unds to buy a 32" TV, VCR and steel stand on wheels. They formed a small ask force to select significant movies to view. The group meets monthly on a pecified Sunday afternoon (or evening) in the church parlor. Major movies can be rented for a few dollars. (Be sure not to charge for the movies, for this is against copyright rules. Serve refreshment, and receive an offering for them.) Appoint one member to be in charge of the discussion, which follows after viewing the film. The discussion leader needs to preview the film before the session. There are many resources available for the discussion leader. Movies are reviewed veekly on many TV programs. Most major newspapers have movie review columns. Magazines such as *The Christian Century* have excellent reviews. Films hat are good entertainment, thought-provoking and good discussion starters are endless. A sampling: (Okay, so here I have included some movies produced after his was written in 1984) "Places in the Heart," "The Color Purple," "A Trip o Bountiful," "The Mission," "A Man for All Seasons," "Philadelphia," "Simon Birch," "Tuesdays with Morrie," "Driving Miss Daisy," "To Kill a Mocking Bird" ("old" and in black and white) but worth seeing again. This list is endless.

29) Display a congregational time chart. Select a wall of a major traffic area (front entrance, narthex, fellowship hall) and place on this wall a roll of newsprint of at least twenty feet. Have a person or committee decorate the chart and divide it into years. You should start your chart with the year your oldest member was born. Then encourage all members to record important dates in their lives: birth, graduation, marriage, when they united with your church, special events, etc. This is an informing and fun activity that allows the membership to feel important and also know others better. Significant events within the life and work of the church can also be recorded. Encourage members to record their events within the first month, and then leave the chart up for another five months.

30) Provide a telephone reassurance ministry. One county seat community used the following format. Seven congregations formed a local telephone ministry. A phone was installed in a small room in one church building. The purpose of the ministry was to provide a way for individuals, who lived alone, to be contacted daily. Each of the congregations provided volunteers for one week on a rotating basis, to make the calls. Any person who lived in the community regardless of church affiliation, or no church connection, was invited to submit their phone number for the program.

Names were secured through information provided from local congregations, and a brief article in the local newspaper. Individual calls were made between 9:00 and 10:30 each morning. Contacts were to (a) be sure the individuals were okay, and (2) to simply make human contact with those persons who lived alone. If the volunteer did not receive an answer, a friend or relative was contacted to be sure the individual was not injured. (The name of the friend or relative was listed on the card of each one contacted.)

In two cases during the first year, when a contact was not made, medical personal were sent to the residence. Individuals had fallen and they could not reach the phone. They were transported to the local hospital.

The small cost for a few materials and the monthly phone bill were divided among the seven sponsoring congregations. Not only were "shut-ins" provided with a ministry of caring; the callers reported great satisfaction with the opportunity to provide this support ministry. (Many "Thank You" notes and comments were received from those who were contacted.)

31) Hold "Come-on-over" times. Select members to host "Come-on-over" events, who will select a time (evenings, or Sunday noon) and invite members into their home for a meal. Hosts may provide the meat dish. Then post these events, each on a separate paper, on your bulletin board. Provide spaces for the number the host can seat. As soon as the list is filled the host phones those attending and assigns other dishes. At the meal each host may provide a time when introductions are made. Allow enough time for participants to share their backgrounds in detail, including favorite pastimes and hobbies. Hosts may also initiate a sharing time around the topic: "What I like about our church." This is a time to accentuate the positives. The hosts could later share these ideas with the church staff.

32) Hold your Maundy-Thursday communion service in your fellowship hall. Jesus shared the bread and cup around a table in the upper room. Christians today can best act-out the Last Supper event by communion around tables. One church follows the following format. The bread and wine for each table is placed in the center. A piano is moved in to accompany singing. Prayers,

mns, scripture readings, anthems and/or solos are interspersed in the service. ıere is a time of table fellowship during which the worship leader asks for each e to introduce themselves; tell about their uniting with the body of Christ; a ief Lenten experience; and complete the statement: "I'm thankful for Jesus cause . . ." At the direction of the worship leader the communion elements are ten at the tables, followed by a closing hymn and a benediction.

33) Purchase a display case. A nice glass display case (6'x4'x2') can be ırchased for around $500. Memorial funds might be used. Be sure it has justable shelves. Place the case in a prominent area. Items to be displayed are nitless. Almost every department in the church can use it. A new display is eded monthly or bi-monthly. Displaying hobbies by members is a sure hit. ther possibilities include – a display of crosses during Lent; Bibles from the nerican Bible Society (P.O. Box 5656 Grand Central Station, New York, NY)163); old hymnals; art/craft work from children in the church school; church storical items; items from other countries, especially where your church has ission work.

34) Develop a relationship with a sister congregation from another coun-y. Secure the address of a congregation from your denominational headquar-rs, or write to the World Council of Churches, 475 Riverside Drive, New York, Y 10115; or Riverside Church, 490 Riverside Drive, New York, NY 10027. ne congregation made a three-year commitment to a sister congregation over-as. The two congregations exchanged letters and pictures monthly. They ayed for each other. They read about each other's society and local communi- using newspapers, magazines, encyclopedias, books and the appropriate nbassy for information. This program enables American congregations to velop a relationship with a sister congregation and reflect together, in the con-xt of a mutual commitment to love and understanding, on the meaning of the hristian faithfulness in each particular place.

35) Make your own communion bread. Many in the churches today can call when some kindly older sister made the bread for communion. This is a st art that needs to be reclaimed. The congregation I serve observes the Lord's ıpper weekly, and for the past four years members have prepared the bread. ne person coordinates the procedure, and members or groups within the ıurch prepare the bread for one month at a time. The variety is great and the ste is good. Who said communion bread had to taste stale? Those who pre-ıre the bread have approached the task with reverence. (Do have commercial--prepared bread on hand in case a mortal baker should forget.)

36) Spice up your church newsletter. In the corridor of a seminary I over-eard one professor say to another, "I've been doing a study of local church ewsletters, and I could sum them up by saying they are boring, dull and trite. hey are an insult to one's intelligence." Work closely, and gently, with the one ho prepares and edits the newsletter. Have a committee work with the church aff and examine a number of back issues. What was important? What was ıarp? What could have been improved? Too many newsletters simply borrow ınk fillers from other newsletters. Get rid of overworked church clichés: Word has just been received" or "Every one is welcome." Of course everyone welcome. Is anyone not welcome? Select only sharp, thoughtful quotes. Have meaningful "Thought for the week" highlighted in a box. Use cartoons and ictures. Enlist persons to be reporters to write about church happenings. A igh school or college student taking a journalism class might welcome the

opportunity. Work at it and make your newsletter the best in your area.

37) Provide a bulletin board for exchange of opinions. Members wh hold a minority point of view on an issue tend to suppress their feelings. Inste of venting their feelings with unsigned letters to church leaders, those who fe their opinions are ignored may post them on the board. This method, whi allows for a variety of points of view, is to establish a place where all are free place material. One church published the following in their newsletter.

> What do you think? The General Board has voted to reserve part of the bulletin board in the areaway for an exchange of views among members. You are encouraged to put up cartoons, articles – your own or something you've read - which expresses your view on important public issues. We rejoice in our differences. Here is a chance to share them openly. See you at the bulletin board!

38) Have prayer at every meeting. Does this statement seem stran within the context of this list? Maybe, but one is amazed at how many boar commission, task-force and committee meetings prayer is never offered. It's n that we have gotten away from it, but too often prayer is just not a part of t agenda. Have your official church body examine this. Encourage every chur group to include prayer in their meeting. Ask this be done for at least one ye Have prayer at the choir practice, at the youth group, at the work day. Th would be an excellent time to examine what ought to be and what ought not be included in prayer. Prayer could become a priority for the year. The past might preach a series of sermons on prayer. Outstanding prayers and praye from the Bible could be reproduced in the newsletter. If prayer was an impo tant part of the life of Jesus, it should be an important part of the life of yo church.

39) Organize a community Thanksgiving meal. A local church provid the model. That church sought to serve older persons, both in their church ar in the community, who spend Thanksgiving by themselves. Seeking to provi an opportunity for food and fellowship for these people they organized a con munity Thanksgiving meal. Reservations were received in advance at a nomin cost. Volunteers prepared a complete meal and it was served in their buildin They also provided for meals to be taken to persons who were not able to co to the building. They provided simple door prizes, and at times special mus that came from area churches. Volunteers to secure and prepare food, to ta meals to homes and to clean-up came from many churches in the area. Tho who eat and those who serve both find it a joyous occasion.

40) Welcome visitors warmly. Like other clergypersons I rarely attend service of worship as a stranger. But when I do I am amazed at how inept v Christians are at greeting strangers. There is something in the Bible about gree ing strangers, (check Hebrews 13:2 and III John 1:5). During a recent summ trip we stopped to worship at a large church in a Midwestern state. I was sens tive as to how I would be received as a stranger. No one spoke to us as we we seated. After worship I planted myself at the side of the center aisle almost da ing anyone to pass me by without speaking. They managed to do so with eas I counted seventeen persons who came within handshaking distance, but n one did so, or spoke to us. First impressions are vital. People want and need be recognized and to feel welcome. One often gets a warmer greeting from t bank teller, service station attendant, and bus driver than they do from tho

within the church! How are visitors received in your church?

41) ____________________

Now that you have read this list you probably said, "I've got two or three ideas that are just as good." I'm glad you do. Now go, try them.

(Your Church, July/August, 1984. An abbreviated version appeared in the 1987 Edition of The Ministers Manual. "Things 41-60" were accepted by Your Church for a future issue; however, the ownership, format and editor all changed; so 41-60 remain known only to me, and God.)

G.E. and Mac, Faithful Laity

"If only there were more like your mom and dad within Christ's Church." This was the warm comment from a long-time family friend following Dad's memorial service. We had held a similar service for Mom two years earlier.

Their bodies were placed side-by-side in a Kansas City area cemetery; but their spirits left a joyous trail of support, as laity par-excellence in Disciples congregations in Nebraska and Missouri. ("Joy Joy" is inscribed on their cemetery headstone, a familiar saying of mother's.)

To the question: "Can anything good come from Hope, Kansas?" Dad, William Wallace McDermet II (everyone called him "Mac," even mother) embodied a "yes" with a meaningful career in social work. Dad evidently got a good start in life from a supportive family. In a file we found a letter from Dad's father, written to Mac on February 13, 1915, when Mac was four years old:

> *My dear son William. Will write you a letter. I want you always to be a good boy and a perfect Gentleman. Always be good and kind to all, be good to your mother. Love and obey her at all times, love and obey your savior. Keep his Commandments and you will have peace on Earth and Earn a home in heaven. Your loving Father WW McDermet*

Mom, (Grace Eleta Lowe) was a PK (Preacher's Kid) who, with her sister Margaret, loved playing "church" in the parsonage. Mom was at the piano, and Margaret was the "preacher." (Their father, W.S. Lowe, was one time State Secretary – now Regional Minister – of Kansas. He would later become the preacher for the Lowe/Anderson Evangelistic Team in the Midwest.)

Mom and Dad met in Lincoln, Nebraska at Bethany High School. Dad was a 120 pound halfback who kept a lock of Mom's hair in his football helmet. They went to Cotner College (a Disciples school in Lincoln.) Mom was in many music groups, and Dad was president of the senior class. They always noted that Cotner died in 1934, one year *after* they graduated. A quote they frequently used was one placed on the chalk board by Cotner's philosophy professor: "Keep an open mind, and a suspended judgment."

Dad wanted to be an engineer, however they were in his words, "a-dime-a-dozen;" so he began a meaningful social work vocation. He kept a balance in job and humor while being the first male director of a county (York) welfare program in Nebraska. Mac received a letter from a small community, with the writer requesting they be given strong consideration for a state-county program. To add to the importance of the issue the letter was signed, "Mare of Henderson."

In 1939 the family moved back to Lincoln where Dad was in charge of personnel for public welfare in all 93 counties. He remarked he had been in *all* 93, giving support to all county welfare staff. The family became active in the Tabernacle (now Southview) congregation.

During this time Mom was providing leadership as president for all the PTA groups of Lincoln. In this position she was able to share in the decision process of Lincoln public schools.

In 1956 the family relocated to the Kansas City area where Mom and Dad became deeply active in one of the largest congregations in the area. Mom was president of all 21 CWF's, Dad was an Elder. Together they chaired the World Outreach Committee, which at that time was the #1 congregation in giving to ıtreach/mission causes, within the denomination.

However, there were some strong differences within the congregation. At church board meeting the National Council of Churches was taking a beating r some social action ministry they were performing – helping the marginalized. he decision was to "hit them (NCC) in the pocketbook," and not send the 500 set in the yearly budget. Instead of continuing the "discussion" within the oard meeting, when Dad came home, he simply wrote a check for $500 and ailed it to the NCC.

G.E. was making her own witness. The congregation wanted to recognize e founding pastor by building an expensive chapel, across the street, in his emory. Mother put forth the suggestion the former pastor be membered/honored with a mission health clinic, in Africa, which would bear is name.

The chapel "won" mainly because 60 new parking spaces went with it, d the congregation had no off-street parking. (To somewhat "pacify" Mom, e senior pastor scheduled her as the first woman to speak in the new chapel.)

In the late 1960's, persons on the peripheral of society, were attempting to rganize, to effectively demonstrate their basic human needs for jobs and housg. The Kansas City cluster of congregations met for the purpose to help/not elp, employ social activist Saul Alinsky from Chicago to organize and provide rong direct witness to the needs of Matthew's Jesus "the least of these." (25:40)

Alinsky, himself, was a "hot issue," not necessarily because he was Jewish, ut for his activism, at times resulting in ugly demonstrations, strong language, d direct confrontations with the powers that be. At the – go with/do not go ith – Alinsky vote, the room was packed, and the discussion was intense. I was resent, representing another congregation, and just before the vote, Dad went the front and gave a 3-4 minute talk supporting the calling of Alinsky, noting e opportunity for the church to help those in need, and our, indeed obligation, get on with ministry. His tone was calm and firm, his reasoning logical and ncere. The vote, by a strong majority, was to call Alinsky, even as the other repsentatives from Dad's church voted, "no."

At age 62, Dad had had enough of the Nixon administration's interest in ollars and not in the social needs of people, so he took early retirement from his deral position from the regional office of the Department of Health, Education nd Welfare.

In 1972 G.E. and Mac moved to the Lake of the Ozarks, and they immeiately became a part of a congregation in Camdenton, a 62 mile round trip. Iere G.E. was a member of the Regional Board; a Board member of the Barton V. Stone NBA Home in Illinois; and chair of the Pastoral Search Committee. Iac was an Elder. Together they commissioned a beautiful/dramatic fourteen oot multi-dimensional cross which hangs above the central baptistery.

In 1981 they retired to Foxwood Springs, a community in Raymore, Iissouri. They united with the "campus" congregation. There Dad and Mom erved as worship greeters, counted the offerings, and they founded the World Outreach Endowment Fund with a significant initial gift. The Fund has since ıultiplied by four times. Monies are used only for projects, equipment, supplies eyond the local church. One of the latest projects was to help send 18 on a mison/work trip to Mexico.

In reflection on our parent's lives, I believe they put into action, what Iarcus Borg put into words: "The Kingdom of God is not somewhere else; . . .

it is a present reality in the message of Jesus."

To the question: "Why am I here, and what can I do with my life?" Mom and Dad answered by putting faith into action. They were always co: cerned about those within the world family. In the 1950's it was Grace Ele who would ask, "But, what about the Palestinians?" (A people without a cou: try.) In a chapel meditation she concluded with these words:

> *There is no separation between me and God. God means the courage in my spine, the service in my hands, the wisdom in my mind, the sympathy in my ears, the love in my heart, the words on my tongue, the vision in my eyes, the direction in my feet, the dedication of my being.*

Mac used to amusingly say, "You know the shortest verse in the Bible 'Jesus wept.'" To which I can lovingly respond that perhaps another verse sur up their lives. In Mark 3:35 the evangelist has Jesus say, "Whoever does the w of God is my brother and sister."

It may be clergy who "preach the Word" yet it is often laity who "turn t Word" into active ministry. Amen.

The Water Buffaloes

I recently moved from one mid-western community to another. ollowing Sunday worship, a church member, and a professional man in the ommunity, invited me to attend his service club. His intention was that I join e club. Their meeting time was convenient for me, so I visited; and within a w weeks I did join. (Good "evangelism," so far.)

After I joined, a number of things happened which I found easily parallel e life and work of a local church. Let's simply refer to my new club as – The 'ater Buffaloes.

Soon after I became a Water Buffalo, the church member who invited me join, stopped attending worship almost completely. I wondered if he really as interested in me, or more in the VCR given to the Water Buffalo who rought in the most new members. He did introduce me to a few fellow Water uffaloes, but I soon found myself on my own. I wondered, how many new urch members are warmly welcomed into membership, and then, boom, they e lost in the crowd.

What really bothered me about becoming a Water Buffalo was that I had carve out a place for myself. There was no orientation to the club, none. I oticed that other Water Buffaloes had large badges with their name and work assification. After a few weeks I rather shyly asked an officer how I could get ne. "Oh," he replied, "Sure, we will see to that, how do you spell your name?" got my badge two months later.

On another occasion I asked about the little Water Buffalo lapel pens ther club members were wearing. "Oh," said the president, "here's one" as he pened the speaker's podium, "and you probably could use a roster of all the embers." Yes, I could, and yes I will.

After being in the club for a few weeks, some of the Water Buffaloes knew was a clergyperson, so I was asked to give the invocation. I did. However, no ne informed me that the person who gives the invocation was also to lead in the ledge of Allegiance. There was an awkward pause.

In a few more weeks, I was asked to secure the program speakers for one onth. Wanting to do my share, I said I would. However, again, I had to take e initiative and ask, "Does the club pay for the speaker's lunch? How long ould the guest speak? Does it matter on what subjects they speak?" The nswers were: "Yes" "About 20 minutes" "Any subject."

Please do not misunderstand me – I like the Water Buffaloes. They are ice people. We have a good "fellowship" together. There are both male and emale Water Buffaloes. Some members are young, some not so young. They ome from an interesting cross-section of the community. But, boy, could they nprove in assimilating a new member into their club! They have a special fund help solve a world problem. I asked the local chairperson of this project for ore information and a pledge card. He smiled and said he would see that I eceived both. But, he must have forgotten, for he never gave me anything.

Membership in a church is far more important than membership in any ub; but do we do any better at incorporating new members into the congrega- on? After they join does the pastor, or members of the congregation provide rientation about the worship and activities of the church? Even among isciples congregations we have different styles of worship. We vary in the man- er we take communion; we vary in stewardship, education, outreach and community programs.

I have learned a lesson from my Water Buffalo friends – don't leave any thing to chance. Get organized, follow-through, make sure you have complete ly explained the: who-what-when-why-where and how's of all phases of the lif and work of your congregation.

Now if I could just find the right Water Buffalo and get him or her to pu my name on the mailing list for our national monthly publication: Tall Grass

(The Disciple, November 1988)

Message appeals to saints and sinners

On a trip in western New York we came upon a church located at th intersection of a four-way stop. Below the name of the church – on their sign was a slogan: "If you're through with sin, come on in." Immediately below tha phrase someone had written: "If not, phone 425-9815."

(The Disciple, December, 1988)

Push Those Church Walls Out

My wife and I are innkeepers. We live in a quiet, tranquil, historic village. 'e provide a space in God's world "away for it all," where our guests may relax, group and become refreshed before they go back into our crazy competitive orld. We enjoy our role of hosting, where we can provide a bit of calmness. ior to inn keeping, I served for 29 years as a pastor in local congregations. I ill serve congregations on an interim basis. Yet, when we made this transition vowed that I would not discuss/debate/demythologize religious issues with iests. They did not come for preaching, but for renewal.

For our meals I fill the role of waiter – not a dumb one, but as a friendly rvant – and I just bite my tongue when the table conversation drifts toward omments which I believe are not compatible with the Christian faith.

Recently I met my most difficult challenge. I was pouring breakfast cofe for two couples when one woman started "grousing" (her term) that their nited Methodist conference had raised the apportionments for their local iurch.

With some irritation she asserted, "It's too bad the conference is doing this we need more dollars for our own church, because *that's where it's at!* We need take care of our own."

I kept pouring and said nothing – for a few moments – then I entered the onversation. (Bed-and-breakfast hosts are often encouraged, indeed invited, to articipate in guests' conversations.)

I reflected that my understanding of the Gospel is that we live in a world mily, and that priority must (not should) be given to sisters and brothers with iajor needs. I continued (in what I hoped was a non-preaching tone) that we iust heed the words of an old hymn to "Rescue the perishing, care for the ying."

I believe our guest was a typical church member. She was sincerely conerned about the ministry of "her" church. However, she needed to *push those hurch walls out* so that all of God's children are included and served.

I shared with our guests my belief that congregations can provide ministry i both places – here *and* there. Local congregational life and work simply takes me and planning, but no big bucks: Bible study, prayer groups, fellowship, and ducational events need a place to meet and some supplies.

Worldwide, "out there" ministry – consisting of feeding, clothing, healing nd sheltering – does require big bucks and we must provide them, gladly.

So, unrehearsed, we had breakfast conversation about the Kingdom of iod. Two or three or more can discuss the purpose of the church, any time, any lace.

Our guests left the table – ready to continue their journey – with the comient: "Great breakfast, and thanks for the chat. It was enjoyable, really."

I responded, "Shalom."

(The National Christian Reporter, November 20, 1992)

On Being Found by the Search Committee

Only two questions were asked: "Do you believe in the Virgin Birth," ar "Does your wife play the piano?" The year was 1960, and my wife, Sheral, ar I were being interviewed/interrogated by the Pulpit Committee (the term f that time) in a small western Kansas town.

That committee turned out to be 21 in number ("We just decided to l the Church Board be the Pulpit Committee."), and they had written to me son weeks earlier that they would like to visit with us. In their initial letter they ha informed me – "We have groan nicely lately." It was a groaning/growing exp rience for all of us.

Regional, economic and cultural idiosyncrasies can come into play durir the pastoral search process. M. Jack Suggs, my professor of New Testament Brite Divinity School, the seminary of Texas Christian University, reflected o the process early in his life. Suggs was selecting a graduate school and was Denver looking over Iliff School of Theology. At the same time he was inte viewed for a possible part-time associate position with Central Christian. Th church interview went well, but toward the end of the meeting, Suggs lit up cigarette. Immediately he could feel "coolness" come over the committe Within this context he committed a regional-religious faux pas.

A few weeks later he was in North Carolina to consider Duke Divini School. Again, he was interviewed by a church committee looking for a studen pastor. This time Suggs decided to ask first, and privately quizzed the chairma "Would this church mind if their pastor smoked?" The stern reply was, "No, w would not mind, but it sure would help if he did!"

Being "called" in the Disciples ministry can be an emotional proce described by a variety of adjectives: hopeful, challenging, drawn-out, frustratin agonizing, humorous, insightful, confusing, rewarding and strongly testing one faith. One regional minister shared with me his analysis: "Disciples don't rea ly have a clearly defined placement system, what we have is a *process.*"

Having shared with clergy friends, I find I am not alone in bewilderme and I not-so-silently shout: We Can Do Better in Placement! Wanderin through this vocational-maze a number of times, I make some reflections fo improving this cherished congregational process.

To the Seeking Pastor

Don't request relocation papers be put into circulation unless you *reall* are prepared and *ready* to move. The process may be clogged, as it is, with thos who *need* to move.

Write a personal letter to those regional ministers where you are willing t live. Even if you do not personally know these agents of the relocation proces let them know you have a keen interest in their region.

Don't make a decision about a congregation depending only on Year Boo reports. Know each situation. For example, there are some great small tow congregations, who have a need for ministry, an adequate salary, and a lovin group of believers.

If a search committee invites you to visit for an interview, ask precisel what process they are using and what will be expected of you.

Still, be ready for anything! Even if the chairperson has seeming lained everything, be alert for unexpected happenings or requests. Three mples will suffice. A congregation asked me to visit and to deliver a sermon. is is an archaic practice, but because of unusual distance and circumstances I the uncommon. After the service it was announced that I would be avail- e for questions from the entire congregation. The chair remarked, "Oh, I ss I forgot to tell you we were gong to do this." Hmm.

At another interview the regional minister sat in on the interview session. ad never heard of this procedure. He played a supportive role, but I was sur- sed and caught off guard.

Following Sunday worship, and back in my study, I was just finishing my e of helpful-father by assisting in dis-lodging a tooth from the mouth of a ing daughter. At this scene two grumpy men appeared asking to "see the pas- "

They were part of a search committee and they were late, having missed service. My family took up temporary residence in the Chapel while I host- their committee of six. They had chartered a plane to bring them across sev- l states, and they were guilt-ridden for being late and "blowing the congrega- ns' money." I provided them with absolution – as well as a protestant could – and some tapes of previous sermons they could play on their return trip. hey did call me to a fourteen year ministry.)

Role-play the interview before your visit. With your spouse, friend, rela- e or whomever, simulate any and all possible questions and situations.

A decade ago I was being interviewed by the search committee for a posi- n as an associate regional minister for a large metropolitan area. They had gun their process with 105 names. They narrowed it to ten, and then to three; as one of the three. They flew me half-way across the country. We shared a al together, and then were cloistered in a small room. After introductions, the irperson's first and only question for me was: "Would you place into circula- n – for possible ministerial placement – the names of clergy who you *knew* re homosexuals?"

I had rehearsed myself for every question but that one. I responded that id not believe a persons' sexual orientation should qualify nor disqualify them service in ministry. That committee did not call me.

Come to the interview prepared with thoughtful questions: "What have n the five most meaningful events in this congregation over the past three rs?" "Of the many responsibilities a pastor has, what three stand out as most portant?" "What do you want to see happening within this church in the next o years?" "What are members willing to do to see that these dreams become lity?"

Go with expectations and reservations. Ask yourself, "Would I/we like to e here?" Notice the warts of the community and be as objective as possible.

Don't be shy about noting your strengths to the committee. There should opportunities to share accomplishments and interests. Share them.

Don't expect that perfect church. Every congregation has weaknesses, ne more than others. Weaknesses may be opportunities for growth and richment!

To the Search Committee

Be truly a representative committee. Make sure a couple of complainers,

and a couple of saints, are members of the committee. Always work with y
regional office! Always! Don't consider a maverick who happens to be the s
ond cousin of a faithful member and who once took a Bible course, can play
trumpet, and is a good dresser.

Do your homework. Complete an in-depth profile of your congregati
Hold listening conferences with members asking them for the characteris
they seek in a pastor.

Establish a time schedule and stick to it as much as possible.

When you contact candidates inform them exactly where you are in
process. "I am calling on behalf of Helping Hand Christian Church in L
Antelope, North Dakota. We are seeking a pastor, and we have narrowed the
to four; you are one of them. Would you be willing to be considered by Help
Hand?"

When you do call a pastor please inform the other candidates they are
longer being considered. The height of rudeness is to have a candidate read i
church magazine that someone else was called to your church, months after y
contacted them.

To the Regional Office

Respond to correspondence. Most regional clergy answer their mail, b
some must be allergic to writing. It is frustrating not to receive at least a n
"Thank you for writing Kimberly, yes; I'll keep you in mind when I sub
resumes to search committees."

Remember the relocation process can be charged with emotion, and t
pastors and their families need periodic encouragement and support. They m
need compassionate love as their searching process drags on and on and . . .

Strive for uniformity within regions. It is disconcerting to receive a lett
"As you consider relocation you need to know that our region works a bit diff
ently at the process." This only adds to one's frustration.

Allow, even encourage pastors to apply for consideration with speci
congregations. This practice is the norm in the business world.

Be candid and objective with both search committees and candidates.
one case I was given two profiles of a congregation – one prepared by the chur
and one by the regional associate. They read like two different congregations!
was grateful for the one by the regional staff person – it was objective.

To the Whole Church

Pastors and all manifestations of Christ's church need to give increas
energy to the search/relocation process, so vital to our total life and work. W
is the role of our DHM Center for Leadership and Ministry in this proce
Should there be a complete listing of all open pulpits, nation-wide, to all cler
at all times? How can we encourage congregations to openly consider calli
women clergy? Should our seminaries continue to heavily recruit students wh
in many cases, we have an over supply of clergy for congregations who pay a l
ing wage for leadership? There are some encouraging findings. Congregatio
have no-interest loans for a down-payment on a house. Some congregations
providing a sabbatical in their package. Most congregations are open to the p
tor's spouse doing their "own thing" concerning their role in the church and t
community.

The search can expand one's depth of human understanding and sense of humor. My most unique experience started with a conference call. After a few minutes I heard a powerful wailing. I was told to simply "hold on." Finally the committee explained that their church building was across from the city fire station, and these interruptions happened often. I was invited to come to their city for an interview.

When Sheral and I arrived we were informed there were co-chairs of the committee, with each one attempting to exert their control of the committee. We were given a tour through their building. We met their church secretary, a most pleasant woman, who happened to be an active member of another church.

We shared a pot-luck meal with search committee members and their spouses. During the informal visiting I was able to chat privately with a search committee member who also happened to be on the faculty of the local university. He informed me he was an Independent Baptist, and found the local Baptist church too "liberal," so he had joined First Christian. (That alone told me much about that congregation.)

Prior to the "official" interview, one of the co-chairpersons announced that spouses of committee members were welcome to ask the candidate any questions. (I was not informed of this procedure before hand.) One gentleman, who happened to be on oxygen, slowly stood and with as much strength as he could muster questioned, "Dr. McDermet, do you preach the Gospel of redemption and salvation with the same vim, vigor and enthusiasm with which you make love to your wife?" There was an awkward and long pause and some of the group went blank. I finally brought forth some response, which seemed to satisfy him.

A few days later I received a note from one of the chairs which read in part: "Dear Dr. McDermet, thank you for your time. We think you are over qualified for us and we do not think we should consider you as pastor." Inside this letter was a hand-written note from their church secretary. "Dear Dr. McDermet, I think the committee really missed the boat on this one, best of luck." Whee!

The call to Christian ministry ought to be a happy and joyous event. However, the process of calling pastors can be filled with hazards, detours and stop signs. We all need to work at making this journey smooth, and for God's sake, meaningful.

The LEGS Fund

Congregations want members to learn and grow and to develop an appreciation of God's world and their place in the world family. Yet few congregations provide financial support so that learning experiences become a reality.

While I was pastor at the Prairie Avenue Christian Church in Decatur, Illinois, the congregation decided to allocate some special funds for this purpose. I was able to work with the stewardship committee in developing a proposal that led to establishment of the LEGS Fund (Laity Enrichment Growth and Service Fund).

The following guidelines are listed with the hope that other congregations might initiate similar programs.

* *Purpose* — To underwrite a variety of individual and group experiences that enriches and develops the life and work of the congregation. These experiences should lead to the growth of both individual members, and the congregation, resulting in greater service with the whole church and in God's world.

* *Examples* — Examples are almost endless. They could include workshops, seminars, retreats held both at the church and at other locations. Growth and service experiences come in many shapes and sizes. Some possibilities are:

> Retreats sponsored by the region > Seminars sponsored by a local or state council of churches > Attendance at the International Christian Women's Fellowship Quadrennial > Bible studies led by a Bible scholar >Mission study/work tours > Videotapes.

Our Decatur congregation invited an English professor from Millikin University who had a special interest in how writers have dealt with grief, to lead a series of sessions on Sunday mornings. Another professor from Millikin, one from the religion department, came for two Septembers and held "fireside chats" dealing with questions, and sharing insights about learning and growing in the Christian faith. Both youth and adults from the congregation participated in a trip to Jamaica sponsored by the region.

* *Supervision* — A committee responsible for the LEGS Fund is chaired by the vice moderator of the congregation's board. Other members include the chair-persons of Christian education and membership committees and the pastor.

* *Eligibility* – Those who have been listed as participating members of the congregation during the calendar year are eligible to receive funds. Individual participants shall not receive more than $150 per year.

Amount Requested: $1 to $50, 100 percent; $50 to $100, $50, plus 50 percent of the amount over $50; $100 and over, 75 percent, with a maximum of $150.

* *Frequency of Participation* — The number of participants for each event shall be determined by the committee. The committee shall periodically publicize a variety of potential events and encourage member participation.

* *Honorariums* — Honorariums shall be paid to resource persons at rates established by the committee and may include transportation.

* *Congregational Enrichment* — Participants are encouraged to share their learning experiences with the congregation's members and groups.

* *Annual Report* — An annual report by the committee to the congregation's board will include expenses, a listing of educational events attended, and the number of persons participating.

* *Annual Evaluation* — The committee will make an annual evaluation of the LEGS Fund and submit suggestion changes for improvement, to the congregation's board.

* *Funds to Establish* — An amount of $5,000 is needed to start the LEGS Fund; which could be taken from undesignated funds.

* *Continuing Fund Support* — Add $500 annually from interest earned on the congregation's checking account to maintain the fund. Members and groups should be encouraged to make periodic gifts to the Fund.

To show concern for the total ministry of Christ's church, our congregation took another $5,000 from undesignated funds to give to outreach causes. Basic Mission Finance received one half of this amount, and the other half went to local outreach causes – including the Decatur Habitat for Humanity, and Dove, a Disciples Reconciliation program.

If congregations give some structure and direction for membership cultivation, and members participate in learning experiences, they will find that everyone benefits: the individual, the congregation, and all persons in God's world.

(Vanguard, J/F/M, 1993)

The Long Walk

An African girl presented a Christmas gift to her teacher. When the teacher unwrapped the gift, she found a beautiful sea shell. Asked where the child could have found it, she told her teacher that such shells come only from a special, faraway beach. The teacher was very touched, knowing the girl had walked many miles, and remarked:

"You shouldn't have gone so far for a gift for me."
The girl looked at her, smiled and replied,
"The long walk is part of the gift."

(The Gifts We Bring, Volume II, August, 1989)

The Newspaper Route

The Des Moines Register

THE INDIANAPOLIS STAR

The Ottumwa Courier

The Post-Journal

The Chautauquan Daily

Urith Dailey Gill

Long before women's liberation was news, Urith Dailey Gill quietly broke new ground for women. In so doing, she gave much of her 86 years in service to the church in Indiana, serving so memorable that to this day members of her first church school class return to Indianapolis annually for a reunion with her.

Urith Dailey was graduated from high school at Greenfield, her birthplace, in 1913. She entered Butler University, then in Eastside Indianapolis, that year and got the same room occupied earlier by her father (Benjamin Franklin Dailey), then pastor of the Greenfield Christian Church.

"When I entered the university, I tried hard to get my father's room." she recalls. "Through our combined efforts, I succeeded, and with a little chisel I put my initials beside those of his on the sandstone window slab."

When the building was razed in 1946, she obtained the windowsill, which is in her yard today as a souvenir.

In 1915 Urith joined Downey Avenue Christian Church in the Irvington part of Indianapolis. She taught a pre-school class of 10 boys 4 and 5 years old.

"Boys only," she says. "That's the way they did it. They couldn't put on their boots, couldn't wipe their noses, they were the cutest little things."

Rather than part with them, she promoted herself with her young boys from nursery to beginner, to primary, to intermediate, to high school.

"It was not according to Hoyle that you promote yourself," she says, smiling, "but I had to; I loved them."

The love and loyalty have lasted six decades. Two of the 10 have died and addresses of two are unknown. But every year the remaining six return to Downey to be with their teacher.

"Our lives were made better by knowing her," says Gwynn Barnett, one of the boys and still a member of Downey. "Being brought up in the church gave us a better outlook on life."

In 1925 Urith married George Gill; her boy's class held a mock wedding and presented a gift to her. The Gills settled down in Irvington. George, an I.U. graduate, was first administrator of the Indiana State Employment Service.

From 1955 to 1959 Urith Gill served two terms as president of the Indiana Christian Women's Fellowship with 22,936 members. In 1959 she was elected as one of two women elders, traditionally the highest office in the Disciples of Christ. Elders, presiding over weekly communion service and counseling the clergy, had historically been men.

Indiana Disciples had been meeting in a state convention for 125 years by 1964, always with a man presiding. That year Urith Gill was elected as the first woman president of the Indiana Christian Church State Convention.

"The convention was held at Clowes Hall in Indianapolis," she recalls. "Clowes had just been open a year and this church convention gave people a chance to see it free, so the place was packed. When the nominating committee made their report and placed my name before the convention, it was very quiet, but it was a unanimous vote."

She presided over the 126th state convention at Marion in 1965. At that time there were 99,003 members in 336 Indiana congregations. "I was not going to get some preacher to make the president's speech – I was going to make the speech. I've still got a copy," she points out.

In that speech she called for help to provide all people the "abundant life."

We should care for refugees, strengthen family relationships, practice humility, efriend those not included in society, and apply our abilities in daily living. We ust help Negroes, migrant farm workers, Puerto Ricans, Mexicans," she said.

Urith and George Gill reared two sons. Both went to school No. 85, lowe High School, Indiana University and the Navy.

Ben Gill today is a vice-president of Amoco in the Chicago office. George . started his journalism career with the Richmond (Va.) *News-Leader*, joined ie Louisville *Courier-Journal* in 1960 and in 1981 was named president.

Today Urith continues to live in her Irvington home. She needs a cane or walking, but she likes a motto that sits on her kitchen table: "Lameness is a indrance to the leg, but not to the will."

"I've been a church person all my life," she says. "I can't imagine life with-ut the church. What is vital are the simple teachings of Jesus. Count your lessings and don't complain about the things that are wrong with you."

ndianapolis Sunday Star Magazine, October 25, 1981. Two pictures were part f the article. One pictured Urith at the 1965 Marion State Convention; the sec-nd was with Gwynn Barnett and John Miller from a 1979 photo inside the anctuary of Downey Avenue Christian Church.)

Jean Brown Wagoner

Jean Brown Wagoner is a Hoosier author whose name did not appear on er first book. She had to be coaxed into ghost writing that publication.

Central Indiana people are probably more familiar with the name of Hilton Ultimus Brown, her father. He was with the *Indianapolis News* for 75 ears, many as vice-president, and was president of the Butler University Board f Directors for 49 years. The summer Starlight Musicals are presented in Butler's Hilton U. Brown theatron.

Jean has etched her own name into Indiana history as author of eight chil-ren's books. She and her twin brother Arch were born in the family home at he southwest corner of East Washington Street and Emerson Avenue on December 19, 1896. Her first schooling was in a cobbler's shop on South Audubon Circle in Irvington.

"Our school burned, so we met there," she says. "In cold weather you ried to get there first to sit close to the stove." She was graduated from hortridge High School.

At Shortridge she wrote for the *Echo,* the school daily newspaper. After igh school she studied at Butler University (then located in Irvington) from 915 to 1919.

"Another girl and I wrote plays to raise money for the 'Y' or Zoology Club," Jean recalls. "I remember one play was 'Safe in Siberia.' It sounded nice. The play contained this scene: Conductor: "This is Venice." 1st girl: "But I don't see any venison." 2nd girl: "Oh, there's a little dear." "Isn't that awful? But he students must have loved it because they packed the little theater in Irvington wo nights to see it," she reminisces.

After her Butler days she taught school for one year at Noblesville. "I was perfectly awful teacher." Jean laughs. For the next six years she was on the staff of the Marion County Criminal Court working with first offenders placed on suspended sentences.

Jean Brown Wagoner joined the Downey Avenue Christian Church in 1909. It was there that she became keenly interested in children. She was in charge of the children's Christmas service one year when the person who was to give the program failed to arrive.

"I decided I'd tell the story of 'The First Christmas Tree,'" she says. "Some of those who heard it thought I had written the story and told my sister Jessica, who was an editor with the Bobbs-Merrill Company, downtown. Jessica phoned me and said, "Why don't you try writing for us?"

"Bobbs-Merrill needed someone to ghost write a book. When you do that you never let anyone know you wrote it, or had any knowledge of it. It went over, and the company wanted to sign me up for my own book, but I couldn't think of anything to write."

The company was publishing a series of children's books about the childhood of famous Americans, and asked Jean to write about one. Her first book which bore her own name was Louisa Alcott: Girl of Old Boston. Five more followed in the series: Jane Addams: Little Lame Girl, 1944; Julia Ward Howe: Girl of Old New York, 1945; Martha Washington: Girl of Old Virginia, 1947; Abigail Adams: Girl of Colonial Days, 1949; and Jessie Fremont: Girl of Capitol Hill, 1956.

During these years she continued to be active in her church where she was asked, "Why don't you write about children from the Bible?"

"My mother had always liked the Old Testament boy David, so I wrote about him." says Jean. Thus, David The Shepherd Lad was published. "I got more favorable comments on it than any book I'd written but you couldn't sell religious books to the schools, so it never sold very well." Still, she followed with another book in 1954, The Captive Lad: A Story of Daniel the Lionhearted.

Jean Brown Wagoner did most of her writing at the dining room table of her home, where she still lives in Irvington.

"I'd write my books out by hand, later I used a broken-down typewriter from a neighbor boy. I used to write during the day, but one afternoon my son Mike said to me, 'Mom, you're not listening. I was talking to you and you didn't hear me.' After that experience I always put my writing away when the boys were home. I do recall one morning after I had stayed up all night trying to finish a book before an 11 a.m. deadline. One of our sons yelled from upstairs: 'I can't find my socks anywhere, mother where are my socks?' My husband Cliff told him, 'Your mother has been working all night, and you will get the benefits from it. You can find your own socks for a few days.'"

Some of author Wagoner's books have been published in foreign languages and she has received many letters from young readers.

"They must have recently sold another batch of books because last month I received letters from students in New England," she says. "I also got a letter from the publisher saying they renewed the copyright on my books for another 50 years."

In 1977 the new Media Center in School 57 was dedicated in her name. In 1979 she received the Golden Embers Award for 50-years service with Campfire Girls; the Service to Mankind Award from the Sertoma Club; and the Alumni Achievement Award from Butler University.

Jean continues to think as a young and lively person. She attends worship t her church when possible and often remarks, "I'm afraid I don't contribute much to the life of the church, I'm deaf as a post," to which I remark, "No, Jean Brown Wagoner, you're deaf as a tree, because a tree is still alive and growing!"

(Indianapolis Sunday Star Magazine, April 25, 1982. A wonderful picture of Jean appeared with the article.)

Martha The Anxious

(Luke 10:38-42)

O My, are the guests here so soon!
Is there a napkin for every person?
Will the food be nourishing?
What about that dessert?
(It looked so good in **Better Homes & Gardens**)
I need Mary to help!
Will my deodorant fail?
Why doesn't Jesus give more notice?

Get out of the kitchen, Martha.
Sit and listen.
And eat from the good portion.
It chews well and digests even better.
Like manna.

(United Methodist Reporter, July 26, 1985)

A Visit to a UCC

It was Parents' Weekend at Carleton College in Northfield, Minnesota. My wife and I attended with our student daughter, Melanie. Carleton has historic roots in the UCC, and two blocks from campus stands the First United Church of Christ. On that Sunday the three of us attended, with Melanie being received as a student member along with other new members.

The service of worship was interesting, and, as a minister in the Disciples of Christ, I want to share my reflection.

The worshipers looked very much like those in our Disciples' congregation "back home." We felt a bit strange when we started to sing "When Morning Gilds the Skies" because the tune was unfamiliar. Then, the choir members smiled, the organist stopped abruptly and started the "correct" tune that we all knew. No difference there.

We all participated in the Sacrament of Baptism. Ah, a problem for us Disciples? I have seen few services where infants were sprinkled, so I was most attentive. The pastor came "into the congregation" halfway up the center aisle. There a deacon held a basin of water and the parents held their child. After saying some meaningful words, the pastor asked the congregation to stand, and then invited members of *any* church to stand. We participated in that baptism by our simple act of standing, repeating a statement from the hymnal and our silent best wishes. It caused me no pain. I felt happiness for the child, her parents, and the church universal.

Baptism will, of course, be an area for dialogue as Disciples and UCC persons consider our possible union. But, as one Disciples' pastor, I had no "our-way-is-right-and-yours-is-wrong" feelings. The area will need much discussion, tempered with a desire to understand and love.

During "moments of concern and sharing" I stood and said, "I bring greetings from a Disciples of Christ Church in Indiana; it's good to be with you." The pastor noted that the Minnesota UCC Conference was planning to be a part of the UCC-Disciples study.

Other concerns sounded familiar: They had raised $3,100 for One Great Hour of Sharing (our Week of Compassion); they needed volunteers to paint the church basement; prayers were requested following a tragic death.

That day happened to be communion Sunday. They conducted the service exactly as the congregation at home does: all are invited to share, to eat the bread individually and to hold the cup so all partake together.

We left the service with a good feeling that we had worshiped with sister and brother Christians. To be sure, there are some thorny problems as we look to possible unity. However ours was a good experience and I recommend it. When possible, Disciples need to visit UCC congregations and vice versa.

(A. D. Magazine, May, 1983)

Monday Morning Mail

Dear Preacher:

This letter is to let you know I stand four-square behind you on this matter of money. I certainly recall vividly the other times I've helped bail you people out of your money binds and I'm prepared to pitch right in again, after all it's my church.

Only last Sunday I was in a foursome at the club playing with Theopholis A. Theist, Lew Therin and the president of our company Pres. B. Tearean. Well, about the tenth green I mentioned to the others that my church contributions sure helped on my taxes.

Theo piped up and said he wouldn't give to a church on a bet. So just to show him up I bet him $5 on the 11th hole. After I beat him with a 20 foot downwind putt I up and tell him I'm donating all my days' winnings to the church. He blew his everlovin' stack, he also blew the 12th hole with a double bogie and got so upset he blew the whole scene and stomped off to the clubhouse.

After things settled down a little, Prez. and Lew both told me they tithe their net earnings to their church. Did I ever pounce on them then; I told them in no uncertain terms that their tithe should be on gross earnings, not net earnings. Well this didn't set to well with them but at least they know how my feelings run on the subject.

I really didn't care if they were miffed, cause we were just finishing the 18th and I had to hurry and pick up the kids at Sunday School. Besides, I'd dropped 20 bucks that morning and didn't want to give them a chance to rub it in.

Back to the subject, all I really wanted to say was to keep up the good work. Last year I gave $90 smackeroos to ole 1st and I know if everyone else kicked in and made the same sacrifice there wouldn't be any money problem. Like I always say "Too many people think a church can run on peanuts, it's a shame we can't tell them to either cough up their share or get out."

How's that for hitting the nail on the head.

Signed: One of Your Faithful

P.S. I'll be out of town Sunday but the first week I can make it I'll see that there are a couple of extra quarters in the place.

Have a Nice Cliché, uh Day

We get it at the bank, bowling lanes and beauty shop.

We get it at the grocery store, gas station and even at the dentist's office.

We get it morning, afternoon and night. We get it on the phone and from the TV news announcer.

"It" is that overdone, non-meaning, terribly trite and boring cliché: "Have a nice day."

Whoever started this saying a few years ago probably thought they were doing humankind a great service. They possibly felt – as many do – that the centuries-old greeting "goodbye" (a condensed form of "God bless you") had lost its punch.

So, "Have a nice day" was a welcome and refreshing change. However, the young delivery man makes his rounds and has me sign his invoice with "haveaniceday." He does not look at me when he says it; in fact, he seems programmed to say it to everyone.

This past August I was being checked-out by the grocery clerk who concluded the transaction with *those* words. I wanted so much to say: "How can I have a 'nice day?' Its 97 degrees, our air conditioning just quit, and my mother-in-law is arriving tomorrow."

I honestly get the feeling that some people don't give a tinker's . . . about your real feelings, and have simply put their mind and mouth into neutral.

In some cases I would really like to say: "Gosh this has been a lousy week, I lost my job, my pet pig died and my rent is due." I wonder if after hearing this I'd still get *those* words.

OK, so what do I suggest we say to each other? There ought to be at least three ingredients in our greetings to other humans: sincere feelings, voice inflections, and eye contact.

Greetings and salutations given with genuineness and sensitivity are as important to humans as flowers are to bees. I suggest some possibilities, and you add to the list: "live," "enjoy," "go for it" "all the best" "peace to you" "shalom." The words, "peace to you" can be spoken with both a religious and secular meaning, either way it can re-enforce ones' personhood.

Shalom is a great Hebrew word that we Decaturites ought to include in our vocabulary. Shalom means more than just peace, (although we might take that). Shalom is a deep relationship between any two people; between a person and God; and between groups and nations.

Shalom is the way God meant our world to be. Shalom means more than simply the absence of hostility and war (again, we will take that). Shalom means a deep concern for all people at all times . . . that the needs of all are fulfilled.

Art Buchwald and his friend were riding in a taxi together, and when they got out his friend paid the driver and then said, "Thanks for the ride. You did a superb job of driving." The cab driver looked suspiciously at him and said, "Who are you, some kind of wise guy?"

Buchwald asked his friend why he praised the cab driver. "I'm trying to bring happiness back into New York City," his friend replied. The friend went on to say, "Suppose the cab driver has 20 fares. That means because I was nice to him, he is now going to be nice to 20 other people. These persons, in turn, are going to be nice to clerks, and waiters and employees and maybe even their own families."

A skeptical Buchwald asked, “Does it work?” His friend said simply, Nothing is lost if it doesn't.”

What do I suggest we say to each other, and how should we use language? simply ask for freshness and creativity; and that we are clear and honest when e converse. Say what we mean, and mean what we say.

Decatur (like any other community) can use all the happiness it can get. am convinced that all our words are either harmful or helpful as we address all umans. So, “keep on keeping on” and “Shalom.”

(Decatur Herald & Review, October 2, 1987)
(The Buffalo News, May 16, 2004)

Say Hello to Martin Luther King

Since I am new to Central Illinois, some friends felt I should tour braham Lincoln sites.

So, a few weeks ago we visited the Mount Pulaski Courthouse, the ostville Courthouse in Lincoln, Lincoln's New Salem and the Old State Capitol nd Lincoln's tomb in Springfield. I saw where Lincoln practiced law, made peeches, served in the legislature, and is buried.

I am sure this involvement with Lincoln lore helped shape my attitude oward the “Broadway vs, Martin Luther King Drive” issue in Decatur.

By chance I was alone in Lincoln's tomb and felt a oneness with what he id in his Gettysburg Address: “. . . dedicated to the proposition that *all* men e created equal.”

Would he have felt renaming a street after Martin Luther King is an nportant step? I can only guess, but I believe he would say, “Yes.” That decidl, at least in my mind; let's look at problems and opportunities surrounding this ossible name change for Broadway:

+ Decatur Postmaster Hazel Showman says a change from Broadway to Iartin Luther King is likely to mean “big problems.” A temporary inconvennce might occur; but in my brief time in Decatur I already know five mailperons by name, and they all impress me as competent carriers who can get the aail to where is needs to go.

+ There will be costs to businesses located on the street. This is an imporant concern, and I have a suggestion. Let's start a fund to meet the costs of hanging letterheads, business cards, identification on trucks and stores, etc. Do ou think Decaturites would be willing to give to this? I would. The Metro. Decatur Chamber of Commerce might help with a temporary task force to eceive gifts and make payments.

+ Decatur businessman Bernard Ephraim has said he would foot the bill or new street signs. Good for him. After they are up let's seize the opportuni- to celebrate this event with a special time.

+ Having selected a special day, residents and businesses along Martin uther King Drive could clean, paint, repair and landscape houses and buildings n the street, creating a look of pride.

+ Mayor Gary Anderson could appoint a committee to organize a celeration of the special day, including a parade (on Martin Luther King Drive of course), and a ceremony. Let's invite high school bands, the Millikin Universi band, Scout troops, and any and all groups to a parade. Maybe some grou would make floats.

Then, at the end of the organized groups all of us could be in the parad – blacks, whites, young, old, liberals, conservatives, moderates – everyone wh always wanted to be in a parade.

+ Let's invite special guests to our parade, and then to share in a celebra tion event in the Decatur Civic Center. Let's invite Coretta Scott King, wido of Martin; maybe Jimmy Carter between his work projects with Habit fo Humanity. Gov. James Thompson would come. Sen. Paul Simon would com bow tie and all. Can you think of others?

+ Leading up to the big day merchants along Martin Luther King Driv could have special sale days, and we Decaturites would patronize.

So where does all of this get us? It gets us to participate in the America dream. It gets us ready to enter the 21st century. It gets us to the place whe we can say, "Yes, there have been some negative pages in our nation's history, bu that's just that – history."

What's in a name? Changing a street is more than changing letters. I this case it is a positive step fulfilling the beliefs of both A. Lincoln and M.I King.

You may say, "Come on Bill, you're a crazy dreamer." King said, "I hav a dream." His dream was to have black and white children learn, live and gro together. Why do so many fear and hate this dream? King wanted open school housing and churches.

He wanted equal opportunities in Dixie, Detroit and Decatur.

It may be time to give our regards to Broadway and say hello to Marti Luther King.

(Decatur Herald & Review, October 15, 1987)

Thankful for Five Kernels of Corn

On Thanksgiving Day five years ago, our grandson Brian was born. Thu this uniquely American holiday became special for us. Without the approval o his mother or grandmother, I have frequently, but affectionately, called Brian ou "Big Turkey."

November is the time when Brian, and the rest of us, need to digest th facts of Thanksgiving. Thanksgiving is not the celebration of a devastating bat tle, nor the anniversary of the birth of a conqueror. It does not commemorat the writing of an historic document.

The day is the expression of a deep feeling of gratitude by our people fo the rich productivity of the land. It's also a memorial to those who passe through dangers and hardships; and it's the harmony of peoples living together

In early New England it was the custom at Thanksgiving to place five ker nels of corn at every place. This was a reminder of those stern days during th first winter when the food of the Pilgrims was so depleted that only five kernel a day were rationed to each person.

The Pilgrim mothers and fathers wanted their children to remember th acrifice, suffering and hardship which made possible the settlement of a free eople in a free land. They wanted to keep alive the memory of that 63-day trip aken in the tiny Mayflower.

They desired to keep alive the memory of that first terrible winter which ook so many lives. They did not want their descendants to forget that on the ay their ration was five kernels, only seven healthy colonists remained to nurse he sick and nearly half their number lay in the windswept graveyard on the hill.

The thanks in Thanksgiving was a celebration because four men returned rom a hunting venture with food. Also, thanks to the agricultural expertise of n Indian, the corn crop was good.

There was peace between the Pilgrims and the Indians. So, Indian friends vere invited to a pitch-in, and they brought most of the meal. Together they ate enison, duck, goose, clams, corn bread, watercress, berries and grapes.

So grandson Brian, this is a time of heavy eating and family gathering.

It is also the time of rats in apartments, drunks in gutters and children on velfare. Somewhere in the middle of our stuffing we ought to feel the need to how compassion for others in our human family.

In our community we are thankful for the Good Samaritan Inn which rovides meals for today's hungry pilgrims; for Love Unlimited Ministries which rovides the necessities of life; for Dove's domestic violence residential shelter, nd for beds provided by the Salvation Army. Thanksgiving is really based on n inner attitude toward life.

An older Decatur woman was confined to her bed in a shabby little room. Asked whether she had anything that she could honestly be thankful for, she ooked at the walls and replied, "Yes, I am thankful for the sunshine through the racks."

A visitor at St. Mary's Hospital Extended Care Unit stopped for a moment o speak to an old gentleman and inquired about his health. "Thank you sir," e said, "I have a great deal to be thankful for. I have two teeth left and they are pposite each other."

We're all turkeys living in a great nation under the watchful care of God. We do have problems, but we can be thankful for the determination and ability o solve those problems.

What we need to do is remind the Brians of our nation that when the ship Mayflower sailed back to England only the sailors were aboard.

(Decatur Herald & Review, November 24, 1987)

Street Smarts Aren't Easy to Come By

Five months ago, I moved from our nation's 11th largest metropolitan area to Decatur. I thought, "Moving around in this city of less than 100,000 will be a piece of cake." Not necessary.

My first discovery was that Decatur has four Main streets – North, South, East, and West. Main streets seem to be a Central Illinois tradition. In Bearsdale there is a Main Street, South and a Main Street, West. In Mount Zion you find Main Street North and South, Main Street West. In Warrensburg one finds Main Street North, East, and South.

I have discovered that Decatur's Main streets are not really the main drags. Eldorado is the primarily traveled street; however, one does not drag Eldorado, one cruises. The "main street" is Pershing, which is not a street, but a road.

It helped somewhat to find there are at least six churches with either their front or back on Church Street. The Holiday Park Swim Club is on North Water, and the Surf Club is on Sandcreek Road. The Decatur Earthmover Credit Union is on Dividend Drive. Ah, now things are beginning to make sense.

However, confusion overtook me when I made my first venture from Decatur Memorial Hospital to St. Mary's Hospital. Driving south on North Main, I was stopped by a train. Fortunately another driver had a deck of cards and four of us engaged in a not-so-brief hand of bridge.

At the end of South Main I knew I had to go left (east) to get to St. Mary's, so I did. But I ended up in South Shores. I now know I should have jogged right, to go left; west to go east on Lake Shore Drive.

I also know that if I want to go east, from the north part of the city, I'm probably ahead to get first to 22nd Street, and then go south. But don't try to turn south onto 22nd from Garfield – you can't. You do avoid the train by going over the Staley Viaduct, not to be confused with the Staley Bridge which goes across Lake Decatur via U.S. 36.

Recently my wife and I made a trip to look for a used car. That trip turned out to be for the birds: Whippoorwill, Bluebird, Hummingbird, Robin, and Oriole. We were looking for Dove Drive. We found it, but the house numbers increased, then decreased, then increased again when Dove crossed Meadowlark. We finally found the house, seeing no hawks on Dove Drive.

The real navigational mystery for me in Decatur is Lost Bridge and Lost Bridge Road. How can it be lost if I keep going over it? When was it lost? How? Who lost it? Where did it go? Did the bridge float down the Sangamon River to Springfield? Who found it? How did they bring it back to Decatur? Did they use helicopters, or did they bring it back section by section? Was there a celebration when they found Lost Bridge? Is there an annual "Founders Day for Lost Bridge?"

I notice that on some intersection signs Prairie is a street, and that on others it is an avenue. At least it is always that road between East William and East Main – except when Prairie gets close to the lake, and then it is between Meadow Lane and Lake Shore Drive.

I now find it best to have a city map at home, at the office, and always in my car. So, if some evening you see a lost soul wandering in your neighborhood, map in one hand, flashlight in the other, it is probably me, looking for an address. Please don't shoot me, just point me in the right direction.

I'm going to stay home tonight and kind of roast by an open fire. We live Chestnut.

(Decatur Herald & Review, January 7, 1988)

More Than Meets the Eye

It was a quiet Saturday afternoon, and my wife, Sheral, suggested I join r on a shopping trip. That's why I was sitting close to the front entrance of nart on Mount Zion Road.

My mind was in neutral, so I almost missed the little boy's question. He s about seven or eight, evidently had just seen his first Amish people, and they d seemed very strange to him.

The boy noticed they were different – plain clothing, black socks and oes, beards, and of course the black hats or bonnets.

Outwardly they seemed so different. Thus he posed the question to his other, "Mom, who are those people and why do they have those funny hats?"

Now my mind shifted out of neutral and vicariously I silently entered the alogue and wondered how his mother would answer his question.

As she zipped her son's coat and made sure his gloves were on, she start-, "I guess they are up from Arthur, they are Amish, and they . . ." The word ıey" was the last word I heard because the pair was out the door. How did she swer the question? I yearned to know.

I was left with my thoughts and I reflected back to the early 1960s when ır family lived among people of another prairie – those of Kalona, Iowa. alona, like Arthur, is a center for both Old Order and Beach Amish. When we oved there, we too, were curious about those "strangely dressed people, "who casionally bore the brunt of cruel jokes. Yet in that community our under-ınding and appreciation of Amish people flourished.

Those were the years when three young daughters kept our home a bee-ve of activity and Sheral one happy, healthy, hoping and harried mother. To lp with the "chores" we had a young Amish girl, Marie S., to assist with the ousework and another Amish girl, Elizabeth M., to baby sit.

In those close relationships, stereotypes died. Marie and Elizabeth were as fferent as any two people you'll know. One was industrious, the other put rth minimum effort. One was outgoing, the other was not. They were both ry human! Once could iron clothes and watch television soaps (something she course could not do at home) faster than any human. We grew to like her ry much, and we enjoyed her use of language such as "make the light out."

Amish are people within our world family who have often received abuse. hey are misunderstood, often because we who are the "true Americans" will not ke the time to understand them. They believe in nonresistance and will not rve in any military capacity. They establish their own schools. They choose ot to be a part of Social Security. Amish live "nonconformed" to the world; us they dress simply and without signs of pride. They support their views with ssages from the Bible. They are excellent neighbors, possess a deep concept of aring, and are quick to help anyone.

As for the K mart mother and her son, I can only hope that what she told him about "those people" was tempered with understanding and kindne Maybe she said, ". . . and they dress that way because it is part of their religio custom. They are nice people. Perhaps we can visit with them sometime."

(Decatur Herald & Review, March 6, 1988.
Also in REC News, May, 1996)

Living Every Minute

I got the part.

So what if no one else was interested in it.

Of course it's not much of a part, only two lines. You could say thr lines, but I simply repeat one of them.

There are advantages to my part. I never really go "on stage" and I ne no makeup, and after Act I, I'm all through.

The role is not really essential to the play. Yet, Thornton Wilder obviou ly thought it important or he would not have written it into the play. How's th for deductive reasoning? Wilder used the part, and two others, to give the aud ence a *feel* for being *in* the play.

I guess that if I wanted to expand my acting credits I could have tried o for the role of the "second Dead Man" in Act III; but then I would actually ha to be on stage. That man has only one line, and I'm happy with my three, I' not greedy.

What I'm telling you is that I'm the "Man in the Auditorium" Thornton Wilder's play "Our Town" which Decatur's Theatre 7 is presenting May.

I've simply got an attachment to the role because I played it when we liv in Kansas, years ago.

Friends will easily call it type-casting. I don't mind. My main line is: " there no one in town aware of social injustice and industrial inequality?" I do receive much of an answer to my question from Editor Webb, so Wilder has n say (forcefully), "Then why don't they do something about it?"

Social activists will be proud, while conservatives may be concerned as possible liberal political activity. Yet no one can really fault Webb's reply to n second question: "We do all we can to take care of those who can't help then selves and those that can we leave alone."

Being the man in the Auditorium doesn't give me a real opportunity hone my skills – just so I don't detract from the atmosphere of the play. I' afraid that I did unwittingly disrupt a Kansas audience when I played the role Howie (the bartender) in William Inge's "Bus Riley's Back in Town." When donned an apron and went behind the bar, the snickers and muffled laughter di not amuse the director. Pastors probably need to stick to certain roles.

I hope you are planning to enjoy "Our Town," not to see if I'll flub m three lines, but to savor Wilder's work of art. Some people find that when the have seen "Our Town" they have actually participated in a religious experienc They won't get an argument from me.

In the third act, Emily (one of the main characters) dies, but she goes bac nto time and relives one day of her youth. She finds meaning in the simplest of hings – flowers, trees, dresses, hot baths, and everyday common conversation vith her family.

Knowing she can never return, Wilder has her almost shout (to all of us), Do any human beings ever realize life while they live it – every, every minute?"

You'll have to see it to really get the effect, but if that statement doesn't grab you; you must be dead too.

"Our Town" is a great happening. That's why I wanted the bit part; to be n it, and enjoy it.

(Decatur Herald & Review, April 8, 1988)

Decatur Pride Emerges

It was an evening filled with hopes and dreams and anticipation.

After 14 years in Indianapolis, my wife, Sheral, and I were making our rek to Decatur. I drove a Ryder rental truck, filled with our prized possessions. Sheral drove the station wagon, stuffed with everything that would not fit into he truck. We were beginning another chapter in our journey in life.

We pondered the meaning of the sign that greeted us at the edge of the city: "Pride of the Prairie." Was Decatur a community of promise, or was that slogan simply a public relations pipe dream?

The only incident that happened late that first evening was when I backed the truck into the guttering on our new home. At least we could start immediately in helping the local economy. A carpenter fixed it for less that $25.

That night was one year ago. So I have some reflections on our first year in Decatur.

We like Decatur very much.

We find the people friendly, warm Midwestern, gracious.

We like the change of seasons and Lake Decatur.

We like to see our neighbors fishing and enjoying the lake.

We love the vivid change of colors in the trees.

We have found the park system to be outstanding for a city of our size.

Although the opportunities for cultural and entertainment experiences are not numerous, they are adequate. We have greatly enjoyed the atmosphere of the Kirkland Fine Arts Center at Millikin University. We got our money's worth as season ticket holders for the Millikin-Decatur Symphony Orchestra. Decatur's community theater – Theatre 7 — also receives our applause. Their final production of "Our Town" was marvelous. We look forward to the '88-'89 season especially, "The King and I" which Decatur's own George Pinney will direct.

We have smiled and hummed our way along with the Greater Decatur Chorale. We enjoy spending a summer Sunday or Monday evening listening to the Decatur Municipal Band. How can you beat the cost – it's free. (One can of food, for those in need – this summer.)

Some of the little things provided by the city of Decatur have not gone unnoticed. We paid more for once-a-week garbage pickup in Indy than we do for twice-a-week here.

Yet the event that really excited me happened last January at 2 a.m. What was that noise outside on the street? Might it be? Could it actually be? Yes, it was a snow plow cleaning our street. I was so excited I almost woke Sheral. Why? During the last 14 years in Indianapolis, never once did the city send a snow plow down our street. The mayor of Indianapolis had said, "Why should we clean the streets, Chicago doesn't; and the city can't afford to." Thus we had each neighborhood family anti-up $25 a year, and we hired a driver with a pick-up and blade to clean "our" street.

Reading our city's newspaper has been a delightful change. I find the editorial policy of the Herald & Review open and thought-provoking. The Herald & Review editorial cartoons and columnists provide a wide spectrum of opinions. That's how it should be. Yes, the Herald & Review needs to provide us with more detailed national and international news. Yes, some local dog-bites-man stories need to be on Page 5 rather than on the front page. However having endured the narrow parochial view of a metropolitan newspaper, I find the Herald & Review refreshing.

Now someone will say, "Bill, haven't you found some areas where you feel Decatur could improve?" My reply is, "Of course I have, but those experiences can be the content of another article."

For now, let the statement be made with a note of pride: "Decatur, you are delightful."

(Decatur Herald & Review, June 24, 1988)

Of Donkey Dens and Elephants

They are only 215 steps apart, yet they are as different at the Cubs and Cardinals. They are going for the same prizes, yet their styles vary.

"They" are the Republican and Democratic headquarters in Decatur. Recently I easily spotted the Republican office as I drove by the corner of Franklin and William streets. I wondered, "Where are the Democrats?" It took two phone calls to find my answer: "They are in the 300 block on North Water, down from K's Merchandise Mart."

Being a political science major in undergraduate school, I thought it would be fun to see both headquarters.

I visited the Democrats first. They had an adequate supply of signs on their front windows, but very little inside. There were five volunteers in the balcony, all working for state Sen. Penny Severns. There was nothing on the walls. At the back was a simple table with a variety of pamphlets. A very pleasant woman was behind the table. I asked if they had any Dukakis yard signs and was told, "It's been hard to get any information out of the Dukakis people in Springfield." However Dukakis buttons were "selling very well."

"How's it going?" I asked. "I don't like some of the things I read in the paper and I don't buy the polls," the woman said. It was her feeling debates would show Dukakis "as the better man." A retired schoolteacher, she's at her post from 11 a.m. to at least 4 p.m.

One of the few posters was a homemade cardboard sign titled: "GOP MENU." It pictured George Bush and Dan Quayle with the caption: "A Turkey and a Quayle."

I then made my brief walk to the GOP headquarters. They, too, had a number of colorful posters in their front windows. They also had a Millikin University football schedule. (The Democrats had Illini schedules on their table.) The GOP had taken advantage of their walls, and I immediately got the feeling they were better organized. There were six desks close to the front door.

The person I met at the first GOP desk was an attractive middle-aged woman, well-dressed and very professional. I asked if I could look around and she said, "Sure." The Republicans go more for red, white and blue. They have at least three American flags, one very large. (The Democrat had an MIA-POW flag.)

One woman was at a desk with information about Jim Edgcomb, opposing incumbent Severns. Seven women were in the back, diligently going through phone books. I asked what they were doing, and was told they were working for state Rep. Mike Tate. To my "How's it going?" the woman at the first GOP desk replied, "Very well, I think Bush has no problem. We have a great location here with fantastic visibility."

I then asked, "How about Macon County?" She responded, "We are really going to have to hustle. It will depend on the swing vote. We have had some young people and a few blacks in who showed interest and registered. But we have to work at it and take nothing for granted, there is no free lunch."

I returned to my car having ventured into two worlds that were both the same, and yet very different. The Republicans were well-organized, assured, confident, and portrayed that they have it all together.

The Democrats seemed very homegrown, no-frills, casual, and honest – what you see, is what you get. On Nov. 8, one of these two groups will be filled with euphoria. The other will be saying, "We'll win it next time."

(Decatur Herald & Review, September 27, 1988)

Yes, there Is Honesty in Politics

What a day off!

I used it to get involved in the political process. I was a volunteer driver for the Democratic party, taking voters to the polls on Election Day.

My first passenger needed a ride because his car would not start. He was more concerned about how he would get his car started than the outcome of the election. My next voter, age 82, lived only one block from her polling place. Having suffered a recent fall, she indeed deserved a ride. She provided me with my first insight to the honesty of Macon County polling places. She wanted to vote the straight party line, but had difficulty making that "punch," in the booth. As I watched from a distance, two judges – one from each party – assisted her and she accomplished her mission.

I was then a taxi for a woman waiting at her apartment door. "My son was going to take me, but he's out of town," she said. "I'm going to vote the straight ticket."

I made three other stops. By then it was close to noon and volunteers were treated to a meal at campaign headquarters. The fried chicken and cole slaw were OK, but the baked beans were soupy and the potato salad contained potatoes that tasted like rocks. Volunteers did not overeat on the free food, except one large man who exclaimed, "Good chicken."

I had a devil of a time finding my next rider, but I was determined. After 20 minutes I found her trailer behind a motel, hidden in a small valley. She informed me, "I used to walk to vote, but I can't no more."

By now I realized that many polling places were in churches. Having a more than average interest in religion, I spent time nosing around church buildings while my clients voted. Most churches kept their noses clean and maintained a church-state separation. However, one church did not.

That church had stacks of material from groups called Presidential Biblical Scoreboard, Decision '88 and American Freedom Coalition. All of this "information" was strongly slanted toward one presidential candidate. You quickly got the feeling that "their" way was the way Jesus of Nazareth would vote if he were punching a ballot.

My next appointment was *the* challenge. I was greeted by two dogs in the front yard. I remembered a childhood lesson: "Don't let a dog know you are afraid." Having reached the front door I was greeted by a picture of a pit bull surrounded by the words "BEWARE" and "NO TRESPASSING." No one responded to my knock, but finally a voice called from a window. After a confusing exchange of words the voice responded, "I've already voted, get the h— off my porch."

I returned to headquarters for a soda and a doughnut.

Then I made a trip to pick up an elderly couple. As we entered their polling place the husband said, "I forgot my glasses." A neighbor at the polls loaned him hers, which helped slightly. The wife had to sign for her husband. Later she went into the booth to assist him.

I finished the day logging 61 miles.

For my efforts I received one meal and one snack, views of Decatur I had never seen before, visits with some nice people, and the experience of seeing helpfulness and honesty at every polling place.

I'll do it again in four years.

(Decatur Herald & Review, November 10, 1988.)

Chorale Baritone has Fear of No. 13

Please send me your best thoughts and vibes on Friday. I would appreciate them especially around 8 p.m.

Point yourself in the direction of the Decatur Civic Center. It would even be better if you were in the audience of the theater, for then you could concentrate your ESP feelings toward the center of the back row of the risers. I'll be standing there as a member of the Greater Decatur Chorale.

My concern is that this concert is on Friday the 13th. If I make it through this one, I'm sure I'll make it through the other five. The theme for the Chorale's winter presentation is "A Piece of Cake," and I hope it is just that.

My problem is that I have triskaidekaphobia – the fear of number 13. This fear is of more than casual concern, for I have injured a knee three times on Friday the 13th.

The first time was as a football defensive lineman when I tried to sack the quarterback; the second was when I tried to dunk a basketball from the free-throw line; and the third time was when I tried to stop a four-man toboggan that I feared was going into a creek.

I have since wised-up and given up all sports, but one never knows when those Friday the 13th demons may attack. There are probably some hiding in the dark backstage recesses in the Civic Center, waiting for chorale members.

My sojourn with the Greater Decatur Chorale began in September when they held auditions. The Chorale's vocal director, Bob Teel, had given an open invitation at the spring concert, "If you like to sing, simply come and just sing a hymn." That rang a bell, so I did.

I had sung baritone with the A Cappella Male Chorus at Nebraska Wesleyan University. That was 30 to 33 years ago. I first had to check the audition date – it was Saturday, Sept. 10, so I was OK.

I have already passed two triskaidekaphobia tests, and that has given me a bit of confidence. WAND-TV recorded the Chorale for a segment on ABC'S "Good Morning America" show. It was aired on December the 13th, but that was a Tuesday. It lasted for 13 seconds, but there were no hitches.

As we prepared for the concerts we were stationed on risers during a rehearsal. That's when I was assigned to the middle of the back row. I'm tall, and that's where I often end up. No problem with the practice, but when it was finished, I forgot where I was and took one step backward. Thank God there were two other members between me and the wall, for they cushioned my fall. I was not hurt, probably because it was Monday the 12th.

I do hope I don't mess up on the 13th because it is a neat concert. Listening to our accompanist, Karen Shaffer-Neece, is a treat. Mary Lou

Ferguson will knock your socks off with "Honey Bun." When Tina Fletcher sings "Doin' What Comes Naturally," you get the feeling the song was written just for her.

As I approach the 13th I have a slight tinge knowing there are 115 in the Chorale. If two don't show there will be 113. I'm wishing good health to all.

Now let me check those possible spring concert dates. Let's see, in May the 13th is – on Saturday. No problem.

(Decatur Herald & Review, January 12, 1989)

Should I Question?

I read a book about doubts.
The author says
we all have them.
She suggests/encourages
    yea-verily
    she implores us
to bring our doubts
out-of-the-closet
and place them on a clothesline
for a fresh airing.
(My God, people will see them.)

Was the Red Sea that wide?
What did Jesus really say?
Just what is prayer?
Is there life after death?
Is there a God?

Doubts lead to growth.
Growth leads to understanding.
Understanding leads to faith.
Faith leads to:
    "My Lord and My God!"

My God.

The Big Spender

It began last fall when my wife, Sheral, was shopping. She was in a shoe store where a radio disk jockey was giving away prizes. He awarded her a coupon good for two movie passes.

A few weeks later I was driving in beautiful downtown Decatur, listening to the radio. That DJ, only one block away, was giving away a Dairy Queen Full-Meal-Deal, and I got it. Now we were able to treat ourselves to an evening out on the town. We can make a little free thrill go a long way!

Between her schedule, and mine, and finding a movie we really wanted to see, this event was not easy to plan. The movie pass expired March 1, so we had to get our act together. Thus on a cold February afternoon we headed for Hickory Point.

We arrived 45-minutes before show time, parked south of J.C. Penney's and took a stroll through the Mall. After enjoying free samples of delicious chocolates we returned to the car. Upon opening the car doors the wind blew both gift coupons out of the car and to the ground. As I reached for them a not-so-gentle southerly wind blew them away. I was not about to lose free food and the movie, so I took off after them. Do you know how easy it is for a 20-mile an hour wind to blow two little pieces of paper across an open parking lot? However, I don't give up easily. The chase was on.

Eight times I almost pounced on the coupons, but they were blown north. After a two-block gallop I knew the large pile of snow at the end of the lot would strop them. As I reached for them the wind easily took them up and over the snow. I had come this far and I was not about to be defeated.

So I tramped through snow a foot deep for about 15 feet. Now I was in the movie parking lot, where I caught both of them!

As I looked up I realized I was providing those who were standing in the lobby with another show. Four or five people were pointing and laughing. So be it – they were paying for their tickets. The cashier said, "Sir, I believe you have a coupon." "Yes," I said, "and I worked for it." She issued me tickets with a wink. There were only a few in the theatre, so I had plenty of space to take off my shoes, shake out the snow, and let them dry.

I clung to my DQ coupon as we entered their store. Determined to continue our thrifty evening, I presented my coupon food for – a drink, french-fries, burger and small sundae. I ordered a glass of water and two spoons. I had another coupon good for 25 cents off another burger. The cheerful clerk said, "You can get a double-burger for only $1.06, without the coupon," which I did. As I fumbled to get the exact change, the clerk smiled and said, "I'll give you the penny if you need it." She was indeed treating me right. "No, I've got it," I said, "after all; I'm the last of the big-spenders."

Chautauqua: It's America's Best-kept Secret

The sign at the entrance reads: "Welcome to Chautauqua – A Center for Education, Religion and the Arts."

For the past six years my wife, Sheral, and I have been enjoying the variety of opportunities at Chautauqua Institution. "Institution" sounds a bit foreboding, but our experiences surely have not been.

Founded in 1874 as training grounds for Sunday school teachers, this 860-acre retreat by Lake Chautauqua is located in the extreme southwest corner of New York state. It is 75 miles southwest of Buffalo, or 45 miles northeast of Erie, Pa.

In the early part of this century, traveling tent Chautauqua's toured the nation in the summer offering cultural stimulation to isolated communities before the days of radio and motion pictures.

Today, Chautauqua retains an atmosphere of Victorian-style homes. We have found Chautauqua (pronounced sha-TAW-kwa) to possibly be the best-kept secret in America.

During its nine-week season (July-August) more than 300,000 will attend public events. Annually more than 2,000 enroll in the Summer School which offers classes in the arts, music, dance, theater and the humanities. Visitors pay a gate fee of $100 a week (less if you stay more than one week) which allows you to attend all the major events, and the events are major. (1988)

Each weekday morning there is a presentation in the covered, open-air amphitheater ("Amp" to the natives), seating 5,500. We have heard Alex Haley, author of "Roots", Richard Coles, Pulitzer Prize-winning psychiatrist, Gov. Mario Cuomo of New York, Jean Shepherd, humorist, and Joan Mondale to just start a list. Each presentation is followed by a question and answer session.

Each Sunday morning the Amp is full for worship. A choir of 150 and a congregation of thousands almost raise the roof. The Department of Religion continues to develop creative and innovative ways to teach and inspire.

Daily worship is led by a diversity of weekly chaplains who present the best in pulpit skills and church leadership. There are a number of continuing education seminars and conferences open to both clergy and laity.

Chautauqua has its own summer schools program covering the spectrum from art to Zen. We have taken classes as varied as creative writing, furniture restoration, opera appreciation and understanding your computer.

The Chautauqua Institution has come into international prominence for two recent conferences on U.S.-Soviet relations. "Good Morning America" presented some of the programs on national TV last August. Visitors participated in all these sessions.

If you want a break from the programmed format, there are recreational opportunities including tennis, an 18-hole golf course, swimming, fishing, boating, windsurfing and sailing. Many residents jog, walk and bike. There is a Sports Club with shuffleboard, lawn bowling and horseshoes. The Children's School offers varied activities for youngsters age 2-6. There is a structured boys and girls program every morning.

Chautauqua has the largest double dip ice cream cone for 75 cents you can find anywhere.

Afternoon lectures are in the Hall of Philosophy, a Parthenon-like structure that is open to the casual coming and going of listeners – most in jeans and orts. Martin Marty, Robert McAfee Brown, James Armstrong, Ernest mpbell and Joan Chitister are among those who have made weekly presentans.

Dr. Karl Menninger, the founder of the famed Topeka Menninger Clinic ide a presentation, and our daughter, Melanie, a psychology major, was able to eak with him afterward. This is another Chautauqua tradition – the famous, d the yet to be famous, in open friendly dialogue.

Evenings find us again at the Amp, where three nights a week the iautauqua Symphony Orchestra is in concert. These 74 musicians are from ijor symphonies across the nation. Interspersed between the symphony prentations are a variety of personalities such as John Denver, Johnny Mathis, The iptain and Tennille, Al Hirt, the Glenn Miller Orchestra, the Gatlin Brothers d Doc Severson. Three operas, in English, are presented each summer.

Accommodations are available for all tastes. The Athenaeum Hotel proles first class rooms with three meals a day for $800 a week for two. (1988) vo desserts are a tradition at every meal in the Athenaeum dining room. The tel is the first commercial property in America to have electric wiring, thanks an early Chautauquan, Thomas Edison. Sheral was the salad chef at the henaeum for one season and combined culinary skills with cultural opportuties.

Several religious denominations have residential houses within the ounds and welcome guests. These include Presbyterian, Lutheran, Episcopal, iptist, United Church of Christ, Unity and Christian Church (Disciples).

One does not have to be a member of that denomination to be a guest. iere is also a Minister's Union. We have stayed in Disciple House for the past c years. Rooms are modest, but adequate, with guests sharing the baths and tchen. Strong friendships are frequently made in this close friendly atmosiere. The cost for one week is $60-$80 for two. (1988) We have toured all nominational houses and find them clean and comfortable.

If you want to enjoy quality music; if you are searching for meaning and owing in knowledge; if you are seeking religious understanding, then you need experience at least one week at Chautauqua Institution before you die. hautauqua is a unique place with a unique program. *Smithsonian* magazine its it this way, "Chautauqua is certainly the best 'whole package' you'll find iywhere."

(This was the *Travel* section article in the Decatur Herald & Review for Sunday, March 13, 1988. Included with the piece were pictures of the thenaeum Hotel, the lakefront with the Miller Bell Tower, and themes for the 1988 season.)

(Portions of this article, with up-dates concerning costs; and comments id pictures about Disciples House at Chautauqua, appeared in the July/August sue of DisciplesWorld, 2004)

But Not For Me

I realize that because I don't do *it*, I am un-Iowan, un-American ar almost un-human. I am very much aware that most adults do do-*it;* and son do *it* many times every day. For years I have been the recipient of startling rea tions such as: "Oh, you don't!" Or "Oh, I just supposed you did." Some pe ple give me a strange look; others simply shrug and ponder with, "hum."

Yes, I have tried *it* in my younger years. However *it* did not satisfy. know how it feels to be in the minority. For me, the *it* – is coffee. I don't drir it, I don't like it. When I tried it, I put so much cream and sugar with it, it w unrecognizable as coffee.

So I've chosen to stagger and stumble through life without java. It has n been easy because coffee is very much a part of my two professions: clergy ar innkeeping.

Coffee is *the* drink in congregations. At church suppers or committ meetings coffee is always the drink. When I make home visits, I am frequent offered cookies or cake, and of course, coffee.

I have attempted to deal with the situation in many ways. One methc has been an attempt at humor. When I am offered coffee I smile and innocen ly state, "No, I don't drink coffee, I'm pure."

My statement is frequently received with amusement; but once was tl source of embarrassment. I was the new pastor in the community, and w attending a women's ecumenical worship service. Following worship I joined tl others for refreshments in the social hall. One member of the congregation I w now serving was proudly introducing me to her friends. When coffee w offered to me she took the initiative and assuredly stated, "Oh my pastor doe n't drink coffee, he's a virgin."

Her face took on the color of a ripe tomato, and she stammered, "Oh n . . . that's not what you told us, the word is 'pure.'" So much for covering m un-human, non-habit with humor.

As an innkeeper I am frequently seen with a coffee pot in my hand. Whe guests look at me and say, "Good coffee," I just smile and nod. I buy it, I mal it, I serve it, I wash coffee cups; but I've learned to never say, "I don't know ho it tastes, I never drink it."

In my senior years some family and friends hope I will become "adul and join them with coffee. However my taste buds call for other beverages.

I seem to march to a different drummer, I take the road least traveled, an I shall not become the Juan Valdez of the mid-west.

So, in my journey through life, if I should come to your door, would yc please let me in, and perhaps offer me hot chocolate or milk?

"Bottoms-up."

'The Far Side' gives us a good old belly-laugh

There it was in *The Des Moines Register* – a letter to the editor degrading ıe cartoons of Gary Larson. Those negative remarks put me in a mild state of ıe blues.

Friends of Gary Larson and his "The Far Side," arise and proclaim with ıe the joys and insights found in his wonderful cartoons. Notice as he takes a b at those who destroy the environment; laugh as he strips away the prejudicial ɔncepts we have harbored for too long; smile as he probes the ridiculous.

In one cartoon we see a native escaping across a gorge with a TV. The cap-on reads: "After reaching the far side, Zasszo cut the bridge (rope) – sending the utraged suburbanites into the river below. Their idol (a television set) was now is . . . as well as its curse."

That cartoon is worth more than a thousand words of commentary on ow contemporary Americans are subject to television.

The problem is simply one of communication and understanding. Some eaders of The Register's comic section may not take the time to ponder and ppreciate the depth of a creative cartoonist.

Humor can come in a variety of art forms, images and provocative words. Spider Man," "Cathy" and "Rex Morgan" may do for some readers, but we all eed to become a bit more avant-garde and sophisticated.

Another Larson gem pictures a quiz-show program called "Trivia 'onight." Next to the host sit two persons – one average, one larger and wiser. Yes. That's Right. The answer is Nebraska. Another 50 points for God, and . . uh-oh, looks like Bob, our current champion, hasn't even scored yet."

Larson's prehistoric cave dwellers are often like us – inquisitive and fool-h – while his bears and ducks and cows are also like us – wise and resourceful nd caring.

What we occasionally need is a good old belly-laugh. Larson provides us vith the opportunity with his outrageous humor. In another "The Far Side" we ee a man reaching for his mail in an apartment house hallway. From the shad-ws behind a stairway, an elephant dressed in a trench coat and hat says: Remember me, Mr. Schneider? Kenya, 1947. If you're going to shoot at an ele-hant, Mr. Schneider, you better be prepared to finish the job."

This type of cartoon is so outlandish that it is capricious. At times life eeds to be lived on the edges, not always in the center. We must learn to laugh t ourselves and reflect on how we have abused others and the world. We can earn from Larson. We can put the ingredients of life in proper priority. We can hink about our common destiny. In another "The Far Side" Larson draws a ransport truck carrying a deadly missile. A sign on the truck reads: "Our lights re on for safety." That is humor with a necessary jolt.

Stephen King may help us understand Larson when King writes:

"You can't tell a cartoon; if you could, cartoonists would be out of busi-ness. A cartoon isn't simply a joke; it's a talented eye combining circumstances nd joke in a clearly recognizable way which cannot be duplicated. You could opy Gary Larson's pictures, just as you could copy Charles Schulz's round-head-d worrywart, Charlie Brown; it's Larson's mind which makes him one of a ind."

As we make our journey in life, Gary Larson helps us to deal with th human condition, while he entertains us, and causes us to ponder our place i society.

(The Des Moines Register, March 1, 1990. Two of Larson's cartoons appeare within this article.)

About 2 cents a Month

I bought gasoline; I went to the show;
I bought some new tubes for my radio;
I bought candy, peanuts and ice cream;
While my salary lasted, life sure was a scream!

It takes careful spending to make money go 'round;
One's method of finance must always be sound;
With habits quite costly, it's vital to save;
My wife spent six bucks on a permanent wave.

The church came 'round begging; it sure made me sore!
If they'd leave me alone, I'd give a lot more.
They don't give me credit for gifts in the past;
I gave them a quarter year before last.

(This poem was found in a file owned by W. S. Lowe, my grandfather, Disciples pastor who served as the State Secretary in Kansas, 1906-1910.)

(The Gifts We Bring, Volume 4)

Gatherings from alongside an Iowa road

At the ages of 54 and 55 my wife and I have an addition to our family. : signed the formal application papers, and after a few months we were proved, so on March 19, 1990, we received our new "baby."

Our adopted child is a two-mile stretch of Highway 1 in Van Buren unty, a few miles west of our Bentonsport home. The Iowa Adopt-A-ghway program began in 1989. It is an innovative program designed to beau-y Iowa's roadsides. In our adoption contract we have agreed to pick up litter, both sides of the highway, at least twice a year, for two years.

However, as in any serious family relationship, we visit our child more fre-ently than required. Almost weekly we pick up discards of a not-so-thought-public. One reason for the extra attention is that God and everyone else ows this section as "our" highway. This fact is clearly spelled out at both ends this road. Six-inch letters: MASON HOUSE INN – BENTONSPORT on o large signs greet all travelers.

A recent publication from the Iowa Department of Transportation states at nearly 100 groups or individuals are applying for the program each month. uring the first five months of fiscal year 1991 we adopters picked up nearly 500 bic yards of trash. This amount filled 100 dump trucks. The Iowa DOT pro-les an extensive list of guidelines on how to maintain your highway while you otect yourself and others from oncoming traffic.

I recently donned my orange safety vest, and armed with a set of large ange trash bags, set off to attend our child, hoping to help build a positive age for the state. Following my journey into those Van Buren ditches I make is semi-scientific report.

We like to drink a lot in southeast Iowa. Budweiser leads in the beer cat-ory followed by Lite, Milwaukee's Best Light and Coors Light; then came rtles & Jaymes Wine Cooler, Bud Light, Busch, Busch Light and Old ilwaukee.

In the soft-drink crowd the volume winner was Mountain Dew with 38.2 rcent of my total "take." Pepsi (in cups, cans and glass) came in with 23.5 per-nt, 7-Up had 11.7 percent, followed by Coke-Cola Classic with 8.8 percent. y list would be too long if I named the others.

Cigarette discards revealed that most smoke Merit Ultra Lights, then arlboro. I also found Virginia Slims Lights and Camel Lights along with ɔpenhagen Snuff. The American public seems to be hooked on the word ight."

Heading the candy-wrapper list was Almond Joy. Two wrappers with triguing sounding titles were Fudge-Dipped Chewy Granola and Hershey's 'hatchamacallit.

In the snack-food category I found that travelers preferred Doritos chips d Planters peanuts. I also found: Lays potato chips, dry curd cottage cheese, eer Nuts, popcorn boxes and a noisy sounding brand – Thunder Crunch pota-chips.

There were endless numbers of non-biodegradable plastic cups and plas-: straws. Lubricants were also hiding in the weeds: Texaco Anti-Free, Shellzone l-Season Protection, Quaker State Motor Oil and WD-40.

I am pleased to report that not everything "out there" is junk food, or bad r one's health. My adventure produced containers that once held: milk, 2-per-

cent milk, chocolate low fat milk, V-8 juice, orange juice, tomato juice a
Gatorade.

My orange sacks also bulged with broken pieces of bottles, truck m
flaps, newspapers, rags, parts of tires, tin pans, a section of a car bumper, t
printed numbers 1 to 250 by an unnamed elementary school student, Io
Lottery studs and one cloth baby diaper (use, of course).

I'll not soon forget picking up pieces of Styrofoam after they had be
mowed into little pieces.

Wait. What is this? And what is that about 20 feel away? Yes, they are
two pair of deer antlers.

Many discards were products not purchased with our county, leading
to believe that most of those defacing our child were visitors.

I will, of course, cash in on all the cans I have collected. That amount w
more than pay for the gas I used for the pick-up. The biggest pay-off is findi
satisfaction in keeping our child, a very small part of God's good Earth, free
debris.

Has this been a good learning experience?

The experience has underscored the need that all Iowans should pract
one habit – do not discard rubbish out the car window. Period.

(The Des Moines Register, July 24, 1991. Included with this article was a pi
ture of our grandson, Brian, with his vest and sack, picking up trash.)

Back Porch Communion

It was Easter Sunday afternoon and I sat moping on our back porch. M
sulking mood was the result of my being unable to preach that day. In fact,
was the first Easter I had ever missed. My stimulating sermon never made it
the pulpit; it was in my desk drawer. I was the victim of the twenty-four-ho
flu.

Now my body felt better, but my soul was sick unto death. I just sat, n
really thinking about anything in particular. I was about ready to nomina
myself as president of the "Poor Me Club" when our grandson, Brian, then th
years and four months old, ventured onto the porch. He sat beside me with h
Easter basket.

"Grandpa" he said, "Do you want some gum or *M&Ms*?"

I selected both.

He then patted my leg and we took our communion, for that is what h
gifts became. I recalled the words from the Psalms, "The afflicted shall eat a
be satisfied." I did, and I was.

Many times God provides not only the bread, but the one who serves t
bread.

(The Disciple, April, 1988, also The Secret Place, April 10, 1994)

Census Taker Gains Insight into People

For the past few weeks I have been a federal bureaucrat, if one can give a temporary U.S. Census Enumerator that label. For $6 an hour, plus 24 cents a mile, I served as a Quality Assurance Enumerator for Davis and Van Buren Counties. As such I logged hundreds of miles on back (sometimes very back) roads of these two picturesque southeast Iowa counties.

My venture into rural Iowa life provided a rich opportunity of experience, and from it I made some reflections, observations and one suggestion.

Even in the gray and brown of March this area of Iowa is serenely attractive. Among the peaceful hills, valleys, streams, rugged trees and shrubs, some great people live in the Des Moines River valley. I spotted eight deer in one day. One almost became my auto hood ornament. Wild turkey, beaver, opossum and squirrels are abundant. Birds are numerous and in great variety.

Yet it was the hardy rural Iowa people that made the door-to-door-days interesting. Census enumerators were greeted with the extremes of, "Good to see you, come in and have a cookie," to "Y'know what I'm gonna do with that damn thing (census questionnaire) – throw it in the wastebasket." The vast majority of respondents were pleasant.

I share some general observations:

+ Rural mail carriers are friendly and helpful.

+ There are 2.3 dogs to every farm home. One exception was the five vicious German shepherds inside a fenced yard. That resident's questionnaire was mailed!

+ When a road sign reads: "Limited maintenance enter at your own risk," don't.

+ There are a lot of good ole boys out there, and a few good ole girls. A census enumerator must check every building to see if it contains any living quarters.

+ The Amish are a positive factor for the area.

+ Older persons, especially those who live alone, are hungry for conversation.

+ Many U.S. flags fly even in inclement weather.

+ There is a lot of barn siding going to waste.

+ I'm sure the "rainmaker" knew I would be out among the elements, so she/he did their darnedest to keep me wet. At least I brought rain to happy farmers.

Now friends and neighbors, an observation, and a suggestion. Most Southeast Iowa cemeteries are neater and better maintained than are some residents' living quarters. I was amazed to see so many: old junk cars, broken appliances, cans and trash, rusty machinery and discarded furniture in front, back and side yards, and on porches. Whatever happened to good old Iowa pride? Is this Iowa? It certainly was not heaven! I am painfully aware that the Per capita Income for area 19 is about $8,000. I know that some of my friends and neighbors are barely "making it." Yet there seems to be a common allergy to house paint. More than one person greeted me with a reflection on their own home: "Ain't fit to live in."

Maybe what is needed is a good old clean-up, fix-up and paint-up week or month. I'm not suggesting that everything become antiseptically aesthetic. However, what would the area look like if everyone simply cleaned the trash from their yard, and spent about $100 on paint? Even renters can make a neat-looking home out of a hovel.

I simply want to challenge my neighbors to make their environment as attractive as they are.

Most rural Iowans are delightful and friendly, and I wish them good health so that I might be able to count them 10 years from now.

(The Ottumwa Courier, April 9, 1990)

Does a spirit sit in the front or back?

A woman approached her friend about buying a ticket for a benefit concert. Her friend replied, "I'm so sorry, but I have something else to do that evening. I'd like to help, but I'll be with you in spirit." The woman responded, "I'm glad you would like to help; where would your spirit like to sit – in a $10, $14 or $20 seat?"

(The Gifts We Bring, Volume II, August, 1989)

In the Plate, and on the Table

A church friend shared this happening with me:

A man from another country was visiting, and we attended worship together. He asked me for an explanation as the offering plate was passed. "I give 10% of my salary as a tithe because of my love for God," I told him. Later, after dining in a restaurant, I put a 15% tip on the table for the waitress. My visitor-friend then asked, "Does that mean you love the waitress more than God?"

(The Gifts We Bring, Volume II, August, 1989)

Doing Time in Line

It happens so often that I believe I'm jinxed. I really do try to avoid the delay. Am I being paid back for those naughty pranks of my youth? I've tried to analyze each situation and plan a tactical move, resulting in a satisfying conclusion. Still in happens over and over: at the drive-up bank, the grocery store, the discount store, even the fast-food restaurant.

My frustrating problem is that when I'm ready to check out, or order, I'm always in the wrong line. Every line moves faster than mine.

I recently entered a hamburger house and saw three lines: one with two people, one with four and one with seven. I quickly took my place in the two-person line – only to discover they were partners in crime, ordering for a school bus filled with 30 junior high kids. I prepared to move to the next line, but by then it had gained three more bodies. I lost again.

When I'm ready to check out at the grocery store I'm always one item over the express line limit. So I ponder the fullness of the carts in the other lines. I finally take a spot in a line that moves smoothly until the woman ahead of me has an item with no UPC code. This results in the checker having to ask the supervisor for a price. The supervisor goes to the intercom: "Fred I need a price check on Sunkist prunes." By the time Fred gets the prune price – you guessed it – those in the other lines are in their cars going home.

The lines at the drive-through banks are also a problem. It never fails that I get behind a customer who wants $1,000 in quarters. And in stores that take charge cards, I'm always behind a person who doesn't have the proper identification, or whose card expired yesterday, or who is returning a purchase.

Believing I'm a person of average intelligence, I've made a list of constructive activities I can do in line:

+ *Isometrics*. Using a cart, steering wheel or counter, I can push and pull. I can pretend Dolly Parton is behind me, looking at me, so I practice excellent posture.

+ *Plan my day or week*. What will I do when/if I get home? What six things do I have to do tomorrow? In what order should I do them?

+ *Start a conversation with others in my line*. "What type of stocks would make good investments?" "Do you believe there's life on other planets?" "Did you see the Letterman show?" "I'm thinking of painting my bathroom orange. Would you sit in an orange bathroom?"

+ *Practice proper breathing*. My voice teacher once said, "You need to stand straight and breathe properly." She would be so proud of me.

+ *Cultivate great thoughts*. For starters: "What's the meaning of life?" My answer should take at least two minutes.

+ *Read*. I will always carry reading material with me. When I'm caught in the wrong line, I can whip out *The New York Times* or *The Christian Century or The New England Journal of Medicine*. I'll educate myself while impressing others.

Having thus prepared myself, I headed for the store ready for the worst, but now knowing that I was an expert in the art of constructive-use-of-time-while-waiting-in-line. I pushed my cart to the check-out counter only to discover . . . I was *first* in line. Well, maybe next time!

(Iowa REC News, October, 1995)

Watch what you say

Our English language: What would we do without it; yet what are we doing with it? In our daily conversations, business transactions and news reporting, we're bruising, abusing, over using and misusing words. We've become sloppy with our language – filling the air with grunts and clichés. Consider there:

+ *Y'know.* This, y'know, is by far, the most overused non-word, y'know, which too many of us are using in our speech. Y'know what I'm-a-say'n?

+ *Gunna* and *gotta*. All too often, we hear people use "woulda," "coulda," "shoulda," "wanta," "gunna" and "gotta." Even the national network newsperson starts the evening reporting with: "We're gunna begin tonight with . . ."

+ *Much, much more.* The furniture dealer says he has a special sale – beds, chairs, tables, lamps, sofas, chests, rugs and much, much more. If the dealer indeed did have more items he would list them. "Much, much more" is a contemporary catchall to entice us to come in and see all the many other wonderful things. Hum.

+ *Uh-huh.* Is this the right one baby? A soft-drink company may think it has a worldwide catching slogan, but I hope "uh-huh" is not the best we have to offer our world family. Does this utterance add to the development of our being? The company also promotes, "Gotta have it." Do these words advance us?

+ *I'm really excited about* . . . This over-worked phrase gives the impression that the project, program or happening is the most unique, wonderful and life-changing event to have ever come down the pike. This phrase should be reserved as a prefix for announcing things like – a cure for cancer, solving world hunger or that the Iowa State Cyclones beat the Iowa Hawkeyes in football!

+ *We're gonna play 'em one game at a time.* Sports announcers and coaches punctuate their observations with this phrase. Have you ever known a team to play 'em two games at a time?

+ *I'm gunna be real honest with you.* Does this mean the person is usually *not* honest with you? If you hear a salesperson use this phrase, be cautions.

+ *And so forth.* My wife says I say this far too often. Her thought? I'm buying time while I think out my next statement.

+ *Uh-uh-uh-uh.* An old one, but a good standby which fills the void.

+ *Well.* We often add this word to start a conversation.

+ *Have a nice day.* I've even received this "send-off" when I was leaving a drug store at 10:30 p.m. There was not much "nice day" time left to enjoy. This all-too-popular "benediction" to a brief encounter, has even been reduced to "Have a good one" or "have a good 'un." Maybe we can get it down to "have a."

What do I suggest we say to each other, and how should we use language? I simply ask for freshness and creativity; and that we are clear and honest when we converse. Say what we mean, and mean what we say.

But I'm gunna be real honest with you. It's hard to, y'know, change our speaking style – no doubt about it. I guess people are gunna utter garbled phrases, one colloquialism at a time. Y'know what I'm-a-say'n? Well, uh, have a nice day.

Peace!

(Iowa REC News, January, 1996)

Going, Going, Gone

Are you looking for a little excitement, entertainment, even a bit of education? Then enjoy a rural Iowa estate auction. Wear old clothes, especially comfortable shoes; and come in a pickup, van or a car with a large trunk. You never know what gem you might be toting home – that "thing" you didn't know you needed.

Your first order of business is to carefully read the auction listing. Most papers contain them, and you can get on the mailing list of your local auctioneers. Be sure you note the correct date, time and location.

After attending a number of auctions I'm learning how to really read the auction bill. Most auction advertisements contain this type of statement:

> NOTICE: All information contained in this ad has been gained from sources considered to be reliable, however, bidders are invited to inspect the property & make their own investigations with respect thereof.

Translation: "What you see is what you get; we won't guarantee nothin."

Learn not to be disappointed. What was advertised as "unique quality" may turn out to really be flea market quality. The words: "Lots of items not listed" may become: "Did we ever clean out the attic and basement!"

Many auctions are a mix of socializing, seeing new places, enjoying the competition of bidding, and the hope of coming away with that true bargain. People come to visit and eat. I recently spotted my neighbor, Sam, at an auction who said, "I just came for the good tenderloin from Lee's grill."

One soon learns lingo special to auctions. Don't look for gender equality. Most auctioneers are men, and when they want your attention will say: "Now listen up boys." When the bidding isn't going well you might hear: "Someone's asleep out there," or "This here's a great item, you gotta fine 'em first."

Indeed, there are wonderful finds at auctions. My wife, Sheral, found a 100 piece set of Duchess Rose China. She said, "I'll stop bidding at $100. She was surprised and pleased when she got them for $25. An antique dealer standing next to her reflected, "It was probably too new, about 1930, for the glass dealers." I recently brought home a 4 foot by 6 foot beveled mirror for $62.50. Wow!

At another auction Sheral spotted a small syrup pitcher. This auction was not proceeding very well, so the auctioneer pushed many boxes together for one bid. "Her" pitcher was in one of the boxes; yet she got it for only $3. However, when she took her prize, leaving the other boxes, the auctioneer told her she *had* to take all 18 boxes! (We sold these gems at our own yard sale, and cleared $137.) Do we qualify as entrepreneurs?

You need to stay alert at auctions. A woman brought a folding chair for her own use – an excellent idea – but she left it to seek refreshments; and when she returned, the auctioneer had sold it. (She did get it back without buying it.)

I pulled a faux pas at an auction. I bought about 20 items, but absent-mindedly brought home only half of them. The next morning I hurried back to the site – and bless honest Iowa neighbors – my treasurers were still there.

Here's some wisdom as you head for an auction. The "junk" small-change stuff almost always sells first. So, come with an ample supply of reading material. (Unless, of course, if you like the small-change stuff.) Don't wave, scratch, nod or blink – or you may find yourself the owner of an unwanted item. Before bidding starts on an item you want, set your limit, as you can easily become caught-up in the rapid escalation of the bidding, and you might be sorry later.

I'm still somewhat of a neophyte at this auction business. One auction was about to end and I was one of a dozen left to bid on items inside an old store. I had done my "research" and had discovered a box of about 75 old Playboy magazines. The auctioneer said, "We're gunna *jackpot* it." I was not familiar with the term which meant: "We're gunna sell all this stuff at one shot from *here* to *here*." I did not bid even when the auctioneer looked at me for a bid. Someone else got the insightful literature. I, of course, wanted the magazines only for their antique value!

I'm checking the paper for the next auctions. You check your paper, and go and enjoy the process, and take home your own gems. Maybe I'll see you there.

From the Other End of the Bed

After working as innkeepers for the past seven years, my wife and I have alized that life isn't very much like the *Bob Newhart Show*. In fact, it's nothing e it.

I had been a church pastor for 29 years in the Midwest, when my wife eral decided to return to Purdue for a second college degree in hotel and staurant management. After she got her degree, we decided to get into the &B industry, and for some years we made trips to New England looking for ur" inn. Nothing developed, so we considered the Midwest, and in June of 89, we purchased an historic inn in Bentonsport, Iowa, built in 1846, the me year Iowa became a state.

Being busy innkeepers (we have nine guest rooms) with no extra help, we d few opportunities for trips or vacations. So realizing that February is a cold d lonely month for us – even in the banana belt of southeast Iowa – Sheral and losed our inn and took off for places east. We traveled to 14 states and cov-ed 3,988 miles in 31 days, during which we stayed in 14 B&Bs. Some of those re through an inn exchange program. Instead of making beds and breakfasts, slept in other beds and enjoyed the breakfasts of others.

What follows are reflections, observations and suggestions that hopefully ll make for better innkeepers and inn keeping?

Most innkeepers are friendly, gracious and genuinely want to be helpful. is, of course, is why many travelers choose to stay in B&Bs instead of motels. warm greeting which makes you feel at home, suggestions of places to eat and lpful directions from the hosts are ingredients that make for a pleasant stay. member that you are the only one who knows where the switch is, where the tra towels and pillows are, and what that unusual sound means, but this is a st-time adventure for your guests. Those are all unanswered questions for em.

Staying in a number of different places, and being strangers in the night, ecame keenly aware of things that go "bump" in the night. At one location I ard the large grandfather clock strike 10 p.m. and 11 and 12 and 1 a.m. When returned to our own inn, I realized that I did not hear the large clock in our rlor; as we sleep three rooms away from it. However, I wondered about guests the rooms directly across the hall and on the next floor. Were they woken on e hour? Innkeepers might consider spending one night in each guest room, us experiencing each room from the vantage of guests.

Pardon our pet

Pets are great, and we enjoy them. But do our guests? At one B&B our st was most apologetic for a cat that was sick all over the inn. Do our person- pets help or harm our business? I think this is an area that innkeepers often erlook simply because they are attached to their animals and believe they ould be a part of the business, whether they are truly an asset or not.

If a significant part of our business revolves around offering our customers pleasant place to sleep, then we must make sure we have comfortable beds. It no fun being 6'3" and trying to squeeze into a short antique bed. On this trip, e most expensive inn had the most uncomfortable bed.

Talk about minimum standards. Here's one of my pet peeves. In our

business, a breakfast surely must consist of more than a store-bought roll a
cold cereal from a box. At a quality B&B, breakfast should be warm and tas
ful. The breakfast table – with its cloth, silverware, dishes and decorations – m
be gorgeous, but if the food is not tasty and plentiful, it's like an empty promi

Thanks for not sharing

Another suggestion: Hosts need to practice a quotation from the O
Testament: "There is a time to speak, and a time to refrain from speaking." Th
is an art, but it can be learned. As hosts, a simple rule might be helpful –
need to *speak less and listen more.* If we are directly asked for information a
suggestions, we gladly give them. At one B&B, our host repeatedly re-told t
details of their family problems. We were also provided with unsolicited infc
mation about a child's illness. Guests, I'd like to remind innkeepers, may not
interested in our own politics or religious beliefs or recent negative experienc
An open exchange with other B&B owners/managers can be rewarding and hel
ful. Still, the incentive rests with the resident hosts to steer the dialogue to o
of mutual interest, maybe saying, "How's it going with your inn?" or "Tell n
about some of the more interesting experiences you've had with guests."

Opportunities to reflect on the beauty of individual personalities a
afforded to many, but even more so with the average innkeeper. I recall a pa
ticular phone call from a prospective bride from "Hicksville." She made t
reservation in butchered English. When I asked her for a method to secure h
reservation she replied, "No, we don't got no credit cards or checkin' account
When the newly-weds arrived, they were in cowboy boots and western garb.
breakfast, I noticed that their linen napkins never left the table. However, wh
they left, they both sincerely thanked us, and about one week later we received
hand-written note from the new bride thanking us "for allowing us to stay
your lovely inn." We have a folder of "Thank You" notes from guests, and th
one we truly treasure. We were the honored ones, as we were able to share in t
most meaningful time of the couple's lives.

Welcome wit

One thing our trip taught us was to continue to cultivate a growing appr
ciation for people, and an expanding sense of humor. For example, one innkee
er told us of a time when two men arrived together requesting accommodatior
This innkeeper quickly showed them two rooms, each with twin beds, but t
couple wanted a room with a queen-size bed. The innkeeper gently suggeste
they could have the twin beds for the same price as the queen. The two gues
maintained, however, that they would prefer the queen-size bed. We are in t
business of letting our guests have what they want – within reason. And whe
we give them what they want, we develop a growing appreciation for people.

Some innkeepers fill guest rooms with dusty flea market finds. Some lways have the same breakfast – always. Some try to Victorianize everything. n our own situation, we have no mountain views, no seaside sunsets, no in round pool, no ski slopes, no five-star restaurant. What we do have is an old eamboat river inn built by Mormon craftsmen while making their famous trek o Utah. Abe Lincoln, Mark Twain, George McGovern and writer Robert Waller ave slept under our roof. We have a cookie jar (with cookies) in each guest oom. We give a full country breakfast at the hour selected by our guests. We ave an abundance of peace and quiet, with shelves full of books for reading leasure. And we try to be helpful hosts. That's about it. We adhere to the notto, "Go with what you've got." Make things clean and neat. And with a lit- e luck, it will be even better next year.

All things considered, our recent trip was a pleasant and positive experi- nce. It was a wonderful opportunity to see innkeeping from the other end of he bed. Hosts were happy and helpful, and accommodations were adequate, ven if they were "short" at times. We are part of a wonderful profession. nnkeepers have been hosting travelers since biblical days. In our days, we may ot be an encore for the *Bob Newhart Show,* but we can be that true home away om home.

(Bed & Breakfast, November/December, 1996)

Innkeeping Escapades

For the past nine years Sheral and I have been innkeepers. It has been crazy trip. We have been challenged to use our wisdom in dealing with th human animal.

We have learned to "go with the flow." Sheral was serving breakfast to couple. She brought them the eggs and sausage course on an oval serving platter. The woman took it, removed her plate, and began eating directly from th platter. Her companion smiled and continued their conversation. Back in th kitchen Sheral wondered: "How do I serve the man?" She prepared anothe "platter" and brought it to him. After breakfast he privately said to Shera "Thanks for being so thoughtful, my friend is really a nice person."

I am versatile at our B&B One weekend we hosted a wedding party. A innkeeper I greeted our guests, and then served as air-conditioner repairman. officiated at the wedding (I am also a clergyperson). Later I served as waiter. A I brought their food the remake was: "Haven't we seen you somewhere before? Indeed.

More honeymooners were guests. Sheral was in the kitchen when sh responded to a soft rap on the door. The bride blushed and said: "I'm sorry, bu we have locked ourselves out of our room." In earlier days our baths were dow the hall. The couple had showered – but returned to a locked room. As Sher unlocked their door she attempted *not* to notice the groom crouched in a ha chair wrapped only in a quilt from the hall. A year later they returned and greeted us at the front door with: "Hi, remember us, I'm the one in the quilt!"

I've caused some of my own embarrassing moments by being too friendly. When a couple appeared at our door I welcomed the gentleman saying: "It nice to have you with us Mr. Smith." Wanting to be inclusive I turned to th woman and cheerfully remarked: "And we're glad you're here, Mrs Smith." M comment was met with a cold stare and the words: "I'm not Mrs Smith!" quickly showed them to *their* room.

Most of our guests eat their breakfast in our "Keeping Room" which is fu of antiques. Whey they arrived, a young family of four was given a tour of th Inn which included a detailed look at the 1884 Buck stove. Prominently displayed is a large possum rack, used when possum was an eatable decades ago The next morning when the sausage was served, the father loudly stated: "O look, they caught a possum for us!" The children's appetite seemed to have le them that morning.

When writer Robert Waller still lived in Iowa he was a guest for five days Each morning he ate breakfast at 4:50 so he could photograph objects in th morning sunlight. He enjoyed his stay and phoned his wife to join him for th final two days. Sheral agreed to prepare a 6:00 evening meal for them. At 7:0 the wife phoned that she could not find the Mason House Inn *in* Bettendor Bentonsport, (37 humans, 7 dogs) is about a two hour drive west fro Bettendorf. They ate at 9:00.

Living in an 1846 Inn we are the ideal place for ghost stories. Whe asked: "Do you have a ghost?" I quickly reply: "Yes, Mary Mason, who died i 1910, is a resident, but she has promised me she will not leave her third floo quarters." On at least three occasions guests have reported at breakfast: "Ther was knocking outside our door about 2:00, was that you?" I could honestly say "No, I was in bed," and I was!

A couple comes every Thanksgiving. Knowing we also have a restaurant ense the woman requested a special evening meal. After the menu was set she d to Sheral: "We're very quiet people, would you two please eat with us." eral responded: "We would be honored." Then the woman seriously quesned: "Do we have to pay for you?"

Sheral has learned to grin-and-bare some comments. A young man commented her on the breakfast remarking: "You're even a better cook than my om. Of course my mom isn't a very good cook." Hmm.

Innkeepers have been hosting travelers since biblical days. In our day we n be that home-away-from-home if we have the wisdom to keep our wit.

He took pride in his "accomplishment"

Seven-year-old Justin had never been to church. Justin's next-door neighor was a minister, Kris Niceperson. After several months of friendly cultivation, stor Niceperson was able to get Justin to attend Sunday school. In class Justin ade a new friend, Robbie; and following Sunday school the two were talking the hall where Pastor Niceperson spotted them.

The pastor asked Justin what he had learned in class. Justin replied that had just learned the Lord's Prayer, and he did a fairly good job of repeating e prayer to his pastor-neighbor.

Pastor Niceperson invited Justin and Robbie to stay for worship, and they d. Immediately after the pastor had led the congregation in the Lord's Prayer, stin nudged his new friend and said, "I taught her that!"

(The Disciple, April, 1989)

That Old Theta Chi House

(In the spring 2002 issue of Archways, the quarterly alumni publicati of Nebraska Wesleyan University, there was a "Call to write" request centeri on: "Where Did I Spend My Free Time While at Wesleyan?" This was the selec ed essay which appeared in the Summer, 2002 Archways. Some of this mater appeared in the Fall, 1967 issue of The Rattle of Theta Chi, the national pub cation of Theta Chi fraternity.)

It was never much to look at. It wasn't even ours – we rented. It ha pened to be painted yellow & brown (Wesleyan's colors). It was crowded. held a basement sump-pump that had to be frequently "unloaded" by pledg (You don't want to know about the contents!). Yet it was home to more than young men. It was the place where I spent most of my free time while at NW from 1954 to 1957.

"It" was the Theta Chi fraternity house at the southeast corner of 50 and Huntington. Some students used to call "it" the "snake pit," (Part of t Theta Chi symbol/pin is a coiled snake).

That space today is only a parking lot. What happened within *that* spa lives within memory. Forty-five years later – still trying to completely discov the meaning of life – I remain deeply thankful for both my class time and fr time at Nebraska Wesleyan.

In the summer of 1954 I decided that I should become more involved college life; so I decided to try out for the Male Chorus (which developed into most rewarding three year experience) and to pledge a fraternity.

I went through rush week. I was impressed by fraternity life, and believed that I was missing some rich experiences. Being a part of a fraterni might indeed fill a void, and I was not to be disappointed.

Pledge life started the list of valuable fraternity experiences. If pled duties were fulfilled we were rewarded collectively; if we blundered, we we punished. We learned that by working together as a unit, we could achieve goal, a most valuable lesson for later life. Many times throughout my frate nity life the necessity to use the skills of each other was evident. We won th Homecoming display award by using the artistry of one member; the electric knowledge of another; the coordinating ability of another; and the brawn of ot ers. Winning the May Fete sing contest was accomplished by the blending trained and untrained voices into a harmonious unit and by following the lea ership of Gary Bacon. Certainly we learned teamwork as we won sports tr phies. We found satisfaction not only in winning, but in developing the nece sity of working together.

I cannot emphasize too much the importance placed on scholarship. Ou average was always higher than the total men's average. Theta Chi provided th structure for coming together to discuss, study and ponder the classroom know edge. It was there in my free time place that I dialogued over the concepts pu forth by professors: Edward Mattingly (Religion) "Do we believe in a God wh simply turns a woman (Lots wife) into a pillar of salt because she simply turne to respond to a cry of help from a neighbor?" Harold Hall (English) "Can lo be uniquely expressed by two old (really old) people just holding hands, whi rocking on their front porch?" E. Glenn Callen (Political Science) "What are th positive elements we find within the consolidation of a city/county form of go nment?" The fraternity encouraged, indeed demanded, that we keep our ades up or not be allowed to participate in the social life.

Yet, what I insist was the greatest benefit from my free time place was the scipline of learning to live together. By eating, studying, playing, singing, orking together, we came to appreciate a person as an individual. We learned being together to evaluate a person, not by his family background, not by his ıysical looks, but we came to respect each individual as a person.

This structure provided for dialogue. True, we may or may not have been phisticated to call it interpersonal relations, but we were learning how to live ithin a community. Is this not an ageless need: to provide structure where ıose of different opinion may discuss the very reasons for living? Learning to) live with others; (2) cooperate; (3) respect others persons; (4) finding success unity – these are some values of my free time at NWU.

My free time space was not always filled with sweetness and blue sky, far om it. I recall the time our national fraternity office was requesting each chapr to vote on what was really a "Caucasian clause" which was the stated or silent olicy of the fraternity. (In short, would we "allow" men of color to be broths?) Some of the reasoning was: "We don't want to embarrass – or make it difcult for – our brothers in the South."

As I remember the final chapter vote was something like: 54 "no", 1 "yes", abstained, (I was one of the two, big deal!) Only Brad from Colorado had the ıts, or insight, to vote "yes." I have often wished I would have said/done someıing more as a child of God. Still, maybe we learn and grow from all situations, e they good or not-so-good experiences.

Yet during the times we discussed prospective pledges, more than once I eard, "What can we do for this person?" In other words we were saying that ot all persons are physically or emotionally attractive at times. Still our purpose as not to just go for the cream of the crop, but we can and should help and evelop persons. I remember the pledging of the handicapped young man from estern Nebraska. He was physically unattractive – and some of the brothers did ot want him – yet we pledged him – and not out of pity. He became a valuble asset to us.

I also make a keen observation that when the school administration needl support from the student body, they could always depend on the Greeks. ireeks were seen everywhere in giving leadership in the life and work of Vesleyan. The Greeks were not an appendage of the University; they were and re part of the main body.

In my free time space I was able to hone my social graces. Rising when a oman enters a room, speaking courteously and distinctly, good table manners, arning not to be sloppy or lazy are traits becoming human beings; or was this nly for the 50s, and not for today?

For my final college year I was able to live in the house as my family ıoved from Lincoln, to Kansas City. Thus my free time became my full time ee time. This was a year of rewarding experiences which I shall cherish forevr. What greater value than learning to live with others.

That spring and summer of '57 are filled with happy memories. I comleted my undergraduate days. Then I married my "Dream Girl" with her Phi Mu sisters and my Theta Chi brothers having all key parts in the service.

So, I treasure reflecting upon what happened within my Wesleyan free time place: cultivating values; developing lasting friendships; learning to live an work with others; accepting responsibility. This helped me to become a signif cant part of the human family – learning in our life's journey – that we are no created to live as individuals, but with community.

He's happy that the report wasn't correct!

A congregation I served in Illinois has a public time of sharing before th Sunday worship service. Good news, sad news, family news – all is shared. On Sunday, a member stood and said, "My wife and I want to share that our daugh ter, Julie, recently passed her CPA (Certified Public Accountant) test."

The member reported later in the week that his family received a sympa thy card from an elderly member who had been in worship. On the card wa the note: "I'm so sorry that your daughter passed away." To an older saint whos hearing is not what it used to be, "CPA" and "passed away" sounded very simi lar.

The proud dad says he appreciates the concern shown by the loving mem ber, but he is happy that Julie is alive and practicing her accounting skills!

(The Disciple, July, 1989)

More Than an Amp Ump

"Umpire – an official who administers the rules in certain team sports, as baseball – SYN. Judge."

— Webster's New World Dictionary

My wife, Sheral, and I have been coming to Chautauqua Institution since ıe early 1980s. In 2001 we retired to the Lake of the Ozarks in Missouri. Iowever, we found we did not fit into the "Branson-type" atmosphere. So ɔppreciating and enjoying the Chautauqua lifestyle, we bought a home fourteen ıiles south of Chautauqua, and moved there in May.

Instead of buying season gate passes, a friend suggested, "Why not see if ou can be ushers at the Amphitheater? You're going to be there anyway." We pplied, passed any security checks, and began "duty" on June 21, opening along ith Frank Sinatra Jr.

This unique experience has been far from dull. I wear a blue vest (called penny), bearing the yellow-green-blue badge of the Miller Bell Tower with the ords: Chautauqua Institution. This symbol of authority/information has been mixed blessing. One Chautauquan liked it and asked, "Can I buy a vest at the ookstore."

Being an usher you quickly find that Chautauquans are not of one mind.)uring the morning devotional hour a couple approached me in the middle of ıe sermon, and asked, "Who is this guy preaching?" I shared the preacher's ame. The response was, "He stinks." Twenty minutes later, a worshiper leav-ıg the Amp said to me, "Best sermon I ever heard."

One morning the 10:45 speaker requested we pass out copies of "An Ode ɔ a Grecian Urn." Some persons remarked, "I remember reciting this in chool." Yet others reflected, "This is a waste of paper."

The usher badge is a magnet for comments, questions and reflections. ;arly in the season former Wyoming senator Alan Simpson had to make a list-ıinute change from Tuesday to Wednesday. A few minutes before his previous-y scheduled talk, a man approached me who was obviously upset saying, Where is Al Simpson?" I explained the change in schedule, to which he replied, But I changed my airplane flight just to hear him!" Like other ushers, at that ıoment I represented the Institution, so I simply listened to him. He left say-ıg, "Thank you."

As an usher you need to be a reservoir of information including the loca-ion of many rest rooms, denominational houses, places to eat, lost and found, ime and place of events, etc. Sheral was even asked, "What are the hours of the ,ucy-Desi Museum?" (It is located in Jamestown.) Ushers learn to receive crit-cism and then suggest that comments can be given on forms supplied at the Colonnade. One gentleman informed me that, "The Hall of Philosophy is too rowded at 2:00, and *you* need to move the sessions to a larger place!" Also, I eceived the comment, "Why doesn't Jared (Chautauqua's organist) play __________?" Another man – pointing to the three screens at the front of the ımp ready to be used as part of the morning lecture – said, "Using screens is just ıot in the Chautauqua spirit. We're becoming just like Disneyland."

There are, of course, Amphitheater rules. This is where some would con-ider that ushers are simply acting like umpires. Individuals must show their gate passes for evening concerts. Ushers learn to not take comments personally su(as, "Oh, give me a break, my gate pass is back in my room" or "I'm a proper owner and I have been coming for 26 years." We simply send those without pass to a specific gate where our supervisor makes a decision.

Probably the number one concern is coffee being brought into the Am Coffee, when spilled, makes a wretched mess, especially when it runs down a inclined floor. A humorous moment was the morning an older (I will n(attempt to define "older") man made his way into the Amp and sat holding a cu of coffee. Barbara, our crew chief, approached him inquiring, "Coffee?" H reply, "No thanks, I've already got some." (He did take the cup outside the Am fence.) A few persons have developed very creative ways to smuggle coffee int the Amp. I'll not share them with you, because their techniques might be em lated.

As an usher I can observe the many sayings displayed on T-shirts. enjoyed – "Wear Me Out" – "You can't beat a South Carolina Woman": and or I still don't understand – "Where it's Flat is Where it's At."

Relationships can develop between ushers and Chautauquans. Over th years I have noticed a lady who almost always wears outfits that match, even the bow in her hair. With some hesitation, and not knowing if I was over step ping my place, I approached her and said, "I enjoy seeing you in matched garb. She responded in a positive manner, even on the day when I said, "Your sock don't match your outfit today." She responded, "They blend." She has now tol me to keep score on her dress, and give her a rating at the end of the season.

Ushers have been audience to moving moments. One woman was vica iously affected by the devotional service, and wept. Later she passed me, smi ing, and said, "This has been a very meaningful morning, I have a sense of dire(tion."

Following the Sacred Song Service in Week 5, titled "Chautauqua Pray for Peace;" Sheral happened to observe an emotional exchange of a Star of Davi and a Cross between two women, one Jewish, one Christian, accompanied wit the words, "Why can't others get along the way we do?"

Ushers do their best to assist. A man lost his small, but expensive hearin aid. Four ushers spent over 20 minutes on their knees searching the Amp floo with no success; the following morning we were informed that the "lost" iter was "found" within the individual's underwear.

Seeing a woman on her knees looking under the Amp bleachers, I aske("Can I help?" She informed me that her black cat was missing, and she wa looking everywhere. We looked, together; no cat was found.

I have learned there are times when a comment is best left unsaic Spotting a member of the Symphony pushing a double bass through the Amp remarked, "I'll bet you wish you had taken up the violin?" The reply was, " would be a rich person if everyone who said *that* had given me a dollar!"

Still, some conversations have been quite fruitful. I noticed a woman sit ting at the back of the Amp, sporting a large scar on her knee. I excused myse and asked if she had a knee replacement; and that I might need one. She pleas antly shared her operation, relating the pros and cons she experienced.

Being an Amp usher carries beyond the Institution grounds. Sheral wa in a grocery store in Jamestown. Checking out, she heard a voice from tw counters over saying, "Oh, ma'am, Oh ma'am." Sheral turned and acknow edged the woman, who then continued, "Ma'am, when does the Symphony star night?"

For twelve years Sheral and I owned a small Inn where we hosted more an 1,100 guests a year. We could recall a few guests who were difficult; and en overlook the 99 percent who were a joy to serve. In the same way, being an mp usher has been a pleasant experience. I have learned that graciousness and urtesy are words that describe almost all Chautauquans.

I sincerely hope that I have been more than an Amp ump who simply lministers rules, but rather one who serves as a welcoming host.

(The Chautauquan Daily, August 18, 2003)

Palestinians Are Humans, Too

I want to establish this fact: I am not anti-Semitic. Never have bee never will be.

My first contact with Judaism was with Herb Friedman. Herb and I we in the same Boy Scout Troop in Lincoln, Nebraska in the 1950's. The Troop w sponsored by a Christian Church (Disciples of Christ). There never were ar "Does he fit-in" questions. Enjoying a meal at Herb's house I remember askir about the large candlestick. The family shared background about their menora (seven branch candelabrum, a symbol of Judaism.) I thought it was meaningfu I still do. As a youth the book Exodus by Leon Uris made a tremendous impre sion on my vicariously experiencing the sufferings of Jews during World War I

I have shed many tears over The Holocaust. As a Christian I am disturbe over the possible fact that (according to John Cornwell) Pius XII may have bee Hitler's Pope. I encourage all gentiles to witness Steven Spielberg's "Schindler List." This movie will leave you with a hole in your heart – but hopefully reflec ing on the film will lead you to a determination that "it" shall never happe again! As humans we need to do everything we can to take the word "suffering out of our contemporary vocabulary.

So.

So, I am greatly distraught over the "activity" of the State of Israel, an their dealings with the "Palestinian Problem," and the media almost always po traying the Palestinians as the bad guys.

The 1948 decision by the United Nations to form the State of Isra forced about three million Palestinian refugees into their own Exodus trek, bu with no Promised Land in sight.

I remind myself that the State of Israel and the sons and daughters c Abraham, Isaac and Jacob are not necessarily interchangeable terms. Wh bewilders me is that the State of Israel (with so many residents or their relativ experiencing persecution) now turns around and causes/permits suffering on th Palestinians.

Since the 1967 war, many Palestinians have spent their lives living unde military occupation. The true reason of the present conflict is the "orderly" vic lence of an Israeli military power (the world's fourth largest; supported b America) over a captive people.

Since 1993, Israel has violated all agreements it signed with the PLO. I failed to halt settlement expansion of Palestinian land. It built roads for Israeli only vehicles. It did not release Palestinian prisoners. It did not provide safe pas sages between the West Bank and Gaza. It did not fulfill a third withdrawal b May, 1999, and it did not open a seaport at Gaza. Thus the continuing violenc is a human response of a people desiring its independence from an Israeli sieg of Palestinian areas.

Much of the American media has bought into the belief that – to use Hebrew Bible story – Israel is little-young-David, while Palestinians/and thei Arab neighbors, are the personification of evil giant Goliath. This has been well-crafted public relations stance provided by Israel for decades.

Are the Palestinians without fault? Hardly. Have they done evil deeds Yes. Will they do them again? Ah, but why not change the question to: "Hov can both Jews and Palestinians live in dignity, equality and justice?"

Now, under the Ariel Sharon Zionistic government, a concrete 30-foo igh, 400-mile-long-wall is being erected to "stop terrorism." However ier will divide many Palestinian farmers from their land, continue to humi. 1em, and will serve as a symbol of the inability of the state of Israel to recogniz alestinians as fellow humans. One is reminded of Robert Frost's "Mending Vall." In that poem the builder "moves in darkness" as he says, "Good fences nake good neighbors." To this statement Frost reflects, "Something there is that oesn't love a wall."

Criticism of the current Israeli policy comes from within the state of srael. Yaakov Perry, former chief of Israel's domestic security service recently aid, "Israel is going in the direction of decline, nearly a catastrophe in almost very area – economic, political, social and security. If something doesn't hapen here, we will continue to wallow in the mud and we will continue to destroy urselves." Speaking directly to the erection of the wall, another Israeli official tated, "The wall creates hatred . . . expropriates land and annexes hundreds of housands of Palestinians to the state of Israel. The result is that the fence chieves the exact opposite of what was intended."

So, living in tranquil Chautauqua County, why should I care about this onflict happening thousands of miles away? I care because I believe we are all art of a world family; and when anyone within my family is hurting, I become nvolved.

I want every human being to be treated with the respect and worth that s at the heart of the Jewish, Christian and Islamite faith.

My hope is that all parties will heed the words of the Hebrew Bible rophet, Amos, and apply them in 2004.

> Take away from me the noise of your songs: I will not listen to the melody of your harps. But let justice roll down like waters, and righteousness like an overflowing stream.
>
> — Amos 5:23-24 NRSV

What is needed is an application of Yahweh's Shalom. "Shalom" is a wonerful Hebrew word meaning more than "peace." It is a salutation which comnunicates an end to racism and hatred; it is a declaration of hope and appreciaion and acceptance. "Shalom" means peace between God and all of God's chilren, whether chosen or adopted.

"Shalom."

(Jamestown Post-Journal, January 4, 2004)

Considering "Why" Jesus Died

Post-Journal has recently provided readers with articles on the movi
ssion of the Christ." Robert W. Plyler gave us an honest "Critical Eye
il 3 review which he titled "Grim and horrible." This was followed b
"Pa ate About 'The Passion'" on April 4. I would like to provide a differen
slant on this film, and a (granted minority) interpretation on the reason and pur
pose of the death of Jesus of Nazareth.

My reflections come within the context of being accepted, loved and nur
tured by the Christian church all my life. I am a retired clergyperson, gratefu
for the insights received from two earned seminary degrees; having, I hope, faith
fully served as a pastor for 43 years.

As we engage in discussion concerning persons, stories, events, and dia
logue from the Bible; I find this statement to be most helpful: The Bible (66 dif
ferent writings) is *not a book about God*; the Bible is a book *about the people o
God*. Within the Bible we find stories of individuals, groups, and nations wh
were faithful, and unfaithful in their relationships to other humans, and to God

Director Mel Gibson has taken the events of the death of Jesus "directly
from the New Testament. However, we must remember that the writers of th
four Gospels were evangelists, *not* historians. As evangelists, they were publi
relations men, promoting the Christian faith. These writers did their wor
decades after the life of Jesus, building their work from oral tradition, and addin
their own embellishment to the events surrounding the life and sayings of th
Nazarene.

Using selected sayings from the Hebrew Bible, the evangelists attempte
to tie-in the concept of atonement with Jesus. The atonement theory is that
Adam and Eve (who may or may not have been actual individuals) "sinned" an
therefore "all have sinned." Thus, the only way to atone for human sin is to hav
God send his son to "make-it-okay" for us, by his pre-planned death. This con
cept simply makes God a murderer. So, Jesus did not die for my sins, or for an
persons' sins, Jesus was killed – by Rome.

What we see in the life and ministry of Jesus is that God loves us as w
are; we call this grace. Lisa W. Davison, a professor at Lexington Theologica
Seminary in Kentucky, is very helpful: "Rather than inherent sinfulness, human
ity needs to be saved from believing that we are unworthy of God's love, that w
must somehow earn God's forgiveness. Salvation involves being liberated fron
the belief that we are not able to live out the image of God that dwells within us
Jesus' death on the cross did not pay some cosmic debt or save humanity fron
sin and death. His death was the natural consequence of how he lived his life
His violent death was the result of his taking seriously God's faith in us and o
calling us to a high level of accountability to God and to one another."

Jesus was killed. Indeed, Gibson's film helps us to "feel" the horror of hi
death (no doubt he takes far too long in depicting the suffering). Yet ask any
one in the medical field and they will inform you that attempting to breath
while "hanging" from a crossbeam is painful, beyond belief. In addition, histo
rians of this time (Philo and Josephus) report that those being crucified wer
often sexual abused and were "hung" on a cross naked. This was to dehumaniz
those being crucified, and to remind everyone who was in total control – Rome

The central force in the death of Jesus was the un-relentless power o
Rome. This power is seen in the person of Pilate. In the movie, Gilson (as d

me Gospel writers) depict Pilate as an indecisive and "understanding" person. istory does not support this depiction. Pilate was a cruel and ruthless ruler, ho seems to have "enjoyed" suppressing resistance. (Philo says he was notori-ıs for "executions without trial.") Pilate was so ruthless that he was eventually lieved of his job by the Romans (of all people) for excessive cruelty. Yet, gospel riter Mathew has Pilate giving into a mob out of fear and thus committing the orst possible "sin" for a Roman official: compromising the authority of Rome.

In the eyes of Rome, Jesus was a trouble-making, two-bit rebel, who was lking about "The Kingdom of God" which was a concept challenging Roman ıle. We, who are followers and believers of the Christian faith, view Jesus ırough completely different lens that did the Roman Empire. Rome killed ıousands of humans a year, what difference in one more?

In the time of Jesus agriculture was the basis of the economy. A small elite ok the surplus from the peasant producers, through taxation. Between one ıd two percent were taking fifty to sixty-five percent of the total agricultural roduction. Those in power might also take the peasant's land. The Roman mil-ary occupation was a constant reminder of who was in charge! The results were crushing taxation, increasing indebtedness, and loss of family farms. Into this orrible condition, Jesus proclaimed the Kingdom of God. For Jesus, the ingdom is not a place, or a future state of affairs, it is present here-and-now ecause God is already king. To some this sounded ludicrous and naive; to oth-:s, it was politically dangerous; to others, it was indeed very good news. For :sus, the Kingdom of God exists whenever and wherever people dare to live as God's will (not Rome's) governed the world. Jesus announced this Kingdom, ıught about it, enacted it, and celebrated its presence. Proclaiming *that* ingdom is why Rome killed him.

As to Gibson's film being anti-Semitic, he emulates Matthew's words, His blood be upon us," (Jews). This is not a statement from God, nor Jesus, ut from writers giving *their* slant on the event. Yes, it is probably true that some :wish leaders did not shed any tears over the death of Jesus, for he was strongly hallenging the status quo. Applying a homiletical question to the crucifixion, e can ask, "And just where are the disciples of Jesus?" In their hour of trial, they *ll* fled! What of us today?

So, where does one go from here? I feel that Gilson's movie has done us service by provoking interest and discussion concerning the person of Jesus, a rst century Jewish rabbi. Some would acknowledge that he was one of the reatest humans who ever lived. For myself, I would say he was *the* greatest. aying this, I do not place myself above anyone who believes in other revelations f God. What I do want to stress is: The greatest facet of Jesus was not his eath; but his words, parables, actions – his life!

(The Post-Journal, May 2, 2004)

Remember your mission

In the 1940s and 1950s, the Christian Church (Disciples of Christ) spo
sored Living-Link Missionaries. Congregations in the United States and Canac
were linked with missionaries who served in foreign countries. During fu
loughs, these overseas-servants-of-God would share their experiences and mi
istry with the home congregation.

Hal and Ruth Heimer were the Living-Link missionaries for Ottumwa's Fir
Christian Church. They visited Ottumwa often. Hal was from Hebro
Nebraska, and Ruth from Rensselaer, Indiana. They were excellent servants
the church. They were gracious and gentle, intelligent and insightful.

I first met Hal and Ruth when our family lived in Kansas. They served fc
many years in Zaire, and then lived in Indianapolis, where I was privileged t
serve as the pastor of the congregation where they were members.

Hal died last month. Ruth continues to live in Indy. They were a cred
to the universal church and they enriched the lives of many. My Webster's
Dictionary defines the word "missionary" as: "One sent out to do religious c
charitable work." Hal and Ruth were sent out years ago to Africa. In 1995, wh
not consider that we who live in Southeast Iowa can be "sent out" as missiona
ies?

One does not have to go to another country to do religious work. That hu
and words of support you gave to a bereaved person; you were a missionar
Those words of guidance and direction you gave as a volunteer at the Ottumw
Regional Health Center; you were acting like a missionary. That potenti
neighborhood fight which you defused with words of reconciliation; weren't yo
becoming a missionary? Going to the store for a shut-in friend; you were a mis
sionary. Working on that Habitat for Humanity home, or supporting th
Ecumenical Lord's Cupboard, weren't you serving as a missionary?

Hal and Ruth served faithfully in their time. They learned another languag
they lived in a different culture, they second-miled-it on many occasions. I'r
grateful for their missionary ministry.

For us, the mission fields where we can serve with love, compassion an
understanding are: Hedrick, Bloomfield, Sigourney, Eldon, Ottumwa
Bentonsport, Albia, Oskaloosa, on and on.

Your mission field is where you are.

(The Ottumwa Courier, June 17, 1995)

My Postlude

In our lifetime we shall journey on a variety of roads. Our travels will tak
us to many locations: hospitals, places of worship, cemeteries, schools, rivers
meal tables, stores, Inns, court rooms, choir lofts and porches. We will mee
saints and sinners, and we will experience a number of relationships. Somewher
along the way, hopefully, we will realize we are not alone as we wander. We ar
grateful for all who have shared our trip; and as we "go" may we continue to lov
God and enjoy God, forever.

Glossary of Publications

A. D. — National publication of the United Church of Christ.

alive now! — Bi-monthly of poems, prayers, meditations by The Upper Room, Nashville.

Bed & Breakfast — Quarterly magazine for innkeepers, Scottsdale.

Bloomfield Democrat — Bloomfield, Iowa newspaper.

Catalyst — Monthly of the Christian Church (DOC) for high school youth from September, 1969 to December, 1976.

The Chautauquan Daily — Seasonal daily from Chautauqua Institution.

The Christian — National weekly, then monthly, of the Christian Church (DOC) from 1960 to 1973.

Christian Church Worship Bulletin Service — Weekly bulletins of the Christian Board of Publication, St Louis.

Christian Leadership — Church of God, Anderson, Indiana.

The Christian Ministry — Bi-monthly for pastors, published by The Christian Century Foundation, Chicago.

The Church Musician — Monthly for music leaders of the Southern Baptist Convention.

Crusader — Monthly newspaper mailed to all members of an American Baptist congregation, Valley Forge, Pennsylvania.

Decatur Herald & Review — Daily/Sunday in Decatur, Illinois.

The Des Moines Register — Iowa's largest daily/Sunday newspaper.

The Disciple — National monthly of the Christian Church (DOC) from 1974 to March of 2002. A merger of The Christian and World Call.

DisciplesWorld — National monthly of the Christian Church (DOC).

Disciplines — Yearly daily devotions book from The Upper Room.

Encounter — Quarterly theological journal of Christian Theological Seminary, Indianapolis.

Family Devotions — Non denominational daily devotions, Lima, Ohio.

The Gifts We Bring — Worship Resources, Church Finance Council, Christian Church (DOC).

The Home Altar — Daily devotional for families with young children, (ELCA).

The Hymn — Bi-monthly of the Hymn Society of America.

The Indianapolis Star Magazine — Indiana's largest daily/Sunday newspaper.

JED Share — Ecumenical quarterly for church educators.

Journal of Church Music — Non denominational quarterly, Philadelphia.

Kansas Messenger — Monthly of the Christian Church in Kansas.

Master Sermon Series — Monthly resources for clergy, Dearborn, Michigan.

The Mennonite — Monthly for General Conference Mennonite Church.

Messenger — National monthly of the Church of the Brethren.

Mid-Stream — Quarterly by the Council on Christian Unity, Christian Church (DOC), Indianapolis.

The Ottumwa Courier — Daily newspaper, Ottumwa, Iowa.

Pension Fund Bulletin — Quarterly by the Pension Fund of the

Christian Church (DOC), Indianapolis.

The Post-Journal — Daily/Sunday in Jamestown, New York.

Power — Quarterly ecumenical youth readings.

Prayers For Public Worship — Edgar Ziegler, Editor, Brethren Press.

Preaching — Bi-monthly for clergy.

REC News — Monthly magazine for the Iowa Rural Electric Corporation, Des Moines.

The Secret Place — Quarterly daily devotional by the American Baptist and the Christian Church (DOC).

These Days — Quarterly daily devotional for three Presbyterian denominations and the United Church of Christ.

United Methodist Reporter — Weekly newspaper for United Methodist congregations, Dallas.

The Upper Room — Bi-monthly daily devotional from Nashville.

Vanguard — Quarterly for church leaders from the Division of Homeland Ministries, Christian Church (DOC), 1969-1998.

World Call — Monthly mission magazine of the Christian Church (DOC), 1919-1973.

The Word in Season — Daily devotional for the (ELCA).

Your Church — Bi-monthly for church leadership.